D1345489

The Business and Management of Ocean Cruises

The Business and Management of Ocean Cruises

Edited by

Michael Vogel

Bremerhaven University of Applied Sciences

Alexis Papathanassis

Bremerhaven University of Applied Sciences

Ben Wolber

Prestige Cruise Holdings, Inc.

www.cabi.org

387.5
VOG

CABI is a trading name of CAB International

CABI
Nosworthy Way
Wallingford
Oxfordshire OX10 8DE
UK

Tel: +44 (0)1491 832111
Fax: +44 (0)1491 833508
E-mail: cabi@cabi.org
Website: www.cabi.org

CABI
875 Massachusetts Avenue
7th Floor
Cambridge, MA 02139
USA

Tel: +1 617 395 4056
Fax: +1 617 354 6875
E-mail: cabi-nao@cabi.org

A catalogue record for this book is available from the British Library, London, UK.

Library of Congress Cataloging-in-Publication Data

The business and management of ocean cruises / edited by Michael Vogel, Alexis Papathanassis, Ben Wolber.
       p. cm.
  Includes bibliographical references and index.
  ISBN 978-1-84593-845-1 (alk. paper)
1. Ocean travel--Management.   2. Cruise lines--Management.   3. Cruise lines--Economic aspects.   I. Vogel, Michael.   II. Papathanassis, Alexis.
III. Wolber, Ben.

  G550.B865 2012
  387.5'42068--dc23

                                                                    2011028632

ISBN-13: 978 1 84593 845 1

Commissioning editor: Claire Parfitt
Production editor: Simon Hill

Typeset by AMA Dataset, Preston
Printed and bound in the UK by MPG Books Ltd

Contents

About the Authors

Mandy Aggett is a Lecturer in Hospitality Management in the School of Tourism and Hospitality at the University of Plymouth (UK), and also acts as the Placement Coordinator for Tourism, Hospitality and Events students. She teaches modules in Front Office and Facilities Management, Managing Service Innovation and Business Management for Service Operations. Mandy's research interests lie in service operations management, services marketing and social media marketing, and she is currently working on a PhD, investigating the impacts of social media on consumer behaviour. Email: mandy.aggett@ plymouth.ac.uk

Dr Borislav Bjelicic is the Head of Group Corporate Communications of DVB Bank SE in Frankfurt/M. (Germany). Before joining DVB, he worked for Deutsche Lufthansa, German Airlines. He studied Business Administration, majoring in Logistics and Transportation Management, and holds a PhD in Economics. Borislav is Honorary Professor for Business Administration and Logistics at the University of Mannheim. He has received several awards for his work, including the Rhenania-Logistics-Award, the Academic Award of the Stinnes-Foundation, and an Award from the Prechel-Foundation. Email: borislav. bjelicic@dvbbank.com

Cordula Boy works for Bernhard Schulte Shipmanagement in Hamburg (Germany). She holds a BA in Cruise Industry Management from the Bremerhaven University of Applied Sciences (Germany) and an MSc in Marine Policy from the University of Cardiff (UK). Cordula gained practical cruise operations experience on board the *MV Europa* of Hapag-Lloyd Cruises. Email: cordula.boy@web.de

Grenville Cartledge is a hospitality professional with well over 20 years' experience of the cruise industry. After graduating from hotel school in the UK he spent the early part of his career in the hotel sector. His first General Management appointment came at the age of 26. He joined Cunard Line as a Hotel Officer on board *Queen Elizabeth 2* and worked his way up to the position of Purser. He has since worked in shore-side operational management roles for Cunard Line, P&O Cruises, Sun Cruises (MyTravel), Louis Cruises (Thomson Cruises) and Saga Cruises. In 2010, Grenville set up his own cruise consultancy and support services company in the UK. He has recently been appointed as Regulatory Consultant to the UK Passenger Shipping Association. Email: gcartledge@ fourgold.co.uk

Dr Philip Gibson is Associate Professor and Programme Manager for Hospitality and Cruise Management at the University of Plymouth (UK). Prior to this, he held various management positions in hospitality and tourism organizations, including P&O Cruises and P&O Ferries, and was the Head of Centre for Tourism at South Devon College in Torquay. He has a PhD from Exeter University. In 2007 and 2008, he was visiting faculty at the University of West Indies in Barbados. Philip is the author of the *Cruise Operations Management* textbook. He is a Teaching Fellow, a Fellow of the Centre for Excellence in Professional Placement Learning and a Fellow of the Institute of Hospitality. Email: P.Gibson@plymouth.ac.uk

Dr Sven Gross is Professor of Transport Carrier Management and Co-head of the Department of Tourism at the Harz University of Applied Sciences in Wernigerode (Germany). He is also a member of the New Zealand Tourism Research Institute based in Auckland (New Zealand). Sven studied Tourism Geography and Economics at the University of Trier and Spatial Planning at the University of Dortmund. Prior to his current position, he was a Management and Community Consultant and a Research Associate at the Dresden University of Technology, where he also earned his PhD. His research interests include tourism and transport, business travel management, as well as tourist market research. He has authored more than 50 publications on these subjects, including nine books. Email: sgross@hs-harz.de

Dr James Henry is based at the University of Otago, Dunedin (New Zealand) where he researches, teaches and consults on business-to-business marketing, channel management, logistics and financial aspects of marketing. He holds a PhD from the University of Otago. James is currently involved in research related to the cruise ship industry. In addition to this, he is actively involved as a speaker, advisor and mentor for a number of industry support projects. Previously he held positions in product design, engineering, business to business marketing and management. Email: james.henry@otago.ac.nz

Dr Robert Kwortnik is a tenured Associate Professor of Services Marketing in Cornell University's School of Hotel Administration (USA). Rob's research focuses on consumer behaviour in service contexts, with special attention to service experience management. His research has appeared in the *Journal of Marketing Research*, *Journal of Service Research*, *International Journal of Research in Marketing*, *Psychology & Marketing*, and the *Cornell Hospitality Quarterly*, among others. He has published articles on the cruise industry and is the lead author of a Harvard Business School case on Carnival Cruise Lines. Prior to his academic career, Rob held a number of professional positions in marketing. Email: rjk34@cornell.edu

Dr Wai Mun Lim is an Associate Professor and Teaching Fellow at the University of Plymouth (UK) and an Associate of the Advanced Institute of Management. She was a tour operator in Singapore prior to embarking on an academic career. Her research interests are in the use of information technology, including internet technologies for distribution and marketing. Wai Mun has consulted for organizations ranging from art design companies to global chain hotels in the use of Web 1 and 2 technologies. She has published widely in the area of technology adoption within the tourism industry and has recently won a grant to investigate the use of technology in small and medium sized hospitality enterprises. Email: W.M.Lim@plymouth.ac.uk

Wendy R. London is an internationally recognized expert in technology law and the use of computers in the law. However, in 2006, she decided to pursue her passion – cruising – and left her first career behind to re-tool for a new one. She completed her Masters in Tourism at Otago University, Dunedin (New Zealand) and is now a PhD candidate at Victoria University in Wellington, investigating the dynamics of cruise passenger spend in New Zealand in the context of power, politics and the role of the ports. Wendy is also CEO of Cruise Strategy Ltd, which offers a wide range of consultancy services to the cruise sector, and the creator of CruiseBubble.com, which promotes authentic New

Zealand goods and experiences to visiting cruise passengers. Email: wlondon@att-global.net

Dr Michael Lück is Associate Professor, Head of the Tourism & Events Department in the School of Hospitality and Tourism, and Associate Director for the coastal and marine tourism research programme area at the New Zealand Tourism Research Institute, AUT University in Auckland (New Zealand). He received his PhD from the University of Otago, Dunedin. Michael has over 10 years of work experience in tourism, and has taught at universities in Germany, New Zealand, Scotland and Canada. His research interests include marine tourism, ecotourism, sustainable tourism, the impacts of tourism, aviation and gay tourism. He has published in various international journals, is founding Editor-in-chief of the academic journal *Tourism in Marine Environments*, and associate editor of the *Journal of Ecotourism*. Michael has edited or co-edited volumes on ecotourism, marine tourism, polar tourism, and the *Encyclopedia of Tourism and Recreation in Marine Environments*. Email: michael.lueck@aut.ac.nz

Dr Edward W. (Ted) Manning is President of Tourisk Inc., a Canada-based consulting firm providing integrated planning for World Heritage sites and tourism destinations, development of measures of sustainability and environmental management solutions. He has worked in more than 50 countries in the creation and implementation of improved methods for planning environmentally and culturally sensitive areas and reduction of the ecological and social footprint of human activities, including cruise tourism. Ted is the lead consultant to the international initiative on indicators of sustainable tourism for the UN World Tourism Organization, advisor to World Wildlife Fund programmes and international advisor to the UN Industrial Development Organization. He has published 23 books and over 90 articles on sustainable development and environmental management topics. He has served as President of the Canadian Association of Geographers, a Director of the Social Science Federation of Canada and a Governor of the Royal Canadian Geographical Society. Ted is also Adjunct Research Professor in the Geography Department of Carleton University and Chair of the Programme Committee of the Canadian Association for the Club of Rome. Email: tourisk@rogers.com

Sarah Neumann is a student of Cruise Industry Management at the Bremerhaven University of Applied Sciences (Germany). Before commencing her studies, she completed an apprenticeship in tramp shipping and worked for a tanker operator. Within the field of safety and quality assurance, Sarah gained experience with regard to maritime regulations, contributed to the quality management system and took over responsibilities as Alternate Company Security Officer. Alongside her studies, she works for a shipping company in the areas of quality, health, safety and environmental systems. Email: sarahneumann85@gmx.de

Cristina Oschmann is a Lecturer in Tourism Management at the Bremerhaven University of Applied Sciences (Germany), a Research Associate at the Institute for Maritime Tourism in Bremerhaven and a Quality Management Consultant. She holds a graduate degree in Business Administration and Tourism Management from the University of Lüneburg and an MA in Adult Education from the University of Kaiserslautern. Cristina has 15 years of experience as a tourism professional, working with tour operators, hotel groups and incoming agencies in different source markets and destinations. Her fields of expertise include incoming services, product management, marketing and sales, project and quality management. Her research interests lie in literary and film-induced tourism, as well as health tourism. Email: to@t-oschmann.com

Dr Alexis Papathanassis is Professor of Tourism Management and Information Systems at the Bremerhaven University of Applied Sciences (Germany) and Co-Director of the Institute for Maritime Tourism in Bremerhaven. He serves as chairman of the Cruise Research Society, has published in the *Annals of Tourism Research*, *Tourism Management*, *International Journal of Tourism Research* and others, and (co-)edited two books on cruise management. Prior to joining academia, Alexis pursued a professional career with TUI, Europe's leading tourism group, as Project Manager and Process Engineer, Business Unit Manager and Business Development Manager. He graduated with a degree in Business Administration from the University of Bath, gained his MSc in Analysis, Design and Management of Information Systems from the London School of Economics & Political Science and received his PhD in Economic Sciences from the University of Hanover. Email: apapathanassis@hs-bremerhaven.de

Joe Rand is currently the Director, Marketing Strategy for Disney Destinations, LLC (USA). In this role, Joe guides domestic marketing efforts designed to drive visitation and resort room nights for both Disneyland Resort in California and Walt Disney World Resort in Florida. In addition, Joe leads domestic multicultural marketing efforts targeting the African-American and Hispanic consumer segments. During 4 of his 10 years with The Walt Disney Company, Joe led the Marketing organization for Disney Cruise Line. In this role, he directed all marketing efforts including brand management, advertising, public relations and promotions, and prepared the business for significant expansion with the debut of two new ships; the *Disney Dream* and the *Disney Fantasy*. Joe graduated from the Rollins College Crummer Graduate School of Business after attending the University of Central Florida. Email: Joe.H.Rand@disney.com

Dr Jacques Roy is Professor of Logistics and Operations Management at HEC Montréal (Canada) where he is also Director of the Carrefour logistique, a university-industry forum on Supply Chain Management, and Director of the research group Chaîne that is conducting research activities in the field of Supply Chain Management. He was also Director, Research and Publication and Director, Training, at the Montréal-based International Aviation Management Training Institute. Jacques graduated with a BSc from the Royal Military College in Saint-Jean and completed his education with an MBA and a PhD in Business Administration at HEC Montréal. Prior to his teaching career, he was employed as an aerospace engineering officer with the Canadian Armed Forces. He also possesses many years of experience as a Management Consultant with several large Canadian corporations and governmental organizations. Email: jacques.roy@hec.ca

Steffen Spiegel is a Lecturer in Cruise Management at the Bremerhaven University of Applied Sciences (Germany) and an independent consultant to tourism companies, focusing on destination and cruise management. Over the past 10 years, he worked for a travel agency and a tour operator, before switching aboard as Shore Excursion Manager, Expedition Leader and Cruise Director on standard and luxury class vessels. He holds a degree in International Tourism Management. Email: Steffen.Spiegel@gmx.de

Andreas Ullrich is Ship Type Manager Passenger Vessels with the International Classification Society Germanischer Lloyd (Germany) where he has been working on ship safety, focusing on passenger ships, high-speed crafts and yachts. Andreas has over 20 years' experience in the fields of fire protection, means of escape and life saving appliances. He is also a consultant to the German Ministry of Transport, Building and Urban Development, representing Germany in working groups of the IMO Sub-Committee on Fire Protection and the Marine Safety Committee with a focus on passenger ships. Andreas studied naval architecture in Rostock. After graduating, he joined the former East German Classification society DSRK and worked in the field of finite element analysis. Email: andreas.ullrich@gl-group.com

Dr Simon Véronneau is Assistant Professor of Operations Management at Quinnipiac University, Connecticut (USA), and an Associate Researcher at the Supply Chain Research Group at HEC Montréal as well as at the Inter-University Research Center on Enterprise Networks, Logistics and Transportation (CIRRELT). He also currently serves as a scientific advisor on the cruise ship wastewater science advisory panel for the Department of Environmental Conservation in the state of Alaska. He holds a PhD in Operations Management from HEC Montréal, and a Master of Science in Transport Management from the Universiteit Antwerpen. Simon's research focuses on global supply chains, transport management and real-time critical operations management. He is a licensed Senior Navigation Officer with work experience in the Canadian Coast Guard, on cruise ships and merchant ships. Email: simon.veronneau@hec.ca.

Dr Michael Vogel is Professor of Business and Tourism Management, Programme Leader for Cruise Tourism Management at the Bremerhaven University for Applied Sciences (Germany) and Co-Director of the Institute of Maritime Tourism in Bremerhaven. He has published on cruise economics, destination strategy, higher education, critical research and epistemology; conducts research for the German Ministry for the Environment on the acceptance of offshore wind farms; leads a major teaching quality enhancement programme; and runs an innovative street magazine with students and homeless people. In 2008, he received the German Higher Education Teaching Award. Previously, Michael worked as a strategy consultant and tourism manager. He holds a graduate degree in Business Administration, an MSc in Environmental and Resource Economics and a PhD in Theoretical Economics. He is also a doctoral student at the Institute of Education, University of London. Email: mvogel@hs-bremerhaven.de

Celia Walters, formerly Head of Hotel Training with Carnival UK, was instrumental in working with the University of Plymouth in order to establish the company's highly successful cadetship programme. She is a visiting lecturer in the School of Tourism and Hospitality at the University and has advised the course manager on planning and development issues relating to employability. Celia is an honorary member of the Cruise Research Society. Email: celia.walters@pocruises.co.uk

Ben Wolber is Vice President, Fleet Purchasing for Prestige Cruise Holdings (PCH), based in Miami. PCH is the parent company of Oceania Cruises and Regent Seven Seas Cruises and the market leader in the upper-premium and luxury segments of the cruise industry. Ben's previous career in the luxury segment of the cruise industry includes the positions of Hotel Manager, F&B Manager and Provision Master on board, as well as Financial Controller shore-side. He holds a degree in Business Administration, used to be a Lecturer in Cruise Management at the Bremerhaven University of Applied Sciences (Germany) and is a Research Associate of the Institute for Maritime Tourism in Bremerhaven. Email: BWolber@prestigecruiseholdings.com

Preface

Cruise lines combine socio-economic, technological and environmental systems in unique ways to form their products. Many managerial functions in the cruise sector deal with tensions, conflicts and uncertainties arising from the interaction of at least two of these systems. The organization of cruise ship management in a hotel department, a technical department and a nautical department, for example, mirrors those three systems, and it is the captain's role to manage the interfaces between the three departments, i.e. between the three systems. Itinerary planning and management needs to strike a balance between the cruise line's economic interest and the passengers' leisure and safety interests, taking further into account the geographical, climatic, nautical and legal conditions, as well as the ship's technical properties. The cruise itinerary, in turn, determines how tour operations and shore excursions, passenger logistics and ship logistics must be managed.

Running a business under such conditions poses particular management challenges. With this book, we aim to capture and document some of the most important and interesting managerial challenges associated with ocean cruises. We believe that there is a need for this book because after decades of double-digit growth, the worldwide cruise sector, including its suppliers and distribution partners, has become a significant employer of people with a wide range of skills and qualifications.

The Need for this Book

While the qualifications required for managerial careers in cruise lines' technical and nautical departments are fairly well defined, this is far less the case for management careers in the hotel department and shore side, e.g. in marketing, product management and tour operating. As a result, the corresponding positions are often filled with experienced 'outsiders' from other sectors. Our book may help them gain a bigger picture of 'The Business and Management of Ocean Cruises' and better understand their own role in this larger context.

The cruise sector's size and growth prospects, the significant financial investments it involves and the challenging management functions it offers have also triggered an 'academization' process. In recent years, many universities have started offering specialist cruise management courses as part of their leisure, hospitality and tourism curricula in order to prepare their students for cruise management careers.

The universities in Bremerhaven (Germany) and Plymouth (UK) have gone even further: in 2003, they launched fully-fledged undergraduate degree programmes with a cruise management focus. In Bremerhaven, the emphasis is on the business aspects of cruise tourism, whereas Plymouth stresses hotel and service operations. Both programmes continue to meet strong demand on the part of both students and the cruise sector.

Judging by the rising number of academic members of the Cruise Research Society and by the strong attendance of its interdisciplinary International Cruise Conferences, we expect many more higher education institutions to implement courses and curricula with a reference to cruises in the future.

However, courses on cruise management share the difficulty that their object of interest is still comparatively sparsely documented. There may be an abundance of tourist guidebooks on cruise destinations and cruise ships, but these books are largely unsuitable for teaching. There is also a growing number of research-based academic journal articles on the cruise industry, cruise tourism and selected aspects of cruise management, yet for many students these articles are too narrowly focused, too detailed or difficult to understand. We cannot think of more than two books that cover the inner workings of cruise lines and of the cruise sector in such breadth and depth that we would adopt or recommend them as textbooks for a cruise management course. With *The Business and Management of Ocean Cruises*, we hope to add a third book to this category.

A Long Genesis

The idea for this book came to our minds in 2006, when CABI published Ross Dowling's edited volume, *Cruise Ship Tourism*. We found it a rich and very comprehensive source of information and in parts also quite useful for our teaching. Its many chapters cover passengers and marketing (cruise demand), destinations and products (cruise supply), impacts of cruising and cruise industry issues. From our point of view, Ross Dowling's book had only one drawback: it was not a book on cruise management. Being involved in teaching on Bremerhaven's cruise management programme, the three of us resolved to fill what we perceived to be a gap in the literature, and to follow Ross Dowling's good example.

In 2007, we developed the book concept and started contacting potential contributors. Our idea was to bring together the perspectives of practising cruise managers and those of academic cruise researchers. Half the contributions should come from each group. Suitable academics would not have been too hard to find, if Ross Dowling had not already included about 50 of them as authors in his book. Since we wanted our book to be complementary to his, we decided not to work with the same authors. Despite this serious restriction, getting academic colleagues to commit themselves to authoring chapters was the easier bit.

Much more difficult proved the recruitment of managers as authors, and unfortunately, it took us a while to find that out. At first, it went very well. At conferences, trade fairs or through personal relationships, we addressed cruise managers who we believed to be capable of writing short chapters about their respective areas of responsibility or expertise. Many felt flattered by being considered and agreed. But when we asked them to produce chapter outlines or first drafts, they discovered how hard it is to verbalize one's tacit knowledge, and how time consuming writing can be, so after a couple of weeks or months several gave up.

In summer 2008, finally, we had all chapters covered by authors who we thought could do the job. Then, in September 2008, Lehman Brothers went bankrupt, the financial markets fell into turmoil, and the shock waves that propagated through the global economy also hit the book project. Within eight weeks, we lost all our non-academic authors except one who had already completed his chapter. The looming economic crisis required the managers' full attention.

We put the book project on hold for almost a year to see how the cruise industry would emerge from the crisis. At the end of the difficult year 2009, when we tried to get back in touch with our former authors-to-be, several of them had moved on to other companies or disappeared. Others told us that pressure at work had increased and that they would have to withdraw from our project. So, after 3 years, we were still ten authors short. This is when we decided to abandon the plan of having half the chapters contributed by practising cruise managers.

In summer 2010, for the second time we had found authors for all chapters. In autumn 2010, we signed the publishing contract with CABI. The last chapter of the book was completed in April 2011. By the time we submitted the manuscript in May 2011, we had recruited a total of 39 authors – and lost 19 along the way.

Structure of the Book

The book is divided into six parts, which are organized to guide the reader step by step from the macro level of the cruise industry to the micro level of operations management on board cruise ships. This way, each part represents the context for the subsequent part. Figuratively speaking, the book gradually zooms into cruise management.

Part I (The Cruise Industry) sets the scene for the book by characterizing the conditions under which cruise lines operate. Chapter 1 (The Demand for Ocean Cruises – Three Perspectives) presents a quantitative, a psychological and a sociological–interpretive perspective on cruise demand. Its aim is to contribute to a richer and more complex understanding of the demand side than that usually offered in industry studies and market research reports. Chapter 2 (Development of the Cruise Industry Structure – the Supply Side) is concerned with the evolution of competition, concentration and barriers to market entry in the cruise sector. It emphasizes the importance of cruise companies' access to capital as a precondition of competition. Chapter 3 (Regulatory Frameworks of the Cruise Industry) gives an overview of the main institutions and conventions at international, supra-national and national level that regulate cruise shipping to ensure the safe, secure and sustainable operation. Chapter 4 (Impacts of Cruising) identifies the impacts expected when cruise ships visit a port. It also addresses the range of environmental and visitor management issues related to ships and their passengers, and suggests how ports and cruise lines can reduce negative effects.

Part II (Cruise Line Corporate Management) includes four chapters that address issues of significance for corporate managers in the cruise sector. The choice of the right strategy is existential. Chapter 5 (Cruise Line Strategies for Keeping Afloat) provides an inventory of strategic options available to cruise lines. Strategies need to be supported by suitable processes, hence Chapter 6 (Core Cruise Operator Processes and Systems: Overview and Challenges) introduces the generic process architecture of a cruise operator and the systems that support those processes. Chapter 7 (Cruise Lines' Purchasing and Logistics Management) takes a closer look at the processes related to a particular corporate function: it examines the complexity of global cruise ship supply chain management. Of special importance in a people business like cruising is the management of human resources. Chapter 8 (Human Resource Management in the Cruise Industry) considers this function in the corporate context and addresses specific HR management challenges such as a scarcity of labour, staff retention, a multicultural workforce as well as training and development from a cruise company perspective.

The three chapters of Part III (Cruise Line Marketing Management) deal with aspects of the marketing mix employed by cruise lines to attract passengers and fill their ships. Chapter 9 (Marketing Communications in the Cruise Industry) introduces the reader to marketing-communications strategies and tactics used by cruise lines to build brands, generate brand awareness and promote brand propositions to target customers. Chapter 10 (Pricing and Revenue Management for Cruises) explains the economic principles of pricing and revenue management as applied in the cruise sector. Static brochure pricing is contrasted with dynamic pricing, and the relationship between cruise ticket revenue and on-board revenue is explored. Chapter 11 (Cruise Packages) describes and discusses the role of cruise-inclusive package holidays for the development of the British cruise market. The combination of two occupancy risks, cruise and flight, together with the intricacies of packaging and pricing, represent interesting management challenges.

Part IV (Cruise Product Management), consisting of four chapters, is concerned with managerial functions related directly to the cruise product. Chapter 12 (Cruise Product Development) raises the question as to whether product development in the cruise sector should be understood as an art or a science, and proposes an answer upon consideration of the product development process. An essential feature of a cruise product is the itinerary. Chapter 13 (Itinerary Planning) explores the parameters that go into the planning of itineraries. One such parameter is the tourist attractiveness of destinations, because it allows marketing it to cruise customers, e.g. in the form of shore excursions. Chapter 14 (Shore-side Activities) considers the management of demand and supply of shore excursions and other shore-side offers. Quality assurance of the cruise product delivery is the focus of Chapter 15 (Service Quality and the Cruise Industry). The chapter highlights established concepts of service quality and discusses the recently developed service concept known as the co-creation of value in the context of cruises.

Part V (Cruise Operations Management) comprises four chapters and focuses on operational management functions on board cruise ships. Chapter 16 (Hotel Operations Management in the Cruise Industry) characterizes key managerial roles in hotel departments and addresses special aspects such as performance indicators, outsourcing and management contracts. Within hotel departments, food and beverage management has undergone major changes over the past two decades. Chapter 17 (Food and Beverage Operations) considers some of the contributing factors and some of the issues and challenges in delivering the level of food service standards now expected by cruise passengers. Chapter 18 (Safety and Security Management) presents the regulations concerning the management of safety and security, with which cruise ships and ports have to comply. The threats of piracy and terrorism are also addressed. Chapter 19 (Cruise Ship Marine Operations) sketches the role of the marine operations by examining both the on-board organization and the shore-side support component.

The final Part VI (Cruise Futures) consists of only Chapter 20 (Cruise Sector Growth – Prospects, Challenges, Responsibilities). It explores multiple relationships between the cruise sector today and its future development possibilities.

Acknowledgements

First and foremost, we thank our authors for their contributions to this book. We highly appreciate the time, effort, ideas and diligence they invested in their respective chapters. For some of them it was the first experience with writing for a publication. Those authors who joined the project at an early stage and submitted their chapters before the financial crisis have shown remarkable patience with us, for which we are grateful. We also thank all authors who generously provided their own cruise pictures and gave us permission to use them in the book, especially Ted Manning.

Our special thanks go to Barbara Voges and Annabel Baxter. Barbara had the questionable privilege of being our proofreader. We admire her stamina and her unfailing good humour. Annabel made sure that the manuscript met CABI's format requirements, checked and completed the references, and re-drew several diagrams, sometimes at very short notice.

We also gratefully acknowledge the financial assistance of the Bremerhaven University of Applied Sciences.

Finally, we wish to thank our families and friends for sharing us with this book project. Without their support and encouragement, we might not have had the energy to complete this long journey.

Michael Vogel, Alexis Papathanassis and Ben Wolber
Bremerhaven and Miami
April 2011

Part I

The Cruise Industry

1 The Demand for Ocean Cruises – Three Perspectives

Michael Vogel and Cristina Oschmann

_____

Introduction

For over 30 years, cruise lines and cruise trade associations have been repeating the same message over and over again: that cruising is one of the fastest growing segments of the tourism industry. Indeed, passenger numbers, cruise line revenues, the number of cruise ships and their berth capacities have been increasing enormously since the late 1970s. New ships keep arriving on the market at an impressive rate, and judging by the published occupancy rates of major cruise lines, it seems that, by and large, demand is keeping up with supply.

However, the real average prices of a passenger cruise day have declined significantly in the last decade, which suggests that cruise lines have had to offer price incentives to fill their ships. What this shows is that demand growth cannot be taken for granted and needs to be actively fuelled by the supply side. In fact, cruise demand has always been supply-led, starting with the invention of leisure cruising by passenger shipping lines whose scheduled transatlantic services were losing passengers to the airlines. The numerous subsequent supply-side innovations in areas like hospitality and entertainment, service delivery, ship design and technology, tour operating and destinations have made cruising more attractive for more people who otherwise might never have demanded a cruise ship holiday.

Demand for cruises may be supply-led, yet in turn it also influences supply. Cruise lines tend to listen very carefully to what their actual and potential passengers say, trying to extract information about their expectations, motives and needs. Cruise lines also analyse other sectors of the leisure industry, study their respective demand patterns and attempt to identify innovations that could be adapted to the cruise ship environment. And cruise lines, at least the most professional ones, scan their horizon for general trends and developments in society that might one day become relevant for the demand for cruises.

So cruise demand cannot be understood independently from cruise supply and vice versa. They are coupled through learning and adaptation processes at the individual, organizational and industrial level. The co-evolution of cruise demand and supply, in turn, is embedded in a larger context of society. Society has its own condition, which inevitably affects the direction and pace of the co-evolution of cruise demand and supply.

In this chapter, we aim to contribute to the understanding of cruise demand by providing three perspectives. The first perspective is largely quantitative and focuses on volumes, prices, distributions and time paths. It corresponds to the perspective conveyed by many market studies. Our second perspective on cruise demand is psychological, emphasizing in particular two aspects that are characteristic for the cruise sector: high consumer involvement and repeat buying. The third perspective, finally, is sociological and interprets cruise demand and the value of cruises for passengers in the context of the postmodern age or, more precisely, of Zygmunt Bauman's concept of liquid modernity.

Cruise Demand: a Quantitative Perspective

Ocean cruising as a mainstream leisure activity can be regarded as an American invention. In 1966, 1968 and 1972, three cruise lines were founded in the USA, which later became the dominant players of the sector: Norwegian Caribbean Line (NCL), Royal Caribbean Cruise Line (RCL) and Carnival Cruise Lines. Leisure cruises had already been offered by various passenger shipping lines as a means to generate additional business for their traditional ocean liners. Scheduled transatlantic services by ship had more and more been made redundant by commercial air travel, so the passenger liners had to be put to other uses. But these three companies especially turned cruising into an increasingly affordable and informal type of holiday.

Historic demand growth

We can assume that, by and large, the cruise sector is and has been in a state of equilibrium. This means that demand and supply are balanced through appropriate market prices. When demand exceeds supply, cruise lines raise their prices until excess demand vanishes; and when supply exceeds demand, prices are cut and/or capacities reduced until a new equilibrium is reached. In equilibrium, cruise demand is equal to the number of cruises sold. Historic passenger numbers can thus tell the story of the evolution of cruise demand.

According to the Cruise Lines International Association (CLIA), which represents over 80% of the worldwide ocean cruise ship capacities, the number of passengers carried by CLIA member cruise lines grew from 1.4 million in 1980 to 15 million in 2010 (CLIA, 2005, 2010, 2011). This more than tenfold increase corresponds to an average annual growth rate of 8.1% over a 30-year period.

The dominance of the US cruise market has begun to crumble. Table 1.1 shows that in 1990, 93% of the CLIA members' passengers came from North America or, more precisely, from the USA and Canada. By 2010, this share had fallen to 74%. And if not only CLIA members' passengers, but the entire cruise global cruise sector with an estimated volume of 18.8 million passengers (Peisley, 2010) are taken into account, the 2010 share of the North American market drops to only 59%.

In the European Union (EU), a total of 5.5 million passengers went on an ocean cruise in 2010, representing a share of 29% of ocean global cruise demand. With 1.6 million and 1.2 million passengers respectively, the UK and Germany were the second and third largest cruise markets worldwide. Italy reported 0.89 million, Spain 0.65 million and France 0.39 million passengers in 2010 (ECC, 2011; numbers include passengers of non-CLIA members).

Cruise passenger numbers in Asia may have reached 1.6 million in 2010 (Cruise Shipping Asia, 2011), corresponding to 9% of the global ocean cruise demand. Rapid economic growth in the region and the formation of a mobile middle class in China and India are the main demand-side drivers of the cruise sector in Asia.

Table 1.2 displays the rates of growth of CLIA members' passenger numbers in North America and in other markets over 20-year, 10-year and 5-year periods ending in 2010. The North American single-digit rates have not only been exceeded by the double-digit rates of other markets; the North American growth rates have been declining whilst in

Table 1.1. Cruise Lines International Association (CLIA) members' passenger numbers.

	(a) North America	(b) Other regions	Total	Share of (a)
1990	3.5 m	0.3 m	3.8 m	93%
2000	6.5 m	0.7 m	7.2 m	91%
2010	11.1 m	3.9 m	15.0 m	74%

Source: based on CLIA (2010, 2011).

Table 1.2. Compound annual growth rates of CLIA members' passenger numbers.

	(a) North America	(b) Other regions	Total
1990–2010	+5.9%	+14.1%	+7.1%
2000–2010	+5.4%	+19.3%	+7.6%
2005–2010	+2.8%	+20.9%	+6.1%

Source: based on CLIA (2010, 2011).

Table 1.3. Absolute growth of CLIA members' passenger numbers.

	(a) North America	(b) Other regions	Total	Share of (a)
1990–2010	+7.6 m	+3.6 m	+11.2 m	68%
2000–2010	+4.6 m	+3.2 m	+7.8 m	58%
2005–2010	+1.4 m	+2.4 m	+3.8 m	37%

Source: based on CLIA (2010, 2011).

other markets, growth has even been accelerating. So while North American demand for ocean cruises is showing clear signs of satiation, demand elsewhere still promises a vast potential.

Moreover, North America has not only fallen behind in terms of growth rates, but even in terms of absolute growth. As documented in Table 1.3, a share of 68% of the increase in CLIA members' cruise passenger numbers between 1990 and 2010 came from North America. Between 2000 and 2010, the share had dropped to 58%, and between 2005 and 2010, the North American market contributed only 37% to the rise in global passenger numbers.

In 2010, the number of cruises sold in North America (i.e. the USA and Canada) represented a share of 3.2% of the local population of 344 million. In the EU, this penetration rate was 1.1% of 501 million

people, and in Asia it amounted to 0.05% of a population of 3.2 billion people. Assuming that the North American penetration rate is achievable also in Europe – which may be a strong assumption – Europe's market potential is 16 million passengers per annum. In Asia, 16 million passengers would only correspond to a market penetration rate of less than 0.5%.

Cruise demand and prices

The growth of the cruise sector has not taken place at constant prices. It is partly the result of the increasing affordability of cruise products for larger parts of the population. Lower cruise ticket prices have been made possible through cost savings resulting from economies of scale due to larger ships and fleets, and through the profitability of on-board business, which allows subsidizing cruise ticket prices (see Vogel, Chapter 10, this volume).

To illustrate the evolution of demand and prices, we use data published by the Carnival Corporation and Royal Caribbean Cruises (RCL) in their annual reports of 2001–2010. These two companies may not be representative of the entire cruise sector, yet with 13.7 million ocean cruise passengers and a combined global market share of 73% in 2010, their data still provide very useful insights.

Figure 1.1 depicts the Carnival Corporation and RCL's passenger numbers as well as the corresponding real cruise ticket per diems, i.e. average real ticket prices per cruise day. The US consumer price index for urban consumers (Bureau of Labor Statistics, 2011) is used to make earlier nominal prices comparable with 2010 prices. Between 2001 and 2010, Carnival's passenger numbers increased by 170% in total or

11.7% per year. Part of this growth resulted from the 2002 merger with P&O Princess Cruises in the UK. RCL grew largely organically by 88% or 7.3% per year.

Real cruise ticket per diems of both companies evolved in a very similar manner. From 2001 to 2010, Carnival's per diems declined by 21.4% in total or 2.6% per year, and RCL's per diems fell by 21.9% in total or 2.7% per year. Even in nominal terms, both companies' cruise ticket per diems went down by an annual 0.4%. The sharp price drops in 2002 and 2009 reflect the cruise companies' responses to the 9/11 attacks in the USA and to the financial and economic crisis, respectively. These reductions were necessary to keep occupancy rates above 100%. Since real cruise ticket per diems never recovered from the 9/11 shock, it is imaginable that they will also not recover from the 2009 economic slump.

Declining prices are not only a phenomenon of Carnival and RCL's North

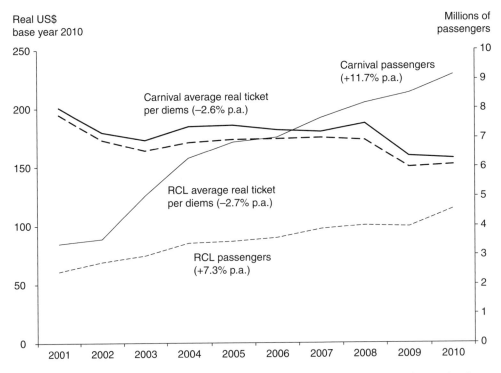

Fig. 1.1. Evolution of Carnival Corporation and Royal Caribbean Cruises' passenger numbers and real cruise ticket per diems 2001–2010. Data sources: Carnival and RCL annual reports.

American home market. In Germany, for instance, where the number of cruise passengers grew at an annual rate of 13.4% between 2001 and 2010, real cruise ticket per diems also fell by 2.4% per annum (DRV, 2005, 2011; Destatis, 2011).

Demand patterns

Cruise demand is strongly influenced by economic, institutional and cultural circumstances. Some of these influences may be largely similar around the globe (e.g. demand for leisure cruises correlates positively with household income), but others are more local in nature (e.g. cruise demand depends on the availability of casinos on board). Hence it would be daring to suggest the existence of universal cruise demand patterns. What we attempt here instead is to point out a few selected patterns that appear to be typical for individual markets.

Price segments

Many attempts have been made to develop price-based sub-segments of the cruise sector (for an overview, see Gross and Lück, Chapter 5, this volume), but so far no international standard seems to have emerged. The segmentation approaches taken by different organizations in different markets are largely incompatible. In the UK, the Passenger Shipping Association defines demand segments in terms of cruise ticket prices. In Germany, on the other hand, the Deutsche Reiseverband (DRV) uses segments defined on the basis of per diems. Table 1.4 contrasts

the two approaches and the respective demand distributions. Similar numbers for the US cruise market do not seem to be published by CLIA.

Length of cruise

In the North American market, the average length of a cruise is less than 7 days. Cruises of 6–8 days are most common with 51% of the market. However, their share is falling in favour of shorter cruises of 2–5 days, which represent over 31% of the demand. Cruises of 9–17 days still have a share of 19% in the North American market (CLIA, 2008a).

In Europe, longer cruises are preferred, as employees enjoy longer paid annual leaves. In the USA and Canada, employed adults receive on average about 13 and 19 days of paid annual leave, respectively, which compares to 26 days in the UK and 27 days in Germany (Expedia, 2009). In the UK the average duration of a cruise increased from 9 days in 2002 to 11 days (12.5 days in winter and 10.5 days in summer) in 2009. In Germany, the average ocean cruise sold was 9.3 days long, down from 10 days in 2002 (DRV, 2005, 2011; PSA, 2010).

Destination choice

For the North American market, the Caribbean is still by far the most important cruise destination. This is reflected by the US cruise lines' capacity allocation. In 2009, a capacity share of 35% (measured in available passenger cruise days) was deployed to

Table 1.4. Price segments and their shares of British and German cruise demand.

Cruise prices	UK market	Per diems	German market
–£500	12%	€75–125	21%
£501–1000	24%	€126–175	29%
£1001–2000	37%	€176–250	26%
£2001–2500	10%	€251–400	21%
£2501–5000	13%	€401–	2%
£5001–	2%		

Sources: DRV (2011), PSA (2010).

the Caribbean, 18% to the Mediterranean, 9% to Northern Europe, 7% to the Bahamas and 6% to Alaska (CLIA, 2010).

For the British cruisers, the most important destination region is the long-time favourite, Mediterranean (39%), followed by Northern Europe (19%), the Caribbean (18%) and the Canary Islands (7%) (PSA, 2010). German cruisers have similar preferences. The Mediterranean (35%) continues to be their most important cruise destination by far, followed by Northern Europe (16%), the Caribbean (10%) and the Canary Islands (10%) (DRV, 2011).

Pre-booking behaviour

The demand for cruises passes through distinct phases, which differ with respect to booking frequencies (bookings per week or month). In Fig. 1.2, which depicts an exemplary booking curve of a cruise departing in late July, the short 12-month booking period is divided into three phases. The first 6 months are characterized by a moderate booking frequency, with a dip during the summer holiday season in August. Early bookings are often made by experienced cruisers who want to secure their favourite cabin on their favourite ship for a particular departure. In general, the more expensive the cruise, the greater will be the share of early bookings.

The second phase in Fig. 1.2, which covers the first quarter of the next year, is associated with a significant increase in booking frequency. In the US market, this phase is referred to as wave period, because, in the first 3 months of the year, demand for cruises builds up like a wave. For the US cruise industry, the wave period represents up to 40% of annual bookings (Coiro, 2011).

During the last 4 months before the end of the booking period and the departure of the cruise, the booking frequency declines again. Late bookings may come from bargain hunters and be triggered by cruise lines' last-minute yield management activities.

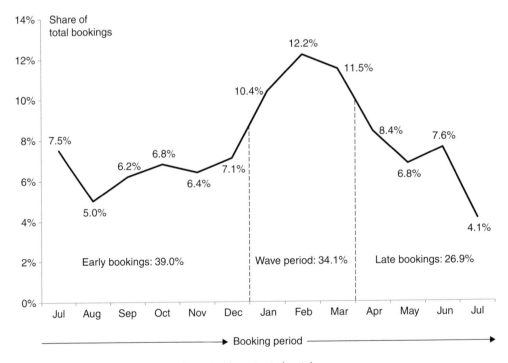

Fig. 1.2. Exemplary booking curve of a cruise departing in late July.

Cruise Demand: a Psychological Perspective

The booking curve in Fig. 1.2 is only a snapshot of a phenomenon that presents itself differently for each departure, each itinerary, each brand, each source market and each year. Some of these variations may be random, but to a much larger extent they reflect the passengers' learned behaviour. In the UK, for instance, the share of late bookings (3 months or less ahead of departure) fell continuously from 34% to 17% between 2000 and 2009, while the share of very early bookings (more than 12 months ahead of departure) rose from 9% to 25% (PSA, 2010, p. 11).

Cruise demand trends such as this are the result of collective learning through social interaction, and it is also social learning through which cruising has become the cultural practice it is now. In other words, cruise passengers are made, not born (though some cruise addicts might disagree).

In this section, we attempt to shed some light on the learning-induced dynamics of cruise demand. To this end, we introduce an explanatory model.

A process model of cruise demand

From a marketing perspective, demand arises when a want is backed by purchasing power. Demand thus presupposes willingness and the ability to pay for something found suitable to satisfy a want. Wants, in turn, are expressions of needs shaped by individual personality, as well as by the cultural and social context. Needs, finally, are states of felt deprivation (Kotler *et al.*, 2003, pp. 13–15). While needs are assumed to be relatively stable, individuals' wants change over time in response to personal development, new experiences and exposure to social and cultural influences. Also people's economic situations and thus their ability to pay are subject to change. Being the result of changing wants and changing purchasing power, demand is an inherently dynamic concept.

To emphasize the dynamic nature of demand, this section of our chapter is based on the process model depicted in Fig. 1.3. It combines elements of Moutinho's (1987, p. 4) and Page and Connell's (2009, p. 76) tourist decision making models with aspects of consumer involvement. Process models 'focus on the way consumers come to have cognitive and affective judgements, intentions and commitments [...]. Most process models are sequential as they suggest an evolution of plans and decisions through different stages' (Decrop, 2006, p. 33).

The starting point of our model is the consumers who wish to satisfy their wants, such as to go on holidays. Wants are backed by a certain purchasing power, which limits the consumers' set of affordable holiday options. The consumers look for information

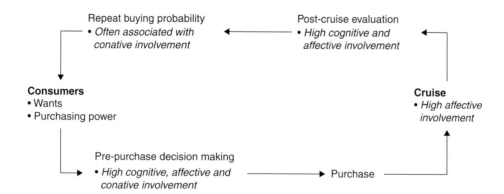

Fig. 1.3. Learning cycle connecting consumer and cruise experience.

on suitable travel offers, consider their respective benefits and costs and try to identify the product promising the best value for money. In Fig. 1.3, the consumers decide to go cruising. After purchasing and experiencing the chosen cruise, the consumers evaluate it, which may influence the probability of future repeat purchases.

This simple model deliberately blinds out many important factors affecting consumer decision making in order to highlight two particular aspects. The first aspect is the role of the consumers. For every stage of the process model in Fig. 1.3, their involvement is necessary. In fact, high consumer involvement is a key characteristic of cruising, and it is the main issue of the next section.

The second aspect highlighted by Fig. 1.3 is the learning cycle linking consumers and the cruise. The majority of cruise passengers pass through this cycle more than once, which means that they learn from their previous experiences and adapt their behaviour, expectations and decisions accordingly. High repeater rates, which may be related to the high consumer involvement, are an essential driver of the cruise sector's sustained growth and success. They might also contribute to the establishment of a distinct cruise culture (Berger, 2004, 2006).

Cruises and consumer involvement

Cruises are an almost prototypical example of a high-involvement product. In marketing, consumer involvement is defined as 'the degree of perceived relevance and personal importance accompanying the brand choice. When a purchase is highly involving, the consumer is more likely to carry out extensive evaluation. High-involvement purchases are likely to include those incurring high expenditure' (Jobber, 2007, p. 123).

Psychologists distinguish between three components of involvement: cognition, affection and conation or behavioural intention. Cognitive involvement refers to the active and rational processing of information. Motivation, awareness and attention are prerequisites of cognitive involvement, and knowledge, learning and recall are its consequences. Affective involvement describes the intensity of subjective experiences or felt emotions. In a positive consumption situation, high affective involvement means that the consumers are passionate about a product, e.g. because it expresses their self-concept. Affective involvement can lead to the shaping of strong attitudes (Lantos, 2011, p. 558). Conative involvement, finally, comprises intention, behaviour and action. In the context of consumption, conative involvement may be understood as 'active search for information, giving advice to others, and communication about experiences one has with a product' (Wirth, 2006, p. 204).

Cruises are fairly complex products. The amount of information to be processed by consumers prior to their purchasing decision is considerable. The significant expenditure associated with a cruise is a major incentive for consumers to get cognitively involved, i.e. to make sure that the product they choose really corresponds to their wants and financial possibilities. In addition to that, emotionally charged product images and descriptions in cruise brochures, guidebooks and on the internet, and the prospect of an enjoyable holiday at sea stimulate also consumers' high affective involvement.

Figure 1.4 lists the reasons of British passengers for choosing to cruise and for selecting a particular ship. Each reason stated is based on the evaluation of information. Some of the reasons reflect high cognitive involvement, e.g. departure date, value for money or loyalty membership benefits. Other reasons seem to have a major affective component, e.g. the enjoyment of a previous cruise, dining or maiden voyage.

Consumers planning a cruise tend not to limit their information search to information channels that are controlled by cruise lines and their distribution partners. Social media are gaining influence fast. Blogs, forums and special interest websites, where

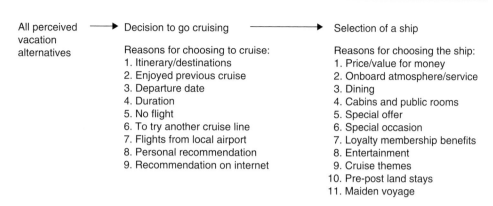

Fig. 1.4. British cruise passengers' reasons for choosing a cruise. Source: based on PSA (2010), p. 10.

experienced cruisers informally post ship reviews, exchange tips and discuss cruising-related topics, are seen by many as more neutral and trustworthy sources of information than brochures and cruise line websites. Also word of mouth and personal recommendations from family members, friends and colleagues are influential factors in the decision making process. The consultation of so many different information sources evidences cruise customers' high conative involvement in the pre-purchase phase.

For Duman and Mattila (2005), the high-involvement character of cruises is not limited to brand and product choice. According to them, 'Cruise vacations are high-involvement, affectively laden experiences [...] cruise vacationers are likely to be guided by their feelings during the vacation and the cognitive evaluation process tends to occur only after some time past the experience' (p. 314). In this broader sense, involvement expresses the extent to which a person is devoted to cruising or the cruise product.

Cruises have no use value. Their value is expressed in experiential categories such as aesthetics, escapism, education (in a non-instrumental sense) and entertainment (Pine and Gilmore, 1999; Oschmann and Vogel, 2006). The passengers' high affective involvement during the cruise is an essential ingredient to the cruise experience. The cruise lines supply the hardware, the service, the itinerary and the daily programme,

but without the passengers' affective involvement, the cruise lines' efforts would be in vain. 'The experience industry can do no more than provide input that the tourist may turn into a tourist experience' (Andersson, 2007, p. 46).

While we agree with Duman and Mattila (2005) about the importance of passengers' affective involvement during the cruise, we question the validity of their claim that the passengers' post-cruise evaluation is primarily a cognitive act. Duman and Mattila's study shows that the perceived value of a cruise is largely determined by affective factors such as hedonics (pleasure seeking), novelty (change from routine, escape, thrill, adventure, surprise, boredom alleviation) and control (multiple options, freedom of choice, calculable risks). Furthermore, the post-cruise evaluation is based on emotionally laden memories, possibly supported by similarly emotionally laden holiday photographs and souvenirs. Under these conditions, the post-cruise evaluation is inevitably a cognitive, as well as a highly affective process.

Post-cruise evaluations seem to turn out very positive. CLIA (2008b, p. 25) reports that 95% of cruisers rate their cruise experience as 'satisfying', and that 44% claim having had an 'extremely satisfying' experience. According to the expectancy disconfirmation model (Oliver, 1980), the classical approach to conceptualizing tourist satisfaction, passengers are satisfied if their prior expectations about the product have been positively disconfirmed. Since it is hard to believe that 95% of all passengers including repeat buyers are consistently surprised by their own positive cruise experience, CLIA's terminology should be taken with a pinch of salt. But even a satisfaction rate of 44% would be remarkable.

Passenger satisfaction, combined with high affective involvement before, during and after the cruise results in high repeat buying probabilities and triggers conative involvement (Fig. 1.3) in the form of information sharing, word of mouth and even proselytism. Large numbers of enthusiastic cruisers engage in their favourite brand's loyalty club, in online discussion forums, in dedicated social networks and virtual cruise communities. Websites like cruise-addicts. com, cruisemates.com or cruisecritic.com would not exist without thousands of cruise passengers willing to invest time and effort into communicating their experiences and keeping each other up to date. Decrop (2006) regards this prolonged involvement as related to hedonic consumption because 'it extends the emotions and moods triggered by the vacation experience' (p. 140).

Repeat buying

For many cruise customers, after the cruise is before the cruise. Their prolonged involvement enables repeaters to bridge the temporal gap between two cruises. The result is enduring involvement, which has been conceptualized as a 'stable trait that represents an individual's degree of interest or arousal for a product on a day-to-day basis; that is, an ongoing, long-term interest' (Higie and Feick, 1989, p. 691). Over time, their interest and concern for cruising, which are associated with ongoing cruise-related information search and transmission, make enduringly involved repeat cruisers very knowledgeable, influential within cruise communities, and often opinion leaders. They act as 'information channels that informally link networks of friends, relatives and other potential travellers' (Reid and Reid, 1993, p. 3) to a cruise brand or to cruising more generally.

The economic potential of these informal ambassadors for the cruise sector (Petrick, 2004) becomes evident when one considers the sector's high repeater rates and large shares of brand-loyal customers. According to the CLIA (2008b) cruise market profile study, 55% of cruisers had taken another cruise in the past. More expensive types of cruises were found to host between 74% and 79% of repeaters, whereas on less expensive cruises the share of repeaters amounted to 40%. Of the cruisers participating in the survey, 21% had taken two or more cruises within the past 12 months. In the luxury cruise segment, this share was 35%. In the UK cruise market, the repeaters' share of bookings rose from 62% to 71% between 2007 and 2009, largely as a result of the economic crisis; 35% of UK cruise passengers booked two or more cruises, and 15% booked three or more cruises in 2009. Also brand loyalty was high: 53% had booked a cruise with the same brand before (PSA, 2010).

Associated with repeat purchasing is the passengers' growing travel experience. More experienced cruisers develop different motives and expectations, which influence their brand and product choices and their evaluation. For instance, prior experience makes cruisers more demanding. More demanding customers are harder to satisfy, and the risk of disappointment and of losing customers rises. The cruise sector's high innovation rates can partly be explained by its significant repeater rates.

Research on the relationship between leisure travel experience and travel motivation led to the development of the travel career ladder model (Moscardo and Pearce, 1986; Pearce, 1993). The model was taken up by Cartwright and Baird (1999), who presented the case of a UK citizen who 'displays a typical progression from family boarding house holiday through to a current "career" in cruising' (p. 19). Unfortunately, they failed to provide evidence for the typicality of this person's travel career. Lumsdon and Page (2004) critically noted that 'we do not fully understand cruise tourists in relation to [...] the travel career ladder' (p. 21).

Other researchers challenged the model itself (e.g. Ryan, 1998), which led to a reformulation referred to as travel career pattern model (Pearce and Lee, 2005). The data on which it is based show that escape, relaxation, novelty and social relationships are the most important factors of travel motivation, irrespective of leisure travellers' travel experience. People with little travel experience are motivated especially by the prospect of stimulation, personal development, self-actualization, security, nostalgia and recognition. More experienced travellers, on the other hand, tend to seek encounters with nature and self-development through host-site involvement, e.g. in the form of experiencing different cultures and meeting the locals (Pearce and Lee, 2005). Because of lack of cruise-specific research, it is not fully clear if these factors of motivation are also behind the demand for cruises.

What is clear, however, is that cruisers with growing experience need to decide for themselves whether they want to remain loyal to a brand or seek more variety. Variety seekers are collectors of different holiday experiences who appreciate novelty as a necessary holiday ingredient. They believe that a cruise is memorable only if it is unlike any other they have taken before. Also, 'variety seeking is an expression of status; it is used to reveal an adventurous, unstable and prospective nature, and to enhance self-image' (Decrop, 2006, p. 137).

Brand loyalists, in contrast, have found what they want. Behavioural brand loyalty is seen as the result of attitudinal loyalty. According to Oliver (1997), attitudinal brand loyalty develops in three stages, which are reminiscent of the three kinds of consumer involvement mentioned earlier and represent a sequential learning process. Customers become 'loyal first in a cognitive sense, then later in an affective sense, and still later in a conative manner' (p. 392).

For cruise passengers, cognitive loyalty can mean that after a good experience with a particular brand they consider booking another cruise of the same brand in order to minimize the risk of disappointment or to benefit from a repeat booking discount. Affective loyalty might be related to romantic moments, enjoyable sensations (e.g. related to food, spa or entertainment) or the particular atmosphere on board. Affectively loyal cruisers seek to revive their cherished memories or to relive their pleasurable experiences they associate with the brand. Conative loyalty, finally, translates into an active commitment to the brand.

High repeater rates and brand loyalty, combined with the self-contained social environment of a cruise (the 'cruise cocoon'; see Vogel, 2004), foster the emergence of ship and brand-specific cultures. According to Sørensen (2003), 'the enforced social interaction within fixed groups on cruises or on organized tours provides mobile settings for tourist cultures to unfold' (p. 9). Over time, self-referential social processes among passengers can lead to the formation of communities of practice (Wenger, 1998), each with its own identity, shared norms, rituals, jargon, discourse and symbols. By interacting with more experienced passengers, first-time cruisers are introduced to the relevant cultural subtleties. They learn what counts (e.g. the number of cruise days and cruises one has completed), what matters (e.g. being a top-tier member of this or that cruise line's loyalty club) and what to avoid (e.g. being caught as a gold member at a reception for platinum members). The socialization passengers undergo on board also covers dress codes, insignia (officers' as well as loyalty club members'), terminology and the appropriate ways of talking about one's past cruises.

There has been some debate as to whether a single, comprehensive 'cruise culture' can be said to exist. Foster (1986) and Berger (2004, 2006) seem to support this position, whereas Douglas and Douglas (1999) reject the idea as 'no more sound than the concept of a single "tourist culture"' (p. 380). In our view, the comparison of cruisers with tourists in general is unsuitable, because cruising is a segment of tourism and as such, it is more homogeneous internally. Moreover, the comparison appears to be based on a rather narrow understanding of culture. If culture is defined as 'a mental map which guides us in our relations to our surroundings and to other people' (Downs, 1971, p. 35) or as 'the collective programming of the mind which distinguishes the members of one group from another' (Hofstede, 1984, p. 21), it is quite imaginable that especially repeat cruisers share what might be considered a discernible common culture.

Cruise Demand: a Sociological Perspective

Leisure cruising may have its own specific (sub-)culture, but more importantly it is a cultural practice. Cruising emerged in Western industrialized societies and continues to be a cultural manifestation of these societies. In this section, we look for conditions and influences of the larger societal context, which may have helped, if not enabled, the development of a mass market for leisure cruises, and which continue to shape it. Figure 1.5 illustrates the embedment of the cruise sector in the larger context of society and the cultural influence that the latter exerts upon the former. The cruise sector in Fig. 1.5 is represented as a simplified version of Fig. 1.3, emphasizing the dynamic, co-evolutionary relationship of cruise demand and supply.

Our sociological analysis is tentative, yet we believe that it merits a place in our chapter on cruise demand. Too many industry and market research reports limit themselves to the summary of consumer and travel agent opinions or to the mere presentation of numbers, leaving it to the reader to make sense of them. We try to provide some guidance to sense-making. To this end, we draw on theories of the sociologist Zygmunt Bauman (2000, 2005).

Modernity, postmodernity, liquid modernity

The 'Big Three' of the international cruise business, NCL, RCL and Carnival, were founded within only 6 years (1966, 1968 and 1972). It is quite remarkable that no pre-existing cruise line managed to keep up with those three companies. We suggest that their creation happened to benefit from a unique window of opportunity, which opened when the Western societies began their transition from modernity to the postmodern age.

For Lyotard (1984), 'this transition has been under way since at least the end of the 1950s, which for Europe marks the completion of reconstruction' (p. 3). Bauman (1992) agrees when he writes that postmodernity 'took its present shape in the second half of [the twentieth] century' (p. 187).

Basically, modernity describes a cultural condition characterized by constant change in the pursuit of progress. Change has a direction and is accepted as an inevitable but only transitory side effect of progress towards a state of perfection. The assumption underlying modernity is that perfection can, in principle, be reached, since the world is seen as controllable, largely predictable and rationally comprehensible for humans.

In postmodernity, however, the belief in a comprehensible, predictable and controllable world collapses. The notion of progress becomes obsolete, and permanent undirected change determines the status quo. We hypothesize that cruising as we know it today is a product of the postmodern age.

Bauman is interested in a particular aspect of postmodernity, namely in the inability of society to hold its shape. He uses the metaphor of 'liquidity' to express the

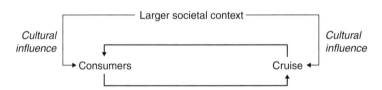

Fig. 1.5.   The societal embedment of the cruise sector.

ephemeral, inexorably transient condition of contemporary (postmodern) society, which, in Bauman's view, is largely related to the restlessness of global capital. Liquid modernity was preceded by solid modernity – an era marked by social cohesion rather than disintegration, tight communities rather than loosely coupled networks, solidarity rather than individualization.

What used to be solid is becoming increasingly fluid: social structures, personal and work relationships, communication habits, lifestyles, even value systems, knowledge, meanings. According to Bauman (2005), '"liquid modern" is a society in which the conditions under which its members act change faster than it takes the ways of acting to consolidate into habits and routines' (p. 1). Instability, uncertainty, lack of orientation, uprootedness – these are just some of the characteristics of life in liquid modernity.

Cruising as an icon of liquid modernity

'The passengers on early cruise ships were well-heeled and well-educated, and facilities on board assumed a certain self-contented independence, with generous provision for reading and writing' (Quartermaine and Peter, 2006, p. 37). Passengers' life on board in those days was a replication of the upper classes' life ashore, including their highly exclusive social norms, tastes and discourses. Middle-class and especially working-class passengers would have felt completely out of place, had they been able to afford a cruise.

Therefore, the ambition of Carnival founder Ted Arison of making cruises accessible for the average holidaymaker required more than making cruises more affordable. Accessibility asked for a cultural shift both on board and ashore. On board, this shift was pioneered by Carnival and their Fun Ships (see Cartledge, Chapter 11, this volume).

Ashore, the shift took place from the 1960s onwards in the form of a 'liquefaction' of previously rigid social structures,

conventions and ways of acting. Liquid modernity, in our view, was the precondition for cruising to grow out of its tiny elitist niche and to become a global industry serving tens of millions of passengers. Today, the demand for cruises reflects the liquid modern condition in so many ways, that cruising can be regarded as an icon of liquid modernity (not only for the liquidity of the sea).

In CLIA's 2010 *Cruise Market Overview*, for example, one reads that 'Cruising is an important vehicle for sampling destination areas to which passengers may return. 80% of cruise passengers agree that a cruise vacation is a good way to sample destinations that they may wish to visit again on a land-based vacation' (CLIA, 2010, p. 1). The possibility to sample destinations without commitment is a strong argument in favour of cruises. For Bauman, the 'looseness of ties' with the places visited and the people encountered, and the 'grazing behaviour' of cruise passengers are key characteristics of liquid life (Franklin, 2003).

Cruise ships move from one stopover to the next without ever really arriving anywhere. Cunard Line's advertising slogan from the 1950s, 'Getting there is half the fun' (Quartermaine and Peter, 2006, p. 34), still implied a final destination. Most cruise itineraries, however, end where they start. There is no progress. In this sense, the circular itinerary perfectly epitomizes the postmodern condition.

In solid modernity, people believed in, and worked for, a brighter future in this life or beyond. Producing was more important than consuming. In the liquid modern age, this relationship has reversed: 'society [...] judges and evaluates its members mostly by their consumption-related capacities and conduct' (Bauman, 2005, p. 82). Moreover, the 'consumerist syndrome consists above all in an emphatic denial of the virtue of procrastination and of the propriety and desirability of the delay of satisfaction' (Bauman, 2005, p. 83). Being a highly conspicuous form of consumption and promising the instantaneous fulfilment of almost any desire, cruises clearly have their place in liquid modernity.

Since 'The "short term" has replaced the "long term" and made of instantaneity its ultimate ideal' (Bauman, 2000, p. 125), people try to compress eternity into their individual life spans. In a world in permanent flux, lightness and speed are more important than constancy and duration. In consequence, a nomadic existence has become a general trait of liquid life. Cruises fully represent these principles: passengers travel with minimal effort (lightness) hundreds of miles while sleeping (speed) to visit a different port every day (nomadism). The duration of visits ashore is unimportant, and also the duration of cruises themselves seems to be losing significance, as large cruise ships carry with them countless attractions, which can be experienced even when there is little time.

Also ship design and interior decoration are expressions of liquid modernity. 'The grand yet eclectic styling of cruise ships is uniquely revealing of popular taste [...] Yet they are important cultural phenomena: mobile self-contained, self-selecting, and inherently transient communities that exemplify the rootlessness and conspicuous consumption of globalized mass culture in the twenty-first century' (Quartermaine and Peter, 2006, p. 78).

Cruising as an escape from liquid life

In some sense though, a cruise can be thought of as a refuge from liquid life. Its attractiveness and value for passengers, then, lies in its relative 'solidity'. Life on board, for instance, promises a degree of reliability, predictability, structure and routine that is hardly found ashore (Vogel, 2004). People who feel overwhelmed or threatened by the fast-paced, turbulent, confusingly complex world surrounding them may find temporary shelter on a cruise. Cruise ships also offer physical protection, or at least the illusion of it, when berthed in port, with their high walls of steel, a moat and a drawbridge, and gatekeepers guarding the entrance. For many passengers, their cruise ship is their castle,

an anachronistic symbol of security in foreign lands and uncertain times.

One of 'the last defensive outposts on the increasingly deserted battlefields on which the war for certainty, security and safety is waged' (Bauman, 2000, p. 184) is community. 'The vision of community [...] is that of an island of homely and cosy tranquillity in a sea of turbulence and inhospitality' (Bauman, 2000, p. 182). The idea of joining a community of like-minded fellow cruisers may give passengers a feeling of belonging and identity, which their restless, mobile daily lives might not have to offer.

Whether this community on board is real or illusive is of no importance, as the differences among the passengers, unlike the differences among people ashore, are 'tamed, sanitized, guaranteed to come free of dangerous ingredients' (Bauman, 2000, p. 99). In a liquid modern world of destabilized and disintegrating social structures and relationships, communication habits, lifestyles, values, knowledge and meanings, 'the myth of community solidarity is a purification ritual' (Sennett, 1970, p. 36).

Concluding Remarks

By providing three very different perspectives on cruise demand in our chapter, we want to contribute to a richer and more complex understanding of this phenomenon. In our experience, market research and industry reports tend to be limited to the presentation of cruise demand data (e.g. time series of preferred destinations and brands, number of passengers with a certain willingness to pay, historic booking patterns, stated purchasing and repurchasing intentions) whilst addressing the possible reasons only marginally, if at all. The reduction of demand analysis to data trivializes the matter and is not particularly helpful for many decision makers in the cruise sector.

The business and management of ocean cruises involves many operational decisions on a day-to-day basis, for which plain cruise demand data may be sufficient as an information basis, since demand can be taken as given. A cruise line's call centre manager, for instance, needs to know when to expect the booking wave period in order to prepare the staff roster accordingly. For such operational management decisions, the quantitative perspective on cruise demand is appropriate.

However, developers of a new on-board restaurant service concept, a new loyalty scheme or anything else aimed at influencing cruise demand will not be satisfied with the information that the customer satisfaction rate is x% and the repeater rate is y%. These marketers would need to know why it is so and how certain modifications on the supply side are going to affect demand. What they need are explanations and, ideally, cause–effect relationships. In our chapter, the psychological perspective on demand provides some insights of this kind.

Strategic decisions entailing significant risks and long-term consequences, finally, ought to be made on the basis of a profound understanding of the network of factors underlying cruise demand. The decision to build a revolutionarily innovative cruise ship or to adopt a radically different marketing communication strategy poses very different questions about the nature of demand. Here, decision makers need to know not only why the repeater rate is y% but whether they can count on high repeat booking rates over the next decade or two, even though in liquid modernity, loyalty tends to be 'a cause of shame, not pride' (Bauman, 2005, p. 9). The sociological perspective may help clarify the larger societal context of cruising and reframe the strategy discussion.

References

Andersson, T.D. (2007) The tourist in the experience economy. *Scandinavian Journal of Hospitality and Tourism* 7(1), 46–58.

Bauman, Z. (1992) *Intimations of Postmodernity*. Routledge, London.

Bauman, Z. (2000) *Liquid Modernity*. Polity, Cambridge.

Bauman, Z. (2005) *Liquid Life*. Polity, Cambridge.

Berger, A.A. (2004) *Ocean Travel and Cruising – a Cultural Analysis*. Haworth Press, Binghamton, New York.

Berger, A.A. (2006) Sixteen ways of looking at an ocean cruise: a cultural studies approach. In: Dowling, R.K. (ed.) *Cruise Ship Tourism*. CABI, Wallingford, pp. 124–128.

Bureau of Labor Statistics (2011) *Consumer Price Index*. US Department Of Labor, Washington, DC.

Cartwright, R. and Baird, C. (1999) *The Development and Growth of the Cruise Industry*. Butterworth-Heinemann, Oxford.

CLIA (2005) *Market Overview Spring 2005*. Cruise Lines International Association, Fort Lauderdale, Florida.

CLIA (2008a) *Cruise Market Overview. Statistical Cruise Industry Data Through 2007*. Cruise Lines International Association, Fort Lauderdale, Florida.

CLIA (2008b) *Cruise Market Profile Study*. Cruise Lines International Association, Fort Lauderdale, Florida.

CLIA (2010) *Cruise Market Overview. Statistical Cruise Industry Data Through 2009*. Cruise Lines International Association, Fort Lauderdale, Florida.

CLIA (2011) Cruise Lines International Association's State of the Industry 2011. Available at: www2.cruising.org/cruisenews/news.cfm?NID=196824 (accessed 16 March 2011).

Coiro, T. (2011) Another 'Tsunami Cruise Wave Season'. Available at: www.prweb.com/releases/directlinecruises/waveseason/prweb8169552.htm (accessed 27 March 2011).

Cruise Shipping Asia (2011, 31 January) Cruise Shipping Asia Goes Full Steam Ahead. Available at: www.cruiseshippingasia.com/c/document_library/get_file?uuid=4a6982ad-d565-4a66-abd8-62c3b6a43b2c&groupId=1115798 (accessed 26 March 2011).

Decrop, A. (2006) *Vacation Decision Making*. CABI, Wallingford.

Destatis (2011) *Verbraucherpreisindizes für Deutschland. Lange Reihen ab 1948*. Statistisches Bundesamt, Wiesbaden.

Douglas, N. and Douglas, N. (1999) Cruise consumer behaviour: a comparative study. In: Pizam A. and Mansfeld, Y. (eds) *Consumer Behavior in Travel and Tourism*. Haworth Hospitality Press, Binghamton, New York, pp. 370–392.

Downs, J. (1971) *Cultures in Crisis*. Glencoe, Beverly Hills, California.

DRV (2005) *Der Kreuzfahrtenmarkt Deutschland 2004*. Deutscher Reise Verband, Berlin.

DRV (2011) *Der Kreuzfahrtenmarkt Deutschland 2010*. Deutscher Reise Verband, Berlin.

Duman, T. and Mattila, A.S. (2005) The role of affective factors on perceived cruise vacation value. *Tourism Management* 26(3), 311–323.

ECC (2011) European Cruise Market by Country, 2003–2010. Available at: www.europeancruisecouncil.com/content/ECC_Stats_2010.pdf (accessed 19 March 2011).

Expedia (2009) 2009 International Vacation Deprivation Survey Results. Available at: media.expedia.com/media/content/expus/graphics/promos/vacations/Expedia_International_Vacation_Deprivation_Survey_2009.pdf (accessed 26 March).

Foster, G.M. (1986) South Seas cruise: a case study of a short-lived society. *Annals of Tourism Research* 13(2), 215–238.

Franklin, A. (2003) The tourist syndrome. *Tourist Studies* 3(2), 205–217.

Higie, R.A. and Feick, L.F. (1989) Enduring involvement: conceptual and measurement issues. *Advances in Consumer Research* 16, 690–696.

Hofstede, G. (1984) *Culture's Consequences: International Differences in Work Related Values*. Sage, Beverly Hills, California.

Jobber, D. (2007) *Principles and Practice of Marketing*. McGraw-Hill, Maidenhead.

Kotler, P., Bowen, J.T. and Makens, J.C. (2003) *Marketing for Hospitality and Tourism*. Pearson Education, Upper Saddle River, New Jersey.

Lantos, G.P. (2011) *Consumer Behavior in Action: Real-Life Applications for Marketing Managers*. Sharpe, Armonk, New York.

Lumsdon, L. and Page, S.J. (2004) Progress in transport and tourism research: reformulating the transport-tourism interface and future research agendas. In: Lumsdon, L. and Page, S.J. (eds) *Tourism and Transport. Issues and Agenda for the New Millenium*. Elsevier, Amsterdam, pp. 1–28.

Lyotard, J.F. (1984) *The Postmodern Condition: a Report on Knowledge*. University of Minnesota Press, Minneapolis, Minnesota.

Moscardo, G.M. and Pearce, P.L. (1986) Historic theme parks: an Australian experience in authenticity. *Annals of Tourism Research* 13(3), 467–479.

Moutinho, L. (1987) Consumer behaviour in tourism. *European Journal of Marketing* 21(10), 5–44.

Oliver, R.L. (1980) A cognitive model of the antecedents and consequences of satisfaction decisions. *Journal of Marketing Research* 17(4), 460–469

Oliver, R.L. (1997) *Satisfaction: a Behavioral Perspective on the Consumer*. McGraw-Hill, New York.

Oschmann, C. and Vogel, M. (2006) Erlebnisplus Landprogramm. *An Bord* 4, 64–66.

Page, S.J. and Connell, J. (2009) *Tourism. A Modern Synthesis*, 3rd edn. Cengage Learning, Andover.

Pearce, P.L. (1993) Fundamentals of tourist motivation. In: Pearce, D. and Butler, R. (eds) *Tourism Research: Critiques and Challenges*. Routledge and Kegan Paul, London, pp. 85–105.

Pearce, P.L. and Lee, U.-I. (2005) Developing the travel career approach to tourist motivation. *Journal of Travel Research* 43(3), 226–237.

Peisley, T. (2010) *Cruising at the Crossroads. A Worldwide Analysis to 2025*. Seatrade Communications, Colchester.

Petrick, J.F. (2004) Are loyal visitors desired visitors? *Tourism Management* 25(4), 463–470.

Pine, J. and Gilmore, J. (1999) *The Experience Economy*. Harvard Business School Press, Boston, Massachusetts.

PSA (2010) *The Cruise Review*. Passenger Shipping Association, London.

Quartermaine, P. and Peter, B. (2006) *Cruise: Identity, Design and Culture*. Laurence King, London.

Reid, L.J. and Reid, S.D. (1993) Communicating tourism supplier services: building repeat visitor relationships. *Journal of Travel & Tourism Marketing* 2(2/3), 3–19.

Ryan, C. (1998) The travel career ladder. An appraisal. *Annals of Tourism Research* 25(4), 936–957.

Sennett, R. (1970) *The Uses of Disorder: Personal Identity and the City*. Alfred A. Knopf, New York.

Sørensen, A. (2003) Backpacker ethnography. *Annals of Tourism Research* 30(4), 847–867.

Vogel, M. (2004) Kreuzfahrt: Reisen im dreifachen Kokon. *An Bord* 5, 17–20.

Wenger, E.C. (1998) *Communities of Practice: Learning, Meaning, and Identity*. Cambridge University Press, Cambridge.

Wirth, W. (2006) Involvement. In: Bryant, J. and Vorderer, P. (eds) *Psychology of Entertainment*. Lawrence Erlbaum Associates, Mahwah, New Jersey, pp. 199–213.

2 Development of the Cruise Industry Structure – the Supply Side

Borislav Bjelicic

Introduction

In the past few years, the structure of supply in the transport markets has undergone momentous change. Increased external growth of transport firms, via mergers and acquisitions (M&A), continues to be central to these changes. In the cruise sector, too, M&A transactions have grown in importance in the past years – owing principally to the globalization of the tourism industry – and have led to a consolidation amongst providers. What is the current supply structure? Is the global cruise market still open to new entrants, and will these operators be able to gain a significant position in the market? These are the two key issues that I attempt to address in this paper.

Competition and Market Development

Competition among firms is the basis for the successful functioning of a free enterprise system. However, the system's success may be threatened when suppliers merge. In the first place, there is the danger that a market's remaining suppliers enter into agreements that effectively restrain competition. Second, an individual provider may acquire market power to such an extent that other

suppliers become dependent – in their conduct – on the market leader. To avoid this happening, it is imperative that markets remain open to entry by new suppliers. In other words, as long as market entry remains a possibility, there can be competition – even among a small number of providers. Domestic competition policies serve the purpose of protecting competition in a nation's free enterprise environment. The globalization of markets requires increasing cooperation among national authorities dealing with competition issues, or, as in the European Union, the design of a common competition policy to safeguard competition.

Friedrich von Hayek has referred to competition as a discovery procedure, as firms perpetually endeavour to find more efficient technologies (von Hayek, 1969). New markets for goods and services emerge mainly by virtue of technological innovations relating to products and procedures. Typically, markets evolve according to a characteristic pattern that is depicted in Fig. 2.1 and may be outlined in the following way. Initially, pioneers enter the market, and since they are not being taken note of or not considered a serious threat, they quickly prosper when their products find acceptance in the market. In the second phase of market expansion, success has become visible, attracting emulators. These comprise not only entirely new entrants but also incumbent providers, which feel threatened by the pioneers' products. Since the number of suppliers is at its highest level in this phase, while price competition is increasing, demand is growing at an exceptional rate. The number of providers entering the market declines. In the next phase, market consolidation sets in, since not all providers are able to reduce costs sufficiently or persevere otherwise in the face of persistent price competition. Alternatively, providers may expand capacities at a rate surpassing growth in demand. Marginal suppliers exit the market, quite possibly including pioneers. During the market consolidation phase, in addition to cases of genuine market exit, M&A also take place. Typically, M&A are explained by the need to adjust company size, to allow for a suitable level of technological and economic efficiency. Hence, at this point one observes a growing trend towards corporate concentration.

To the extent that new players enter the market at this stage, one encounters mainly firms that direct their investments toward special market niches. Market entry motivated by rapid acquisition of a large market share is a rare phenomenon at this stage, for such a strategy entails a massive commitment of capital. In this phase, when the market is in a state of high consolidation, it is far more likely to observe market entrance by providers attacking the business models of the incumbents – by putting in place their own innovative business models. In as much as the established providers attribute little credibility to these new arrivals, or refuse to take them seriously, the start of a new market cycle might be in the making, where those offering new business models assume the role of pioneers. As an example from the transport sector, consider the airline market entry by Ryanair in 1985, introducing the Low Cost business model to European air transport. While the new carrier was barely taken seriously by incumbent airlines in the early years, at the end of the day Ryanair triggered a massive restructuring in European air traffic, inducing numerous emulators to enter the market and causing considerable strain to established operators (Bjelicic, 2007). Of course, sooner or later a new market cycle gives rise again to market consolidation along with market exits, M&A.

Since the assumption is usually made that restraints on competition are more

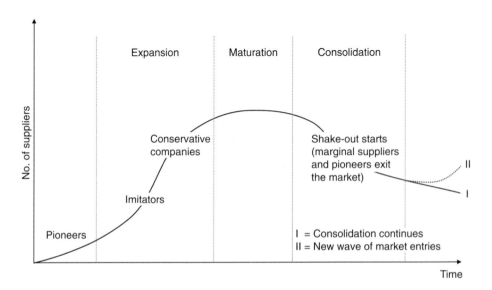

Fig. 2.1. Market development phases.

likely if there is a higher degree of corporate concentration in the market, the various forms of exercising control over activities related to mergers have become important tools for competition policy. The task of competition policy is to safeguard markets against anti-competitive practices by market participants, price-fixing agreements between suppliers being a case in point.

Notably, large mergers in the offing have to be reported to the authorities dealing with anti-trust and monopoly issues, which examine repercussions for the competitive environment. It is of paramount concern to establish whether a market position that results from a merger or an acquisition is likely to restrain competition. In order to assess the nature of an envisaged merger, it is necessary to define the type of market in question. A market may be delineated both in geographic terms and in terms of products. In determining the relevant product market, consideration is given to the various aspects of the competitive relations between products. The delineation of the relevant geographic market focuses on defining one or more market areas affected by the merger.

Historic Development of the Supply-side Structure in the Cruise Industry

The development of the supplier structure in the cruise industry has followed the pattern described above, with differences vis-à-vis other markets relating to the temporal extension of specific developmental phases. As early as the 19th century, pleasure cruises were being offered. Thomas Cook, the pioneer of the tourism industry, offered cruises (Quartermaine and Peter, 2006) for the first time in 1894. Like recreational travel in general, in those days cruises were aimed at the affluent. To the extent that dedicated cruise vessels were available, they could be compared with large luxury yachts. The time of mass tourism had not arrived yet. In the early 1960s, mass tourism would begin to develop against the backdrop of growing prosperity

among consumers and the general increase in leisure time. Industry pioneers like Knut Kloster and Ted Arison were quicker to anticipate the development than others. They were also quicker than others to anticipate the inevitability of the eclipse of scheduled passenger line voyages, in the face of competitive pressure exerted by the substitute services offered by airlines; their vision enabled them to embark upon the cruise business by redeploying converted liners.

Geographically, routes between the USA and the Caribbean would form the central region of growth in the cruise industry. In 1966, the Norwegian vessel operator Knut Kloster and his associate Ted Arison established Norwegian Cruise Lines (NCL), offering cruise voyages departing from Florida to tour the Caribbean. The first vessel to be used for the purpose was the *Sunward I*, originally built to serve as a car ferry. The second vessel, the *Starward*, still has its car decks. The *Skyward*, NCL's third vessel, was the first one without car decks, providing only cabins. Later on, Ted Arison left the company and established Carnival Cruise Lines in Miami in 1972, commencing operations with the *Mardi Gras*, converted from a former liner (*Empress of Canada*). Furthermore, in 1968, Norwegian operators established the shipping company Royal Caribbean Cruise Line. The company's headquarters was also located in Miami. Over the next years, Miami emerged as the hub of the US cruise market (Quartermaine and Peter, 2006).

Having caused the demise of scheduled passenger line voyages on the North Atlantic route, aircraft turned out to be an indispensable auxiliary for cruise operators. The dramatic increase in air traffic in North America meant that growing numbers of people were able to travel quickly and cheaply to Florida, the departure point for Caribbean cruises. In this way, aircraft became a momentous factor – triggering the subsequent phase of rapid market expansion. At this stage, increasing passenger numbers allowed for the building of larger vessels – with lower operating costs – which, in turn, entailed offerings at attractive prices, thereby fuelling further demand.

Compared with the North American market, developments in Europe are still lagging behind. The percentage of the population that had been on a cruise was close to 3% in North America during 2009, while the corresponding figure for Western Europe was a mere 0.97%. However, the rate of demand growth has been higher in Europe than in North America for some years. Whilst demand for cruises in the North American market increased by 51% between 2000 and 2009, the growth rate in Western Europe was 148% during the same period (GP Wild, 2010). Asia is still in the early stage of market development. A number of socio-demographic factors provide an explanation. However, a relatively affluent middle class is growing increasingly in Asia, which will form the basis for rapid market expansion in the coming years, along with a trend toward an increase in leisure time.

The trend toward ever larger vessels, providing an ever-widening range of on-board entertainment has been accompanied by a need for more capital, which, in turn, has been an important factor giving rise to increased market consolidation and the attendant reduction both of the number of independent providers (thanks to M&A) and the number of market entrants since the mid-1980s.

Of all cruise operators, Carnival has had the most powerful impact on the way the supply-side structure has developed. Figure 2.2 shows the most significant M&A transactions during the past 20 years; 1988 saw the first takeover by Carnival, involving Admiral Cruises, followed by the acquisition of Holland America Line in 1989. In 1997 followed the takeover of Costa Crociere, a Genoa-based shipping company built on a history of takeovers and mergers relating to French and Italian shipping interests. A year later, Carnival acquired Cunard, the renowned and traditional British shipping company. With the takeover of P&O Princess Cruises (POPC), concluded in 2003, Carnival's external growth reached a new apex.

Initially, it was Royal Caribbean that intended to merge with POPC, and actually submitted a bid. The bid was reviewed both by the German competition authority (Bundeskartellamt) and the UK Competition Commission; both cases resulted in approval of the notified merger. The report of the UK Competition Commission was published on 19 June 2002 (Competition Commission, 2002). However, the case was rendered obsolete when Carnival made a hostile takeover bid in December 2001, an effort that finally met with the approval of POPC's shareholders.

In April 2002, the European Commission decided to initiate proceedings in accordance with the Merger Regulation (Commission of the European Communities, 2003). For this purpose, it was necessary to determine the relevant geographic market, and the relevant product market. A momentous issue; if the defined market is larger, then an individual supplier's market share will be correspondingly smaller. The likelihood of a merger giving rise to a dominant position will therefore be diminished.

Concerning the geographically relevant market, in its argument, Carnival emphasized the existence of international markets, since oceanic cruise operations are marketed worldwide: vessels, not being tied to specific routes or areas, may be bought, chartered and deployed anywhere in the world. By contrast, the European Commission concluded that markets for oceanic cruise operations were still predominantly of a national nature. Accordingly, the UK, Germany, France, Italy and Spain were defined as sub-markets requiring separate examination.

Regarding delineation of the relevant product market, Carnival considered that the market for recreational travel should be regarded as pertinent, since cruises may be substituted by other types of recreational travel, including sojourns in holiday clubs and all-inclusive hotels. The European Commission did not accept the argument, instead regarding the market for oceanic cruise operations as the relevant product market. Moreover, consideration was given to the question as to whether geographic sub-markets comprise separate relevant markets for 'Premium' and 'Economy'

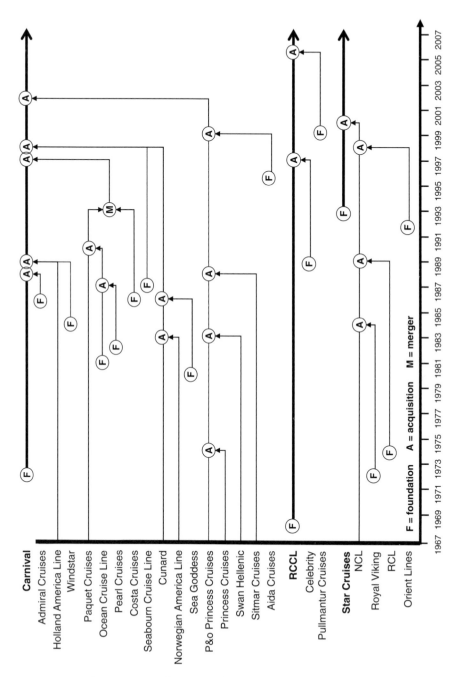

Fig. 2.2. Mergers and acquisitions in the cruise industry. Source: compiled by the author. RCCL, Royal Caribbean; NCL, Norwegian Cruise Lines; RCL, Royal Cruise Line.

cruises. However, the European Commission was unable to delineate clearly 'Premium' against 'Economy' offerings, concluding therefore that there was a single market for oceanic cruise operations.

Despite the European Commission's somewhat narrow definition of the markets, it concluded that 'the proposed concentration will not create or strengthen a dominant position as a result of which effective competition in the common market [...] would be significantly impeded' (Commission of the European Communities, 2003, p. 2). A certain contribution to the European Commission's view was its consideration that domestic markets remained open to new entrants. Concerning the British market, it was determined: 'The ability for new entry and expansion has been proven by recent history in the market' (Commission of the European Communities, 2003, p. 41). The same conclusion was drawn with regard to other markets included in the examination. The conclusion refers to market entry by tour operators, who were able to use their established brand names in marketing newly offered cruises, and to benefit from well-established channels of distribution. These providers had access to used and chartered vessels, for which additional reason market entry was not impeded.

Unlike the European Commission, the UK Competition Commission was not able to arrive at a precise delineation of the relevant product market. '[...] we were not able to reach a conclusion on the appropriate product market for our inquiry [...]' (Competition Commission, 2002, p. 3) and further: 'We have not been able to come to a single view on these issues. Some of us considered that cruises are part of the wider holiday market, while others prefer the view that cruises constitute a separate market, or series of markets'. Regarding the issue of whether the market may be considered open to new entrants, the UK Competition Commission derived an affirmative assessment: '[...] the conclusion that we draw [...] is that barriers to entering the cruise business are not insurmountable – especially for those with existing experience

in travel or tourism' (Competition Commission, 2002, p. 19). Particularly with respect to the ability of new entrants to access vessels, the UK Competition Commission was of the opinion that in view of plans by large cruise operators to order numerous new builds, there will be an influx of older, used vessels into the second-hand market within the foreseeable future (Competition Commission, 2002).

The intended merger was also approved by the US Federal Trade Commission, which considered the market for oceanic cruise operations to represent the relevant product market, while confining examination of the issue of the geographically relevant market to cruises being offered to North American clients (Federal Trade Commission, 2002a). However, the decision was a close one, being based on a 3:2 majority: two members of the US Federal Trade Commission considered that the merger could indeed restrict price competition, and published their diverging view in a 'Dissenting Statement' (Federal Trade Commission, 2002b).

In the end, Royal Caribbean lost out in the bid for POPC to rival Carnival, as the shareholders confirmed Carnival's higher offer. Hence, apart from the takeover of Celebrity Cruises in 1997, and of Spanish operator Pullmantur Cruises in 2007, Royal Caribbean's growth has essentially been organic.

While Royal Caribbean was established in 1968 and Carnival in 1972, Star Cruises is a company of relatively recent origin, having been founded in 1993 and focusing on Asia. Since taking over NCL in 2000, the newly established shipping company has been able to close the gap somewhat on the two big providers. In August 2007, Star Cruises sold 50% of its NCL shares to the US private equity investor Apollo Management.

The cruise shipping franchise of Mediterranean Shipping Company (MSC) has seen very strong growth over recent years. Established in 1970, MSC – which is also active in global container shipping – entered the cruise shipping market in the mid-1980s.

Supplier Structure and Market Share in 2010

Aggregate global cruise shipping supply amounted to 393,800 lower berths (LB) in mid-2010 (all data derived from GP Wild, 2010). Looking at the supply-side structure, which is depicted in Fig. 2.3, the four key operators – Carnival Cruises, Royal Caribbean Cruises, Star Cruises and MSC – together accounted for close to 325,000 LB, equivalent to 83% of the overall capacity. At 48%, Carnival alone represented almost a half of global cruise shipping capacity. Carnival's market share was achieved mainly by virtue of strong external growth (see above). The remainder of aggregate global supply – just under 69,000 LB or 17% – is distributed amongst numerous small to medium-sized operators who largely specialize in expeditions or exclusive luxury cruises.

An examination of the global cruise shipping market in terms of distinct product segments reveals further characteristics of the supplier structure. Depending on the criteria of delineation, market segmentation in terms of products offered yields five segments (Fig. 2.4). According to the GP Wild method of delineation, the mass market is covered by the 'Standard' and the 'Deluxe' segment. Other publications refer to the 'Standard' segment as the 'Contemporary' segment, while the 'Deluxe' segment is described as the 'Premium' segment. In these segments, mid-size to large cruise liners and even so-called mega-cruise ships are deployed. The increasing range of on-board activities, targeting mass-market clients, has boosted deployment of larger vessels because of the need physically to accommodate a growing number of sport and entertainment facilities. However, these two product segments cannot be differentiated in a clear-cut way, i.e. differences in the level of comfort and luxury are often incremental.

The 'Deluxe-Plus' and the 'Super-Deluxe' segment differ from the mass market in terms of pronounced exclusiveness and upscale ambience and amenities. In these segments, smaller vessels tend to be deployed. The 'Super-Deluxe' segment is sometimes referred to as 'Ultra-Luxury',

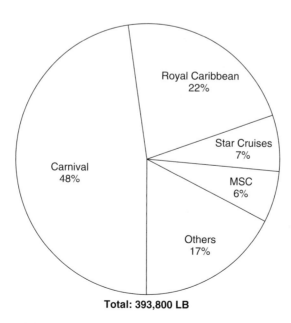

Total: 393,800 LB

Fig. 2.3. Market shares of the four key operators. Source: GP Wild (2010). MSC, Mediterranean Shipping Company.

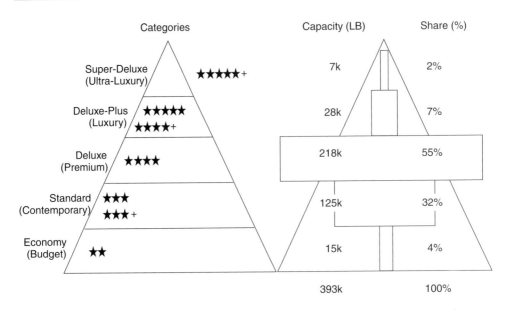

Fig. 2.4. Product segments and their shares of total capacity. Source: compiled by the author. LB, lower berths.

whereas the 'Deluxe-Plus' segment is also known as the 'Luxury' segment. Deployment of smaller vessels tends to be a hallmark also of the 'Economy' segment, which is primarily intended to attract younger clients – by offering low-price cruises to initiate the target group into the market – as well as those attracted by expeditions offering unusual routes and destinations. This segment, which also includes operators offering cruises to the Arctic and Antarctic regions, is also sometimes referred to as the 'Budget' segment.

Categorizing globally-deployed cruise liners by product segments according to the method used by GP Wild, the two segments of the mass market accounted for 87% of total capacity (in terms of LB) in mid-2010, while 9% are accounted for by the two 'Luxury' segments and 4% by the 'Budget' segment. A closer look at the situation in the five product segments reveals the picture shown in Fig. 2.5.

In the 'Deluxe' segment, which represents 55% of total capacity, Carnival commands a share of 49.6%, followed by Royal Caribbean with 25.4%. In the 'Standard' segment, which accounts for 32% of total capacity, Carnival has a share of 57.8%, while Caribbean's share is 10.5%, i.e. this particular segment, especially the lower stratum, is characterized by a comparatively large number of competitors.

By contrast, at 63.3% of available capacity in the 'Deluxe-Plus' segment, Royal Caribbean has a stronger market position than Carnival with 12%. However, this segment represents only 7% of global cruise shipping capacity. In the 'Super-Deluxe' segment, Carnival's Seabourn brand has a share of 23.5% of total capacity (based on LB). Representing an aggregate share of 52% of total capacity, the two operators Silversea and Crystal Cruises are the leading providers in this segment. Royal Caribbean does not participate in the segment. According to the GP Wild classification, Carnival only operates two vessels in the 'Economy' segment, accounting for a 10.7% share of supply capacity. Note again that the segments in question are classified in terms of vessels deployed. It is quite possible that e.g. a company like Carnival, in fact, competes for business in the 'Economy' segment by offering lower day-rates for vessels regarded as belonging to the 'Standard' segment.

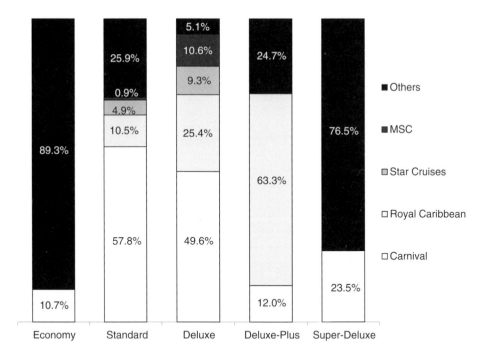

Fig. 2.5. Market shares of the four key operators in the five product segments. Source: GP Wild (2010). MSC, Mediterranean Shipping Company.

It is worth noting that the concentration of supply is the highest in the mass market: of the overall mass-market capacity of just under 344,000 LB, the four big operators (Carnival, Royal Caribbean, Star and MSC) together account for an aggregate market share of 87.3%. In contrast, the supply structures in the budget and luxury market segments are much more fragmented.

More difficult than determining supply capacity is the task of measuring market share in terms of demand. This was, and remains, a central issue in the competitive assessment of a proposed concentration. Thus, absolute figures on passengers are rather inexpedient in determining market share, since they do not reflect the length of a cruise, i.e. companies that tend to offer shorter cruises would be ascribed an inflated market share. Accordingly, measurement of market share on the basis of passenger cruise days would appear more appropriate. While the European Commission employed this method in its examination of the proposed concentration as

regards Carnival/POPC, owing to lack of data, it was not able to calculate market share in terms of turnover.

Prospective Development of the Supply-side Structure in the Cruise Industry

Only a few years have passed since the European Commission approved the proposed concentration relating to Carnival/POPC – not least in view of expectations that domestic markets were going to remain open to new entrants. In this connection, the European Commission drew particular attention to the possibility of market entry by tour operators. Since then, concentration amongst tour operators in Europe has produced a new line-up – one that needs to be taken into consideration in assessing proposed future concentrations relating to cruise shipping. Hence, in 2007, owing to changes in the environment regulated by competition law, tour operator TUI and cruise operator Carnival were compelled to give up plans to establish a joint venture pertaining to cruise operations; in September 2007, both companies withdrew an anti-trust filing (TUI AG, 2007a). Just a few weeks later, in December 2007, TUI and Royal Caribbean announced the launch of a new joint venture to serve the cruise market, notifying the European Commission of the proposed concentration in early February 2008 (TUI AG, 2007b). In the following month, the European Commission granted its approval of the proposed joint venture, in which each partner holds a 50% stake. The joint venture commenced operations under the brand name TUI Cruises, targeting the product segment defined by 'Premium' cruises. Since then, possible expectations for a stronger engagement of additional tour operators have not materialized.

Future cases will demonstrate whether the competition authorities maintain their view that competition in the cruise markets is ensured by the possibility of market entry. In the mass market for 'Standard' and 'Deluxe' cruises, increasingly demanding consumer expectations drive capital requirements to finance new vessels. This will provide a limiting factor for market entry by new suppliers. After all, as of 2009, average manufacturing costs per LB were approximately US$220,000 for very large vessels in the 'Standard' segment. The purchase price for a single mega-cruise ship, with a capacity of 3000 LB ranges between US$500 million and US$600 million, depending on specifications. In the ultra-luxury segment, however, prices per LB reached close to US$550,000 in 2009 (GP Wild, 2010). This translates into considerable purchase prices for new 'Ultra-Luxury' vessels; having an average capacity of 400–500 LB. Rates for used and chartered vessels follow this trend. It is the 'Budget' segment where market entry – involving relatively moderate capital expenditure – is most likely to occur, since this product segment rather deploys smaller and older vessels, demanding total investments of more restricted size.

Going forward, capital will increasingly turn into a barrier to market entry for new entrants during the years to come, affecting the structure of cruise shipping providers and particularly the issue of keeping markets open to new operators. Considering the increased investment required for both new and used vessels, on account of growth in size and a higher level of specifications, it is unlikely nowadays that new entrants will be able to gain sizeable market share within a short timeframe – unless they can be sure, from the very beginning, of massive support from investors and financial markets. Hence, access to financing or capital will play a larger role than before in maintaining competition among market participants on the international cruise shipping markets.

In principle, cruise shipping operators have various sources of financing at their disposal: primarily bank loans, export financings, the capital market and private equity (Tucker, 2010). Typically, private equity investors have a medium-term to long-run time horizon. They collect large amounts of capital from investors, using the funds to invest very selectively in specific companies. An example is provided by Apollo Management, having initially acquired Oceania Cruises (a smaller operator in the 'Deluxe-Plus' segment), a company in which Royal Caribbean had also been interested. Supported by the financial strength of their investors, Oceania was able to order two mid-sized vessels from the Fincantieri shipyard, each accommodating 1260 passengers, at a price per vessel of approximately US$500 million (Oceania Cruises, 2007). In 2007, Apollo subsequently acquired a shareholding in NCL and paid the owner, Star Cruises, US$1 billion for a 50% stake. A 12.5% stake was later passed on to TPG Capital. Whilst retaining a 50% interest in NCL, Star Cruises could use the proceeds from the sale to look for new, additional vessels to ensure further growth (NCL, 2008). Finally, by the end of 2007, Apollo announced (and in January 2008 concluded) the takeover of Carlson's shipping operator Regent Seven Seas Cruises (RSSC), which is active in the

'Ultra-Luxury' segment. Typically, private equity investors are looking for an initial public offering (IPO) as an exit route. In October 2010, preparations for an IPO of NCL were initiated by submitting a Registration Statement to the US Securities and Exchange Commission. Fundamentally, an IPO provides new avenues for the acquisition of capital to fund corporate growth. The IPOs by Carnival in New York in 1987, and by Royal Caribbean in 1993, are examples that may well prove attractive enough to be emulated by new IPO candidates in this shipping segment.

Summary and Conclusion

At present, international cruise shipping is characterized by a high level of concentration among suppliers in its core mass-market segment. In contrast, the low-end (budget) and high-end (luxury) cruise shipping segments do not yet exhibit such a degree of concentration. Continuation of effective competition will depend crucially on the extent to which markets remain open to new entrants. In this context, access to capital will play an important role, both for new entrants and to support incumbent operators in their efforts to expand capacity. Given the prevailing positive outlook for future global demand for cruises, it is fair to assume at present that banks, investors and other stakeholders have a general interest to invest in this sector. In particular, the Asian market holds interesting prospects for the future, since the entry of new market players is most likely to occur from this region, albeit supported by regional financing.

References

Bjelicic, B. (2007) The business model of low cost airlines – past, present, future. In: *Handbook of Low Cost Airlines*. Erich Schmidt Verlag, Berlin.

Commission of the European Communities (2003) Commission decision of 24 July 2002, declaring a concentration to be compatible with the common market and the functioning of the EEA agreement (Case No COMP/M.2706 – Carnival Corporation/P&O Princess). *Official Journal of the European Union*, L 248.

Competition Commission (2002) P&O Princess Cruises plc and Royal Caribbean Cruises Ltd; A report on the proposed merger, presented to the Parliament by the Secretary of State for Trade and Industry.

Federal Trade Commission (2002a) Statement of the Federal Trade Commission concerning Royal Caribbean Cruises Ltd./P&O Princess Cruises plc and Carnival Corporation/P&O Princess Cruises plc, FTC File No. 021 0041.

Federal Trade Commission (2002b) Dissenting Statement of Commissioners Sheila F. Anthony and Mozelle W. Thompson, Royal Caribbean/Princess and Carnival/Princess, FTC File No. 021 0041.

GP Wild (2010) Cruise Industry Statistical Review 2009–10, GP Wild (International) Ltd.

Norwegian Cruise Line (NCL) (2008) NCL Closes $1 Billion Investment by Apollo. Available at: www.ncl. com/nclweb/cruiser/cmsPages.html?pageId=InvPR_010708 (accessed 15 March 2011).

Oceania Cruises (2007) Apollo Management L.P. makes strategic investment in Oceania Cruises. Available at: www.oceaniacruises.com/corporate/mediacenter.aspx (accessed 15 March 2011).

Quartermaine, P. and Peter, B. (2006) *Cruise – Identity, Design and Culture*. Laurence King, London.

Regent Seven Seas Cruises (2007) Apollo Management Unit Prestige Cruise Holdings Acquires Regent Seven Seas Cruises. Available at: http://cruisetalk.org/2008/02/apollo-management-unit-prestige-cruise-holdings-acquires-regent-seven-seas-cruises.html (accessed 15 March 2011).

Tucker, A. (2010) Calmer waters for the cruise industry. *Jane's Transport Finance* 25 November, 6–9.

TUI AG (2007a) TUI and Carnival withdraw anti-trust filing for joint venture. Available at: www.tui-group.com/en/media/press_releases/archiv/2007/20070905_tui_carnival_withdrawal (accessed 15 March 2011).

TUI AG (2007b) TUI AG and Royal Caribbean Cruises Ltd. announce joint venture to serve German cruise market. Available at: www.tui-group.com/en/media/press_releases/archiv/2007/20071210_tui_cruises (accessed 15 March 2011).

Von Hayek, F. (1969) *Der Wettbewerb als Entdeckungsverfahren*. Freiburger Studien, Tübingen.

3 Regulatory Frameworks of the Cruise Industry

Cordula Boy and Sarah Neumann

Introduction

Shipping is an international industry, connecting parties from various parts of the world. The sea presents the 'world's greatest highway', whose 'use is enjoyed by all nations and the continuance and safeguarding of that use is essential' (Donaldson, 1994, p. 12). In October 2010, the world fleet consisted of some 50,054 ships, which were registered in more than 150 countries, with their beneficial ownership frequently to be found in other countries again (Marisec, 2011). To regulate their interactions and to ensure the safe, secure and sustainable operation of this industry, a regulatory framework has been developed.

The market alone would be overstrained in regulating itself, due to its international nature and the sometimes abstruse construction of its stakeholders. Therefore intervention on state level is required as the market itself fails. This is why institutions at international, supra-national (e.g. the EU and its European Maritime Safety Agency) and national level (national governments and local authorities) have been formed to regulate this international industry. Since the beginning of the 21st century, an additional level can be added: the corporate level. Companies implementing corporate social responsibility practices and other voluntary corporate schemes can more and more frequently also be found in the shipping industry. Apart from the above-mentioned institutions, industry specific associations have formed, which promote the needs of the market and monitor developments. For the cruise industry, the Cruise Lines International Association (CLIA), which was formed in 1975, serves as a non-governmental organization consulting the International Maritime Organization (IMO; CLIA, 2010a).

As the cruise industry is one sector of the shipping industry, cruise companies have to adhere to the same international rules and regulations as any other shipping sector. Yet, maintaining a high safety standard in this part of the shipping industry is especially in the focus of public concern, bearing in mind that cruise ship operators are responsible for the lives of several thousand people. Figure 3.1 gives an overview of the regulatory framework of the shipping industry. The individual components are discussed in the following.

International Maritime Organization

The IMO is the agency of the United Nations responsible for 'safe, secure and efficient shipping on clean oceans' (IMO, 2011).

© CAB International 2012. *The Business and Management of Ocean Cruises* (eds M.Vogel *et al.*)

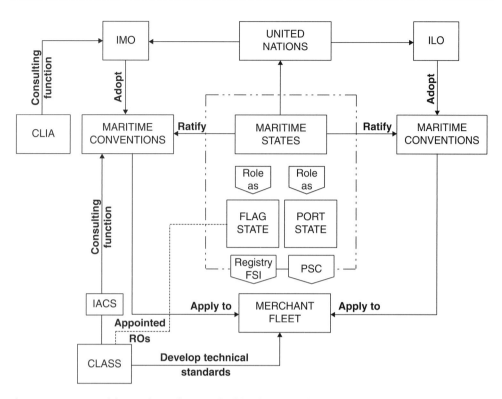

Fig 3.1. Overview of the regulatory framework of the shipping industry. Source: based on Stopford (2009). IMO, International Maritime Organization; ILO, International Labour Organization; CLIA, Cruise Lines International Association; FSI, flag state inspection; PSC, port state control; IACS, International Association of Classification Societies; RO, recognized organization.

Formerly, the IMO was known as Inter-Governmental Maritime Consultative Organization, officially established in 1948 during an international conference held by the United Nations in Geneva. The organization was renamed the International Maritime Organization in 1982. Since then, the IMO works on the development and maintenance of a comprehensive regulatory framework, comprising issues such as 'safety, environmental concerns, legal matters, technical co-operation, maritime security and the efficiency of shipping' (IMO, 2011). In order to achieve this, the IMO has advanced the adoption of a number of conventions, as well as codes and recommendations concerning maritime security and environmental protection. The conventions are drafted by the corresponding specialist committee or subcommittee within the IMO (Fig. 3.2). The two important committees are the

Maritime Safety Committee and the Marine Environment Protection Committee. Every draft created by one of the (sub)committees concerning a new convention is submitted to a conference with delegates from all member states. Currently, the IMO has 169 member states and three associate members whose voting rights are assigned according to registered tonnage (IMO, 2009a). At the end of a conference a final text is adopted, which is then to be ratified by governments in order to be enforced. However, a state is solely responsible for enforcing a particular convention once it has adopted and integrated it into national law.

In general, IMO conventions can be grouped into three main categories: Maritime Safety (see Neumann and Ullrich, Chapter 18, this volume), the Prevention of Marine Pollution, and Liability and Compensation. In the past, new conventions

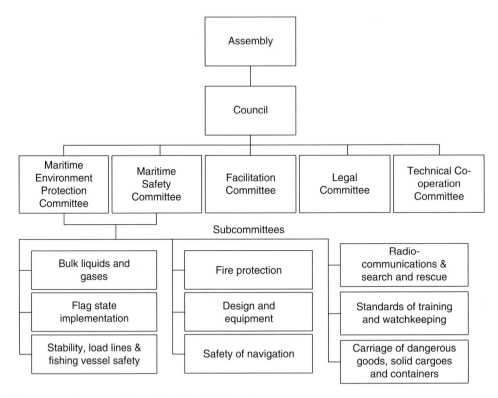

Fig. 3.2. IMO structure. Source: based on IMO (2011).

have often come as a response to tragic ship incidents, as e.g. the *Titanic* disaster, the capsizing of the *Herald of Free Enterprise*, and the *Prestige* or the *Erika* oil spills. The most important conventions regulating the maritime industry include the following:

- The 1982 United Nations Convention on the Law of the Sea, the 'overarching framework governing activities of vessels' (Gianni, 2008) in the maritime industry comprises 320 articles and nine annexes, regulating all general aspects of ocean space, such as 'delimitation, environmental control, marine scientific research, economic and commercial activities, transfer of technology and the settlement of disputes relating to ocean matters' (IMO, 2005).
- The International Convention for the Safety of Life at Sea (SOLAS), 1974.
- The Convention on International Regulations for Preventing Collisions at Sea (COLREGS), 1972.

- The International Convention on Load Lines, 1966.
- The International Convention on Tonnage Measurement of Ships, 1969.
- The Convention on the Prevention of Marine Pollution by Dumping of Wasted and Other Matter, 1972.
- The International Convention on Standards of Training, Certification and Watchkeeping for Seafarers (STCW), 1978, amended in 1995.
- The International Convention for the Prevention of Pollution from Ships (MARPOL), 1973.

At present, major conventions exist for virtually every aspect of the shipping industry. Certain conventions are of particular relevance for the cruise industry, such as the Athens Convention relating to the Carriage of Passengers and their Luggage by Sea, 1974, which regulates the liability for damage suffered by passengers carried on seagoing vessels.

As the IMO functions are of 'consultative and advisory nature' as stated in Article 2 of the IMO Convention, it has no authority to adopt or amend conventions itself, as its mandate only allows it to 'provide for the drafting of conventions, agreements or other instruments and to recommend these to governments and intergovernmental organizations and to convene such conferences as may be necessary' (IMO, 2011). The procedure of amending and updating the conventions changed in the 1970s. Previously, amendments needed, similarly to conventions, to be accepted by a certain number of member states (usually two-thirds). As this was a lengthy process and often led to the failure of enforcement, nowadays, the concept of 'tacit acceptance' is applied: an amendment enters into force at a particular time (e.g. 2 years, minimum is 1 year) unless before that time objections to the amendments are received from a specific number of member states. The new concept resulted in speeding up amendment processes (IMO, 2011).

International Labour Organization

Similarly to the IMO, the International Labour Organization (ILO) is a specialized agency of the United Nations dealing with labour-related issues. Since its foundation in 1919, delegates from each of its member states, currently 183, meet in Geneva at the International Labour Conference on a yearly basis. Having a tripartite structure, its delegates consist of government representatives, employers as well as worker delegates. Thus, in case of maritime conventions, both ship owners and seafarers are represented. Among its objectives are the enhancement of social protection, the creation of greater opportunities for women and men to secure decent employment and income, the strengthening of social and work-related dialogue as well as the promotion and realization of labour standards worldwide (ILO, 2009). These standards are formulated in the form of conventions, which are ratified by member states and become mandatory after coming into force.

The ILO's most relevant convention for the maritime sector is the Maritime Labour Convention, which was adopted on 7 February 2006 during an International Labour Conference in Geneva. It is a combination of 68 previous conventions related to seafarers, which have been adopted over the last 80 years and will enter into force 12 months after ratification by at least 30 ILO member states with a total share of at least 33% of the world's gross tonnage. Until 8 June 2011, the new convention had been ratified by 12 countries, including the Bahamas, Liberia and Panama, being the leading flag states in terms of registered cruise ships (ILO, 2011).

The Maritime Labour Convention applies to all commercially operated ships regardless of private or public ownership, with the exemption of fishing vessels, traditionally built ships and warships. Ships over 500 GT need to carry the corresponding Maritime Labour Certificate. Issuing and supervision is the responsibility of the flag state (MLC, Article II).

When enforced, it is expected that ship owners will benefit from this convention insofar as the quality of service, because of the avoidance of unfair competition, will increase. This is because shipping companies and flag states operating substandard vessels will be forced to adapt to the new regulations and therefore be forced to adjust freight rates. Additionally, crew motivation will increase, which will have a positive impact on operational safety, as the Maritime Labour Convention enforces seafarers' fundamental rights and enforces minimum standards on board. The convention addresses the general welfare of all seafarers, regardless of their nationality or the flag the ship they are working on is flying, by ensuring decent working and living conditions, regulating the minimum standards for the payment of wages, maximum hours of work, health and safety protection, accommodation requirements, provision of food, as well as social security and medical care (MLC, Article VI).

This will have a major impact on the cruise industry, particularly on cruise ship design. In the past, the limited available space for passengers was increased at the expense of crew cabin sizes. Once the Maritime Labour Convention enters into force, new cruise ships have to be built in conformity with new crew cabin size requirements.

The Maritime Labour Convention is the first convention that addresses flag states, port states and labour-supplying countries alike. The new convention is frequently referred to as the missing fourth pillar of maritime regulations (e.g. Mathisen, 2007), as so far, shipping has only dealt with hardware, safety and the environment via key IMO conventions (SOLAS, STCW, MARPOL). The new Maritime Labour Convention now also includes the missing 'human element' and thus enhances safety of shipping by addressing issues such as fatigue, recruitment and retention. The convention can be imposed on any ship calling at a port whose country has ratified the convention and thus made it part of the governing law under the new regulations: 'port state enforcement officials can detain, fine or refer violations back to the flag state' (Aichele, 2006, p. 35).

Flag States

The flag a vessel is flying is more than just a colourful piece of cloth flying from the stern of ships: it expresses the ship's country of registration; moreover, it is a symbol of its nationality. Every ship can be seen as a 'floating piece of the country where it is registered' (Wood, 2006, p. 400) and therefore, it has to adhere to its laws. The United Nations Convention on the Law of the Sea (UNCLOS) determines that every ship sailing the seas has to be assigned a nationality (Article 91):

> Every State shall fix the conditions for the grant of its nationality to ships, for the registration of ships in its territory, and for the right to fly its flag. Ships have the nationality of the State whose flag they are entitled to fly. There must be a genuine link between the State and the ship.
>
> (United Nations, 2001)

It is further stated that a 'genuine link' is required between the flag and the ship. However, the nature of this link has not been specified. Although this link is obvious for national flagged ships, the situation is different for foreign flagged ships. The 1986 Convention on the Registration of Ships was aimed at clarifying and strengthening this 'genuine link'. However, this convention never entered into force. UNCLOS (Article 94) implies that the responsibility for the compliance of ships with international regulations lies with the flag state. Therefore flag states are required to perform inspections on a regular basis, issuing and renewing certificates, which state conformance with international accepted standards. Alternatively, flag states can delegate this task to a classification society. However, as not all flag states take their responsibilities seriously, enforcing international regulation is backed up by port states in the form of vessel inspections to ensure compliance to international regulation.

Thus, flag states play a significant role in the global shipping industry. For a long time, it has been commonly acknowledged that within the range of flag states, significant differences exist regarding the degree to which these duties and responsibilities are met.

Traditionally a distinction is made between national flag states (traditional registers) and open registers. National flags comprise the major independent shipping authorities, as e.g. the original EU member states and Japan. Their main characteristics include (Coles, 2002):

• comparatively high labour costs (in accordance with domestic wage level);
• strict labour regulations (hours of work, social security etc.);
• strict safety regulations (more regulations and more rigidly enforced);
• manning requirements (certification and nationality); and
• taxation based on company's profits.

Yet, these traditional registers have also taken responsive actions to developments in the shipping industry. To remain competitive vis-à-vis open registers, many traditional flag states have introduced state aids for shipping, as e.g. shipping tonnage tax or other (fiscal) incentives (reduced rates of income tax, less contribution for social security etc.) to retain their national fleet. The tonnage tax scheme allows taxation based on tonnage rather than profits and has been introduced by many European countries following the 1997 EU State Aid Guidelines (Marlow and Mitroussi, 2008).

Another responsive action towards open registries is the creation of second or international registers.

Open registries

An open registry is a ship registry, which is comparatively easy to enter, as there are virtually no entry restrictions. They are commonly also referred to as 'flags of convenience' (FOC), a term introduced by the International Transport Workers' Federation (ITF), a 'federation of 654 transport trade unions in 148 countries, representing around 4,500,000 workers' (ITF, 2010). In 1974, the ITF defined these flags as follows: where beneficial ownership and control of a vessel is found to lie elsewhere than in the country of the flag the vessel is flying, the vessel is considered as sailing under an FOC. Another definition describes FOCs as:

national flags of those States with whom shipping firms register their vessels with a view to maximising their private benefits and minimising their private cost by avoiding: (a) the economic and other regulations and (b) the conditions and terms of employment of factors of production that would have been applicable if their vessels were registered in the countries of their national origin
(Metaxas, 1985, p. 15).

The 32 countries that have been declared FOCs are listed in Table 3.1.

The main reasons for registering ships under an FOC instead of a traditional registry are the following (Metaxas, 1985; Skourtos, 1990; Ready, 1998; Chin, 2008; Dickinson and Vladimir, 2008):

- tonnage taxes instead of taxes on profit generated on board;
- low annual fees;
- low registration fees;
- lower operational cost, especially with regard to crewing costs;
- no manning requirements, freedom to choose nationality of crew;
- minimal safety, labour and environmental regulations;
- flag state allows ownership and control of its vessels by non-citizens; and
- entering the registry is easy.

Table 3.1. Flags of convenience in alphabetical order.

Antigua and Barbuda	Honduras
Bahamas	Jamaica
Barbados	Lebanon
Belize	Liberia
Bermuda (UK)	Malta
Bolivia	Marshall Islands (USA)
Burma	Mauritius
Cambodia	Mongolia
Cayman Islands	Netherlands Antilles
Comoros	North Korea
Cyprus	Panama
Equatorial Guinea	Sao Tome and Príncipe
French International Ship Register (FIS)	St Vincent
German International Ship Register (GISR)	Sri Lanka
Georgia	Tonga
Gibraltar (UK)	Vanuatu

Source: ITF (2010).

Labour costs constitute the major differentiating factor (Bergantini and Marlow, 1998). Flying the flag of an open registry implies that also non-nationals, seafarers from 'low wage countries' are allowed to work on board. Spruyt (cited in Wood, 2006, p. 401) calculated the costs of an Asian crew in comparison with a northern European crew on a 24-member ship; the difference amounted to US$698,400 annually. Although this number already seems considerable, for some parts of the shipping industry, implications of the system of open registries are even more significant: transferred to the context of the highly labour-intensive cruise industry, where often 1000 crew members work on board one single cruise ship, cost savings enabled by flying an FOC are tremendous. Therefore, it is not surprising that Liberia, Panama and the Bahamas, all belonging to the category of open ship registries, are those countries that are most frequently found on the stern of ocean going ships.

In 1948, the ITF launched the Flag of Convenience Campaign, which was intended to eliminate FOCs and thus to protect seafarers from exploitation. Though FOCs could not yet be eliminated, the ITF 'succeeded in enforcing decent minimum wages and conditions on board nearly 5000 FOC ships' (ITF, 2010). For compliance with these standards, ITF issues a Blue Certificate or 'Blue Card' to the respective vessels. This compliance is continuously monitored by ITF inspectors worldwide.

Chin (2008) summarizes the benefits of the system of FOCs as minimal regulatory power plus the obfuscation of ship owners' legal and financial accountability and liabilities, as well as no taxation on revenue these owners generate at sea. She indicates the existence of a paradox created by this system: affirming nationality by stripping nationality of its meaning (Chin, 2008, p. 9). In 1998, FOCs accounted for 55% of the total number of ship losses and 66% of total tonnage lost, while at the same time presenting 20% of the total number of ships and 47% of total tonnage (Alderton and Winchester, 2002).

For a long time, a bad reputation was attached to FOCs (Hill, 2003; Gianni, 2008).

However, this traditional view is no longer justified (Llácer, 2003). A study by Alderton and Winchester (2002) found out that it is no longer appropriate to generalize the performance of FOC states. It was revealed that there are obvious differences between FOCs and traditional flags but similarly, also within the group of FOCs itself. In their study, traditional maritime states scored highest in terms of performance, followed by second registries and established open registries. New entrants to the open register market (Belize, Equatorial Guinea, Bolivia and Cambodia) scored lowest, while having the highest growth rates. These emerging FOCs operate their registry solely as a 'commercial service' by incorporating only 'minimal regulatory burden' (Alderton and Winchester, 2002), whereas established FOCs more and more comply with international standards, because of a more effective port state control (PSC) (Alderton and Winchester, 2002; Alderton, 2004). This finding is confirmed by the significant decrease in the number of ship detentions by port states over the past 10 years (Fig. 3.5). Hence safety standards are increasing, which can be traced back to a more effective PSC by enforcing international regulation.

International ship registers

International or second registers are another category of ship registries. Their creation can be seen as a movement of traditional maritime states towards open registries, whereby FOC legislation is seen as a benchmark. Second or international registers are said to be a kind of 'halfway house to open registries', combining the benefits of open and traditional ship registration (Selkou and Roe, 2004, p. 103). The first second register to be introduced was the Norwegian International Ship Register in 1987, soon followed by similar models such as the German International Ship Register and the Danish International Ship Register (Coles, 2002; Johns, 2009).

Their aim is to relax certain aspects of ship registration, mainly regarding manning requirements to enable benefits of global sourcing, while at the same time remaining under a national flag, and thus ensuring the access to capital markets, a highly developed infrastructure and maritime know-how, as well taxation benefits and lower crew costs. However, the success of retaining vessels in national fleets by the introduction of international ship registries is only limited, especially for labour intensive sectors of the shipping industry such as e.g. the cruise industry, since whoever has the opportunity to save 100 DM (Deutsche Mark, former German currency) will make use of this offer, although he has an alternative option to reduce his costs by 50 DM (Däubler, 1988). This applies for the choice between an FOC (in form of the 100 DM cost savings) and the entry into the second register (50 DM cost savings). As the cruise industry is the branch of shipping with the highest proportion of labour costs, this effect becomes even more apparent: hardly

any cruise ship can be found in second registers of traditional maritime states.

Vessel flags in the cruise industry

Figure 3.3 gives an idea of how ship registration is distributed in the cruise industry. It illustrates that only a few states dominate the cruise flagging business.

The cruise industry highly depends on the system of open registries. In 2008, two-thirds of the cruise ship fleet was sailing under an FOC. Therefore the meaning of FOCs in the cruise industry is significant. It is even higher than for the rest of the global merchant fleet where this percentage amounts to approximately 50% (Flottenkommando, 2008). It seems that flying an FOC is the optimal solution for cruise ships, as it is, from an economics point of view, the only viable option, given its comparatively high proportion of labour costs, while

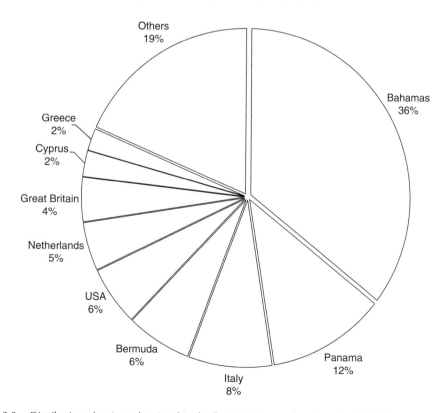

Fig. 3.3. Distribution of registered cruise ships by flag state. Source: based on Ward (2008).

at the same time, negative aspects combined with an FOC seem to be minimal, as safety standards have increased. This dependence is expected to increase even further, as ships are getting bigger, and thus, more and more crew is needed. Therefore the cost pressure is immense. Guests do not seem to mind. On the contrary, they benefit from low prices. FOCs are what 'makes it possible for them to offer cruises [...] at a much lower cost' (Dickinson and Vladimir, 2008, p. 64). The system of FOCs has made cruising affordable for the broad mass and is the basis for the annual growth on the cruise market, which has been observed in the past few years (CLIA, 2008; The Passenger Shipping Association, 2009). Hence, the industry in its present shape depends on this system, as eliminating FOCs 'would be financially devastating to the cruise industry' (Schulkin cited in Wood, 2006, p. 402).

Classification Societies

Classification societies are non-governmental organizations, which establish and maintain technical standards for the construction of ships. Their concern is the safety of ships and the cargo where, in contrast, flag states focus on the safety of people on board (van Dokkum, 2007). Their role regarding safety and security of shipping is laid down in Chapter 18 (Neumann and Ullrich, this volume).

The construction of ships is carried out and supervised by representatives of classification societies based on the defined standards of the class. A certificate of class proves compliance with these standards and is re-ensured through surveys carried out at regular intervals. Furthermore, these certificates present a significant basis for the insurance of the vessel. The renewal of certificates takes place within a 5-year circle on cargo ships, which require annual endorsements. Cruise ships even have to undergo annual renewal surveys, as the respective certificate is only valid for one year. Surveys include visual examinations of the vessel, 'detailed checks of selected parts, witnessing tests,

measurements and trials where applicable' (IACS, 2011). When deficiencies are identified, the ship owner is informed through recommendations or condition of class statements by the classification society and has to rectify the identified items within a given period in order to retain class. The annual renewal survey includes 'an inspection of the structure, boilers and other pressure vessels machinery and equipment, including the outside of the ship's bottom' (IMO, 2009b). For this survey, the vessel will usually have to dry-dock for a certain time, depending on its size, age and works to be carried out.

In addition to the above, classification societies may act on behalf of flag states as so-called Recognised Organizations. This right of delegation is laid down in SOLAS and other international conventions. The IMO has defined minimum standards Recognised Organizations have to fulfil in order to represent flag states. The administration transfers to a Recognised Organization of a flag state the right to carry out flag state relevant inspections on board a vessel, which includes the issuance and withdrawal of statutory certificates (IACS, 2011).

In 1968, the International Association of Classification Societies (IACS) was formed. At present, it consists of 11 internationally recognized classification societies. IACS closely cooperates with the IMO, providing technical knowledge and acting as consultants. The members of IACS are listed in Table 3.2.

Port States and Port State Control

Port states have the right to enforce laws on foreign flagged ships in their coastal waters. Since they implement legislation, the duty of enforcement also rests with the flag states, although this has been proven to be quite inefficient for several reasons. Some maritime states 'lack the expertise, experience and resources necessary to do this [enforcement] properly' (IMO, 2011). Ships trading worldwide may not even call at ports of their flag state, which makes it difficult to

Table 3.2. International Association of Classification Societies (IACS) members in alphabetical order.

American Bureau of Shipping (ABS)	Korean Register of Shipping (KR)
Bureau Veritas (BV)	Lloyds Register (LR)
China Classification Society (CCS)	Nippon Kaiji Kyokai (Class NK)
Det Norske Veritas (DNVC)	Registro Italiano Navale (RINA)
Germanischer Lloyd (GL)	Russian Maritime Register of Shipping (RR)
Indian Register of Shipping (IRS)	

Source: IACS (2011).

inspect the vessels except at regular inspection intervals. Furthermore, flag states may not emphasize this enforcement with top priority. This lack of proper implementation and enforcement results in low safety standards and high casualty rates.

PSC plays a major role in improving these standards through inspections of foreign flagged vessels calling their ports. These inspections shall verify the condition of the vessel and the compliance with international regulations with regard to safety, manning and operation of the vessel. PSC takes all relevant conventions (SOLAS, MARPOL, Load Line, etc.) into account. Port states are already preparing to expand their inspections once the Maritime Labour Convention comes into force. It is a back-up to the regular flag state inspections and helps to identify sub-standard ships. The right of port states to carry out these inspections is laid down in IMO resolutions (A.787(19) as amended by A.882(21); MSC.159(78)), as well as in several conventions (SOLAS, MARPOL, Load Line, STCW, ILO, Maritime Labour Convention, COLREGS, Tonnage Convention) (DNV, 2008).

A port state aims at inspecting 25% of the vessels calling at its ports. These inspections are not announced, and any vessel may be subject to them. Vessels are chosen based on a target factor, taking type, age, flag and PSC history of the vessel into account. Vessels registered under an FOC usually have a higher target factor and thus, are inspected more often.

On 1 January 2011, a new inspection regime has come into force in the port states adhering to the Paris Memorandum of Understanding on Port State Control (Paris MoU, 2008). From that date on, vessels are subject to inspection on a regular basis. Furthermore, the target factor, which determines the intervals of inspections, has become more reasonable and less random.

PSC inspections cover many areas on board a vessel. All deficiencies detected will be reported, also stating the timeframe and rectifying actions that have to be taken. These actions include for example necessary repairs, and whether the attendance of a flag state representative or the classification society is required. In case of a major deficiency, which creates a threat to safety, health or the environment, the vessel can be detained until rectification, irrespective of any commercial effect this may cause. Detentions involve not only delays and costs for operators, but may even lead to reputation damage, as the detention notification of a vessel is available to the public. This fact puts even more pressure on cruise lines, which depend on their image when attracting customers.

Amongst the major reasons for detentions, fire safety measures, life-saving appliances and safety of navigation were to be found (ABS, 2010). In 2009 a total of 12 passenger ships and ferries were detained after inspections in a Paris MoU port. This equals 1.2% of inspected passenger ships and ferries (Paris MoU, 2009). No detention of a cruise vessel was reported.

PSC inspections have shown to be most effective when countries join together in regional agreements (IMO, 2011). Within these regional agreements, it is possible to exchange information between the port states and to standardize inspections. Currently, a total of nine Memorandums of

Understanding (MoUs) on PSC are in force (Fig. 3.4).

The Paris MoU, the first regional agreement, which came into operation in 1982, ranks flag states in its annual reports on a Black/Grey/White List, based on the inspection-detention ratio of the respective state. The annual reports and lists are available on their website along with statistical information on number of detentions and deficiencies identified. These statistics provide evidence for the effectiveness of PSC by showing a decrease in detentions since 2000 (Fig. 3.5).

Through concentrated inspection campaigns PSC started to focus on certain areas

(e.g. safety of navigation, lifeboats), in addition to the regular PSC questionnaire.

USA Requirements

The number of reports and inspections required in the USA goes well beyond international standards. In order to avoid delays or fines when entering the ports, vessels and vessel operators have to meet a range of national requirements outlined below. The USA are not a member of any regional PSC agreement. PSC in US waters is carried out by the United States Coast Guard (USCG)

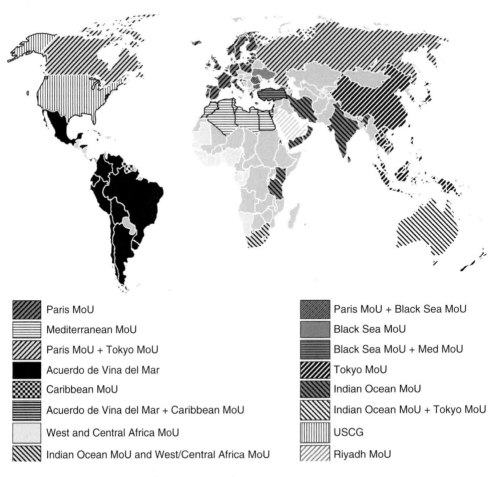

Paris MoU		Paris MoU + Black Sea MoU	
Mediterranean MoU		Black Sea MoU	
Paris MoU + Tokyo MoU		Black Sea MoU + Med MoU	
Acuerdo de Vina del Mar		Tokyo MoU	
Caribbean MoU		Indian Ocean MoU	
Acuerdo de Vina del Mar + Caribbean MoU		Indian Ocean MoU + Tokyo MoU	
West and Central Africa MoU		USCG	
Indian Ocean MoU and West/Central Africa MoU		Riyadh MoU	

Fig. 3.4.   Regional agreements of port state control. Source: DNV (2000).

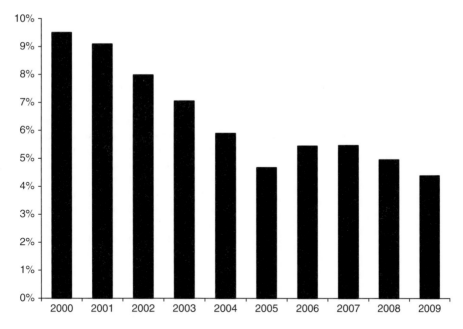

Fig. 3.5. Detentions in percentage of inspections. Source: Paris MoU (2009).

and enforces international requirements, as well as US requirements.

In addition to random inspections of foreign flagged vessels, the USCG requires each vessel calling at a US port to be inspected at least annually. Within regional PSC agreements, inspections of vessels are similarly intended to be on a 12-month-basis, and yet, no actual system is in place. Instead, inspections are somewhat random, not following defined intervals. This will be changed by the New Inspection Regime. Each vessel calling in the USA for the very first time or for the first time after over a year certainly will be inspected. Arrival information of foreign passenger vessels is reviewed, and any of these vessels carrying US citizens is then targeted for PSC, which will enrol the vessel in the control verification examination (CVE) for foreign passenger vessels (USCG, 2008). Upon successful completion of this inspection, a Certificate of Compliance is issued which is valid for up to 1 year. Again, cruise ships face even stricter regulations and are subject to quarterly re-inspections (CLIA, 2010b). Just like any other port state, the USCG has the authority to request rectification of any

detected deficiencies prior to the vessel leaving the port.

Vessel Sanitation Program

Cruise ships calling at US ports are not only subject to PSC by the USCG but also to unannounced inspections, at least twice a year, by Environmental Health Officers of the Vessel Sanitation Program (VSP). This is applicable for ships 'that have a foreign itinerary, call on a US port, and carry 13 or more passengers' (CDC, 2005). Depending on the size of the cruise vessel, an inspection may be completed within 5–8 h.

The VSP was established in close cooperation with the cruise industry in order to provide a 'safe, healthful environment for all passengers at sea' (CLIA, 2010c). Based on points listed on the report for each inspected item the vessel's score is evaluated; 86 points out of 100 or more are considered satisfactory scores. A failure in compliance, meaning an unsatisfactory score, will result in a re-inspection within 4–6 weeks (CLIA, 2010b). The Center for Disease Control (CDC) makes these scores available on their homepage for all inspected cruise vessels. Similar to a PSC detention, this may cause not only delays and involve costs, but damage a cruise line's reputation.

Cruise Vessel Security and Safety Act of 2010

On 27 July 2010, President Obama signed the Cruise Vessel Security and Safety Act of 2010. The Act amends Chapter 35 of Title 46 of the existing Unites States Code, which compiles the federal law of the USA. It establishes requirements ensuring safety and security on board cruise ships, since crimes on cruise ships and the lack of reporting procedures are recognized as a problem of increasing significance. This becomes apparent when observing the alarming developments in the cruise industry regarding the number of sexual assaults and people overboard cases. Statistics show that in the time between 2000 and 2010, a reported number of 142 people went overboard during a cruise, some of whom died (Cruise Junkie dot com, 2010). It was reported that the FBI investigated 184 cases of sexual assault between 2002 and 2007 alone (CNN, 2009). This number only comprises the amount of known cases in the USA. It can be anticipated that the number of unreported cases is even more disturbing.

To counteract this development, major requirements introduced by the Act under §3507 'Passenger vessel security and safety requirements' comprise the following:

- standards of construction and design: ship rails at least 3.5 feet tall; peep holes in cabin doors; security latches in passenger staterooms for all vessels whose keel is laid after enactment; new technology for detecting passengers fallen overboard;
- video recording for crime investigation;
- establishment of a security guide providing detailed safety and legal information to passengers;
- sexual assault preparedness including necessary medical equipment and at

least one person certified for conducting forensic sexual assault examinations; and

- log book and reporting requirements with regard to criminal incidents.

The Cruise Vessel Safety and Security Act 2010 will enter into force 18 months after the Act is adopted, and immediately for vessels with a keel laying date after 27 July 2010. It applies to any ocean-going passenger vessel that is authorized to carry more than 250 passengers, provides on-board sleeping facilities, and embarks or disembarks passengers in the USA. In case of violation, punishments include civil penalties up to US$50,000 or criminal penalties up to US$250,000 and 1 year in prison. Furthermore, vessels may be denied entry to US ports.

From the date of enactment to its final entry into force in 2012, the cruise industry is facing new challenges. Until the beginning of 2011, guidelines for the implementation and training and certification requirements shall be issued, which will become mandatory for cruise lines. Crew members and on-board security personnel will have to undergo new training and achieve certification 'on the appropriate methods for prevention, detection, evidence preservation and reporting of criminal activities' (Cruise Vessel Safety and Security Act 2010). Furthermore, the requirements outlined above will have to be fulfilled by the operators of cruise vessels. This may involve constructional adjustments of existing vessels, installation of new technologies on board, development and implementation of new procedures regarding training and reporting requirements, thus adding to the costs cruise lines are facing.

Additionally, any incident-related data will have to be made available via the internet, naming cruise lines and providing information about the crimes committed on board their vessels. Therefore, apart from facing additional costs, also the reputation of a cruise line will possibly be affected by the Cruise Vessel Safety and Security Act of 2010.

USA Disability Act

The Americans with Disabilities Act of 1990 was established to prohibit the discrimination based on disabilities. Title III of the act is concerned with public accommodations and commercial facilities; therefore it is also applicable for cruise ships. The title ensures equal rights for the usage of public accommodation through barrier-free constructions. This act applies to all cruise ships calling at US ports irrespective of their flag.

Case Studies

The Maritime Labour Convention and the cruise industry

One of the features contained in the new Maritime Labour Convention, which is especially relevant for cruise lines, is the broad application of the convention. As per Article II, paragraph 1 'seafarer means any person who is employed or engaged or works in any capacity on board a ship to which this convention applies' (ILO, 2006). This includes not only regular crew members but also staff, artists, hairdressers etc. on cruise ships and thus immensely increases the number of people on board affected by the requirements of the Maritime Labour Convention.

Title three of the convention refers to accommodation and recreational areas, which in most cases will have a constructional effect on the ships, and therefore applies to vessels built on or after the date of enforcement of the convention. One of the areas of concern is the size of crew cabins. As outlined above, the size of crew cabins is significantly small in order to increase the available space for passengers. The minimum size of crew cabins has therefore been defined by the Maritime Labour Convention: a cabin for two persons, for example, must have a minimum size of 7.5 m², and a cabin for four persons 14.5 m², which is generally still less than that which can be found on a cargo vessel of comparable size.

Furthermore, the title defines minimum sizes of beds and the setup of cabins. Thus, cabins have to be located above the load line of a vessel. At present, on board most cruise ships, a significant number of crew cabins is located below the water line.

As staff members count as seafarers under the Maritime Labour Convention, the requirements for hours of work and hours of rest also apply to them. These requirements will be applicable for all vessels once the convention enters into force. It will save all seafarers, including staff, from exploitation and shall prevent any accidents resulting from fatigue, which is an issue of growing concern in the maritime industry. The maximum hours of work may not exceed 14 h within 24 h (see MLC title 2, regulation 2.3). This is also the maximum interval allowed between two rest periods. Moreover, the hours of rest may not be divided. Thus, for a 14-h working day, in the worst case, the seafarer is entitled to 10 h of rest, which may be divided into no more than two periods, one of which must last for at least 6 h. Depending on the policy of cruise lines, this new regulation may require more staff on board and thus increase costs.

Another requirement of title three of the Maritime Labour Convention may be a challenge on some cruise ships: open space deck of adequate size is to be available for all seafarers when off duty. This may be problematic on those ships where currently all deck space is reserved exclusively for passengers.

The ITF and cruises

Apart from the ILO, the ITF also attempts to improve seafarers' living and working conditions. The case of cruise vessel *Mona Lisa* in 2006 illustrates the power of the ITF in defending seafarers' rights. The vessel was subject to a routine ITF inspection during a port stay at Amsterdam, the Netherlands. It was detected that the ITF contract was not met and the crew, mostly from south-east Asian countries, was paid about only a third of what owners were obliged to pay. In one particular case, a crew member was paid

US$575 instead of US$1150, which he was entitled to according to the contract. In total, 52 crew members were affected, and the owners faced a claim of about US$100,000. Two weeks after the inspection, the outstanding amount was paid in the presence of an ITF representative (ITF, 2007).

Apart from illustrating the work of the ITF in the shipping industry, this case also gives an example of the problems existing on board cruise ships. Rather than substandard living and working conditions such as those outlined above, problems on cruise ships are of a different nature.

References

ABS (2010) Reducing the Port State Detention Factor. Pre-Port Arrival Quick Reference Guide. American Bureau of Shipping, Houston, Texas. Available at: www.eagle.org/eagleExternalPortalWEB/ShowProperty/BEA%20Repository/References/Booklets/2010/PrePortArrivalQRG (accessed 26 March 2011).

Aichele, R. (2006) Clear rules avoid harassment incidents. *Cruise Industry News* 16(2), 34–35.

Alderton, T.B. (2004) *The Global Seafarer – Living and Working Conditions in a Globalized Industry*. International Labour Office, Geneva.

Alderton, T. and Winchester, N. (2002) Globalisation and de-regulation in the maritime industry. *Marine Policy* 26, 35–43.

Bergantini, A. and Marlow, P. (1998) Factors influencing the choice of flag: empirical evidence. *Maritime Policy and Management* 25(2), 157–174.

CDC (2005) Vessel Sanitation Program Operators Manual. Available at: www.cdc.gov/nceh/vsp/operationsmanual/OPSManual2005.pdf (accessed 7 March 2010).

Chin, C.B. (2008) *Cruising in the Global Economy*. Ashgate Publishing Limited, Aldershot.

CLIA (2008) *2008 CLIA Cruise Market Overview: Statistical Cruise Industry Data Through 2007*. Cruise Lines International, Fort Lauderdale, Florida.

CLIA (2010a) About CLIA. Available at: www2.cruising.org/about.cfm (accessed 8 April 2010).

CLIA (2010b) Safety Standards. Available at: www2.cruising.org/industry/safety.cfm (accessed 7 March 2010).

CLIA (2010c) Technical and Regulatory. Available at: www2.cruising.org/industry/sanitation.cfm (accessed 7 March 2010).

CNN (2009) Sexual assaults on the high seas come under scrutiny. Available at: http://edition.cnn.com/2009/TRAVEL/06/22/cruise.sexual.assault/index.html (accessed 14 August 2010).

Coles, R. (2002) *Ship Registration: Law and Practice*. LLP, London, UK.

Cruise Junkie dot com (2010) Crews and Ferry Passengers and Crew Overboard 1995–2010. Available at: www.cruisejunkie.com/Overboard.html (accessed 14 August 2010).

Däubler, W. (1988) *Das zweite Schiffsregister- Völkerrechtliche und verfassungsrechtliche Probleme einer deutschen 'Billig-Flagge'.* Nomos, Baden-Baden.

Dickinson, B. and Vladimir, A. (2008) *Selling the Sea – An Inside Look at the Cruise Industry*, 2nd edn. Wiley, Hoboken, New Jersey.

DNV (2000) DNV Guide to Preventive Maintenance and Port State Control. Available at: http://exchange.dnv.com/PortStateControl/Default.htm (accessed 24 April 2010).

DNV (2008) *Port State Control Course*. DNV Academy Hamburg, Hamburg.

Donaldson, J. (1994) *Safer Ships, Cleaner Seas: Government Response to the Report of Lord Donaldson's Inquiry into the Prevention of Pollution from Merchant Shipping*. HMSO, London.

Flottenkommando (2008) *Jahresbericht 2008 – Fakten und Zahlen zur maritimen Abhängigkeit der Bundesrepublik Deutschland,* 21st edn. Deutsche Marine, Glücksburg.

Germanischer Lloyd (2010a) Maritime Labour Convention, 2006. Available at: www.gl-group.com/en/7581.php (accessed 19 April 2010).

Germanischer Lloyd (2010b) *Implementation Workshop ILO Maritime Labour Convention*. Germanischer Lloyd, Hamburg.

Gianni, M. (2008) *Real and Present Danger: Flag State Failure and Maritime Security and Safety*. ITF/WWF, London/Oslo.

Hill, C.J.S. (2003) *Maritime Law*, 6th edn. LLP, London.

IACS (2011) Classification Societies – What, why and how? Available at: www.iacs.org.uk/document/public/explained/Class_WhatWhy&How.PDF (accessed 27 April 2011).

ILO (2006) Maritime Labour Convention 2006. Available at: www.ilo.org/wcmsp5/groups/public/---ed_norm/---normes/documents/normativeinstrument/wcms_090250.pdf (accessed 25 July 2010).

ILO (2009) Maritime Labour Convention 2006: Action Plan 2006–2011. Available at: www.ilo.org/global/What_we_do/InternationalLabourStandards/MaritimeLabourConvention/lang--en/docName--WCMS_088034/index.htm (accessed 7 July 2010).

ILO (2011) Ratification of the Maritime Labour Convention. Available at: www.ilo.org/ilolex/cgi-lex/ratifce.pl?C186 (accessed 8 June 2011).

IMO (2005) UNCLOS. Available at: www.imo.org/dynamic/mainframe.asp?topic_id=1514&doc_id=7602 (accessed 29 May 2010).

IMO (2009a) IMO Documentation. Available at: https://imo.amsa.gov.au/public/parties/imo-members.html (accessed 13 April 2010).

IMO (2009b) SOLAS Consolidated Edition 2009. CPI Books Limited, Reading.

IMO (2011) IMO website. Available at: www.imo.org (accessed 29 April 2011).

ITF (2007) Teurer Besuch im niederländischen Hafen. ITF Seeleute Bulletin 21(8).

ITF (2010) Flag of Convenience Campaign. Available at: www.itfglobal.org/flags-convenience/index.cfm (accessed 23 January 2010).

Johns, M. (2009) Rückflaggung: Deutsche Reeder erfüllen Versprechen. Deutsche Seeschifffahrt 2, 18–19

Llácer, F.J.M. (2003) Open registers: past, present and future. Marine Policy 27, 513–523.

Marisec (2011) Shipping and World Trade – Number of Ships (by total and trade). Available at: www.marisec.org/shippingfacts/worldtrade/number-of-ships.php (accessed 27 February 2011).

Marlow, P. and Mitroussi, K. (2008) EU Shipping taxation: the comparative position of Greek shipping. Maritime Economics and Logistics 10, 185–207.

Mathisen, O. (2007) A better life at sea. Cruise Industry News 71, 18–19.

Metaxas, B. (1985) Flags of Convenience – A Study of Internationalisation. Gower Publishing, Aldershot.

Paris MoU (2008) Port State Control Annual Report 2008. Available at: www.parismou.org/Publications/Annual_reports/ (accessed 30 April 2011).

Paris MoU (2009) Port State Control Annual Report 2009. Available at: www.parismou.org/Publications/Annual_reports/ (accessed 30 April 2011).

Ready, N.P. (1998) Ship Registration, 3rd edn. LLP, London.

Selkou, E. and Roe, M. (2004) Globalisation, Policy and Shipping. Edward Elgar Publishing Limited, Cheltenham.

Skourtos, N. (1999) Die Billig-Flaggen-Praxis und die staatliche Flaggenverleihungsfreiheit. Heymanns Verlag, Göttingen.

Stopford, M. (2009) Maritime Economics, 3rd edn. Routledge, New York.

The Passenger Shipping Association (2009) The Annual Cruise Review 2008. The Passenger Shipping Association, London.

United Nations (2001) United Nations Convention on the Law of the Sea (UNCLOS) 1982. Available at: www.un.org/Depts/los/convention_agreements/texts/unclos/closindx.htm (accessed 7 July 2009).

USCG (2008) Navigation and Vessel Inspection Circular No. 03-08. Available at: www.uscg.mil/hq/cg5/nvic/2000s.ASP (accessed 20 July 2010).

Van Dokkum, K. (2007) Ship Knowledge. AJ Enkhuizen, Dokmar.

Ward, D. (2008) Complete Guide to Cruises and Cruise Ships 2008. Berlitz Publishing, Princeton, New Jersey.

Wood, R.E. (2006) Cruise Tourism: A Paradigmatic Case of Globalization? In: Dowling, R.K. (ed.) Cruise Ship Tourism. CABI, Wallingford, pp. 397–406.

4 Impacts of Cruising

Edward W. Manning

Introduction

The growth of cruise ship tourism has significant impacts upon destinations. As with all forms of tourism, cruise tourism brings a broad range of social, economic and cultural impacts, both positive and negative to host ports and their surrounding ecosystems and communities. As many as 11 ships have visited the island of Cozumel in a single day. Up to seven mega-ships tied up at the same time to piers in tiny Sint Maarten in the winter of 2011 (Fig. 4.1). Ships often carry more passengers and crew than the resident population of ports like Grand Turk, Skagway (Alaska), islands in the Maldives, the Falklands or Bonaire. When these floating cities visit tiny communities, or disembark hundreds of tourists an hour to visit interesting villages and fragile ecosystems, changes are inevitable. Because ships normally visit for only a few hours in each port, the impacts of visitors are often more intense and more concentrated than in other forms of tourism. As well, because the impacts are often dispersed across many small jurisdictions (some of which are tiny island or coastal nations with little planning capacity and limited influence on large international cruise companies), the ability to create sustainable solutions effectively is limited.

In this chapter, the objective is to identify clearly the range of impacts expected when a cruise ship or ships visit a port, to address the range of environmental management and visitor management issues that relate to the ships and their passengers, and to define a suite of means that ports and cruise lines can use to reduce negative effects and, in some cases, optimize benefits associated with cruise ship visits. The chapter also examines the components of the ecological and social footprint of cruise tourism and some of the means emerging to limit the per capita and per ship impact of cruising, and to integrate cruise tourism into the destination planning process.

Planning for Cruise Tourism

Some destinations become aware of the need for planning and managing the impacts of cruise tourism only when these impacts occur. New destinations, in contrast, have some ability to anticipate and plan for the impacts of cruise tourism. In the 1970s, cruise tourism often arrived in a destination as a single visit by a ship carrying fewer than 600 passengers. It was often able to pull up to an existing freight dock, and a few hundred visitors would often make their own arrangements to see the port or

Fig. 4.1. Seven-ship-day in Sint Maarten. Source: E.W. Manning, Tourisk Inc.

surrounding attractions. While there was some stress on nearby infrastructure – particularly restaurants, washrooms and taxis, the visitors would add some custom to local shops. In many ports, there was little specifically aimed at the visitors, unless it was there to serve the needs of shore-based tourists.

In the past decade, this has changed dramatically in many destinations. A single large ship can carry over 5000 passengers and, for popular ports, several can arrive at the same time. Because the market favours weekend departures, home ports like Fort Lauderdale (Florida), Civitavecchia (Rome) or Vancouver (Canada) are packed on Saturdays and Sundays. Similarly, because the largest market is for 7-day cruises, the ports most chosen to visit are within a 7-day return sailing itinerary from the departure port, and ports visited on the cruise are most crowded mid-week. In the western hemisphere, ports such as Cozumel, Charlotte Amalie, Acapulco or Skagway have six to ten ships in port mid-week, but are sometimes empty at weekends. These destinations have little capacity to influence

itineraries and therefore have to try to accommodate the volumes on the visit days.

This has considerable impact on the level of infrastructure, crowd control, services, tour buses and boats, and numbers of guides and retail staff needed. Does the port build docking space, toilets, bus parking, etc. for the ten-ship day, or plan and build for a lower level of demand? How many taxis does the port need – enough for the 20 peak days, or to serve the community all year round? These questions are not easy to answer. When the arrival of a cruise ship is a rare event, a port can commandeer all the buses within 100-km radius to serve the tourists – and deploy school buses for basic transport or for organized tours (e.g. about 10 days a year in Puerto Chacabuco, Chile), but if there are more visits, this type of solution can be seriously disruptive to the local community.

In response to possible negative effects of cruise tourism, the Hawaiian island of Molokai in 2003 turned down the prospect of cruise ship visits (Travel and Leisure, 2003) and continues to fight any proposals for visits from cruise ships. The harbour of

Kahului Maui also has ongoing public protest as of 2010, aimed at stopping current cruise ship visits (Save Kahului Harbour, 2007). In this chapter, a number of approaches are examined regarding how cruise tourism can be managed, considering the scale of the ship, the destination and the overall cruise package, to deal best with the impacts of cruise tourism and to capture benefits, where possible, for the destination.

Carrying Capacity: Considerations for New or Expanding Destinations

In planning to accommodate visitors, there are several elements to consider for new destinations or those seeking expanded cruise ship visits.

Infrastructure

Infrastructural considerations are usually the simplest to address:

- direct capacity – number of berths, capacity of water and sewage facilities, administrative capacity regarding customs agents, pilots, port police, loading and offloading equipment; and
- related capacity – number of buses, taxis, drivers, guides, translators, organizers, tourist police.

Note that current infrastructural limits can be changed – by investment. Destinations need to consider whether they have sufficient assurance that the port or attraction will continue to attract visitors over a period long enough to justify the investment. Cruise lines often change ports – for security, economic or visitor satisfaction reasons – and major facilities or services may be left unused.

Social

Is the host community prepared to accommodate the tourists? Social impacts include increased contact with foreigners who may have different customs and behaviours than local residents. Noise, occupation of spaces (churches, restaurants, parks, beaches etc.), which were previously the exclusive use of the local community, will occur. New facilities may be built enhancing job opportunities, while in other cases local shops may be replaced by new ones. Some community members may receive benefits – while others may not. Who wins, who loses? In some cases, the tourist impact will be concentrated (e.g. tours to a small village site or game sanctuary). See the Social Indicators section and Protected Areas section of *Indicators of Sustainable Development for Tourism Destinations: A Guidebook* (WTO, 2004) for greater detail on key factors, which affect communities. In other cases, the high street shops, which serve the community, may be displaced by those catering to the visitors – selling souvenirs, jewellery, electronics or local crafts.

Environmental

Cruise ship environmental impacts are of two types – those associated with ship operations and those associated with tourist activities. While Conservation International (2008) has created guidelines for ship operations, which are a key point of reference for control of pollution, much less attention has been focused upon onshore effects, and actions by cruise ship visitors have received less attention. There are a number of specific areas of concern:

- Impacts of shore tours on ecological resources. Specific guidelines are available for tours such as those produced by Green Globe 21 (2011) and are a good point of reference for management of visitor impacts. Specifically, control of numbers, timing and behaviour are of concern. There is also a standard for cruise ship certification available from this source.
- Impacts of sea tours on fragile ecology (notably reefs). The WWF Mesoamerican Caribbean Reef Eco-region initiative has identified some substantive steps – notably inventory of sensitive areas,

awareness and negotiation of conditions of access for tours and mitigation methods (Kramer *et al.*, 2002). Specific capacity and behavioural guidelines (again see Green Globe 21 as an example) would be very useful. There is a capability to negotiate where ships can anchor, which ecosystems are to be accessible to them, and the conditions of access.

- Impacts of levels of use on natural systems. Tourism planning requires understanding of the sensitivity of each element of the ecosystem to different use levels. Indicators can be established to monitor key elements of sustainability – and should feature large in any tour planning (including group numbers, timing, staging, behaviour management).
- Onshore tourist waste management. Tourists will create waste, both solid and liquid. Sound waste management needs to be a central element in any tour management. Specific suggested management guidelines and indicators can be found in the waste management section of the WTO guide (WTO, 2004).
- Resource consumption (water, energy). Like any tours, those associated with cruise ships need sound resource management. The UNWTO indicators guidebook (WTO, 2004) water and energy sections provide key indicators, as does the section on cruise ship destinations. Note that managed tours can avoid water consumption in water short areas (bring it with you; schedule stops where water or energy are more readily available). For some water-poor destinations, cruise tourism may be a solution, as most cruise ships bring their own water supply and can load fresh water in other destinations where fresh water is more abundant.

Economic

Arrival of cruise ships and their passengers is normally expected to stimulate economic activity. Some may be direct – purchase of fuel, water, payment for berthing, port fees etc. Most of the economic impact will, however, be traced to the tourists and their activities. The industries that are most likely to benefit from the visitor activities are: transportation (taxis, buses, automobiles, boat rentals), tour operators (including organizers, guides), selected attractions (mainly those marketed as part of tours or shore activities by the tour staff on the ship) and shops (mainly those located close to the dock, or marketed directly by the ship activities staff, often via paid advertisements through shopping arrangements; Fig. 4.2). The main beneficiaries are jewellery shops, craft merchants and local specialities, such as spices, art and clothing.

While there may be some benefits to other sectors, in most locations, other types of shops may not see significant gains. Restaurants will often get little custom (unless part of tours), as tourists often return to the ship to eat food they have already paid for. Liquor stores may sell little, as most ships do not permit purchases for consumption on board; on most lines, bottles that are purchased are taken from the passengers and stored for them until they disembark at their home port. General merchandise shops may sell a very limited range of items. While some purchase of general items may occur (e.g. snacks, toiletries, hats, rainwear, items forgotten when packing), this is unlikely to be significant. Casinos in some ports will not necessarily attract cruise passengers: while some passengers may visit an onshore casino, most ships have their own casinos, and this will greatly reduce attendance.

While it may seem logical for cruise ships to provision with local products, this rarely happens. Most provisioning occurs in the home port, and even fresh produce or water is seldom taken on at other ports. For example, most (American-based) cruise lines sailing from Buenos Aires to Santiago, a popular route in the southern summer, carry mainly California wines, even though Chile and Argentina are a source of many of the world's best wines and some of the vineyards are visible from the ship. Produce is loaded for the cruise at the home port. Even if the kitchen is running out of some

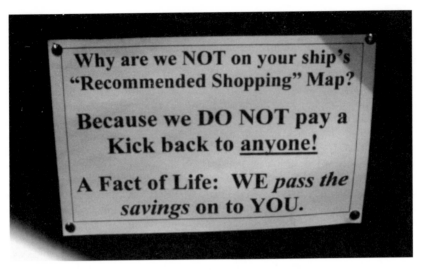

Fig. 4.2. Sign revealing kickback practices in Ketchikan Alaska. Source: E.W. Manning, Tourisk Inc.

products, new provisions are seldom loaded, as the arrangements are not in place for such provision.

At the same time, there will be some spin-off effects from tourist spending. For some destinations, the investment stimulated by cruise and other visitors can help to create critical mass for some services – those with a tourist focus, enhancing such elements as public safety, range of shops, restaurants and availability of health services. At the same time, cruise tourism can be very seasonal (up to 80% of the Caribbean cruise ships re-deploy to Alaska, northern Europe, the South Pacific and the Mediterranean from April to October) exacerbating the seasonality of other Caribbean tourism. Many service shops will close in the off-season – depriving locals of both access to services and of employment for that period.

Greening the Ships

A cruise ship is a *de facto* floating resort hotel, and some of the larger ones now feature resort-type facilities such as wave riders, water slides and ice-skating rinks. As a consequence, the ship will have all of the challenges and opportunities

that relate to greening a hotel and the resort facilities, as well as those related to its transportation function. Like any 1500-room hotel, a cruise ship consumes energy, uses water, produces waste and uses toxic substances (e.g. paint, solvents and cleaners). According to the work by Sweeting and Wayne (2003), the principal issues relating to the operation of the ships themselves relate to air emissions, ballast water containing non-native species, hazardous wastes (e.g. cleaning waste, photo shop waste paints), solid waste, oily bilge water and the direct effects on fragile ecosystems such as coral reefs.

Over the past decade, many lines have strengthened their environmental policies and most now have a senior officer with the title of environmental officer on board. The major global cruise lines companies Carnival (Aida, Costa, Cunard, Disney, Holland America, Iberocruceros, Princess, P&O, Seabourn, Windstar), Royal Caribbean (Azamara, Celebrity, Pullmantur, CDF Croisières de France) and Star Cruises (NCL) along with most others marketing North America, have, through the Cruise Lines International Association (CLIA) committed themselves to meeting international laws (e.g. MARPOL regarding marine pollution), as well as all state and national standards for pollution in the waters where they travel. While there has been significant improvement in how liquid waste from ships is managed, there is still risk, particularly in confined waters or near fragile ecosystems, which must be monitored and requires continuous vigilance to prevent contamination. The US states of Alaska and Florida, which are the key hubs for cruise travel in the western hemisphere, have been leaders in establishing more stringent laws, and because they contain many ports, have been important in influencing overall cruise ship environmental practice. Some Alaska ports (e.g. Juneau) are now installing dedicated transformers and electrical connectors on the docks so that ships do not run the engines when in port – substituting hydroelectricity for hydrocarbons for the time the ships are docked. Such facilities are not in more general use, and may not be of any advantage in many ports (particularly small islands) where onshore power is generated by similar hydrocarbon-powered equipment. An independent rating of cruise ship energy efficiency is now available, but is not based on third party audit. One of the conclusions is that the larger ships tend to be more efficient per person, but more research is needed to clearly test the rough correlation and to determine what are the main factors affecting footprint per passenger. Mark Hannafin of Frommers Guides summarized some of the results in a recent article (Hannafin, 2011). The original data for ships can be found in the Vessel Energy Efficiency ratings (www.ShippingEfficiency.org). One of the most efficient ships as of 2011 is the current largest, Royal Caribbean's *Allure of the Seas*.

Destination Management: Impacts on the Port and Town Centre

The locus of greatest impact in most destinations is the wharf and immediate surrounds of the port. Impacts on environmental and other sensitive destination assets and infrastructure occur. In many destinations, the ships will tie up near the centre of town. This ease of access is considered a plus by many cruisers, as they can leave the ship on their own rather than requiring a tour. Popular ports, such as Nassau (Bahamas), St Thomas (Virgin Islands), Acapulco (Mexico), Stockholm (Sweden) or Ajaccio (Corsica), have dock space right in the centre of the port, and many tourists will choose to walk around the town and market areas, and may make more than one tour to town (returning to the ship for lunch or to unload purchases).

Because in these types of port so many visitors return to the ship for lunch, and the ship leaves before supper, restaurants built in anticipation of cruise visitors have frequently been closed because of lack of custom and replaced by more tourist retail. Those taking short tours (3–4 h) may also have the opportunity to have more than one experience. Where a ship has to use tenders to take passengers ashore, or docks some distance from a town or commercial centre, there may be little opportunity to shop or interact with locals, unless this is provided on a tour leaving from dockside. Often those taking longer tours or going diving, fishing, rafting, hiking, riding, visiting distant attractions etc. will have nearly no opportunity to spend money in the destination, rushing past the dockside vendors to board a bus and hurrying on return to make the ship's departure time.

Extensive port area development has occurred in many intensively visited ports involving tourist targeted retail shops, most predominantly jewellery and electronics shops (e.g. St Thomas, Ketchikan). Main streets of existing ports are now dominated by jewellery and tourist clothing shops (e.g. Cozumel, San Juan), and there is a new trend to construction of new dedicated cruise port facilities that also incorporate extensive shopping (e.g. Turks and Caicos, Costa Maya) aimed nearly exclusively at cruise visitors. These trends have clearly affected the mix of retail, seasonality of trade and employment opportunities for local residents.

In addition to investment in existing and new port facilities, some lines have taken a further step – that of creating their own private destinations. Holland America (Half Moon Cay), Disney (Castaway Cay), Princess (Princess Cays), Royal Caribbean (Coco Cay) and Norwegian (Great Stirrup Cay) have all created private tropical island ports in the Bahamas. Royal Caribbean has also created Labadee (a gated peninsula in the north of Haiti), where passengers can disembark for a beach day, and where, as with the Bahamian destinations, all facilities and attractions are owned and managed by the cruise line.

As in a Club Med, visitors are segregated from any contact with locals other than those employed to serve them, and on-site impacts are carefully managed as part of an exclusive resort site. There are some advantages in quality of experience, control of risks and capture of revenues for the cruise line. Also these sites help provide ports that are a short sail from the world's largest cruise hubs in Florida – useful in cruise planning – ensuring that ships arrive back in the principal home ports of Miami, Fort Lauderdale and Port Canaveral early on Saturday or Sunday, or providing a first day experience on itineraries that require longer periods at sea to reach ports like San Juan, St Thomas or Sint Maarten.

Port and tour managers need to consider these factors – and design the offer to try to optimize destination benefits, as well as visitor satisfaction. According to UNEP (1999), 'The cruise ship industry provides another example of economic enclave tourism.' Non-river cruises carried some 8.7 million international passengers in 1999. On many ships, especially in the Caribbean (the world's most popular cruise destination with 44.5% of cruise passengers), guests are encouraged to spend most of their time and money on board, and opportunities to spend in some ports are closely managed and restricted. The numbers have risen greatly in the succeeding decade. According to Cruise Market Watch (2011), in 2011, there were 19.7 million international passengers, more than double the 1999 numbers, with 14 new ships on order, most with over 3000 passengers. The cruise watch site also notes that as the new

large ships come on line, the older ships are being deployed to new destinations in Asia and Europe and new ports from Napier (New Zealand) to Nosy Be (Madagascar), Petropavlovsk (Russia), Longyearbyen (Svalbard; Norway) and Easter Island (Chile) are being added to the worldwide cruise offer.

Managing Tours and their Impacts

Variety is an important element for many visitors, and a significant percentage of passengers desire tours and experiences while in port. As a result, tours are provided. Most ships will provide a range of tours and activities, which can be bought on shipboard and are organized by the cruise line. Also, local official and unofficial tour guides and drivers meet most ships to take passengers to markets, beaches, scenic points and other nearby attractions. These tours have impacts on many sites in and near to the host destinations.

Visitor management is a key factor in the reputation of a port. Where it is done well, passengers are provided with hassle-free experiences and a variety of opportunities, and this can enhance the reputation of a destination. Cruise lines monitor passenger reactions carefully and are very sensitive to the complaints they receive, related to the quality of the experience, the tours, security, environmental conditions and local reception and in recent years, which ports are best and worst perceived by passengers. Note that some destinations (e.g. la Guaira in Caracas, Venezuela, or North and West African ports) have been dropped from the schedules of most lines in recent years because of visitor problems (mainly perceived security issues) and dissatisfaction with the quality and variety of experiences.

The factors delineated above lead to the following:

- Most visits to ports are for 12 h or less (less time on shore if the ship needs to leave early to get to its next destination or if tenders are required to reach the shore).

- Most passengers leave the ship at least once in each port, if only to look around the dockside and shop.
- Cruise lines provide a wide range of tour options to respond to the interests of their passengers.
- Tours and experiences must be designed to allow tours to return passengers to the ship before it must leave.
- Tours therefore tend to concentrate visits on specific sites during a specific time of day.

To take just one example, Lamanai Belize, a fascinating temple site in the Belize interior, receives all its visitors for lunch. To get there while the ship is in port (most arrive between 8 and 9 am) those on the tour are normally the first off the ship, go directly to the bus when the tender reaches shore, and leave for the launching site for boats that will take them up the river to the ruins. Boats must move quickly on the river to reach the site in time to leave visitors the opportunity to walk around the site and have lunch. As a result, most see much less wildlife on the river than they would if boats could go more slowly, and some wake damage is evident. To make certain that the visitors are back on the ship in time for departure, the same trip is made in reverse, giving those on the tour 15 min on the dock at most to buy curios before they must get back to the ship.

This example illustrates several aspects of onshore impacts:

- Any tours will focus on areas within 2 h travel from the ship (or in the above case, which stretches the limit, nearly 3 h travel).
- For half-day tours (which permit passengers to take a second tour or to spend the rest of the day on their own in the destination), the distance is closer to 1 h maximum travel from the ship.
- Logistics dictate that most tours will reach the same sites at the same time – hence ten buses at the cathedral at once, or six busloads of visitors in the wildlife reserve at the same time.

As noted above with respect to the immediate surroundings of the port, tour destinations have a challenge relative to the impact of the visitors. Most arrive at the same time for the same reason. While some shore operators have tried to juggle itineraries (send half the buses to do the sightseeing route in reverse), the targeted sites must try to manage the large numbers who arrive simultaneously. How many parking slots for buses are needed?

How many washrooms are needed when six buses all arrive for 20 min at the colourful market, pretty waterfall or fishing port? The author personally observed a fist-fight between tour bus drivers on top of Meteora, Greece (a very long day trip for cruise tours from Athens or Thessaloniki), when the last parking slot was occupied and another driver blocked the exit to the lot with his bus.

As was discussed regarding portside facilities, tour sites also have a dilemma. Do you need a parking lot for 20 buses? How many guides are needed? How many seats? Is the site sufficiently hardened to allow the visitors to see the sights on their own, or will wardens, security staff or other staff to manage the tourists be required? Each site is unique. Where visits occur all year round, whether from cruise ships or other visitors, it is easier to justify investment in infrastructure and staff. If the site is only targeted once or twice a week for a few hours, and not used in the off-season, the ability to invest in site management is diminished. Like the portside shops, many cruise tour destination sites may close when the ships are not in port. Guides will need alternative sources of income, but not ones that conflict with cruise season.

While there have been some initiatives to involve the cruise lines in the provision of site improvements and training, most is still provided principally by the local government or private sector in the host sites, based on the revenues they are able to extract from the visitors – via tour charges (bus, boat rentals, scuba gear, fees for site entry, souvenirs and food sold on site). In most destinations, tips from the visitors remain a significant component of earnings for guides and bus drivers.

Visitor management

Cruise tourism is in many ways analogous to day tourism, but tends, as noted above, to be even more concentrated in space and time because of the constraints associated with the length of port stay of the ship. As with all tourism, tourist behaviour is also a concern for destinations. To some extent, cruise tourism distils and can reinforce some of the behavioural issues. A study of tourist behaviour in Dominica (Christian, 2001) concluded that 'cruise ship excursionists are less likely than stay-over ecotourists to be sensitive to the environmental consequences of their actions.' David Weaver, also referring to Dominica experience (Weaver, 2004), noted several factors associated with cruise ship excursionists – including their focus on a few sensitive sites, clustering and crowding, litter, loss of ground vegetation, soil erosion and damage to trees in sites targeted by tours. At the same time, he noted that the cruise tours had provided the impetus and wherewithal to begin to harden and manage impacted sites like the Emerald Pool. He also noted that high visitor numbers disguise lower numbers of visitor days (because of the concentration of visits on a few days).

One Black Sea cruise to Odessa sent 12 busloads of tourists simultaneously to an historic church. At the time the church was holding an investiture of a new prelate – a significant ceremony involving the Metropolitan and key personages. When 400 chattering tourists, armed with flash cameras disgorged into the church, the ceremony was interrupted and disharmony was clear (the author was there at the time, on a study of visitor management in Ukraine). Both better planning and crowd control could have avoided this problem, at least sequencing visits, and ideally rescheduling the tour so that the buses arrived after the ceremony was completed.

While there are many knowledgeable and 'civilized' tourists, significant numbers can be insensitive to the host community and its ecosystems. This is amplified by the following factors associated with cruise ship tourism:

- Ships may visit many countries on a trip – few tourists have the interest or incentive to learn much about a destination culture or ecosystem they will only visit for a day or a few hours.
- Tourists in large groups often do not behave as they do at home – instead a group or even mob mentality can occur – hence excessive drinking, loud behaviour, showing off – behaviours that may be completely out of character with their normal behaviour at home where there is community peer pressure and the norms are known. This can result in offence to local communities and destruction of ecosystems unless controlled and managed by guides and coordinators.
- All cruise lines are not the same. Some target knowledgeable niche markets; Seabourn or National Geographic tours focus on sensitive sustainable tourism, educational experiences and market to those interested in ecology, history etc. Other lines target different segments – stressing partying (Carnival), or family experiences (Disney), shore experiences (National Geographic) or elegance (Celebrity, Holland America) – each of which will bring a different type of tourist to the destination.
- A destination known as a fun place (e.g. Cancún) is likely to be featured in cruises aimed at young partying visitors and will target action trips, motorized jungle tours, jet skis etc. A destination stressing ecotourism, sports or adventure (Dominica, Costa Rica) is more likely to be featured in the cruise itinerary of a ship stressing eco-adventure or exploration, and is likely to bring older travellers seeking educational tours. Cruises featuring historic and cultural destinations (Baltic) are likely to attract a different genre of tourist from those visiting beach and diving destinations. Large ships may have a mix of all these.

Destinations have some ability to influence the offer – related to how they are portrayed and which natural or cultural assets are featured in their own advertising, or in the tours, which are packaged for sale to the cruise visitors. There is also a strong need to have site management in place before the visitors arrive. The author has on several occasions been on cruise tours to new destinations where the cruise tours have arrived before adequate site management is in place, and where infrastructure is insufficient to handle the numbers.

Tour site planning

In their paper on planning sustainable tourism destinations, Manning and Dougherty (2000) delineate a procedure based on risk management approaches, which suggests that key site assets be identified and their sensitivity to each level and type of tourism be examined before tours are permitted. The key assets and sensitivities are best identified through a participatory process where the community is directly involved. In this same paper, a number of methods to manage and mitigate tourism impacts for heavily visited sites are identified; this framework is used here to address the specific issues related to cruise tour sites:

- Demand Management – using a range of marketing, pricing, quota, and other systems to limit the numbers to those that are ecologically or culturally sustainable (for example limiting the number of tourists allowed ashore at a time in Antarctica, or putting on a limited number of buses to fragile ecological sites in Costa Rica).
- Zoning – used on site to keep the visitors in areas where there is carrying capacity for them, and limiting numbers to other parts of a fragile site. Where visitors go to protected areas, wardens or marine park managers can work with the tour operators to direct walking tours or diving to areas that will not be damaged, yet still provide the experiences the tour participants desire.
- Facility Design – for areas that are frequented by many tours, hardening of paths, creation of viewing platforms

over natural attractions, parking and eating areas can help greatly in access for tourists while eliminating negative site impacts. Where the tour bus just stops at the side of the road, there is both danger to the visitors and risk of damage or trespass.

- Crowd Management – there are many techniques, which can be used to spread out tourists so that they will have less intense effects on fragile systems. Route design to keep visitors on paths, timing of entries so that only small groups are on site at any one time, and use of guided vehicles (e.g. small boats through wetland attractions) can all be effective in restricting the number of visitors in one place at one time.
- Behaviour Management – 'Keep your hands in the boat – the crocodiles bite' (sign on Zambezi river cruise boat). Where there are competent guides, the negative impacts of tourists on communities and ecosystems can be greatly reduced. Guides who take tourists through, for example Brimstone Hill Fort in St Kitts or ruins in Olympia, Greece, can ensure that tourists do not walk on walls, take home a souvenir piece of the ruin or place their name on the structures. These same guides enhance the experience for the tourists by making sure that they see the sloth hanging from the tree on the Canales de Tortuguero tour in Costa Rica or do not miss the immense beaver dam in Tierra del Fuego.
- Facilities Management – an emerging trend for attractions is the establishment of EMS (environmental management systems), which take a comprehensive approach to control of key risks and use design tools and low impact technologies to reduce the impact on the environment and on nearby communities. The same approaches, which many hotels and resorts have been adopting, can be applied to visitor centres, retail sites and attractions. For a more extensive review of best practice for managed sites and resorts, see Best Practice for Resorts (Manning, 2005).

- Clean-up – one of the elements often forgotten is the need for clean-up of the sites that are visited. Not all tourists are prepared to carry their rubbish for the entire tour. Therefore, convenient and sufficient receptacles are critical. Because not all tourists seem to be able to hit the receptacle, and because they become full, waste management is essential. One real concern is that not all destinations have effective garbage collection or disposal sites – yet level of cleanliness is one of the most frequent complaints by tourists in many destinations.
- Monitoring – the UNWTO *Guidebook Indicators of Sustainable Development for Tourism Destinations* (WTO, 2004) is designed to inform the tourism industry of the best ways to understand the state and impacts of tourism. This document has specific sections on cruise tourism, site impacts of visitors and sets of indicators for specific targeted sites such as beaches, ecological sites, built environments and small islands. It is very difficult to manage impacts without information, and the creation and use of a monitoring system is a critical element in successful management of the impacts of tourism, especially cruise tourism.

Managing Cultural Impacts

In addition to the impacts described above, there is increasing understanding that there are important cultural impacts on destinations. Some may be considered positive, such as opportunities to learn and use new languages, while others may lead to local perceptions of risk and unacceptable impacts on their own culture and particularly that of youth. These impacts are not unique to cruise tourism, but as noted earlier, exaggerated by the scale of arrivals.

Because the new opportunities related to increased cruise visitors will require staff capable of interacting with the visitors, knowledgeable of the destination and capable of speaking the languages of the visitors, the arrivals may mean new and better jobs for those with the right skills and knowledge.

In UNWTO indicators workshops held in some cruise destinations (e.g. Cozumel, Phuket, Croatian coast), participants noted that many cruise guides were formerly professionals, including school teachers – because they have the education and linguistic capability to succeed in the job. It was also noted that this could in fact take necessary educated personnel from jobs where they were needed, even leaving vacant positions for nurses or teachers, which may not be refilled. This could, if not well managed, result in a net social loss to the community.

A key question for communities is how much of their culture they wish to share, and whether this is negotiable. When a cruise ship lands at the San Blas islands, most residents put on colourful native dress and sell crafts and photos to the tourists (Fig. 4.3). Visitors significantly outnumber residents on the tiny islands. It is unclear whether the massive influx has helped to preserve local culture, costume or crafts or has altered it completely. Ten minutes after the last tender leaves for the cruise ship, the locals put their jeans and T-shirts back on and go home. A thorough study of the actual cultural, economic and environmental effects of this type of tourism would be very valuable to this and to other destinations. In communities where public consultations have been held on the impacts of mass tourism, the results have not always been clear. One of the best studies, done in Barbados (Doxey, 1975), identified a sequence of steps, which illustrate the community impacts of mass tourism as they evolve:

1.   Welcome – as the community responds positively to new tourism, seeing the arrivals as new opportunities.
2.   Opportunism – as the visitors are seen as a reason for new development such as craft stores, purchase of new tour buses, tour boats, building new attractions.
3.   Saturation – where the numbers begin to impact on current lifestyles, and some locals lose amenities (tourists are sitting in

Fig. 4.3. San Blas cruise vendors in traditional dresses. Source: E.W. Manning, Tourisk Inc.

my seat at my local pub; there is no room at the dock for my boat; prices are now rising to beyond what I can pay).

4. Anger – where tourists are seen as the source of problems – litter, crime, traffic, water pollution.

5. Alteration – where the destination is rebuilt to serve the tourists and locals move away. In this scenario, echoed as well in Plog's cycle, tourists (and cruise lines) can decide that they do not want to go there anymore.

Neither the sequence detailed by Doxey (1975) nor the decline first analysed in some sites in Plog's (1974) cycle or in Butler's (1980) work on destination life cycle is inevitable. Even so, some ports have lost visits because of real or perceived risk of crime, violence or decline of amenities. Several ports in North and West Africa have lost cruise visits in recent years because of security and the perception of the reception that visitors receive. Many destinations now have courses for those who deal directly with tourists, and the curricula of some Caribbean island schools contain modules that deal effectively with tourism in the community, the importance to the economy, and the need for locals to be welcome hosts to sustain this element. A tourism common core curriculum has been developed for use in many of the English-speaking destinations (Caribbean Tourism Learning System, 2007).

Integrating Cruise Planning and Community Planning for Destinations

To establish and sustain successful cruise tourism, it is important for destinations and the cruise industry to get together to plan jointly the cruise tourism and the sustainability of the destination. This has not been the norm for the industry. Also, some destinations, particularly those in developing countries, may have no comprehensive planning capacity. While it is possible to initially become a destination with occasional use of existing facilities or tendering to town docks, long-term solutions will be desirable for most.

In the web document Managing Cruise Ship Impacts: Guidelines for Current and Potential Destination Communities (Manning, 2008), a set of guidelines has been developed in association with WWF Canada and Caribbean partners to assist in assessing the costs and benefits that may be associated with cruise tourism. A series of steps is identified, which may assist destinations in assessing whether they want cruise tourism, and provides some guidance in how to integrate destination and cruise planning. Some of the key recommendations are:

- Use a participatory process involving all stakeholders to consider cruise tourism development or expansion.
- Do a thorough analysis of the destination's strengths and weaknesses, opportunities and potential liabilities. In this process, identify key assets and the potential range of experiences available in or near the destination.
- Understand what the cruise lines seek, in terms of facilities, onshore capacity and tours, and what the constraints are from the point of view of the company (distance from next port, time likely to be able to spend in port, services needed).
- Develop a plan – with clear goals. What are the limits to acceptable change? What leverage does the destination have in dealing with cruise lines?
- Do an objective analysis of prospective impacts; ideally, this could be in the form of a Strategic Impact Assessment covering social, economic and environmental issues and sensitivities.
- Consider in advance who will be the visitors, what they will do while in port, and what attractions will be involved. Move towards a joint visitor management plan with the local authorities and ideally also with the cruise companies actively involved.
- Make sure that there are site and visitor management plans in place for targeted sites where the visitors will concentrate. This should include social, environmental and economic elements.

- Objectively examine the real costs and benefits of cruise tourism. Some potential destinations noted above have decided not to welcome cruise ships. Others have been successful in obtaining changes in how or when passengers come ashore, and have obtained assistance from cruise lines in preparing onshore venues and with key infrastructure.

Success Stories in Partnering

There are now a number of success stories where improved partnering between jurisdictions, destinations and cruise lines (and their associations) have yielded benefits to all. The Alaska initiative (cited above) shows how several destinations within one desirable cruise region were able to establish strong regulations for emissions – currently the strongest in force (Alaska Cruise Association, 2011). Similar initiatives are occurring in the Caribbean as part of the initiative to establish a Sustainable Tourism Zone for the Caribbean. A number of potential cruise passengers are seeking information on the ecological footprint of ships and cruise holidays. Increasingly, the policies and practices of cruise lines are part of the information readily available to those choosing holidays including identification of onshore activities designed to help communities, preserve reefs or rainforest and assist local education. Sites like the Cruise Critic (2011) assist potential passengers in finding information about the ships. The Green Cruising section of this site provides up-to-date information on the policies and practices of each of the major cruise lines. Despite this, it is not yet possible to obtain comparative footprinting of packages or of individual ships as it is now for many land tours in Europe.

Cruise tourism is a form of mass tourism. For that reason, most of the tools and approaches that have been developed to manage mass tourism, along with a number that deal with large-scale day tourism and visitor management in fragile sites, are the tool kit necessary for cruise ship destinations to try to make certain that they remain sustainable and obtain the greatest net benefits possible from this rapidly growing tourism sector.

References

Alaska Cruise Association (2011) Environment and Safety. Available at: www.akcruise.org/group.cfm?menuId=151 (accessed 28 March 2011).

Butler, R. (1980) The concept of a tourist area of life cycle of evolution: implications for management of resources. *Canadian Geographer* 19(1), 5–12.

Caribbean Tourism Learning System (2007) Tourism Studies Core: Revised Curriculum Handbook. Available at: www.onecaribbean.org/content/files/Tourismstudiescommoncore.pdf (accessed 28 March 2011).

Christian, C. (2001) Morne Trois Pitons: Dominica's experience with ecotourism. *World Heritage Review* 23, 52–61.

Conservation International (2008) New Agreement works to Balance Cruise Ship Tourism and Conservation. Available at: www.conservation.org/sites/celb/news/Pages/051208_new_agreement_cruise_ship_tourism_conservation.aspx (accessed 28 March 2011).

Cruise Critic (2011) Green Crusing. Available at: www.cruisecritic.com/articles.cfm?ID=528 (accessed 28 March 2011).

Cruise Market Watch (2011) Cruise Market Watch Announces 2011 Cruise Line Market Share and Revenue Projections. Available at: www.cruisemarketwatch.com/blog1/articles/cruise-market-watch-announces-2011-cruise-line-market-share-and-revenue-projections/ (accessed 28 March 2011).

Doxey, G.V. (1975) A causation theory of visitor related irritants: methods and research inferences. In: *Impact of Tourism: Sixth Annual Conference Proceedings of the Travel Research Association.* San Diego, California, pp. 195–198.

Green Globe 21 (2011) The Worldwide Environmental Standard for the Tourism Industry. Available at: www.psillakis.com/environment/Green%20Globe%2021%20Leaflet.pdf (accessed 28 March 2011).

Hannafin, M. (2011) New Website Rates Energy Efficiency of Cruise Ships. Available at: www.frommers.com/articles/7167.html (accessed 28 March 2011).

Kramer, P.A., Kramer, P.R. and McField, M. (eds) (2002) Ecoregional Conservation Planning for the Mesoamerican Caribbean Reef. World Wildlife Fund. Available at: www.summitfdn.org/foundation/pdfs/wwf_mesoamerican.pdf (accessed 28 March 2011).

Manning, E.W. (2005) Best Practice for Resorts. Available at: www.tourisk.com/content/projects/downloads.htm#resort (accessed 28 March 2011).

Manning, E.W. (2008) Managing Cruise Ship Impacts: Guidelines for Current and Potential Destination Communities. Available at: http://tourisk.org/content/projects/downloads.htm#cruise (accessed 28 March 2011).

Manning, E.W. and Dougherty T.D. (2000) Planning sustainable tourism destinations. *Tourism Recreation Research* 25(2), 3–14.

Plog, S.C. (1974) Why destination areas rise and fall in popularity. *The Cornell Hotel and Restaurant Administration Quarterly* 14(4), 55–58.

Save Kahului Harbour (2007) Available at: www.savekahuluiharbor.com/cruise.php (accessed 28 March 2011).

Sweeting, J. and Wayne, S. (2003) *A Shifting Tide: Environmental Challenges & Cruise Industry Responses.* Center for Environmental Leadership in Business, Conservation International, Washington.

Travel and Leisure (2003) Molokai's Dilemma. Available at: www.travelandleisure.com/articles/molokais-dilemma (accessed 28 March 2011).

United Nations Environmental Program (1999) Environmental Impacts of Tourism. Available at: www.unep.fr/scp/tourism/sustain/impacts/environmental/mainareas.htm (accessed 28 March 2011).

Weaver, D. (2004) Managing ecotourism in the island microstate: the case of Dominica. In: Diamantis, D. (ed.) *Ecotourism: Management and Assessment.* Thomson Learning, London, pp. 155–163.

WTO (2004) *Indicators of Sustainable Development for Tourism Destinations: A Guidebook.* United Nations World Tourism Organization, Madrid.

Part II

Cruise Line Corporate Management

5   Cruise Line Strategies for Keeping Afloat

Sven Gross and Michael Lück

Introduction

Imagine a container shipping company with a 100-year history. They have been successful in their operations over many years, and are financially healthy. However, because of increasing competition, they plan to diversify. The CEO has decided that expanding into the cruise industry could be an attractive and viable move, given the great deal of media exposure cruising has received over the past years, and based on the positive experiences of competing container shipping companies, which have also entered the cruise business.

To prepare this move, a number of strategic questions need to be addressed, including:

- What will be the cruise line's competitive advantages?
- What services will be offered on board?
- How will the company behave towards competitors?
- Which customer segments will the cruise line serve?
- How will the revenues be generated, and which growth concept will be pursued?
- Which cooperation partners will be selected – if any?

To deal with these fundamental questions in a systematic way, a guideline sketching the available strategic options would be of value to the company. However, while literature concerning cruise line segmentation and ship classifications is readily available, there appears to be a lack of strategic guidelines. Such guidelines could include an analysis of various aspects of the cruise industry, including the different ways to categorize cruise lines and cruise ships, the different business systems, potential markets and market segmentation strategies, pricing strategies and other revenue-generating activities. Important data for the decision-making can be acquired through a portfolio of analyses, such as of demand and competition, and by scanning the (business) environment.

This chapter will introduce and provide an overview of, and a systematic approach to, the various strategic options available to cruise lines.

Background

Strategies set the frame of action or map the route ('How do we get there?') to ensure that implementation of all operative (tactical) instruments is goal-oriented. Moreover, strategies are oriented towards the achievement of a certain market position and should systematically take into account the opportunities and threats of the company; thus they represent a set of medium and long-term principles (Becker, 2006; Freyer, 2007). Strategies are therefore, by their nature, 'constant' instructions, guidelines or maxims by means of which a concrete framework, as well as a certain amount of entrepreneurial action, is determined. Thus they are a central connector between the objectives on the one hand and the current operational measures of acting and reacting on the other (Becker, 2006).

There is a lack of literature that deals particularly with the strategic orientation of cruise lines. A review of scientific publications concerning cruise ship tourism between the years 2000 and 2007 does not list any work that examines this topic (Casey, 2007); however, Cartwright and Baird (1999) offer some thoughts on the subject in *The Development and Growth of the Cruise Industry.* In contrast, the segmentation of the cruise product and the classification of cruise lines have been discussed in various publications. These are the first indications of a strategic orientation of cruise lines (Table 5.1).

Strategies of Cruise Lines

The corporate strategy of a company consists of several elements, which are also referred to as strategy modules or strategy chips. Different basic modules have been developed in the relevant literature, for example by Becker (2006), Freyer (2007) and Porter (1999). Following this literature, a range of strategy modules and the respective

Table 5.1. Cruise-related segmentation and classification approaches in the literature.

Author	Segmentation and classification categories	Sources
Bull (modified by Hall)	River, canal and lake cruises; special interest; extended ferry 'mini-cruises'; short ocean cruises; long-distance ocean cruises	Bull, 1996; Hall, 2004
Cudahy	Upscale companies, mass market cruise companies, niche market cruise lines and bargain basement cruise companies	Cudahy, 2001
CLIA	Budget, contemporary, premium, luxury cruise, luxury sailing, exploration/soft adventure and niche	Hall, 2004
DVB	Budget, contemporary, premium, luxury, ultra luxury	DVB, 2006
Econoguide rating	Cruise line rating: rusty tubs; oldies but goldies; middle of the fleet; a cut above; luxury; ultra luxury. Cruise ship rating: 1–6 stars	Sandler, 2007
Hobson	Mass market; middle market; luxury market; speciality market	Hobson, 1993
Lloyd's	Super deluxe, deluxe plus, deluxe, standard and economy	WTO, 2003
Schaefer	Budget lines, premium lines and luxury lines	Schaefer, 1998
Stern's Guide to the Cruise Vacation	Category A = deluxe; category B = premium; category C = standard/mass market; category D = economy	Stern, 2006
Ward/Berlitz Guide	Ten different categories: 5 stars plus to 1 star	Ward, 2007
World Tourism Organization	Life-style classification: Standard; Premium; Luxury	WTO, 2003
Wild	Super deluxe, deluxe plus, deluxe, standard and economy	Wild, 2007

CLIA, Cruise Lines International Association.

options they offer for the positioning of a cruise line will be introduced and developed in the following sections for the purpose of illustration.

Business model

The classical categorization of shipping businesses stems from traditional freight shipping. Here, shipping lines can be divided into liner trade, tramp trade and charter. However, modern cruise passenger shipping does not entirely fit into any of these three categories. Tramp trade in passenger shipping is rare to non-existent (freighter travel being a notable exception), and thus not applicable. Cruise lines operate in a different way from those in the classification mentioned above. They are a relatively new category, complementing the liner and tramp trade. In addition, a shipping company might operate using a mix of the cruise line and the liner trade categories. The classification depends on the *modus operandi* of a cruise line for offering passenger transport, and will be explained in the following sections.

Liner trade (also called scheduled services) offers connections between two or more sea or river ports, which are used in a regular cycle (according to a published schedule). They have an obligation to operate according to their published schedule, irrespective of the number of booked passengers. Scheduled service providers can operate sea cruises, river cruises or ferry services. In addition, in recent years cruise specialists offering passages on scheduled freighter traffic have increasingly extended their business segments. Because of the growing importance of airline operations – 1958 was the last year in which more passengers crossed the Atlantic Ocean by ship than by plane – today cruise liners only rarely offer liner trade, and therefore this business system has lost almost all of its former importance.

Notable exceptions are Cunard (with the *Queen Mary 2*) and the Norwegian Coastal Express 'Hurtigruten', which has been in existence for more than a hundred years. The Hurtigruten service calls at 34 ports daily between Bergen and Kirkenes and has, over the years, served a combination of transport functions: for mail, goods and passengers. In addition to its vital importance to many local communities as a carrier of passengers and freight, it has also developed into an internationally recognized cruise operator. The tourist market has become its most important source of income, accounting for about 50% of its total operating revenues.

Another fact, which distinguishes it from other cruise companies, is that Hurtigruten is supported by the State (Sletvold, 2006; Hurtigruten, 2007). In addition to scheduled services, operators such as Hurtigruten use some of their ships during the slower times of scheduled business as classical cruise ships, for example, in the southern hemisphere during the austral summer.

While tramp and liner are potential options, cruise ship tourism today is dominated by cruise lines and companies that offer charter contracts. Most common are cruise lines, which primarily operate their

Table 5.2.   Selected strategy modules of cruise lines.

Strategy module		Strategic options
Business model		Cruise line, liner trade, charter, tramp trade
Geographical scope		Regional/national, international, global
Competition strategy	Strategy type	Cost leadership, differentiation, focus
	Competitive conduct	Conflict strategy, cooperation, consolidation
(Main) source of income		All-inclusive fares, low fares and high on-board revenue
Customer orientation		Mass market strategy, segmentation strategy, nice strategy

Source: based on Freyer (2007) and Pompl (2002).

own vessels or those leased under their own brand name. This applies to sea and river cruises, but also to special forms of maritime tourism (e.g. cruises on large sailing yachts, freighter cruises). These cruise lines, and agents specialized in the charter business, rent (charter) anything from large vessels to small pleasure craft, vessels with fewer cabins, or yachts, either to private individuals or to tour operators. A factor common to all business systems is that they can be operated on the various known shipping routes, which are inland waters, canals and rivers, as well as oceans (Pompl, 1994; Schaefer, 1998).

Geographical scope

The two main points to address in this strategy are the spatial distribution of the customers, and the geographic regions in which the cruises will operate. If a cruise line decides to appeal to international customers in addition to regional and national customers, a variety of product development aspects have to be taken into consideration, such as specific requirements for the cruise product (e.g. choice of food, multilingual staff, entertainment programmes, cabin and ship design, access to/from the port), a customized international marketing, and potentially the establishment of overseas agencies in large international markets (Freyer, 2007).

An ocean cruise line has the choice, either to operate globally, or exclusively in waters in close proximity to their home port, thus operating internationally, but not globally. Following decades of growth in their home markets (North America and Asia), more recently the 'Big Three' (Carnival, Royal Caribbean, Star) cruise corporations shifted to a global growth strategy. In order to increase their long-term competitiveness, they developed new markets using a relatively similar product. For example, in order to increase their market share, new ships of the US-based Carnival Corporation (e.g. through Costa, Aida, Iberocruceros) and Royal Caribbean (through Pullmantur and TUI Cruises) were

planned and scheduled to operate in European waters (Schuessler, 2008).

Competition strategy – strategy type

With customers and competitors in mind, it is necessary to decide how to achieve competitive advantages. Referring to Porter (1999), the three strategic options are cost leadership, differentiation and the focus strategy.

With cost leadership, a company pursues the goal of becoming the most inexpensive producer within the industry. When its strategy is one of differentiation, a company attempts to be unique, or to be considered unique, to rate highly with the customers. The provider chooses one or more of the characteristics that are considered important by a large number of consumers, and takes up a unique position in order to come up to the customers' expectations. For this uniqueness, the company can demand higher prices. There can be more than one successful differentiation strategy within a sector, as long as several characteristics are of equal value to the customers.

When following the focus strategy, a company chooses a segment or a group of segments within a sector and provides customized offers, which preferably preclude competition. With an optimal adjustment of this strategy to fit the specific target segments, the company aims to achieve a competitive advantage, even if this does not mean an overall competitive advantage (Porter, 1999).

Cost leadership

When applying the cost leadership strategy, a company aims to be the producer with the lowest cost base. The main tools related to this strategy (at times also used to gain access to new markets) are aggressive pricing strategies. There are numerous reasons why a company might have a significant cost advantage. These include cost degression through economies of scale, company specific technologies, cost advantages in the purchasing department, or alternative distribution and communication strategies (Porter, 1999).

Carnival Corporation is widely accepted as a cost leader in the industry, and of thus employing an aggressive pricing strategy. 'Carnival's pricing continued to lead the industry, with an average price point per person per day of about US$175, compared with an industry average of US$235' (Kwortnik, 2006, p. 292). The basis of the cost degression in the cruise ship industry is the trend of increasingly large ships, and the subsequent reduction of the cost per unit. According to the 2008 edition of the Berlitz *Guide to Cruising & Cruise Ships*, 23 out of the listed 33 ships with a size exceeding 100,000 GRT belong to the Carnival Group, underlining Carnival's cost leadership (Ward, 2008).

Differentiation

The differentiation strategy is, for example in today's airline industry, still the dominating strategy. A large proportion of contemporary air transport is generated by large network carriers operating internationally. These 'high quality carriers' attempt to differentiate their products from those of competitors by offering upper market products, in the hope that customers will develop preferences for their offers. In the current worldwide cruise market, premium and luxury ships account for almost 30% of the cruise capacity (in lower berth [LB] terms) (DVB, 2006). Cruise lines in this segment also attempt to establish an image or a brand, so that (potential) passengers perceive the cruise line to be unique in a certain sector, and are willing to pay a higher price. Nevertheless, research shows that:

[...] the consumer was unable to compare and contrast cruise products. Whereas the consumer can readily distinguish between a Mercedes and a Volkswagen, the same audience, when it comes to the cruise industry, is far from clear as to what distinguishes certain Premium brands from certain Contemporary brands. Such lack of knowledge is hardly surprising, the reality being that the lines between certain brands

are often blurred, all of which works against the ability of target audiences to differentiate. [...] The crucial challenge is to develop a series of positive associations through branding; a marketing strategy designed to promote appropriate messages and images that will serve to stimulate the purchase of a specific cruise product.

(DVB, 2004, p. 26)

Focus strategy

The niche strategy is most often applied by smaller providers in particular markets or for particular themes (e.g. food, wellness, photography, art, wine, dancing) and customer groups (e.g. seniors, families, nudists or the gay community). These include, for example, adventure cruises, expedition cruises, freighter cruises or round-the-world cruises. 'In these cases the cruise experience itself is more important than the square footage of cabins, number of restaurants on board or large entertainment offers. What is more important is the uniqueness of the itineraries, the low passenger capacity and the individuality of the holiday experience' (DVB, 2004, p. 25).

Freighter cruises follow the standard freighter routes, hence the long duration of many such trips. With computerized cargo vessels now requiring fewer officers, the cargo companies involved are selling the usually well-appointed and spacious accommodation to customers who seek a different cruise experience.

Generally, no individual sectors are sold; passengers need to have a great deal of time available. Port schedules are relatively flexible compared with the regular cruise ships. No special activities or entertainments are provided for passengers, either aboard or ashore, although some ships may have small swimming pools and libraries, also intended primarily for officers. Passengers take their meals with and eat the same food as the officers. Passenger numbers are very low, generally between two and 12, depending on space, but this form of alternative cruising is so popular with special interest cruisers [...] that accommodation is often booked out many months in advance.

(Douglas and Douglas, 2001, p. 335)

An analysis of providers of freighter cruises on the German market shows that there are a minimum of eight providers, some of which only act as agents.

Other niche providers are, for example, ChristianCruises.Net, Bare Necessities Tour & Travel, and RSVP Vacations; however, these do not operate their own ships. Bare Necessities Tour & Travel has been offering more than 40 nudist cruises since 1991. By chartering large ships like the *Carnival Legend* and small yachts like the *Star Flyer*, the company offers a wide range of tours. RSVP Vacations also specializes exclusively in *ad hoc* trips (especially gay and lesbian cruises), and charters ships from large cruise lines. ChristianCruises.Net is a travel agency that specializes in cruise groups with Christian entertainers and ministers. The company books its customers on cruises of other providers (e.g. Royal Caribbean's *Liberty Of The Seas* or the *MS Oosterdam* of Holland America Line) and organizes additional entertainment offers on board, which are specifically designed for the customers of ChristianCruises.Net (Bare Necessities, 2008; Christian Cruises, 2008; RSVP Vacations, 2008).

Competition strategy – competitive conduct

Competition strategies include the options of solo attempt, cooperation and consolidation; however, these theoretical differentiations are characterized by smooth transitions in practice. A cruise line can also pursue different strategies for different markets. The most basic distinction is between cruise lines 'going alone' (internal growth) and those collaborating with other (cruise) companies (external growth). These forms of collaboration range from loose partnerships, such as working groups or communities of interest, to mergers (consolidation).

Conflict strategy

The conflict strategy, also referred to as competition-oriented strategy or 'solo attempt', usually implies individual (relative) market strengths, i.e. possible unique selling propositions. Particularly service and cost advantages are the basis for the choice of this strategy. easyCruise with their innovative concept of low-cost cruises is noteworthy as a current example. They redefined budget cruises by providing a 'no frills' option, where the customer can generally expect to pay extra for every product or service rendered. EasyCruise sought to set the access price as low as possible (*EasyCruise Life* ticket prices start at €30 per cruise day) in order to lower or even eliminate the financial access threshold to cruising and therefore to create a completely new clientele (DVB, 2006; Gross *et al.*, 2007; easyCruise, 2008).

Cooperation

With an existing cooperation strategy, usually comparable providers try to strengthen their market position and aim to expand it together. Besides collaboration in national and international associations (for example, Cruise Lines International Association, Florida-Caribbean Cruise Association, Verband Deutscher Reeder), which are especially conducive to political lobbying, rationalization of production through standardization and public relations, there is a lot of cross-company cooperation. The latter, above all, pursues the goal of saving costs (e.g. in the areas of purchasing and distribution), process simplification and an extended offer for cruise customers (also with the objective of cost saving and simplification of processes). Cruise companies cooperate with hotel companies, car rental agencies, airlines, hospitality or cultural institutions in terms of customer loyalty programmes (or participate in such programmes of other tourism service providers), and non-touristic partners (e.g. soccer clubs, car manufacturers).

In addition to vertical cooperation, there are some cases of horizontal cooperation. For example, Royal Caribbean Cruises lent support to Color Line, a Norwegian ferry-cruise line, in the design of the two new cruise ferries *Color Fantasy* and *Color Magic*.

The cooperation of Royal Caribbean Cruises and TUI AG is a special case, since it could fit into both the horizontal and the vertical categories (TUI AG, 2008). After having received approval from the antitrust authorities, TUI and Royal Caribbean Cruises created a cruise line named TUI Cruises in the premium cruise sector for the German-speaking market, which has been operating since May 2009. This constitutes a horizontal cooperation. However, since TUI is a fully vertically integrated corporation (including, for example, travel agencies, package tour operators, airlines, incoming agents, etc.), this collaboration between TUI and Royal Caribbean can also be seen as a vertical cooperation.

Consolidation

Mergers with or shares in other cruise and tourism companies are a phenomenon that has long been familiar to the cruise industry. Horizontal cruise business consolidation began in the USA towards the end of the 1980s in the 3–4 star segments. One of the driving factors for this development was the trend to build larger ships with increasing entertainment offers, requiring a greater amount of capital. This led to market consolidation, reducing the number of independent operators through take-overs and mergers. Cruise industry consolidation has been particularly prominent since the second half of the 1990s and the early 2000s (see Table 5.3 and especially Bjelicic, Chapter 2, this volume). While in the majority of these cases, separate brands have been maintained to compete in different

cruise market segments, at least a dozen cruise brands have disappeared during this period (Hall, 2004).

> Globalisation of the cruise sector has also led to increased internationalisation of ownership and further concentration in this business, with a massive shakeout steadily reducing the number of players. Cunard's famed QE2, introduced in 1969, is illustrative. Cunard was acquired by Trafalgar House, a British multinational conglomerate, two years later in 1971. (...) In the 80s and early 90s, Cunard purchased several Norwegian ships and the Royal Viking name, but in 1996 Trafalgar House was taken over by the Norwegian company, Kvaerner ASA. Two years later, Kvaerner sold Cunard to US-based Carnival Corporation, which promptly merged it with its luxury-end Seabourn Cruise Line.
>
> (Wood, 2000, p. 352)

As a result of the rapid pace of mergers, acquisitions and bankruptcies in the sector over the past two decades, Carnival Corporation, which in 1973 owned just one ship, has grown to a corporation that today operates 11 cruise lines (Carnival Cruise Line, Holland-America Line, Cunard Line, The Yachts of Seabourn, Costa Cruises, Aida, P&O Cruises, P&O Australia, Princess Cruises, Ocean Village, Iberocruceros), operating 88 ships (Carnival, 2008b). Carnival Corporation has thus had the most significant influence on the development in the supply structure (see also Bjelicic, Chapter 2, this volume). In summary, the buzzword globalization, which came in vogue in the 1980s, can increasingly be applied to the worldwide cruise market. Especially the 'Big Three' dominate the worldwide cruise

Table 5.3. Selected examples of consolidation in the cruise sector during the late 1990s and early 2000s.

Company	Took over
Royal Caribbean	Celebrity Cruises, Pullmantur Cruises
Carnival Corporation	Costa Cruise Lines, Cunard, P&O Cruises, Princess Cruises, P&O Australia, Swan Hellenic, Aida, Ocean Village
Norwegian Cruise Line	Majesty Cruise Line's ships, Orient Lines
Cruise Holdings	Dolphin Cruise Line

Source: Hall (2004).

market and extensively pursue the strategy of concentration: Carnival Corporation & plc, Royal Caribbean International, and the Star Group control around 80% of the world's cruise market in terms of berth capacities (WTO, 2003; Schuessler, 2005).

Shares and acquisitions can be found not only among the cruise lines, but also in other areas. As a combination of cruises and hotel stays (sail & stay) becomes increasingly important, some cruise lines have acquired hotels or shares in hotels. Shares in airlines, bus and tour operators, and call centres are also known, as illustrated in the following examples:

- In addition to cruise operations, Carnival owns Holland America Tours and Princess Tours – two Alaskan tour operators. Holland America Tours operates 16 hotels and lodges in Alaska and the Yukon Territory of Canada, over 560 motor coaches, and 24 domed rail cars, which are run on the Alaska Railroad (Schaefer, 1998; Carnival, 2008a).
- Since 1971, Cunard has had a share of 66.6% in Heavilift Cargo Airlines (Schiffspost, 2008).
- AIDA holds a share in Call4Cruise, a service centre for AIDA ships and Costa Cruise Lines. Moreover, there is SeeLive Tivoli, a joint venture of AIDA Cruises and Schmidt's Tivoli theatre company developing and carrying out entertainment programmes for AIDA (Aida, 2008).
- In Belize,

> Royal Caribbean invested US$18 million in co-ownership of the Fort Street Tourism Village. Opened in November 2001,

> Tourism Village is where all cruise passengers are tendered from cruise ships. The port charge is US$5 per passenger, 80% of which goes to Tourism Village. Receiving US$4 for every cruise passenger landed, Royal Caribbean will recoup its investment in six or seven years.
>
> (Klein, 2005, p. 110)

Cruise lines are not the only businesses acquiring shares in other service providers, which offer services at different stages of the production chain (e.g. hotels, airlines or bus operators) or ancillary services (e.g. port, excursion and incoming agencies). Other service providers, too, have discovered the cruise market for themselves:

> Needing to maintain market share following competitive pressures on its resorts, Club Med entered the cruise sector in the early 1990s with the construction of luxury sailing boats. Hyatt Hotels took a half-stake in Royal Caribbean in 1988. […] The Disney Corporation entered the cruise business in 1998 after a long-previewed publicity campaign promoting cruising as a complementary product to the theme park visits in Florida.
>
> (Hall, 2004, p. 108)

(Main) sources of income

Traditionally, the (main) source of income of a cruise line is either revenue from ticket prices, which already include all ancillary costs, or a low ticket price complemented by high revenues on board and/or from shore excursions (see Table 5.4 and Vogel, Chapter 10, this volume).

Table 5.4. Revenues of Carnival Corporation and RCL 2005–2007 (in million US$).

	Carnival	RCL	Carnival	RCL	Carnival	RCL
	2007		2006		2005	
Cruise revenues						
Passenger tickets	9,792	4,427	8,903	3,838	8,399	3,609
On-board/other	2,846	1,721	2,514	1,390	2,338	1,293
Other revenues	395	n/a	422	n/a	357	n/a
Total revenues	13,033	6,149	11,839	5,229	11,094	3,735

Source: based on Carnival (2008a) and RCL (2008).

All-inclusive fares

Even if a trend away from the all-inclusive concept can be noticed, there are still all-inclusive cruises, offered, e.g. by Hapag-Lloyd on board the *Columbus* (the ticket price includes all beverages, leisure facilities and up to ten shore excursions (Hapag-Lloyd, 2008), by NCL as part of their Freestyle Cruising concept (see Cartledge, Chapter 17, this volume) and by Pullmantur Cruises. The larger cruise lines in particular are increasingly shifting away from the 'real' all-inclusive concept on their cruises.

> In the past cruise ships were sold as 'all-inclusive holidays', i.e. once the fare was paid, there were few extras to pay for items other than those of a personal nature such as for shopping, alcoholic drinks and of course, end-of-cruise tips. Today that has all changed and the all-inclusive element has given way to a 'user-pays' situation. This includes on-board revenue centres that include optional 'extra-tariff' restaurants and food outlets, mini bars, recreational activities and same-day newspapers. Onshore revenue generators include land based tours and shopping programmes.
> (Dowling, 2006)

Low fares, high on-board and other revenue

Today, there are prices for cruises that were unthinkable a couple of years ago, for example, a 7-day cruise being advertised for US$400 a person, or daily rates from €30, like those of *easyCruiseOne* (Schmidt, 2005). This raises the question as to whether these cruises really are as cheap as they seem to be, or if there is another strategy behind this. The cruise lines say that with additional revenue they are able to keep the basic costs for the passengers low(er) and that therefore broader levels of the population can take part in cruise ship tourism. Moreover, passengers are responsible for their own behaviour and free to decide on which extras to spend money. Although this is probably true to a certain extent, there is evidence that ships are increasingly being designed in a way that encourages passengers to stay on board longer, the result being that the expenditures off board will end up with the cruise lines as well.

Large resort ships travel by night and are in port during the day, but provide little connection to nature and the sea, the ship being the destination (small town takes to water), increasingly designed to keep you inside the ship, spending money.

(Ward, 2008, p. 11)

The opportunities for cruise lines to generate additional revenues on and off board are manifold (Table 5.5) and represent a growing share of the total revenue. On-board spending is an important part of cruise line revenue, with figures often reaching 35% of the total revenue.

> A recent study, carried out by the North American company Market Scope, states that, on three, four and seven-day Caribbean cruises, passengers under 45 years of age spend an average of US$357, 45 to 65-year olds spend US$345 and the over 65s spend US$242. Most is spent on gambling and drinking, together representing 50% of the total. Spending on sightseeing trips and playing sports on-land is US$124, US$144 and US$94 for the age groups previously described, while spending in on-board franchises or shops is US$103, US$116 and US$124 respectively. Europeans tend to spend less than their US and Canadian counterparts, with an average of US$30 spent in on-board shops.
> (WTO, 2003, p. 130)

Casinos or particular zones with slot machines, video poker and similar games are nowadays offered on almost every ship, whereby European ships tend to have smaller casinos than American or Asian ships. There are cruises that have a clear focus on gamblers and cruise lines, such as Caravela (India), Jimei Group (Hong Kong and China), Palm Beach Casino Line (USA), SeaEscape (USA), and Sun Cruz Casinos (USA), and have special offers for this customer group (Seereisen Portal, 2007). NCL offers, for example, a 'Casinos at Sea Players Club' and a 'Casinos at Sea Players Program' (NCL, 2007). From casinos ashore, it is known that high yields can be gained. Therefore, it is easily understandable that a consequent orientation towards gamblers constitutes a profitable source of income for cruise lines.

Table 5.5. Examples of on-board revenue sources.

Source of on-board revenue	Examples
In-room entertainment including gambling, internet access, or cell phone connections; internet cafés	'Most ships now have internet-connect centres, where you can surf the net at a cost of US$0.50–0.75 a minute. Computers link almost all functions aboard the latest ships. Interactive TV systems let you order wine, arrange shore excursions, play casino games, shop, and order pay-per-view movies, all from your cabin.' (Ward, 2008) 'There has also been an increase in the availability of satellite telephones, Internet and e-mail in each cabin.' (WTO, 2003)
Photographer	'Professional photographers take pictures (…) of passengers throughout the cruise. They cover all the main events and social functions, such as the captain's cocktail party. The pictures can be viewed without any obligation to purchase, but the prices may surprise. The cost is now likely to exceed US$10 for a postcard-sized color photograph, and a 10×8-inch embarkation photo abroad. Queen Mary 2, for example, is a whopping US$27.50.' (Ward, 2008)
Shopping	'The distribution of revenue generated on-board for NCL cruises, excluding the bar and gambling, is as follows: clothing/fashion (31.6%), jewellery (31.9%), gifts (11.5%), perfume (8.5%), spirits (3%), sweets (2.5%), tobacco (1.7%), cosmetics (1.3%) and others (8%).' (WTO, 2003)
Sports	For example, lessons with golf professionals, computer-generated golf courses, ice skate hire and ice skating on a small rink, rock climbing on an artificial wall.
Wellness, spa and beauty parlour	'Body pampering spas are among the hottest passenger (revenue) facilities at sea, with more space than ever devoted to them (example: Costa Concordia has 21,000 sq. meters of spa space).' (Ward 2007); Massage (50 min): c. €88–110 (Golden and Brown, 2006)
Extra-tariff restaurants, bars, disco	'"Alternative" restaurants are hot – particularly aboard the large resort ships […]. These are typically à la carte restaurants where you must make a reservation, and pay to dine in small, intimate places with superior food, wines, services and ambiance. Some ships, such as many in the NCL and Star Cruises fleets, have up to ten different restaurants and eateries […] These usually cost extra – typically between US$15 and US$50 a person, but the food quality is decidedly better, as is presentation, service, and ambiance.' (Ward, 2008)
Dry-cleaning and laundry services	'Per item c. €2–6, some ships have coin-operated machines for passenger use' (Golden and Brown, 2006)
Babysitting	Private babysitting in the room or group babysitting. Private babysitting for two children around €8 per hour and €5–7 for group babysitting (Golden and Brown, 2006)
Art auctions and galleries, wine auctions	'On many cruise lines, especially those in the mid- to upper-price range, you'll find an on board art gallery or auction.' (Sandler, 2007)

Cruise lines do not always operate the casinos on their ships themselves. Also by issuing concessions to specialized casino operators, they participate in the casino profits. Century Casinos, for example, has a concession contract with Oceania Cruises based in Miami, for the operation of three casinos on Oceania's cruise ships, a contract for the operation of casinos on two Silversea Cruises ships, and a concession contract for the operation of a casino on board the world's first luxury housing estate at sea (*The World of ResidenSea*) (Century Casinos, 2007).

In addition to on-board revenue, some cruise lines place a strong emphasis on shore excursions.

Almost one-third of Royal Caribbean's profit in 2002–03 was derived from shore excursions. Shore excursions are convenient for passengers and often sold as safer than independent sightseeing. The 50–80% of passengers who buy an excursion in any particular port pay a premium for the convenience. As little as one-half to one-third of the cost goes to the shore excursion provider. [...] The cruise lines selling shore excursions also provide port lecture and port shopping programmes where passengers receive a map marked with preferred stores. They are told that the recommended stores give the best prices and the cruise line will warranty what they buy. As the small print on some maps notes, merchants pay referral fees to be listed. The amount can be significant. A retailer in Nassau reported in 1995 that he 'pays more than US$100,000 a year in such fees to one cruise line alone'.

(Klein, 2005, pp. 93–94)

Customer oriented strategies

Demand-focused strategies build a vital element in a company's strategic decision-making. These can include a mass market strategy, or more diverse market segment-oriented strategies. In the case of the latter, the whole market is to be (sub)divided into sub-markets that are as homogeneous as possible. Market segmentation helps to identify target groups, and their needs and wants, and thus to customize the supply and marketing activities. Marketing literature identifies a number of criteria for market segmentation (Freyer, 2007):

- socio-demographic criteria (e.g. age, income, gender, residence);
- behaviour-related criteria (e.g. choice of mode of transport, length of stay, destination choice);
- psychographic criteria (e.g. lifestyle, personality related traits, such as allo-centrism/psychocentrism); and
- geographic criteria (e.g. origin of tourists, destinations).

With the aid of socio-demographic and behavioural criteria, information relatively easy to obtain, cruise lines are able to customize their offers for the needs of their clientele, and subsequently their marketing to specific target groups. The Cruise Lines International Association, GP Wild and DVB, for example, applied socio-demographic segmentation in their respective studies.

> Based on a socio economic approach one can, broadly speaking, break the ocean cruise market down into five segments: the Ultra Luxury segment (five star plus), the Luxury segment (five star), the Premium market segment (four star), the Contemporary segment (three star) and the Budget segment (two star). [...] The Ultra Luxury segment is an exceedingly small part of the overall cruise market. In terms of the US, operators were effectively targeting one per cent of the leisure population, which in 2001 amounted to approximately 580,000 people. These all frills cruises are designed for wealthy pleasure seeking clientele aged 45+ with an average gross household income in the region of US$200,000, representing less than 3% of the travelling US population. The quality for this segment, a cruise product needs to deliver something akin to be a pleasure loving and opulent experience.
>
> (DVB, 2004)

The 'Big Three' target various customer groups (market segments) with the offer of different brands. Kwortnik (2006, p. 289) contends that 'Carnival Corp. emerged as the largest cruise company in the world, with at least one brand positioned in each of the four main segments.' It is conceivable that after having been satisfied with a recent cruise, customers might book cruises in a higher segment for their next cruise holiday. Different brands may also be part of a strategy to service different national markets. A certain brand may be well known to consumers in some countries, but is not necessarily recognized by consumers in another country (see market area strategy) (Weaver and Duval, 2008).

In addition to socio-demographic criteria, cruise lines may segment markets according to different cultural etiquette and preferences (DVB, 2006). Examples include the increasing offerings with casinos and gaming opportunities on board American or Asian vessels, and specific dietary offers:

> German passengers tend to prefer breads (especially dark breads) and a wide variety of cheeses for breakfast and lunch. [...] The French like soft – not flaky – croissants, and may request brioches and sweet pastry items. Asian passengers like food with many different 'mouthfeel' textures. [...]. Australian passengers like to have 'vegemite' to spread on bread and toast.
>
> (Ward, 2008)

Another option is the psychographic market segmentation. A combination of demographic and psychographic criteria has been developed in order to identify specific behaviour-related typologies, forming distinct target groups. Often, these typologies are given concise labels, and illustrated with photos, caricatures or alliterations. As a further development of the establishment of typologies, specific lifestyle typologies have emerged, because travel behaviour is seen as an expression of the general consumer and lifestyle behaviours (Freyer, 2007).

Vogel (2005) applied to the cruise industry Plog's (1991) six psychographic typologies, ranging on his continuum from allocentrics ('venturers') to psychocentrics ('dependables'). He looked at the historic development of the cruise industry, and the tourist types taking cruises over the years. He found that at the beginning of the cruise sector's development, cruise lines were particularly focused on the psychocentrics. Later on, NCL with their 'Freestyle Cruising' concept targeted more the near-psychocentrics, and easyCruise is currently geared towards the near-allocentric tourists. Given this development, Vogel suggested a shift in orientation for some of the German cruise lines catering primarily for the psychocentric passenger. He cautioned that a shift towards the mid-centric range would be necessary in order not to get stuck in a psychocentric dead end of the market (Vogel, 2004, 2005).

Mass marketing is an undifferentiated strategy, and aims to target the whole – heterogeneous – market, without the knowledge of how to reach whom. The idea is to address as many potential customers as possible, with one or very few products. This type of strategy is based on the assumption that sales increase and cost benefits can be achieved through economy of scales. The advantage of such an approach is that it is not necessary to conduct detailed, expensive market analyses. Critics argue that this strategy wastes a lot of (financial) resources and thus is deemed inefficient. In addition, too many competitors make use of the same strategy, and thus, it is suggested that such strategy is likely to be successful only on monopolistic or oligopolistic markets.

However, Carnival Cruise Lines' president and CEO, Bob Dickinson argued that demographic segmentation was irrelevant for Carnival because there was no prototypical Carnival customer, except the person who cruised to have fun: 'If you have a vacation destination that has a wide bandwidth of choice, you're casting a bigger net, and you're going to get more fish' (Kwortnik, 2006, p. 293). While this indicates that Carnival is using an undifferentiated strategy because they have only one customer group – the fun loving cruiser – they do use a differentiated strategy by targeting different customer groups with different ships.

Conclusions

The outlined strategic options are elements or modules for a corporate strategy of a cruise line. Depending on the company, the strategy will vary. Certain elements that are considered particularly important may be strongly emphasized, whilst others that are found less significant may be neglected in the overall strategy formulation. In addition to the corporate strategy for a cruise line, further partial strategies for different business units can be developed if deemed necessary, for example, for different business segments (American vs Italian customers, Caribbean vs Mediterranean itineraries) and/or subsidiaries of a cruise line.

The generalization of strategies is not advisable, since a strategy that works well for one cruise line may not work for another. The same applies to a 'best combination of strategies', because successful combinations depend on a number of factors, such as the particular product(s), competition, the economic environment, and the cost structure of the respective cruise line. Most importantly, it is never a good idea to choose a strategy by 'gut feeling'. Rather, decision making should be founded on sound information, and based on a variety of analyses (e.g. of competition, of demand, operational, environmental), and the interpretation of resulting data (through, e.g. SWOT-analyses, life cycle and portfolio analyses). Subsequently, the chances are much higher for a successful portfolio of a company's strategies.

References

Aida (2008) AIDA Kreuzfahrten. Available at: www.aida.de (accessed 28 February 2008).

Bare Necessities (2008) Welcome to Bare Necessities Website. Available at: www.cruisenude.com/german/cruisehomeger.html (accessed 29 February 2008).

Becker, J. (2006) *Marketing-Konzeption: Grundlagen des ziel-strategischen und operativen Marketing-Managements*, 8th edn. Vahlen, Munich.

Bull, A.O. (1996) The economics of cruising: an application to the short ocean cruise market. *Journal of Tourism Studies* 7(2), 28–35.

Cartwright, R. and Baird, C. (1999) *The Development and Growth of the Cruise Industry*. Butterworth-Heinemann, Oxford.

Carnival Corporation & plc (2008a) *Annual Report*. Carnival Corporation, Miami, Florida.

Carnival (2008b) Our Brands. Available at: http://phx.corporate-ir.net/phoenix.zhtml?c=200767&p=irol-products (accessed 17 October 2008).

Casey, B. (2007) Cruise ship tourism research: a critical overview. In: Lück, M., Gräupl, A., Auyong, J., Miller, M.L. and Orams, M.B. (eds) *5th International Coastal & Marine Tourism Congress: Balancing Marine Tourism, Development and Sustainability*. School of Hospitality & Tourism and New Zealand Tourism Research Institute, AUT University, Auckland, pp. 236–241.

Century Casinos (2007) Wir über uns. Available at: www.cnty.com/no_cache/print/de/corporate/unternehmen/unternehmensprofil/ (accessed 13 August 2007).

Christian Cruises (2008) Welcome To: Daughters of God Cruise! Available at: www.christiancruises.net/DaughtersOfGod.htm (accessed 29 February 2008).

Cudahy, B.J. (2001) *The Cruise Ship Phenomenon in North America*. Cornell Maritime Press, Centreville, Maryland.

Douglas, N. and Douglas, N. (2001) The Cruise Experience. In: Douglas, N., Douglas, N. and Derret, R. (eds) *Special Interest Tourism: Context and Cases*. John Wiley & Sons, Milton, Australia, pp. 330–354.

Dowling, R.K. (2006) The cruising industry. In: Dowling, R.K. (ed.) *Cruise Ship Tourism*. CABI, Wallingford, pp. 13–17.

DVB Bank (2004) *DVB Research & Strategic Planning: The Cruise Industry and its Outlook 2004–2007*. DVB Bank, Rotterdam.

DVB Bank (2006) *DVB Research & Strategic Planning: The Cruise Industry and its Outlook 2006–2010*. DVB Bank, Rotterdam.

easyCruise (2008) easyCruise celebrates success of first year. Available at: www.easy.com/archive/14.03.06ECR.html (accessed 5 August 2008).

Freyer, W. (2007) *Tourismus-Marketing. Marktorientiertes Management im Mikro- und Makrobereich der Tourismuswirtschaft*, 5th edn. Oldenbourg Verlag, Munich.

Golden, F.W. and Brown, J. (2006) *European Cruises and Ports of Call*, 4th edn. Wiley, Hoboken, New Jersey.

Gross, S., Grotrian, J. and Sonderegger, R. (2007) Transferring the low cost strategy to ship, bus and rental companies. In: Gross, S. and Schröder, A. (eds) *Handbook of Low Cost Airlines: Strategies, Business Processes and Market Environment*. Erich Schmidt Verlag, Berlin, pp. 293–314.

Hall, D. (2004) Ocean cruising: market dynamics, product responses and onshore impacts. In: Pinder, D. and Slack, B. (eds) *Shipping and Ports in the Twenty-first Century: Globalisation, Technological Change and the Environment*. Routledge, Oxford, pp. 99–120.

Hapag-Lloyd (2008) Hapag-Lloyd Kreuzfahrten: Willkommen an Bord. Available at: www.hlkf.de (accessed 12 February 2008).

Hobson, J.S.P. (1993) Analysis of the US cruise line industry. *Tourism Management* 14(6), 453–462.

Hurtigruten Group ASA (2007) *Annual Report 2006*. Hurtigruten, Narvik.

Klein, R.A. (2005) *Cruise Ship Squeeze: The New Pirates of the Seven Seas*. New Society Publishers, Gabriola Island.

Kwortnik, R.J. (2006) Carnival Cruise Lines – burnishing the brand. *Cornell Hotel and Restaurant Administration Quarterly* 47(3), 286–300.

Norwegian Cruise Line (2007) NCL's Casinos at Sea. Available at: www.ncl.com/nclweb/cruiser/cmsPages.html?pageId=CasinoIntro (accessed 27 August 2007).

Norwegian Cruise Line (2008) Urlaub wie ich will. Available at: www.ncl.de (accessed 12 February 2008).

Plog, S.C. (1991) *Leisure Travel: Making it a Growth Market…Again!* John Wiley & Sons, New York.

Pompl, W. (1994) *Touristikmanagement 1: Beschaffungsmanagement*. Springer, Berlin.

Pompl, W. (2002) Internationale Strategien von Luftverkehrsgesellschaften. In: Pompl, W. and Lieb, M.G. (eds) *Internationales Tourismus-Management: Herausforderungen, Strategien, Instrumente*. Verlag Vahlen, Munich, pp. 183–208.

Porter, M.E. (1999) *Wettbewerbsvorteile: Spitzenleistungen erreichen und behaupten,* 5th edn. Campus Verlag, Frankfurt.

Royal Caribbean Cruises Ltd (2008) *2007 Annual Report*. Royal Caribbean Cruises Ltd, Miami, Florida.

RSVP Vacations (2008) RSVP. Available at: http://rsvpvacations.com (accessed 3 March 2008).

Sandler, C. (2007) *Econoguide Cruises: Cruising the Caribbean, Hawaii, New England, Alaska, and Europe,* 5th edn. Globe Pequot, Guilford, Connecticut.

Schaefer, C. (1998) *Kreuzfahrten: Die touristische Eroberung der Ozeane*. GERAG, Nuremberg.

Schiffspost (2008) History of the Cunard Line Ltd. Available at: www.schiffspost.com/flotte_air06x.htm (accessed 29 February 2008).

Schmidt, O. (2005) EasyCruiseOne. Available at: www.seereisenmagazin.de/easycruiseone.htm (accessed 29 July 2008).

Schuessler, O. (2005) *Passagier-Schifffahrt: Ein Handbuch fuer Reiseverkehrskaufleute in Ausbildung und Praxis,* 2nd edn. DRV, Frankfurt/M.

Schuessler, O. (2008) *Der Kreuzfahrtenmarkt Deutschland 2007 – Die Branchenanalyse des Deutschen ReiseVerbands*. DRV, Berlin.

Seereisen Portal (2007) Willkommen im SeereisenPortal. Available at: www.seereisenportal.de/rubriken/reedereien-veranstalter/casino-schiffe.html (accessed 13 August 2007).

Sletvold, O. (2006) The Norwegian Coastal Express: moving towards cruise tourism? In: Dowling, R.K. (ed.) *Cruise Ship Tourism*. CABI, Wallingford, pp. 223–231.

Stern, S.B. (2006) *Stern's Guide to the Cruise Vacation,* 17th edn. Pelican, Gretna, Louisiana.

TUI AG (2008) Royal Caribbean Cruises Ltd and TUI AG complete joint venture for TUI Cruises. Available at: www.tui-group.com/en/pressemedien/press_releases/2008/20080422_tui_cruises_closing.html (accessed 6 August 2008).

Vogel, M. (2004) EasyCruise: Die Erweiterung der maritimen Farbpalette. *an Bord – Das Magazin für Schiffsreisen und Seewesen* 4, 52–54.

Vogel, M. (2005) Psychographie der Kreuzfahrt. *an Bord – Das Magazin für Schiffsreisen und Seewesen* 6, 56–59.

Ward, D. (2007) *Complete Guide to Cruising & Cruise Ships 2007,* 16th edn. Berlitz, London.

Ward, D. (2008) *Complete Guide to Cruising & Cruise Ships 2008,* 17th edn. Berlitz, London.

Weaver, A. and Duval, D. (2008) International and transnational aspects of the global cruise industry. In: Coles, T. and Hall, M.C. (eds) *International Business and Tourism – Global Issues, Contemporary Interactions*. Routledge, Abingdon, pp. 106–123.

Wild, G.P. (2007) *Cruise Industry Statistical Review 2006*. G.P. Wild International, Haywards Heath.

Wood, R.F. (2000) Caribbean Cruise Tourism: Globalization at Sea. *Annals of Tourism Research* 27(2), 345–370.

WTO (2003) *Worldwide Cruise Ship Activity*. World Tourism Organization, Madrid.

6 Core Cruise Operator Processes and Systems: Overview and Challenges

Alexis Papathanassis

Introduction

> Being nice to people is just 20% of providing good customer service. The important part is designing systems that allow you to do the job right the first time.
>
> (Heskett *et al.*, 1997, p. 7)

A successful service provider, especially one offering a complex, expensive, emotion-centred service bundle, such as a cruise, is more than a loose collection of well-meaning, friendly individuals. It is a system consisting of motivated, well-equipped individuals taking purposeful and coordinated action to deliver 'ocean dreams' – a number of different ones. In other, more modest words, it is about the consistent passenger-satisfying interplay between people, processes and information systems infrastructure.

The aim of this chapter is to introduce the generic processes of a cruise operator, the systems that support those processes, and to explore the challenges posed by the evolution and trends of the cruise sector.

Core Cruise Operator Processes and Systems: Generic Overview

Examining the process architecture (Fig. 6.1) of a typical cruise operator involves a consideration of the main activity groups, their background, rationale and interrelationships. The focus here will be on core processes supporting processes (Porter, 1985) performed by the accounting and controlling departments, IT operations units, etc. are not described because they tend to be fairly standardized and/or regulated across sectors and are thus outside this chapter's specialized domain.

Moreover, specified roles and responsibilities are purposively excluded in order to accommodate the differing organizational structures evident in the cruise sector. Cruise operating extends beyond cruise ship operations and tends to enjoy less standardization in terms of role descriptions and responsibility domains (e.g. Captain, Cruise Director, Food & Beverage Manager). 'Ship-peripheral' roles are defined and responsibilities allocated depending on the organizational origin and history, culture and size of each specific cruise operator. Generally, one may safely expect that the smaller a cruise operator, the lower will be the segregation of process responsibilities and the more widely encompassing the roles and job descriptions. The separation between 'what' is being done and 'who' is doing it, in conjunction with the focus on core processes enhances the applicability and relevance of this chapter's contents.

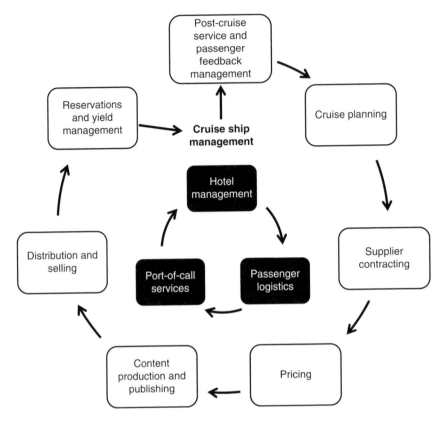

Fig. 6.1.   Generic cruise operator process architecture.

Cruise product planning

The birth of a cruise product, similarly to any other organized package, is backed by a marketing strategy and the corresponding product development, pricing, promotion and distribution policies. The formulation of a cruise marketing strategy ought to be founded on the findings of formalized and extensive marketing research. Marketing research involves the processes and methods employed to understand the target market's requirements, preferences and commercial potential.

Strategic level: deployment planning

This is especially relevant when acquiring and (re-)deploying a new vessel in order to:

- obtain the required financing (internally and/or externally);

- justify the action to internal stakeholders and investors;
- determine the requirements for the vessel's (re-)design;
- set the itinerary planning framework (i.e. matching ship design versus itinerary restrictions and target market preferences and requirements); and
- draft the market deployment roadmap (i.e. distribution, promotion, pricing range) and business development plan (including financial planning, revenue forecasts, investment appraisals).

It is worth mentioning that the utilization scope of marketing research extends beyond the single-instance market introduction strategy, feasibility study and investment case.

Tactical level: service development planning

Deploying a vessel and introducing it in the market involves significant financial commitment and capacity utilization risk. In conjunction with the sector's inherent segment and infrastructure related switching costs, consistently high levels of customer satisfaction and market relevance are the cornerstones of commercial sustainability. In this sense, effective marketing research and its integration in a cruise operator's tactical and operational management represent an ongoing necessity.

Through the direct and indirect collection, analysis and interpretation of customer feedback (see further below), cruise operators are able to draft service-level maintenance and improvement requirements. In turn, these are fed into the detailed planning for the next cruise season.

Operational level: cruise itinerary planning

This level of planning essentially involves a detailed blueprint of the ensuing cruise holiday. More specifically, the following components are decided upon:

- cruise duration and departure dates;
- ports of call;
- transport options from and to the home port;
- on-board events and excursion offers;
- material and supplies delivery requirements (i.e. expendables, food and beverages);
- subcontractor needs (e.g. entertainers, temporary service staff); and
- nautical specifics and contingencies (e.g. fuel, weather conditions, route, safety and security, ship repairs).

On this basis, the corresponding suppliers and partners are identified and targeted for contract negotiations. Over time, itinerary planning assumes a recurrent character, expediting the entire process and reducing complexity costs. In other words, once successfully implemented, an itinerary plan is not discarded, but reused as a benchmark for future plans. Apart from reducing process costs and duration, re-usability allows cruise operators to concentrate their resources on continuous improvement and/ or new cruise-offer development (i.e. service development planning).

Cruise component supplier contracting

The cruise itinerary planning phase delivers the contracting requirements. Negotiation targets and restrictions are set, cruise component suppliers are contacted and negotiations are initiated. Key cruise component suppliers include:

- transportation companies (e.g. airlines), to bring the passengers from and to the home port;
- pre- and post-cruise programme suppliers offering land-based accommodation, tours and events, etc.;
- ship chandlers delivering expendables, food and beverages; and
- incoming agencies or destination management companies, assisting with port formalities, the organization of tender and excursions.

Contracting issues and quality imperative

The geographic variability of itineraries and the multiplicity of suppliers dilute the potential of purchasing economies. On the one hand, there is a multiplicity of small to medium sized enterprises (SMEs), each operating in a limited geographical scope (e.g. regional incoming agents, local accommodation suppliers), which hinders contract standardization and hence condition transparency and comparison. Apart from the volume of contracts and negotiation costs involved, this also limits the bargaining possibilities of cruise operators; especially when compared with those of conventional package tour operators.

Another set of factors posing bargaining restriction is the polarization and irregularity of capacity requests. More specifically, there are either small transport allotments for passengers arriving to or departing from the home port or large numbers of transfer and excursion allotments when arriving at the ports of call. Moreover, for the larger proportion of suppliers, serving a particular cruise represents an irregular event, being effectively a supplementary aspect on top of their 'bread-and-butter' business (i.e. packaged tours).

With perhaps a few exceptions, airlines and incoming agents cannot survive solely on their cruising-generated income. Particularly for incoming agents cruise ship visits also involve a considerable excursion capacity risk. Excursions are booked on board shortly before arrival at the destination. In conjunction with the date and time restrictions (i.e. cannot split excursion participants over separate days or time periods), this renders capacity planning for incoming agents practically impossible. Too few buses mean lost revenue and dissatisfied customers. Too many buses may imply foregone revenue from non-cruise-related excursions. Cushioning this capacity risk from either side ultimately means a higher end price. In the eyes of the guests, high prices can be justified by differentiation, exclusivity and quality. Therefore, one may argue from a contracting point of view, a focus on exclusivity and quality is not a conscious strategic choice but a sector-inherent obligation.

All in all, from a cruise operator's point of view, contracting is a complex, effort-intensive process exacerbated by their relatively limited negotiation power. Therefore, maintaining long-term, close relationships to suppliers is essential in order to:

- reduce process complexity costs (i.e. lower costs of locating, selecting, contacting and bargaining with suppliers);
- secure exclusive services and incentivize suppliers to deliver service quality.

Cruise Pricing

At a macro level (i.e. different cruises of the same vessel), prices differ according to season. At the micro level (i.e. for one and the same cruise), the main price differentiators are calculated in the form of supplements to the standard cruise product:

- Cabin types: in comparison with hotels, the number of different room or cabin types on cruise ships is three to five times higher. Cabin types are determined mainly on the basis of location (inside/outside, deck), size, occupancy and facilities (e.g. balcony).
- Pre- and post-cruise arrangements: this refers to ancillary holiday components (e.g. hotel stays, tours, events) or the customization of the standard cruise package (e.g. different airport, airline or booking class).
- On-board consumption and excursions: variable consumption elements during the cruise such as alcoholic drinks, meals in speciality restaurants, photo and hairdressing services, souvenirs, clothing, cosmetics and most importantly excursions represent a significant opportunity for revenue. Cruise operators take advantage of tax benefits and currency differences in order to generate profit, whilst providing an attractive price for their guests.

Pricing–capacity risk trade-off

Generally, full board is the most common arrangement on cruise ships. All-inclusive offers have traditionally been largely unattractive for cruise operators because of their impact on on-board revenue and reduced choice for the customers. None the less, taking into account the increasing size of ships, commoditization of cruising (Dickinson and Vladimir, 1997; Weaver, 2005) and guest demands for financial planning certainty, it is understandable that all-inclusive cruises also have their supporters. Even so, the inclusion of alcoholic drinks in all-inclusive offers tends to be restricted to certain products (e.g. spirits are excluded), times (e.g. included only until 23:00 h) or both.

A tendency towards more inclusive services is not just evident in board arrangements, but also in other revenue-generating areas such as sports activities and facilities on board, even excursions. Essentially, it signifies a gradual transfer of pricing risk from the customer to the cruise operator, in exchange for reduced capacity risk. If priced attractively for the market segment, all-inclusive cruises make it is easier to fill the ship and minimize the waste of supplies, consumables and resources. On the other hand, if the included offering fails to meet the passengers' expectations, it may result in dissatisfaction, negative word-of-mouth and eventually in empty capacity.

Euphemistically stated: pricing right must also result in the right price!

In terms of process requirements, all-inclusive offerings underlie the need for effective integration of marketing research and demand forecasting in the pricing process. The objectives here are calculability and predictability (Ritzer, 1993, 1998; Weaver, 2005), to minimize price-planning risk. Pricing must be strictly value-based (see Vogel, Chapter 10, this volume), since getting the price wrong for a whole all-inclusive package is more serious that getting it wrong for one or two items.

The main deliverable of a pricing process is a pricing table, which gets published. Such a table usually consists of:

- rows with cabin types and columns with seasonal prices (which usually incorporate transport and catering costs); and
- listings of the different supplement conditions and prices (e.g. airport fees, indicators for excursion prices, pre/post-cruise programme prices).

Finally, price lists (in the form of a data feed or manual list) are provided in order to update the points of sale on board before departure.

MIS Support: Data Warehousing and Mining

The observed growth and commoditization of the cruise sector, associated with increases in ship capacities, cost pressures and intra-sector competition, add to management complexity and planning risk in the aforementioned processes. Larger market and commercial scale renders planning errors and opportunity costs more expensive than ever.

From a process management perspective, there is an ever-increasing need for more proactive and analytical decision making to maximize revenue and margin potential. Therefore, management information systems (MIS) are becoming increasingly important for planning, purchasing for and pricing a cruise.

Traditionally, cruise operators possess an abundance of detailed historical data related to customers' preferences and consumption history, as well as sale development patterns. Moreover, a large part of this information is electronically stored in a variety of data depositories within computerized reservation systems (CRS) and property management systems (PMS). Combining and enriching such data in a data warehouse (i.e. central data depository or database), and providing the functionality to summarize and dynamically query it, enables highly efficient and more effective decision-making. This exemplary type of IT set up is illustrated in Fig. 6.2.

Such a set-up involves significant data modelling, development and interfacing costs, and hence it is economically justifiable only for cruise operators with large and/or numerous cruise vessels.

Content Production and Publishing

Once the cruise package is assembled and the pricing tables are set, the product can be prepared for distribution and selling.

Brochure publishing

As for holiday packages, brochures are the most widely used sales support media in the cruise sector. A typical brochure contains information concerning: prices and fees, lodging, ship facilities, itineraries, conditions, legal issues, health and safety and quality indicators. Following production, mostly with external partners, brochures are:

- made available to distribution partners (mainly travel agencies);

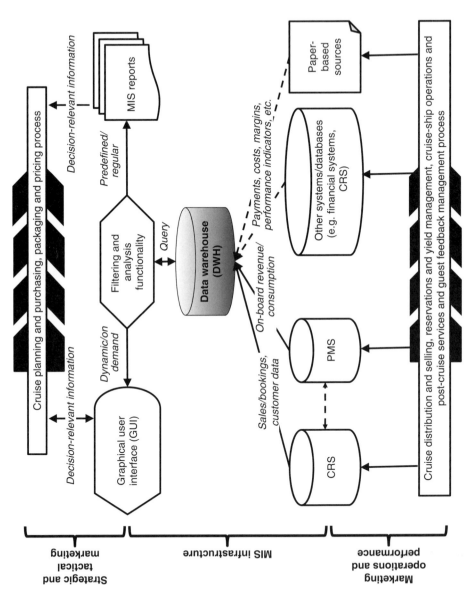

Fig. 6.2. Generic cruise management information system (MIS) setup. CRS, computerized reservation systems; PMS, property management systems.

- published electronically on the cruise operator's website; and
- distributed directly to potential customers (direct sales).

Beyond brochure publishing and the four 'E's of cruise content management

Bearing in mind that a cruise is a bundle of services, it is subject to inseparability and intangibility (Bitner *et al.*, 1993). A cruise, or any other service for that matter, is produced and consumed simultaneously (i.e. both activities are inseparable), and it is a subjective (intangible) experience that cannot be readily inspected before consumption. In other words, booking a cruise means more than renting a cabin bed and having a few meals on a ship.

By implication, it could be asserted that what is actually being sold is not a cruise holiday but its informational representation, hereafter referred to as 'content'. Potential customers use this representation as a basis for their purchasing decision and expectations. In combination with previous experiences and the interpretation of provided information (e.g. friends' recommendations, internet-based customer reviews, press), cruise content determines the commercial success and market sustainability of a particular cruise offer. It follows that aligning the perceived reality of an actual cruise and the accuracy of its representation is a strategic competence for a cruise operator. A gap in this equation implies lost revenue or disappointed guests; and ultimately reduced profitability. Managing this reality–representation gap (content management) can be reduced to the following requirements (the four 'E's):

- Content (E)nrichment: By increasing multimediality (i.e. photos, ipix, clips, TV/videos). This reduces the abstraction of a description reducing customers' perceived risk and uncertainty.
- Content (E)nlargement: Through the inclusion of additional content objects (e.g. destination or attraction specifics); by purposively detailing each object so

that guests can efficiently navigate through the entire description; and by incorporating external information sources (e.g. guest reviews) and content.
- Content (E)volution: By setting controls and procedures aimed at maintaining the content and ensuring its accuracy and relevance over time.
- Content (E)xperience: By incorporating content consumption into the cruise experience (e.g. sales and promotion events, virtual tours, interactive games) and by infusing cruising experience to content consumption (e.g. ship visits, short trips).

Traditionally, content creation essentially involves assembling and publishing a set of single-page textual descriptions and the inclusion of images (i.e. photos, maps, logos).

Workflow-supported and media-rich content

The improved interactivity and multimediality of the internet extend the notion of content creation from a periodical assembly process to an ongoing development process. Multilayer and multi-source content (i.e. linking content from internal, as well as external sources), navigation and usability, stress the need for information architecture and standardization, formalized workflow management and technological skill acquisition.

Current initiatives such as the Royal Caribbean's virtual guide to the *Freedom of the Seas* on www.freedomoftheseas.com or Costa Cruises' Second Life version of the *Costa Serena*, apart from being good examples of media-rich and interactive content, both illustrate and underline this point.

Distribution and Selling

The cruise sector is known to enjoy and encourage customer loyalty (Toh *et al.*, 2005). More specifically, and subject to definition and measurement restrictions, the average cruise repeater rate ranges between 55% and 70%. One may justifiably suspect that this is one of the reasons direct distribution channels (direct mailings, internal hotline, company website) dominate cruise operators' retail preference. In other words, the most 'encouraged' way to obtain information about or book a cruise is directly via telephone to an internal hotline or indirectly through a selected travel agent partner.

Reservations: data monopolization and workflow control

When utilizing external, indirect retailers (e.g. travel agencies), cruise operators are restrictive in terms of partner selection, content availability and booking scope. By monopolizing reservations and thus customer data, they protect their customer base from the competition.

The other reason is the content and consultation intensity associated with selling a cruise. Toh *et al.* (2005) claim that it takes an average of 14 telephone calls between the customer and sales staff to conclude a sale. Non-specialized travel agents, both in terms of the cruise product and target market, are not optimal in this sense.

Migrating from its niche status towards the mass market, with the corresponding capacity expansion and competitive pressures, the sector will increase the focus towards the acquisition of a new (and younger) customer base. Consequently, cruise operators will gradually need to widen their retailing scope and extend their distribution network. Amongst other things, this raises the need for further developing and elaborating their multi-channel strategies and dealing with issues related to: the degree of price and content parity across channels, degree on intra-channel distribution exclusivity or competition, channel partner relationship management and control.

Strategic IT-connectivity imperative

From a systems perspective, this implies an incentive (if not a need) for strategically developing inter-organizational systems.

Selective interfacing and technical standard adoption are essential elements in implementing a multi-channel strategy. Champy (2002) argues that as organizations and sectors evolve, process re-engineering needs to extend beyond the boundaries of a single company and include its supplier and distribution network. Skill in vertical cross-engineering is crucial for creating and sustaining a strategic leverage in competitive sectors. 'The openness and ease of information dispersal is the key to mobilizing a company and its customers, suppliers, and partners for a common purpose' (Champy, 2002, p. 8).

Through providing selective access to their internal systems, cruise operators can prioritize, negotiate and extend the scope of suitable retailers, without compromising customer data and without losing ownership and control of pricing levels and content management.

Reservations and Yield Management

As selling commences, reservations are made through the various stationery and online distribution channels. Each reservation initiates a workflow (in most cases semi-automated) involving:

1.   Transport and cabin availability request.
2.   Selection of bookable elements and discount options.
3.   Entering customer data (i.e. name, surname, address, payment method, comments/special requests).
4.   Updating transport and cabin inventory in order to adjust availability (see 1).
5.   Production and dispatching of travel documentation (vouchers, tickets, etc.).
6.   Invoicing and payment.

The main advantage of performing this workflow with the support of a CRS is that cruise operators have an updated view of their inventory. The ability to monitor capacity development in real time is the very essence of inventory management and capacity risk minimization.

Labour-intensive reservations workflow and inventory management

With the exception of a couple of large cruise operators, the level of reservations automation and interfacing in the cruise sector is relatively low in comparison with the rest of the tourism industry, where large-scale CRS are deeply embedded in tour operator processes and supply chains.

Theoretically, the predominance of PMS on cruise ships allows a fairly sophisticated cabin inventory management and is a solid basis for customer relationship management. None the less, the absence of electronic interfaces to CRS renders PMS practically unproductive in terms of reservation processing and sales-closure. In effect, manual or semi-automated (in form of data export/import) interfacing means that the data flow between land-based retail and ship's inventory is labour intensive and time consuming. In turn, labour intensity and time delays spill over to inventory management. An uninterrupted and integrated data flow between inventory and front-office sales paves the road towards automation and optimization of cruise-operators' inventory management (e.g. automatic triggering of yield management activities based on certain events or states in the reservations development).

This challenge entails more than costs and reaction times. As already mentioned, more extensive distribution networks and retail scope are core ingredients for sustaining the sector's growth. These are ultimately enabled by a 'democratization' of booking potential. Either way, the predominance of paper-based selling media, non-standardized content and labour intensive reservation workflows will most probably be challenged in the medium term.

'Silent' yield management

Unlike for airlines and packaged tourism, price-driven, aggressive yield management is still rather uncommon in the cruise sector. To begin with, cruise operators enjoy very high occupancy rates. According to Toh *et al.* (2005), this is related to a variety of factors related to inherent structural advantages and common management practices in the sector. Cruise bookings are characterized by a relatively long individual planning horizon, stricter cancellation deadlines (in order to receive full refund) and considerable deposits. These characteristics discourage cancellations and contribute to a negligible no-show rate.

Moreover, it is important to remember that the cost base of cruise operators consists mostly of fixed (owned or contracted) capacity elements, the risk of which cannot be readily transferred (see above – limited bargaining power). On the one hand, high fixed costs are a motivator for discounting, while on the other they pose limits on the extent of its practice. Hence the scope of price-based yield management activities is mostly limited to seasonal variations, which also happens to prevent dissatisfaction caused by price comparisons among passengers. In the confined space of a cruise ship, encouraging social interaction between guests over a longer period of time increases the probability of guests discussing the specifics of their respective deals and comparing them to those of others.

Notwithstanding, non-monetary yield management practices are more frequently employed:

- cabin upgrades or 'lucky cabins';
- complimentary excursions or other extras; and
- merchandizing.

Once again, these are not extensively publicized (hence the term: 'silent') and are usually offered either to pacify individual discount requests or attract particular customer groups.

Cruise Ship Management

Managing cruise ship operations can be seen as a 'moment of truth', where all the efforts, results and deliverables of the previous processes materialize in the undoubtedly well-deserved holiday for the cruise passengers. Ship operations can be grouped under the following activity domains:

- passenger logistics and port-of-call services: embarkation and check-in, port handling (i.e. port formalities, provisioning), excursions organization, security controls and safety/emergency drills, medical support, check out and disembarkation; and
- hotel management: catering (food and beverage management), passenger support services (information, complaint handling, excursion escorting), housekeeping, facilities management, revenue management, on-board entertainment (e.g. shows, animation, activities, lectures).

Quality and the service engineering imperative

Consistently aligning service practices with customers' expectations is the basic definition of service quality. Hence, the explicit definition, documentation and standardization of service practices is quintessential, not for cruise operators alone but the entire tourism sector.

Tourism is often described and perceived as a people-centred business, dominated by charismatic, eternally smiling, fun-loving, helpful and, to a certain degree, idealistic individuals. Combining the performance of such people with pleasant weather, good food and a comfortable bed is the stuff holiday dreams are made from. Blending those ingredients with a marine environment encapsulates the essence of a successful cruise. The question is: is cruise quality simply about good weather, good food and being nice to people?

According to Heskett *et al.* (1997), profitable service provision depends on the ability to consistently 'produce' positive service encounters, which in turn is a function of aligning service capability with customer requirements. The authors define service capability as the effective combination of:

- employee recruitment and training processes;

- support systems (accessible, up-to-date, correct and relevant information to decide and perform their service tasks);
- governance structures (latitude to meet customer needs – i.e. freedom to act without authorization – clear limits on and expectations of employees); and
- compensation and incentive practices (job satisfaction, positive reinforcement, employee retention).

The basic idea is that the right people, when accordingly trained, informed and incentivized will ultimately produce positive service encounters and remain motivated through the customer recognition and interaction associated with consistently delivering this level of service. Or simply: good service is not just about smiling, but having a reason to do so!

In the cruise sector, responsibilities and procedures tend to be very well defined, regulated, trained, implemented and controlled. This is partly because of naval regulations and traditions, and reinforced by the quality focus and service standards adopted by cruise operators. Arguably, this relatively high-degree of service engineering allows cruise operators to maintain smooth daily operations and service levels in spite of relatively high staff turnover and diversity.

Nevertheless, it is worth mentioning that high levels of service engineering are limited to the ship's boundaries. External service suppliers (e.g. incoming agents, transport companies) do not necessarily share the same history, traditions, or even priorities. Assuming that a cruise holiday is a bundle of on-board and shore-side services, the discrepancy between service standards needs to be addressed. Passengers book a cruise on the basis of a set of service standard expectations, which are reinforced during their stay and service consumption on board. When confronted with different standards off board, disappointment and complaints may occur.

Finally, increasingly larger ships, evolving demographics, emerging market segments, regulatory changes and cost pressures imply new givens and altered expectations. These impact on the composition, governance and practice standards for human resources on board and pose new challenges for managing the practices and standards off board.

Property management systems (PMS)

PMS such as Fidelio Cruise are integrated systems widely utilized to support hotel operations on ships and land-based hotel units. They support, but are not limited to:

- check-in and check-out;
- security management;
- room management;
- on-board retail (e.g. shops, amenities, excursion sales); and
- financial transactions (on-board payments, master billing).

Apart from their operational value (i.e. reduction of manual effort, reduction of mistakes and miscommunication), these systems indirectly serve tactical purposes by enabling operational efficiency and by supporting service engineering. With reference to the latter, they contain and, to some extent, enforce a:

- standardized and comprehensive passenger data model: capturing services provided and consumption and matching it to the customers' master data (i.e. name, address, reservation ID); and
- consistency in service delivery practices: PMS functionality and data maintenance imposes a workflow (especially in the back-office) for its users.

Their strategic potential lies in their electronic integration with CRS, equipping retail with more extensive sales support and enhancing inventory management.

Post-cruise Services and Passenger Feedback Management

Cruise operators regularly conduct on-board satisfaction surveys, encourage informal feedback from passenger-facing personnel and systematically collect, document and analyse passenger complaints and requests. This analysis serves:

- Complaint settlement: complaints are dealt with by promptly removing their cause and/or by compensating guests to appease them (e.g. by providing complimentary drinks, excursions, vouchers). In the majority of cases, complaints are dealt with informally on the spot (i.e. not after the cruise) by guest-facing personnel to prevent escalation and minimize guest dissatisfaction. Should responsibility lie with external suppliers, compensation costs/penalty fees are negotiated with the partners.
- Customer relationship management: the results of guest satisfaction surveys and positive feedback in general are often utilized for public relation purposes and are publicized in newsletters, homepages, etc.).
- Cruise product development: survey results and customer feedback, if analysed and interpreted sufficiently, could be particularly useful as a deliverable to the subsequent cruise planning and contracting, highlighting areas for improvement.

Cruising and web 2.0

Traditionally, cruise passenger feedback has been paper-based and confined within the boundaries of cruise operators. The advent of the internet and web 2.0, characterized by the emergence of specialized rating sites, blogs and online forums, is increasingly playing a central role for cruise holiday selection (Papathanassis, 2007). Addressing these developments in the existing processes and marketing strategy poses an array of questions regarding the conduct and effectiveness of cruise operators' own marketing research as well as the form and extent of utilizing externally generated feedback.

Future Challenges and Needs

This chapter has provided an overview of the main cruise operating processes, highlighting challenges involved and elaborating on the role of technologies and systems related to them. If anything, it could be argued that the growth of the cruise sector and the demand for cruises confirm the effectiveness of current practices and infrastructure. None the less, there are a number of:

- sector trends, e.g. larger ships, mass personalization, increasing costs, mass cruising, overcrowding, evolving guest base and preferences; and
- technological and competitive developments, e.g. online distribution, digitization, IT convergence and standardization, new entrant and complementary service competition;

that call for adaptation and innovation in the way cruises are organized and operated. The corresponding process and IT infrastructure requirements are summarized as follows:

- 'Management by wire': optimization of strategic and tactical marketing (i.e. planning, purchasing, pricing) enabled by the installation and utilization of MIS. Alternatively, this can be seen as improving the efficiency and sustainability of the information flow between land and sea.
- 'Content richness and convergence': enrichment and digitization of cruise content to aid cruise holiday representation and reduce the perceived risk and uncertainty for potential customers. On this basis cruise operators can pave the road towards more extensive distribution and supplement their multi-channel strategies.
- 'Cross-engineering and virtual integration': Champy (2002) argues that as organizations and sectors evolve, process re-engineering needs to extend beyond the boundaries of a single company and include its supplier and distribution network. Through standardization and interfacing, cruise operators can integrate and align supplier processes and systems with their own landscape. Potential benefits include increased quality control and favourable strategic positioning.

Closing Words

If you can't describe what you are doing as a process, you don't know what you're doing.
(W.E. Deming, cited in Morgan and Liker, 2006, p. 336)

The capacity explicitly to describe and justify an organization's processes is a basic requirement for any purposeful and coordinated effort. Arguably, this may well be the very difference between incidental success and effective management; a difference that becomes apparent as sectors reach maturity and as companies face fierce competition and adverse market conditions. Knowing how and why a company does what it does is a prerequisite for the adaptation and change enabling long-term survival. Obtaining and maintaining the capability to apply this knowledge renders the option of organizational success a realized choice (Faehnrich, 1998). Understanding a service organization's processes, information infrastructure and their interrelationship is the foundation of effective management.

The generic cruise operating process architecture, and main contribution of this chapter, serves as an analytical framework providing a basic structure enabling:

- systematic examination of processes and their interrelationships, within a situation and/or company specific context;
- the further development of a sector-relevant, commonly accepted terminology, addressing strategic, structural and infrastructural issues. The existence of a common language enables a concrete consideration of those issues and the communication required to address them adequately; and
- training and education of those new to the sector by providing a brief, but none the less comprehensive, overview.

For those with experience and knowledge in the cruise sector, a lot of what has been mentioned may appear obvious and intuitive, reducing the usefulness of such an analytical framework. On the other hand, applying it in a dynamic fashion to explore the feasibility and implications of different re-structuring scenarios (e.g. mergers and acquisitions activity) may reveal indirect or hidden challenges and opportunities.

One very important aspect of motivation is the willingness to stop and to look at things that no one else has bothered to look at. This simple process of focusing on things that are normally taken for granted is a powerful source of creativity.

(DeBono, 1992, p. 46)

References

Bitner, M.J., Fisk, R.P. and Brown, S.W. (1993) Tracking the evolution of the services marketing literature. *Journal of Retailing* 69(1), 61–103.

Champy, J. (2002) *X-Engineering the Corporation: Reinvent Your Business in the Digital Age*. Hodder and Stoughton, London.

DeBono, E. (1992) *Serious Creativity*. HarperBusiness, New York.

Dickinson, R. and Vladimir, A. (1997) *Selling the Sea: an Inside Look at the Cruise Industry*. Wiley, New York.

Faehnrich, K.P. (1998) Service Engineering – Perspektiven einer noch jungen Fachdisziplin. *Information Management* 13, 37–39.

Heskett, J.L., Sasser, W.E. and Schlesinger, L.A. (1997) *The Service Profit Chain: How Leading Companies Link Profit and Growth to Loyalty, Satisfaction, and Value*. Free Press, New York.

Morgan, J.M. and Liker, J.K. (2006) *The Toyota Product Development System. Integrating People, Process and Technology*. Productivity Press, New York.

Papathanassis, A. (2007) Online auf See mit Kreuzfahrt 2.0. *An Bord* 1, 62–64.

Porter, M.E. (1985) *Competitive Advantage*. Free Press, New York.

Ritzer, G. (1993) *The McDonaldization of Society: An Investigation into the Changing Character of Contemporary Social Life*. Pine Forge Press, Thousand Oaks, California.

Ritzer, G. (1998) *The McDonaldization Thesis: Explorations and Extensions*. Sage, London.

Toh, R.S., Rivers, M.J. and Ling, T.W. (2005) Room occupancies: cruise lines out-do the hotels. *Hospitality Management* 24, 121–135.

Weaver, A. (2005) The McDonaldization Thesis and Cruise Tourism. *Annals of Tourism Research* 32(2), 346–366.

7 Cruise Lines' Purchasing and Logistics Management

Simon Véronneau and Jacques Roy

Introduction

This chapter examines the complexity of global cruise ship supply chain management (SCM) through a field study of a Florida-based cruise company's practices in re-supplying ships globally. The study focused on three main goals: describing the key components of a cruise ship supply chain and the key characteristics of the suppliers involved (Bowersox et al., 2000); assessing, through a feasibility study, the viability of new technologies in this complex global supply chain (Grover and Malhorta, 2003) and providing insight into how technologies can improve supply chain efficiency (Doerr et al., 2006); and investigating how the relationship between the cruise line and its hundreds of suppliers affects the supply chain (Golicic and Mentzer, 2006). Through field observations and semi-structured interviews, key features of the supply chain and the suppliers were uncovered and best practices identified.

A supply chain consists of all parties involved, directly or indirectly, in fulfilling a customer request, including the manufacturers, suppliers, warehouses, retailers and customers (Chopra and Meindl, 2004). Managing global supply chain networks is a complex task. With the current globalization of trade, supply chains are growing in importance. Indeed, in order to remain or to become more competitive globally, companies are increasingly outsourcing work to lower-cost regions, a practice called off-shoring. As a result, companies enjoy lower production or purchasing costs but incur additional transportation, warehousing and inventory holding costs. If the savings of the former are to offset the expense of the latter, a company employing off-shoring must make strategic decisions involving a host of interconnected relationships.

Global sourcing, which can roughly be defined as the purchasing of goods and services from international sources, is not without risks, some temporal, some logistical. First, it necessarily increases the supply chain's total cycle time and congestion at ports. Second, capacity or quality control problems with foreign suppliers may delay product delivery. Third, increased globalization is defined by competing forces. Product variety has certainly increased, but as the variety of products expands, the life cycle of any individual product shrinks. Shorter product life cycles combined with longer, global supply chains have contributed to supply chain uncertainty (Sheffi, 2001). Currently, complexity and uncertainty are unavoidable features of supply chains.

In the cruise industry, supply chains are truly global. It goes without saying that ships have long played a leading role in trade and the spread of civilization. We know, for example, a fair amount of detail about Greece's long history of shipping and other modes of water transport (Harlaftis, 1996). Given the nature of the tourism product offered by the cruise industry today, the supply chain functions as an integral part of the service to the consumer. To see this, one need only look at the variety of food offered to passengers on board. A cruise line cannot offer such variety and guarantee, for example, fresh produce to thousands of consumers around the world without taking into consideration the importance of such a function. Like other industries, the cruise sector is acknowledging the importance of SCM by appointing high-level managers with titles such as vice-president SCM and director of logistics.

The supply chain challenges today's cruise industry faces are a result of the exponential growth the industry began to experience in the 1980s and which promises to continue unabated (Marti, 1992; Hobson, 1993; Marine Log, 2007). Cruise ship deployments are now more than ever global. For example, with the saturation of the Caribbean market, passengers are demanding new itineraries; in response, cruise lines have relocated a significant share of their fleet to the fast-growing European cruising market segment (CIN, 2009).

Supplying cruise ships presents unique challenges. Even conventional supply chains face difficulties in time management, minimum safety stock and global markets, all of which combine to detract from the efficiency and robustness of a given supply chain. The additional complexity faced by cruise ships and the specific circumstances from which these complexities arise are points to which we will return.

Given the paucity of research on cruise ship operations and supply chains, the research for this chapter was inductive in nature (Cooper and Schindler, 2005). The research methodology focused on a multi-method (Brewer and Hunter, 1989) inductive field study (Van Maanen, 1988; Fetterman, 1998). This methodology combines the advantages of three methods: formal semi-structured interviews, participant observations and empirical data gathering for cost-benefit appraisal. The tripartite approach is designed to capture a more complete picture by looking at a problem from multiple, different perspectives (Jick, 1979). An ethnographic lens (Van Maanen, 1988) and other participant–observer techniques were employed to observe key employees and to record their daily interactions and challenges.

This paper is divided into three main sections. The first and following section cover the general issues involved in re-supplying ships; the second section reports the key findings from the research project; and the last section discusses the findings and outlines implications.

Cruise Ships and Maritime Supplying: Past and Present

The world tonnage, including the important distinction of average ship tonnage, has been growing steadily (UNCTAD, 2005). The steady increases in tonnage indicate that more and more supplies find their way to ships for transport or use. In the past, the responsibility for re-supplying ships fell to the ship chandlers, who used to re-supply ships of every nation but who now are found only in literature. A type of ship chandler still exists today, but today's chandlers are much closer in operations to the average suppliers or a mere reseller. In the days of the traditional chandler, good service and small gifts to a ship's officers and captains ensured continuing business. The following excerpt, from Joseph Conrad's *Lord Jim*, provides an interesting glimpse into the offices of the chandler of days gone by:

> A vast, cavern-like shop which is full of things that are eaten and drunk on board ship; where you can get everything to make her seaworthy and beautiful, from a set of chain-hooks for her cable to a book of gold-leaf for the carvings of her stern; and where her commander is received like a brother by a ship-chandler he has never seen before. There is a cool parlour, easy-chairs, bottles, cigars, writing

implements, a copy of harbour regulations, and a warmth of welcome that melts the salt of a three months' passage out of a seaman's heart.

(Conrad, 1999, p. 3)

The job of liaison between a ship's captains and officers and ship chandlers fell to the water clerks, the forebears of today's cruise ship industry's sales representatives or account managers. Once again Conrad's *Lord Jim* offers a revealing snapshot of another bygone trade:

A water-clerk need not pass an examination in anything under the sun, but he must have ability in the abstract and demonstrate it practically. His work consists in racing under sail, steam, or oars against other water-clerks for any ship about to anchor, greeting her captain cheerily, forcing upon him a card, the business card of the ship chandler, and on his first visit on shore, piloting him firmly but without ostentation to the ship chandler.

(Conrad, 1999)

The main categories of supplies carried and listed by the ship chandler were as follows: dry stores, provisions, cabin supplies, deck supplies, engine supplies, bonded stores, petroleum product (Jones, 1973). Today, supplies for a major cruise ship mainly fall into the following categories: marine, hotel, fuel, and technical purchasing. The bulk of supplies on a loading day are destined to the hotel food and beverage operation. As an example a cruise ship with a capacity of 3600 passengers will require for a 1-week voyage 11,300 lbs (5126 kg) of beef, 2600 lbs (1179 kg) of lobster, 2600 lbs (1179 kg) of bacon, 3700 bottles of wine and 10,300 soda cans (Avery, 2006). The fuel purchasing department is self-explanatory; a large fleet of cruise ships requires good fuel management practices similar to the hedging practices in aviation described by Rao (1999). The importance of the first two categories for SCM will be dealt with further below.

Findings: Cruise Ship Supply Chain Issues

The keys to success for the cruise supply chain are planning and coordination. The following long-term planning model as outlined in Fig. 7.1 exemplifies their

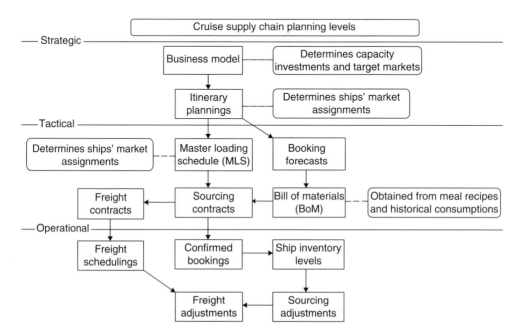

Fig. 7.1. Planning for consumable products with dependent demand. Source: Véronneau and Roy (2009a).

paramount importance. As is suggested by the various planning levels, decisions must be made years in advance and refined as the departure time for a specific voyage approaches. At the strategic level, decisions are typically made 2–5 years in advance of departure; at the tactical level, 8–16 months in advance; and at the operational level, from a few hours to a few months.

The global nature of the trade

The logistical demands specific to cruise ships are many, perhaps the most salient being the global nature of their supply chains. To satisfy these demands, cruise ships must exercise a fair amount of adaptability to variability. Because the itineraries cruise ships deploy cover all main tourists markets, they must be adjusted according to seasonality and yearly demand. Different itineraries mean different operating conditions. To adapt to varying local conditions and operations, ships' agents are hired to represent the company in specific cities and to facilitate communications with local contractors and government authorities. Certain supplies are acquired locally, e.g. produce, but most are shipped from the main logistics centre in Florida. The necessity for cruise ships to re-supply operations at varying global endpoints brings with it a host of less obvious but no less important challenges. For example, operations must be coordinated across different time zones and brought in line with international laws and restrictions governing supplying, which vary from country to country.

The above discussion is not to suggest that the cruise sector is immune to the challenges common to global supply chains in other sectors of business, such as information integration and waste reduction. Indeed, the cruise sector must not only overcome these challenges but do so within a set of constraints particular to cruise ship SCM. These constraints involve replenishment, mobility and variety, each of which is discussed at length below.

Replenishment issues

One challenge specific to the cruise ship SCM is the narrow window of time within which ships can replenish. This window is not only narrow, but open at most once a week and typically only once every 2 weeks. Meeting the re-supply window is a challenge both for the basic operations of the ship and for the maintenance of optimal service. Continuous replenishment at its optimal rate, therefore, has a granularity of a week. The actual, physical transit of goods must take place within a very narrow window of time, typically 4–6 h, and the window does not widen in proportion to a ship's tonnage. Newer, bigger ships face the same constraints on re-supplying as smaller ones, in addition to the obvious operational challenges that come with increased size. Already new designs have neglected to allow for enough space and time for the flow of luggage, deficits that impose yet further constraints on the other supplies that must transit.

Given the current structure of supply chains and the necessity of replenishment lead-time, the commitment to a given supply level is made weeks before the ships set sail; therefore, any anomaly in consumption level is frozen in the normal re-supply lead-time, which exceeds the cruise length. If we apply the theory of the tactical cycle, according to which the tightest operation cycle time is the key to a sustained operations advantage, as discussed in Véronneau and Cimon (2007), the lead-time for replenishment would need to be shorter than the cruise duration to stay within cycle and allow for most effective responsiveness. Replenishment deficits resulting from anomalous consumption would be obviated by a reduction in lead-time, which would, in turn, allow more flexibility and move re-supply operations towards a pull system.

The mobile nature of re-supplying ships

Another concern at the strategic and tactical levels is the mobile nature of supply points. Seasonal changes in ship itineraries and frequent relocations in response to market demands pose the two most significant challenges to global re-supply. Moreover, the cruise industry, unlike most other service industries, must resupply operations at varying global endpoints. The practical upshot of these variable endpoints is that a ship's port must be repositioned. Often resulting from this repositioning is a kind shock to the supply chain, a phenomenon dubbed 'double loading' by cruise company employees. The season of a ship's repositioning has come to be known as the 'double loading season' because replenishment lead-time increases when the ship gets repositioned.

For example, the 2-day replenishment lead-time of a ship with a winter port in Miami will increase to 4 weeks with the ship's re-positioning to Europe. Consequently, for the 3 weeks before arriving in Europe, the logistics centre must load the same ship twice a week, once for local needs and once in anticipation of the ship's arrival in Europe. The phenomenon of double loading is attributable only to varying endpoints and yet, despite its resultant shock to the distribution centre in the form of doubled operation time and the expense of overtime pay, no reference to this particular set of circumstances could be found in the supply chain literature. One might wonder why ships in Europe are supplied by logistic centres located in North America. The answer is twofold: first, there is a lag in adapting to a newer worldwide deployment and second, many cruise lines prefer to centralize their purchasing activities and source such items as meat from the USA in order to ensure better control on food safety. Hence the main thing that is supplied locally is fresh produce, while the vast majority of the remaining supplies come from North America.

Bigger ships

As mentioned above, the replenishment problem is compounded for newer, bigger ships, which have the same time-window constraints as smaller ones, in addition to unique and novel operation challenges. Still, ships continue to grow. For example, Royal Caribbean International launched in December 2009 the world's biggest cruise ship, *Oasis of the Seas*, with a 220,000 gross registered tonnage (GRT) and 5400 passengers capacity, a capacity 60,000 GRT and roughly 2000 passengers more than the world's second largest ship, *Freedom of the Seas*, owned by the same company. Already previous recent designs have neglected to allow for enough space and time for the flow of luggage, which poses a major constraint on other supplies that have to transit. Unlike luggage, supplies like food cannot be precisely quantified before a ship sails.

The need for real-time visibility

A major problem with the supply chain is the real-time visibility of demand (Christopher, 2000); this, when coupled with multiple tiers of members in the chain, amplifies the bullwhip effect described by Forrester (1958). The term bullwhip effect describes the increased variability in demand as one moves back up the supply chain. It is conjectured that inter-enterprise IT systems will be a prerequisite for success in the next decade, since they enable and facilitate transparency (Kemppainen and Vepsäläinen, 2003). One critical aspect of this logistic information integration is the real-time acquisition and recognition of distribution information (Hou and Huang, 2006). Therefore, one main goal of IT integration in the supply chain is to mitigate the bullwhip effect as well as to increase cooperation between members of the given chain by sharing useful information with them (Fabbe-Costes, 2000). Achieving these goals would allow for new process development and fail-safe mechanisms to be put in place.

Discussion and Implications

This research project was based on the premise that, to our knowledge, no research existed on how large cruise ships worldwide successfully re-supplied, so that seldom, if ever, are they without a product on board. The absence of research suggested there is an opportunity to understand which best practices exist in the large-ship SCM domain and to investigate how other domains could benefit from such practices to improve their supply chain efficiency and profitability. We started this research project by asking the following questions: what are the challenges of managing a global supply chain with dynamic supply locations? And what characterizes this unique domain of service supply chain? It was found that this supply chain has characteristics unique not only to the type of operations, but also to the industry, such as narrow time windows and moving supply locations. While the moving supply points for large masses experienced by the cruise industry are similar to those of a military supply chain, the cruise industry's heavy focus on service quality for the final customer is more in line with large resort supply chains. Hence, some principles of both types of supply chain are present in a cruise supply chain, which is best understood as a hybrid between a military and a hospitality supply chain because of its combination of global reach, worldwide mobility, and attention to service quality for the final customer, the tourist.

A number of measures must be taken to ensure sustained service operations abroad in the face of three main challenges:

- sustaining a continuous, large global deployment while maintaining service quality for the final customer;
- sourcing a large variety of products in large volume, which requires a dedicated team of commodity specialists; and
- planning for and negotiating the narrow time window on turnaround days.

In light of these challenges, sound operations management principles, well-used technology and sustained quality relations with the suppliers become crucial to the enabling of sustained quality operations in the cruise line supply chain.

Discussion

It is clear from the findings of this research project that there are numerous key elements that must be present in order for the cruise line supply chain operation to be successful. From the results of this field study, a number of best practices can be outlined to aid cruise companies dealing with various SCM challenges and to serve as models for other service industries in their efforts to overcome similar challenges. These key elements of best practice are as follows: long-term planning, service quality, technology and sourcing, each of which is discussed further below.

Long-term planning

As with the military's long-term planning, which can extend to 3 years in certain cases, advanced work is essential to ensure cruise line deployment success. Scouting locations and future service providers and suppliers has proven essential. While on location, scouts network with local suppliers to secure an agent to represent the company in the future. Local agents have detailed knowledge of regulations specific to their area as well as established connections with local authorities. Therefore, a comprehensive roster of reliable local service providers and suppliers is vital.

This long-term planning is an imperative since the time window for re-supply is quite narrow, as shown in Fig. 7.2. Given the volume of supplies and the lead time required to reach the ships globally, careful attention must be paid to loading dates, loading ports, and local sourcing possibilities. Since produce is sourced locally, it is paramount that ports chosen for turnaround day must offer not only fresh but also, and perhaps more importantly, safe produce, so as not to risk contaminating a ships' food supply.

Communication

For enterprises having global operations spread over many locations, it is essential to

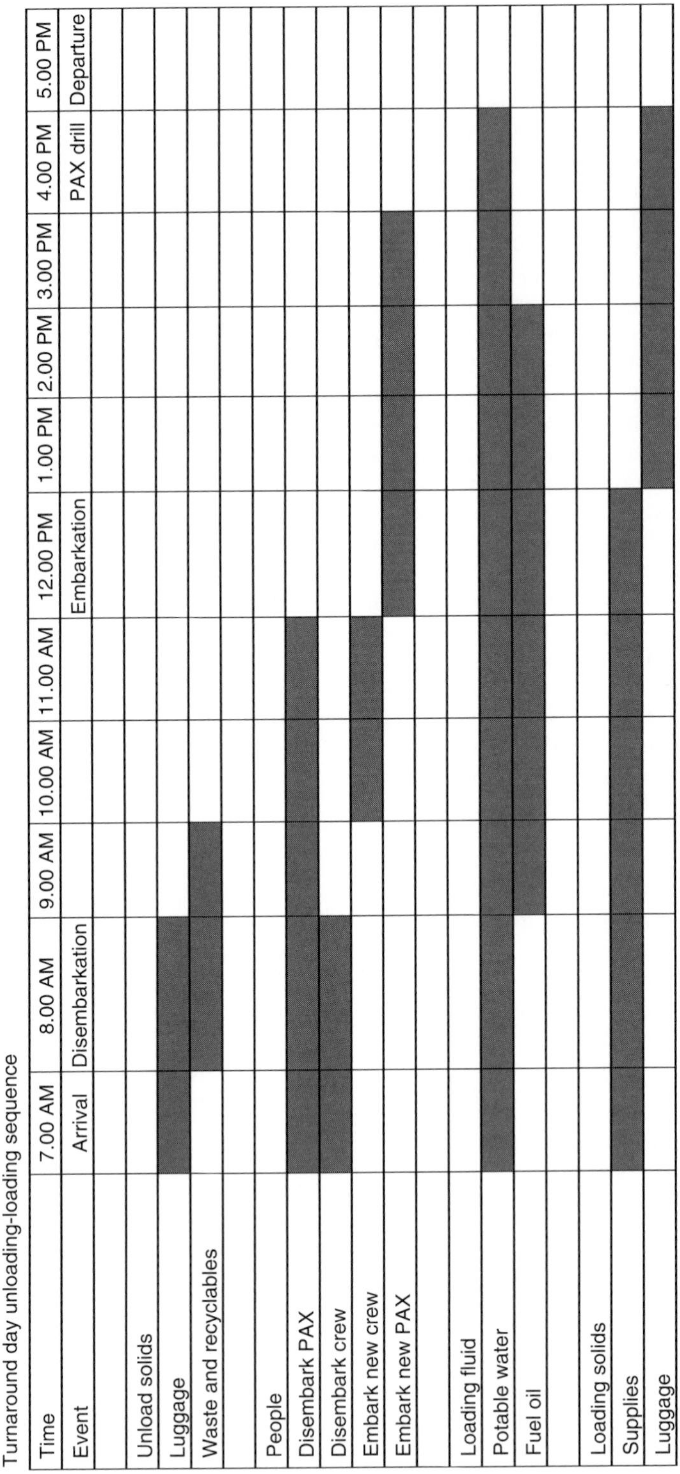

Turnaround day unloading-loading sequence

Time	7.00 AM	8.00 AM	9.00 AM	10.00 AM	11.00 AM	12.00 PM	1.00 PM	2.00 PM	3.00 PM	4.00 PM	5.00 PM
Event	Arrival	Disembarkation				Embarkation				PAX drill	Departure
Unload solids											
Luggage	▓	▓	▓								
Waste and recyclables		▓									
People											
Disembark PAX	▓	▓	▓	▓							
Disembark crew		▓	▓	▓							
Embark new crew				▓	▓						
Embark new PAX						▓	▓	▓	▓		
Loading fluid											
Potable water			▓	▓	▓	▓	▓	▓	▓	▓	
Fuel oil			▓	▓	▓	▓	▓	▓	▓		
Loading solids											
Supplies	▓	▓	▓	▓	▓	▓	▓				
Luggage							▓	▓	▓	▓	

Fig. 7.2. Typical turnaround day at port. Source: Véronneau and Roy (2009a).

have a good communication infrastructure with a centralized database and an intranet accessible 24 h a day. Since operations truly go around the clock and span several time zones, the time of the day at headquarters is irrelevant. In this time-sensitive environment, the capacity for a continuous flow of communication and timely response is crucial. One way to improve communication flow would be to establish an operations centre for the continuous monitoring of inventory levels, transportation lanes and incoming reports. Centralized and continuous operations oversight would allow for timely decisions and proactive management of the supply streams while providing a corrective for the potentially inefficient response likely to follow a late-night call from a ship requiring head-office actions to a sleeping manager in another time zone.

Such asynchronous communication needs are very recent developments for the cruise business, which was, in the past decade, largely concentrated in the Caribbean, an area spanning only two time zones. The recent global deployment of ships calls for new business practices adaptable to these needs. For example, the current robust intranet that supports operations via satellites across multiple time zones is essential for global deployments. Finally, in order to improve communication richness and meaning, it was found that boundary-spanning initiatives were beneficial in ensuring seamless communications from one department to another.

Service quality in service supply chain

For service-centred organizations, it is essential that service culture be passed upstream towards the suppliers and service providers. It was found that the best method for doing so is the socialization of suppliers through informal means. While service industry workers might consider it common sense to place great emphasis on service quality, suppliers, who typically work within manufacturing supply chains where quality means meeting specifications, might require acculturation to the demands of final usage. Service supply chains, unlike their manufacturing counterparts, require a common goal of service satisfaction for the final customer, which is achieved through well-rendered services and quality supplies and materials supporting service delivery.

A measure of the seriousness with which on-board service quality is taken in the cruise industry is the ubiquity of customer-satisfaction surveys, which are given out after every cruise. Since quality is paramount on board and cruise passengers' assessment of quality depends largely on food and beverages, the current perception of stockout costs tends towards the infinite. A company will not hesitate to airlift meats or other items in the name of keeping a diverse, consistent and quality offering. Though these emergency airlifts come at a premium and usually result in an internal inquiry of the expenditure, managers are allowed recourse to them to keep the ship fully stocked with all of the supplies that passengers would expect to find on their cruise.

Technology and RFID

Technology plays a crucial role in the coordination of and the communication within the supply chain and can also serve as a major efficiency enabler in three ways. As described by Véronneau and Roy (2009b), the various tiers in the supply chain all require time-sensitive information exchange through their information system network. First, the intranet, as well as the robust internal email system, facilitates the internal coordination of logistical activities; second, the supplier's Internet portal facilitates the coordination of the supply chain; and third, RFID (radio-frequency identification) technology or an integrated material tracking system can improve labour efficiency and visibility throughout the supply chain. It is clear from previous studies, as well as from the results of this research, that RFID can provide direct benefits, such as labour reduction and potential savings, by offering real-time visibility. Using RFID can reduce the labour required in tracking and tracing, a benefit sufficient in itself to justify the implementation of tags.

Supplier relations sourcing

An important characteristic of a cruise supplier is the flexibility to meet a specific demand outside the normal scope of the supplier's responsibilities. But the ability to meet a demand alone is insufficient; responsiveness is also crucial, since time windows are so narrow. To acculturate a supplier to service-industry needs, an online portal available to registered users has proven useful in the areas of communication, coordination and socialization. The socialization of the supplier is very important for a service-focused supply chain if the emphasis on service quality and the alignment on the goal of final customer satisfaction are to be achieved; socialization builds a certain relational capital, which was found to be highly desirable in a fast-paced service supply chain.

When significant relational capital is achieved, the relationship benefits. For example, sufficiently socialized suppliers may be willing to focus all their effort on fulfilling requirements if they understand the nature of the demand and the mutual benefits of meeting an atypical or special request. Though it may seem counterintuitive, relational capital may also accrue as a result of competition. A cruise company would do well to practise open bidding and to encourage competition within the supplier pool, even if the competition is only in an oligopolistic market. Failure to maintain competition may tip the balance of power towards the supplier, who may then become complacent. When complacency is combined with the supplier's inside knowledge of certain supplies, the company may find the supplier wields two forms of power over it. Even when the relationship is going well and significant relational capital has accrued, an open-bidding strategy can be an effective way to keep the supplier from slipping into a monopolistic complacency.

Implications

As a result of this project, a new avenue of research has been explored, and other, branching avenues are now open for further research. The findings show that there is a need for more research on cruise ship management issues. The project provides new data on the supplier-service provider dyad and its key characteristics, as well as a better understanding of technology's viability in a complex global supply chain, with its relevant costs and potential benefits. Furthermore, the supplier relationship exploration reveals new, previously undocumented phenomena in classic supplier relations, which warrant further investigation. An example of such is the employment of suppliers as local agents to help deploy in a given market.

As discussed above, the long-term planning model outlined in Fig. 7.2 can serve as a basis to further explore the demand-forecasting problem. Another important best practice that could be applied outside the cruise industry is the building of a collaborative relationship with foreign suppliers in order to use them as local agents. This potential for application warrants in-depth investigation to determine, on the supplier side, whether this is also common to other domains. Traditionally, lean principles have been seen as being mostly beneficial. The finding of this research shows that when deploying in a new foreign market, employing strict lean principles to strive for minimal waste could be detrimental to the on-board service quality. Deploying globally into a foreign market with an unknown demand pattern can result in two outcomes: a perfect forecast that meets the demand, or a demand that is outside the forecasted pattern. Hence, a trade-off has to be made between service quality and a minimum inventory yielding zero waste. Given the current mindset of total passenger satisfaction, with zero stock-out of products, lean principles cannot be fully applied since extra inventory and resultant waste have to be built into the deployment plan.

The best practices of a specific supply chain can be useful for research into other fields with similar constraints, such as humanitarian supply chains, military supply chains, and other service supply chains. The research also clearly shows the need to investigate further the service supply chain realm to understand this unique area of SCM. Because a cruise company is service centred, it takes a radical approach to stockout costs, which are not assigned a dollar value, but rather reclassified as unacceptable options. This approach differs greatly from that of traditional manufacturing supply chains, which tend to quantify the value of a stockout for inventory planning purposes.

These research findings can be beneficial to other hospitality settings in which service SCM is a growing area of focus. Examples of such include large resorts and theme parks as well as large hospital complexes. Finally, these findings may prove useful to employees of cruise line departments outside SCM who have a limited understanding of SCM and its implications for the cruise industry.

References

Avery, S. (2006) A supply chain's voyage to world class. *Purchasing* 135(10), 76–81.

Bowersox, D.J., Closs, D.J. and Stank, T.P. (2000) Ten mega-trends that will revolutionize supply chain logistics. *Journal of Business Logistics* 21, 1–16.

Brewer, J. and Hunter, A. (1989) *Multimethod Research: a Synthesis of Styles*. Sage Publications, Newburry Park, California.

Chopra, S. and Meindl, P. (2004) *Supply Chain Management: Strategy, Planning, and Operations*, 2nd edn. Pearson Prentice Hall, Upper Saddle River, New Jersey.

Christopher, M. (2000) The agile supply chain: competing in volatile markets. *Industrial Marketing Management* 29(1), 37–44.

CIN (2009) *Cruise Industry News Annual Report 2009*. Cruise Industry News, New York.

Conrad, J. (1999) *Lord Jim*. Oxford University Press, New York.

Cooper, D. and Schindler, P. (2005) *Business Research Methods*. McGraw-Hill, New York.

Doerr, K.H., Gates, W.R. and Mutty, J.E. (2006) A hybrid approach to the valuation of RFID/MEMS technology applied to ordnance inventory. *International Journal of Production Economics* 103, 726–741.

Fabbe-Costes, N. (2000) Le rôle transformatif des SIC et TIC sur les interfaces multi-acteurs de la distribution et de la logistique. In: Fabbe-Costes, N., Colin, J. and Paché, G. (eds) *Faire de la recherche en logistique et distribution?* Vuibert, Paris.

Fetterman, D. (1998) *Ethnography Step by Step*. Sage, Thousand Oaks, California.

Forrester, J. (1958) Industrial dynamics – a major breakthrough for decision makers. *Harvard Business Review* 36(4), 37–66.

Golicic, S.L. and Mentzer, J.T. (2006) An empirical examination of relationship magnitude. *Journal of Business Logistics* 27, 81–108.

Grover, V. and Malhorta, M.K. (2003) Transaction cost framework in operations and supply chain management research: theory and measurement. *Journal of Operations Management* 21, 457–473.

Harlaftis, G. (1996) *A History of Greek Owned Shipping. The Making of an International Tramp Fleet, 1830 to the Present Day*. Routledge, London.

Hobson, J.S.P. (1993) Analysis of the US cruise line industry. *Tourism Management* 14(6), 453–462.

Hou, J.-L. and Huang, C.-H. (2006) Quantitative performance evaluation of RFID applications in the supply chain of the printing industry. *Industrial Management and Data Systems* 106(1), 96–120.

Jick, T.D. (1979) Mixing qualitative and quantitative methods: triangulation in action. *Administrative Science Quarterly* 24, 602–611.

Jones, J.W. (1973) Accounting practices in ship chandlery. *Management Accounting* 55(2), 28–30.

Kemppainen, K. and Vepsäläinen, A.P.J. (2003) Trends in industrial supply chains and networks. *International Journal of Physical Distribution & Logistics Management* 33(8), 701–719.

Marine Log (2007) Building boom. *Marine Log*, 14–19.

Marti, B.E. (1992) Passenger perceptions of cruise itineraries: a Royal Viking Line case study. *Marine Policy* 16(5), 360–370.

Rao, V.K. (1999) Fuel price risk management using futures. *Journal of Air Transport Management* 5(1), 39–44.

Sheffi, Y. (2001) Supply chain management under the threat of international terrorism. *International Journal of Logistics Management* 12(2), 1.

UNCTAD (2005) *Review of Maritime Transport.* United Nations Conference on Trade and Development, New York.

Van Maanen, J. (1988) *Tales of the Field: on Writing Ethnography.* The University of Chicago Press, Chicago, Illinois.

Véronneau, S. and Cimon, Y. (2007) Maintaining robust decision capabilities: an integrative human-systems approach. *Decision Support Systems* 43, 127–140.

Véronneau, S. and Roy, J. (2009a) Global service supply chains: an empirical study of current practices and challenges of a cruise line corporation. *Tourism Management* 30, 128–139.

Véronneau, S. and Roy, J. (2009b) RFID benefits, costs, and possibilities: The economical analysis of RFID deployment in a cruise corporation global service supply chain. *International Journal of Production Economics* 122, 692–702.

8 Human Resource Management in the Cruise Industry

Philip Gibson and Celia Walters

Introduction

It takes no genius to recognise that a hospitality business stands or falls on the staff it employs – on the welcome they provide, on the efficiency with which they perform their tasks and on their ability to interact with their colleagues and with the customers.

(Bob Cotton, Chief Executive of the British Hospitality Association in the foreword to Boella and Goss-Turner, 2005, p. xv)

The cruise industry is a blanket term that implies an amalgam of different types of activities, which, when taken together, reflect the core business practice of managing a floating resort. It is patently a maritime business involved in both transportation and the provision of tourism experiences. In addition, it is concerned with leisure and all that falls under this title in terms of sport, recreation, entertainment, beauty, health and therapy. However, more than anything, the cruise industry is most closely related to hospitality.

The word hospitality is an ancient term that has been applied relatively recently to encapsulate the business activities concerned with combinations of elements to do with food, drink, accommodation, service, ambience and environment (Jones, 1996;

Brotherton, 1999). A contemporary consideration of the term would note that the components include:

- the notion of a host conferring hospitality to the guest who is away from home;
- the interactive nature of the act of hospitality between provider and receiver;
- the combination of tangible and intangible elements that make up the 'product'; and
- the centrality of the guest's well-being in terms of security and comfort (Brotherton, 1999).

In this respect, bearing in mind the criticality of the marine context and the scope of operations, the cruise industry can comfortably acknowledge that both industries share the need to source similar skill sets and competencies.

According to Mabey et al. (1998), the quality of the human resource (HR) underpins success for all organizations. This statement is worth even greater emphasis when considering labour oriented service industries (LaLopa, 1997) such as those in the tourism, hospitality or leisure industries. In recent years, the cruise industry and the hospitality industry have both experienced extremely high levels of growth and, in turn, this growth has had significant effect on the demand to secure quality labour. This latent opportunity suggests that these two industries should figure prominently in the minds of potential employees, yet Boella and Goss-Turner (2005) believe that in the UK, the world of hospitality has not seen significant positive improvement in respect of the status of the industry as an employer. The authors cite many reasons for this situation including: the lack of unionization; reluctance because of competitive pressure to charge higher prices for products; and a reliance on a secondary labour market (i.e. one that has a tendency to be high turnover, low pay, temporary or part-time and used by those who are seeking short term benefit).

The cruise industry may be dwarfed in scale by the hospitality industry: according to Gibson (2007), it is estimated that 49.3 million people were employed in hotels (one sector of the hospitality industry) in 2005, whereas approximately 310,000 were employed on cruise ships, but cruise businesses can present various points of differentiation, which can help to raise its status as an employment option. First, the industry is still relatively young, so opportunities are as yet embryonic and full of potential. Second, while the jobs may involve hard work and long hours, features that are commonplace for many employees who are seeking to succeed, the ever-changing geographical setting can be both invigorating and motivating. Third, the cruise ship as an entity is home from home to the crew and, as such, it has the potential to become a place of real social meaning and importance – developing into a community in harmony.

This chapter will consider the HR function in context and reflect on practice as undertaken by P&O Cruises, a leading UK cruise brand. Thereafter, key issues such as dealing with a scarcity of labour, addressing staff retention, managing the multicultural workforce and training and development will be addressed. While initially the chapter will consider all areas of sea-based cruise business employment, in the latter stages it will focus predominantly on hotel services (including hotel services management),

which is the largest employment sector in the business. It should be noted that most cruise companies also employ parallel HR functions for shore-based personnel.

Case Study: P&O Cruises – There's a World Out There!

P&O Cruises claim to have invented cruising and to have been pioneers throughout the industry's early stages. Among the many milestones that punctuate the company's progress can be found reference to William Thackeray, the novelist famous for many works, including *Vanity Fair*, who in 1844 was given free passage to write about his trip in the Mediterranean: P&O Cruises' first consultant marketer. In the early 21st century, P&O Cruises is operated as a leading British brand by owner Carnival Corporation, with six ships, each of which has a distinctive personality. This case study intends to illuminate what P&O Cruises does in terms of recruitment and training for hotel crew and identifies issues relating to this HR function.

P&O Princess PLC joined Carnival Corporation in April 2004 thus creating the world's largest cruise company (see Bjelicic, Chapter 2, this volume). The merger has created interesting new opportunities for P&O Cruises. The brand retains its set of core values, but the brand identity has been refined and sharpened in line with their evolving target markets. One positive example of this exercise can be seen in terms of the way subtle changes have been put in place to ensure Cunard Lines, previously a competitor and rival in pre-merger times, and P&O Cruises now complement each other with different offerings for different markets. Carnival Corporation also provides P&O Cruises with other distinctive advantages because the parent company has the scale and flexibility to deploy ships as appropriate according to demand across the globe. It takes 5 years to build a ship but 3 weeks to re-brand it.

P&O Cruises has historical connections with the Indian subcontinent stemming from colonial days, and the majority of recruits still tend to originate from Goa and Mumbai. Word of mouth is the most powerful method of communication for sourcing crew although the Internet is becoming increasingly popular (Fleet Maritime Services India, 2008) and newspaper adverts and job fairs are also utilized. Over the years, there is increasing competition from other industries to recruit skilled staff in India. P&O Cruises have developed a network for recruitment with Magsaysay, an agent in the Philippines, to target specific recruitment covering deck, technical and hotel. The company also targets Bangladesh, France, Canada and Singapore for hard to fill posts such as chefs, and in general terms it does not preclude broadening the search to other countries, should the need arise.

In relation to pursers or hotel managers, the company targets suitable candidates from the UK who have an appropriate hospitality background and preferably a degree qualification. Recently, P&O Cruises introduced a cadet programme for the hotel department for students enrolled on the BSc (Hons) Cruise Management at the University of Plymouth. These students are invited to apply for the cadetship during their second year, with a view to undertaking a 1-year training programme intended to give a thorough grounding in preparation for employment as an assistant manager when they complete their degree.

The galley (kitchen) presents challenges in terms of sourcing appropriately trained personnel, and P&O Cruises prefer to develop their team by recruiting lower level employees and then developing them on-board. Unlike many shore-based catering businesses, P&O Cruises' chefs use the full array of culinary skills from béchamel to bakery, producing goods from raw materials. The company has found good levels of success working with the Culinary Academy of India in Hyderabad, who run 3 months trainee chef and 4 months 1st Commis Chef courses. Successful trainee recruits join P&O Cruises and then undertake in-house training by participating in the scheme known as 'Passport to 1st Commis', a hybrid version of a vocational qualifica-

tion for trainee chefs. A Bangladeshi catering college was also identified that had adopted similar UK training qualifications and also placed food production students in the UK and Ireland for work experience and training before progressing to work on P&O Cruise ships.

Over the years, it became relatively difficult to source laundry personnel. P&O Cruises found a solution to this problem when they created a strategic arrangement with a large-scale commercial laundry in Goa that was familiar with contracts from clients such as Marriott Hotels. The type of scale and equipment in the laundry was therefore similar to that found on board a typical cruise ship. Successful recruits are sent for training and development to the laundry for a 3-month period before onward deployment to the cruise ship.

Once on board, crew can progress to more advanced positions leading to enhanced pay and rewards. The majority of Indian crew enter on the lowest paid positions such as a food and beverage assistant (FBAS), undertaking tasks such as operating the potwash or acting as galley porter, or as accommodation assistants (ACAS), cleaning public areas and toilets. The company recognizes that, relatively speaking, it is usually only a short time before these early recruits progress from FBAS to buffet assistant or from ACAS to room service because of prior experiences and the tendency for the Indian recruits to work hard and apply themselves to the job. Onward progression can see the FBAS becoming a junior waiter, assistant waiter, waiter or assistant bar stewards, bar steward, assistant bartender and bartender, and the ACAS being promoted to assistant cabin steward, night steward, officer steward and cabin steward. Successful employees can progress to be supervisors (these positions come with silver stripes to denote rank) and, in a few cases, to be managers (with gold stripes). However, P&O Cruises has a brand pillar that identifies the need to maintain 'Britishness' and this suggests that there is a commensurate requirement to aim to ensure that the majority of officers are British.

Recruits receive a generic 3 days' general company induction shore side to prepare the individual for life at sea and what to expect. Included in this induction are the history of the company, the company's vision and brand architecture, fleet regulations, marine safety and security, health and safety and food safety, the company's customer service initiative and a ship visit. Job specific inductions are undertaken by line managers on board. All Indian joiners also undertake basic job skills and complete a food safety qualification. Shipboard inductions are undertaken to augment what has been done ashore so that safety training is in place, fleet regulations are clear and customer service objectives are understood. New recruits are allocated a 'buddy' as additional support. It is normal practice for junior officers to receive a 2-week induction to familiarize themselves with the ship, the people on board, the operation and to receive a handover from the outgoing post holder that they will replace. The officer 'handover' is often supported by notes relating to the work at hand, and that virtually could be seen as a form of a job orientation manual.

Thereafter, the Hotel Services and Entertainment department has devised a training tool intended to support the development of key skills and knowledge in a systematic and transparent manner. Each individual, irrespective of rank, is given a training record card and a target to ensure the trainee attains 'experienced worker' standard within a month. In addition, fleet regulations demand regular training to cover specific issues such as dealing with lock-in alarms in refrigeration units (devices to alert colleagues if a kitchen operative gets trapped in a walk-in refrigerator) and manual handling. This framework for training is supported by peripatetic trainers who travel with the ship and provide support to supervisors to make sure training is effective.

Management training poses distinct problems. In delivering management training at sea, the demands of the job are a constraint because of the routines of the job. The company has found uptake variable when delivering management training ashore during periods of leave and as a result the target group is less focused than intended. The mix of ships, patterns of leave and changing managers can mean the logistics of applying the outcomes of training into operations is not as easy as it might first appear. It would seem that training on board creates best opportunities for supporting improvements or developments because it takes place in close proximity to operations.

A system of appraisals is undertaken as part of the training regime to underpin the process of staff development. This process makes use of performance assessment and infers that staff development is a potential outcome, as is the potential for promotion or progression. In some respects the company could recognize a need for staff development as a result of data received in the customer service questionnaire (the CSQ is a key performance indicator for the cruise company), and in broader terms this type of data could result in targeted trainer activities focusing on selling skills and customer service delivery. Financial rewards can be made in the form of bonuses for key staff achieving revenue targets and CSQ results. Good practice is also rewarded formally through the C.R.U.I.S.E. awards (see Aggett and Lim, Chapter 15, this volume) and, informally, individuals in teams may be recognized for exceptional service by their line supervisor or manager with occasional one-off prizes such as extra time off, a spa treatment or a box of chocolates. Ultimately, the company aims to retain its personnel by undertaking good training, providing benefits that are valued, by managing them well and giving good prospects.

A Consideration of Current Practice

International human resource management (IHRM) is cited as a modern-day phenomenon, which has taken on increasing importance in line with international business growth (Briscoe and Schuler, 2004), yet the cruise business is such that since its inception it has always operated internationally.

Arguably, in its formative days, the cruise companies acted pragmatically, using domestic forms of a functionally oriented personnel management, influenced by specific tasks such as sourcing crew from overseas, rather than a strategically focused IHRM (Lundy, 1994). As time has passed, the cruise industry has taken on more complex forms with brands evolving to target distinctive international markets and, along with that, more sophisticated models of IHRM have become established.

The leading and largest cruise company, Carnival Corporation, demonstrates its international credentials in a number of ways. In terms of targeting international markets, the corporation operates Carnival Cruise Lines, Holland America Line, Princess Cruises and Seabourn Cruise Line in North America; P&O Cruises and Cunard Line in the United Kingdom; AIDA Cruises in Germany; Costa Cruises in southern Europe; P&O Cruises in Australia; and Iberocruceros in Spain. It owns two tour companies and is listed in both the New York and London stock exchanges (Carnival Corporation, 2007). The company has its head offices in Miami, Florida and London. The various cruise brands also have head offices in Miami, Seattle, Washington, Santa Clarita in California (all in the USA), Southampton (UK), Genoa (Italy), Rostock (Germany) and Sydney (Australia). Carnival Corporation is an example of a cruise company that is international because of its core purpose in offering cruise holidays, its target markets, its HR and its business outlook. In essence, it can be referred to as a global company because it is 'blind to national borders' (Briscoe and Schuler, 2004, p. 41).

IHRM differs from human resource management (HRM) in that: the international arena requires managers who are experienced and skilled in international contexts; the multicultural workforce can be demanding because of the notion that different people from different cultures act differently; and conducting business internationally means dealing with international laws, conventions and practices (Tayeb, 2005). The cruise ship setting epitomizes

the challenges of IHRM because of the potentially diverse international locations within which cruise ships ply their trade, the multinational and multicultural workforce and the need for managers, when managing people, to be sensitive to the environment in order to achieve success.

The cruise industry is configured in such a way that it is difficult to identify precise figures relating to employment. By examining studies undertaken by Charlier and McCalla (2006), analysing data provided by the Cruise Line International Association (CLIA, 2006), then making adjustments to the calculations to take patterns of contract into account, it can be estimated that there were approximately 310,000 officers and crew employed on cruise ships worldwide in 2004. According to the International Maritime Organization (IMO, 2007) the world trading fleet comprised 47,681 vessels, 12% of which were passenger ships (concerned with the cruise and ferry business). The cruise industry employs approximately a quarter of all seafarers (International Labour Office, 2007), which, unsurprisingly, is a disproportionate number of people on board compared to the other sectors.

Jobs on cruise ships are diverse but tend to follow a pattern relating to the key departments: hotel, engineer, electro-technical and deck. P&O Cruises' 76,000 GRT cruise ship *Aurora* caters for a British market and carries 1900 passengers plus 842 crew (Table 8.1), creating a crew to passenger ratio of 1:2.25. Of these, 70.6% are employed in operating the hotel department and a further 15.2% are concerned with entertainments and services (including medical): this equates to 85.8% involved in customer services activities. The remaining 14.2% of the crew are occupied in deck, engine and electro-technical departments. Of the total ship's company, 9% are officers (with the majority hotel and entertainment officers) and 91% are ratings (includes supervisors). Among the more unusual occupations to be found on board are: the art auctioneer, the horticulturalist, the bandleader, the seamstress, the librarian, the butler, the cyber-study manager, the TV

Table 8.1. Ships complement by department on P&O Cruises' *Aurora*.

Aurora	Number by rank	Number by dept	% of total
Deck: officers	11	51	6.1
Deck: ratings	40		
Engine: officers	13	56	6.7
Engine: ratings	43		
Electro-technical: officers	6	13	1.5
Electro-technical: ratings	7		
Medical: doctors	2	6	0.7
Medical: nurses	4		
Hotel: officers	29	594	70.5
Hotel: ratings	565		
Entertainments: officers	10	73	8.7
Entertainments: ratings	29		
Entertainments: guest	34		
Revenue (shops/spa)	49	49	5.8
Grand total	842	842	100

operator, the waste disposal operator and the computer technical support manager.

This large-scale operation can be compared to the 2112 GRT *Hebridean Princess*, which has a ship's complement of 38 crew looking after 49 guests. This creates a ratio of crew to passengers of 1:1.3. The *Hebridean Princess* is one of the smallest cruise ships in the world and among the 23 hotel staff are two pursers, six chefs and a tour guide. Some 60% of the crew are hotel or guest oriented. These examples give an indication of the contrasting scale of employment issues on cruise ships and the relative focus in managing the HR aspects of planning for the different departments. The contrast is stark in respect of quantities of personnel, but the changing trend in new ship construction suggests the future will see cruise companies continuing to build large vessels, to capitalize on the resultant greater earning capabilities, thus adding to the demand to both source and retain the best people for the various jobs. According to Seaview (2008), the average size of new cruise ships constructed in 2007 was 93,200 GRT while in 2008 this figure is expected to be 121,900 GRT. In contrast, in 1997, the average size of a new build cruise ship was just under 64,000 GRT, and in 1987 it was 33,900 (Colton, 2007).

Sourcing Personnel

The scale of the task in securing a high calibre crew with the range of skills and necessary attributes to work on contract at sea is daunting. The three major employers in the cruise industry – Carnival Corporation, Royal Caribbean Cruises and Star Cruises/ Norwegian Cruise Line (NCL) – account for some 145,000 employees with approximately 109,000 ship-based personnel. If the figures presented for *Aurora* are representative, this means these three corporations are seeking to operate their ships using over 93,500 hotel and entertainment staff and 15,500 deck and technical personnel (Fig. 8.1). Taking into account leave patterns, or lengths of contracts, the cruise companies need to factor in additional personnel. This equates to 1.5 posts being required for every member of staff on a 6 month contract, 1.4 posts for staff on 9 month contracts and 1.6 posts for every officer contract.

Each individual vessel requires its own set of skilled professionals and it follows that while scale, in terms of size of vessel, brings its own peculiar challenges, mega-cruise ships create opportunities to reduce personnel costs by maximizing efficiencies of labour. In addition, cruise

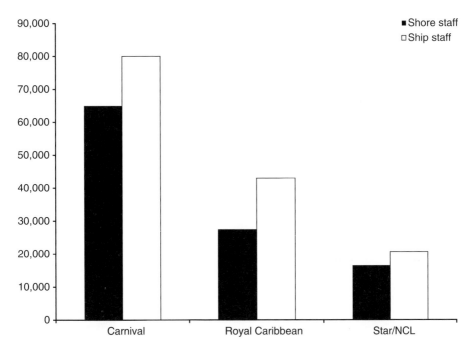

Fig. 8.1.   Number of staff in 2007. Source: corporate websites. NCL,Norwegian Cruise Line.

brands targeting mass or large-scale markets have definable service standards, which, while of high calibre and offering a broad range in terms of choice, are frequently less labour and skill intensive than smaller more niche luxury markets. A vessel such as the *Hebridean Princess* is intended to ensure a different level of service to one such as the *Aurora*. The size of the ship (smaller ships require a higher proportion of technical to hotel staff) and the type of service levels that are required to underpin cruise brand have a bearing on the ratio of crew to passengers.

The two largest corporations are confidently constructing ships that exceed 100,000 GRT and Royal Caribbean, as well as taking delivery of three 158,000 GRT cruise ships, have two new vessels under construction that will exceed 220,000 GRT. This implies that while Royal Caribbean may operate fewer vessels (Figs 8.2 and 8.3) than Carnival, the total passenger capacity to ship ratio is likely to increase and the on-board HR operating costs for Royal Caribbean are likely to decrease.

The sheer numbers of crew involved mean that cruise HR teams have to be strategic in how they source, recruit and build capacity (Foss and Pedersen, 2004). One significant strategy is to outsource aspects of crewing by using recruitment agencies. Most cruise brands adopt this approach to varying degrees. In some cases, the agencies are used to address hard to fill vacancies that require skills, qualifications and experience. In other cases the agents are used to source skilled, semi-skilled or unskilled employees (and sometimes to provide elementary training) from specific locations around the world, to ensure labour costs are minimized and the best type of employees are found. Some cruise brands devolve responsibility for virtually all aspects of on-board personnel by paying a recruitment agency a total solutions fee to source, provide and manage the personnel on board. This approach can be taken for elements of the operation, e.g. the hotel function or the deck and technical function. Irrespective of whether the HR function is managed entirely in-house, with or without

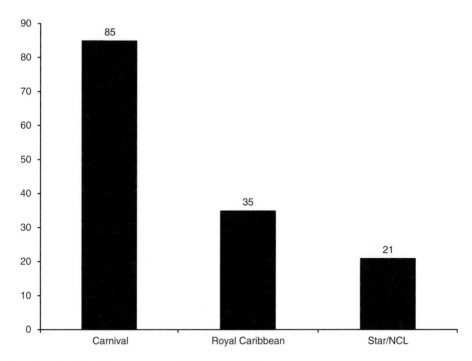

Fig. 8.2.   Number of vessels in 2007. Source: corporate websites.

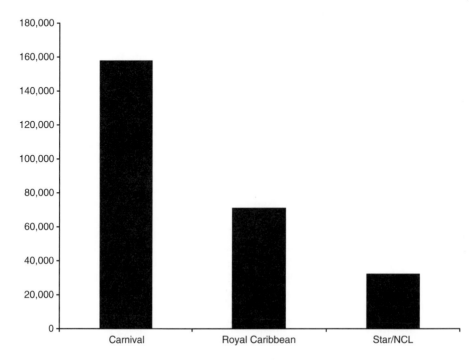

Fig. 8.3.   Passenger capacities in 2007. Source: corporate websites.

outsourcing, there remain significant challenges in terms of meeting the needs of crewing requirements in a growth market with considerable internal and external competition.

In order for cruise brands to target specific markets, they must ensure that the product and services are designed and configured to meet (and exceed) customer expectations. In line with this, the personnel on board are expected to possess certain attributes and qualities. For customer-facing staff, invariably, that means competence in communicating to a level and in a language that is required. This is one major factor that influences the geography of staffing for cruise brands. Cruise brands are configured with markets in mind. The majority of cruise passengers are English speaking, from the USA or UK, and on cruise ships servicing these markets, the officers tend to originate from English-speaking countries or other countries where the requisite job skills are likely to exist and where the standard of English language teaching is high, while the crew originate from countries that are generally known to provide employees who are in a strong position to acquire the required job skills and who have the capability to meet language requirements (Gibson, 2008). It follows that, on German, Italian, Spanish and other cruise brands with a nationality or language focus, a similar strategy is employed.

The aforementioned P&O Cruise ship *Aurora* employs 202 British (spread across all departments), 26 Pakistanis (deck department only), 486 Indian (hotel and entertainment departments), 116 Filipinos (engine, electro-technical, hotel and entertainment departments) and ten Nepalese (Deck Department). Passengers are predominantly from the UK. In contrast, on one cruise in the Mediterranean, *Grand Princess*, a ship operated by Carnival Corporation brand Princess Cruises had passengers from 64 countries on board (although the majority were from the USA) and the crew originated from 54 different nations (Gibson, 2005). Each cruise brand has its own specific reasons for electing to crew ships with particular nationality orientations.

P&O Cruises has a long history of crewing its vessels as it does, and this particular world-view is well recognized by the loyal customer base. Market recognition and acceptance are important to P&O Cruises as part of their aim to maintain the brand dynamic in a fast moving evolving industry. In addition, since Carnival Corporation acquired P&O Cruises, the HR function has been maintained out of Southampton and involves satellite activities with agents located in the target recruitment companies.

Princess Cruises has a different historical background, which has led to the evolution of its own set of HR practices. When P&O Cruises acquired Princess Cruises in 1974 and Sitmar Cruises in 1988, it was decided to merge the Italian-based Sitmar brand with the Los Angeles-based Princess brand to make a larger and stronger Princess Cruises, leading to what is known as absorptive capacity (Cohen and Levinthal, 1990), or the ability to derive advantage from the accrued knowledge when one company takes over another. This resulted in the incorporation of a sizable Italian crew complement to add to the previously combined US/UK influence on staffing – a hybrid mix that can still be identified to this day. Their HR effort is centred on Princess Cruises' head office in Santa Clarita in Los Angeles and involves similar network arrangements with agents in strategic locations across the globe. Both Princess and P&O Cruises have unilateral approaches to recruiting hotel and entertainment staff (although Princess Cruises' head office also contributes in varying degrees to the personnel function of P&O Cruises Australia) but have bilateral arrangements for key personnel in deck and engine departments.

The type of complex arrangements that exist to procure staff have evolved for pragmatic reasons in an effort to ensure the HR function keeps up with the demands placed on the industry relating to constant growth. Yet, however familiar cruise customers are with international patterns of staffing, as traditional HR become less available, cruise companies are being forced to widen their search. The cruise business is not immune to the realities of globalization. As Briscoe and Schuler (2004) highlight, the world of business has changed for many reasons, including: improving education worldwide raising expectations and capabilities; increased travel leading to greater awareness and stimulating demand for products and services; rapid development of communications and technology; growing trade and international competition; and mass emigration. This global market place requires businesses to source the best labour at the best price in order to maintain a competitive edge.

Cruise companies can capitalize on the international agreement known as Flags of Convenience (see Boy and Neumann, Chapter 3, this volume) in order to reduce crewing costs and minimize related tax liabilities (Gibson, 2006b). In many respects the agreement, which was established to ensure fair competition at sea by providing opportunities for ships to be registered to nation states that are members of the International Maritime Organisation, is a constraint as well as being an incentive. This is because cruise operators are unable to change the method of crewing and increase wages and conditions without incurring what may be a debilitating increase in costs and it would be business suicide to concede such a financial advantage to other cruise operators. The industry may be growing exponentially but competition is critical. Faced with this reality, it is less likely that richer nations would be targeted to source the army of customer-facing personnel that are required for the hotel departments on board cruise ships unless a strategic advantage is derived from sourcing such individuals.

Managing the On-board Community

Cruise operators are faced with the challenge of operating their vessels with officers, crew and staff who are on board for lengthy contracts. This has a multiplicity of impacts. In the first place, the types of relationships that are formed and maintained are important for stability. The personnel enjoy a lifestyle on board that is bound up with primarily professional duties balanced by social or rest periods, both on and off the vessel. This community is defined by the individuals engaged in the close and frequently overlapping work and social domains (Lave and Wenger, 1991). In this scenario, those whom you work with you socialize with, too. The resultant levels of camaraderie can be powerful but equally avoiding those who are disliked can be problematic. When it is harmonious, the social setting can engender a positive working culture that is self-sustaining and highly rewarding at a personal and professional level. When the work–life balance lacks equilibrium and staff fail to get along, there is a tendency for individuals to become involved in morale-destabilizing activities such as gossiping or disrespectful practices. Contracts change and people both leave and join the ship, constantly fracturing the social reality and creating the potential for a new community of practice (Gibson, 2006a).

The cruise company's HR team functions within this naturally occurring socio-professional setting, aiming to develop teams that are suitably prepared for the working environment and emotionally equipped to deal with the unique maritime world. Cruise brands adopt various approaches to addressing the problem of equilibrium on board. In many respects, the cruise ship setting is controlled by international maritime law and the command structure in place to ensure judicious management. Zero tolerance practices exist for a whole range of anti-social behaviour and actions. Personnel who transgress standing orders or company regulations are most likely to be de-shipped as quickly and quietly as possible, to ensure the working environment is protected for the benefit of the majority. Cruise brands employ trainers who are either peripatetic or are attached to specific vessels. They work with departmental managers, and the on-board crew office managers to ensure orientation, induction, health, safety, security, skills and knowledge training are conducted effectively and efficiently.

The crew office on board a cruise ship is the hub of personnel activity. It is frequently located centrally on the cruise ship in a crew area so that it is easy to access. The crew office maintains crew records, deals with new crew members signing on to ship's articles (the legal record that ensures crew are administered in accordance with maritime regulations), or signing off when departing. The office liaises with the company head office, to maintain close contact in pursuance of crewing the vessel to meet operational requirements. This can entail dealing with unforeseen events such as disciplinary issues, health problems or compassionate leave. The office usually offers a service to send money home for crew members or to provide banking and financial services. In effect, the office deals with all personnel matters on board.

The Cruising Context and Human Resources – Challenges

As has been described in the previous section, the HR element, when managing the cruise industry, is unique. It is imbued with a number of complex characteristics, which in isolation are challenging enough for any industry but, when addressed in combination, becomes multifaceted and highly intricate. A list of issues that arise as a result of studying the environment in the previous section of this chapter exemplifies this claim:

- The cruise ship is a skills rich and technically sophisticated environment (whether related to deck, engineering or hotel departments).
- Most contemporary cruise ships, and virtually all new build vessels, require in excess of 1000 crew to operate the ship.
- The majority of cruise companies derive tax advantages by contracting crew through offshore offices.
- Cruise companies use a variety of methods for recruitment although many rely on recruitment agents to source personnel.

- Cruise personnel are employed for lengthy contracts, which can be anything between 4 and 10 months without days off, with on average, an expectation of 10 h of work per day.
- Cruise personnel live and work on board thus generating strong interpersonal dynamics.
- The cruise ship environment is highly regulated to ensure the ship is operated safely, to maintain discipline and to establish equilibrium for the ship's company.
- Cruise companies tend to recruit a multinational workforce with resultant requirements to cater for cultural differences.
- Growth in the industry means that cruise companies are competing with each other and other industries (while passenger ships account for only 12% of the world fleet, they employ the majority of personnel) in order to attract and retain suitable personnel.
- Growth is associated to the introduction of new ships and the problems of dealing with HR issues on a grand scale.
- Every crew member will have, in addition to their main job, a safety role to perform on board the ship.

A constant theme that has emerged in this chapter relating to IHRM and managing cruise ships is concerned with culture. According to Confucius, 'all people are the same, it's only their habits that are different' (Schneider and Barsoux, 2003, p. 3). Major cruise corporations are keen to replicate brand values on board ships to attract target markets and, as part of this drive, the HR and how the crew do their job are central elements when defining the brand. As Tayeb (2005) declares, managing HR is complicated by the opportunity for variety within the socio-cultural environment. Cruise managers are faced with the task of ensuring that the multicultural crew, possessing a broad range of personal knowledge and beliefs, can provide the services and products as proscribed by the architects of the brand. This task can be further complicated when the passengers are also multinational.

Costa Cruises have established training schools in key locations, such as Manila in the Philippines, to prepare their employees for working on board, to understand brand values, corporate culture and to raise multicultural awareness about passengers and crew (Anon., 2007). The training includes language classes and promotes understanding about the expectations of clients who may be from different parts of the world (Anon., 2006b). Costa is not alone in aiming to inculcate a corporate culture and to take active steps to prepare personnel to meet the multicultural demands of the job. Trainers from P&O Cruises work closely with agents to ensure their crew is in the best position to join the workforce on board by visiting hotel schools in India. Cunard Line operates the White Star Academy, an on-board training and staff development team intended to ease the transition from shore to ship. Princess Cruises have introduced 'Princess U', an online learning portal for staff to use in order to improve product and work-related knowledge and skills.

According to Schneider and Barsoux (2003), culture, as a shared pattern of behaviour, exists nationally, regionally within countries, across borders (in country clusters), within industries, within professional circles and at corporate level. Geographical culture can be influenced by place, history, politics, economic forces, religion or language. The authors highlight the problems, which can occur when cultures clash, developing friction and serious outcomes for corporate entities and, coupled to this, that these clashes can be difficult to identify. For cruise brands such as P&O Cruises, the cultural nuances are relatively well understood. By concentrating recruitment and targeting specific nationalities, the company is building on its knowledge base and merging the geographical cultural elements to the corporate cultural elements. For another cruise brand with greater degrees of cultural diversity, the potentials for experiencing cultural clashes are increased, and managers can be faced with a different scale of problem.

Summary and Conclusions

Ultimately, the cruise industry is faced with serious challenges to source, recruit, train and retain high-quality crew to meet the needs of expanding fleets and passengers' service expectations. The challenge is exacerbated by competition, in terms of both other cruise companies and from other growth industries that are looking to secure the same types of skilled employee, and by the ever-increasing demands of the customer. However, the cruise industry has matured and developed in terms of the level of sophistication employed in managing its HR and it is well placed to face these challenges with intelligence and confidence.

Despite changing perceptions relating to working at sea, there remain strong attractions and concomitant rewards and cruise HR specialists can capitalize on these strengths to raise the profile of the industry as a profession for professionals. The multinational environment can provide a refreshing example of a world in equilibrium, where fellow workers enjoy each others' diversity rather than become entrenched in positions of conflict and where the differences define barriers.

Undoubtedly, the industry is faced with problems concerning crew shortages and in addressing unacceptable high levels of turnover, yet examples exist, which show that long-term planning can work. Holland America Line was reported as stating that 12.5% of their officers and crew had attained over 10 years' accumulated service, which was put down to the fact that the company is consistent, fair and positive when managing their staff (Anon., 2004). These issues were further examined at a recent Miami Seatrade Cruise Shipping Convention where best practice in attracting and retaining staff was addressed as a critical issue (Anon., 2006a), and it is clear that the industry is not addressing the problems from an uninformed position.

References

Anon. (2004) All work and no play? No way! Available at: www.cruiseindustrynews.com/index. php?option=com_content&task=view&id=807&Itemid=58 (accessed 16 March 2008).

Anon. (2006a) Miami Seatrade Cruise Shipping Convention. Available at: www.cruiseferryex.com/NASApp/ cs/ContentServer?pagename=mtevents/homen&mtevent=cfx07&section=confe&conf=hem&page= hem_agenda (accessed 16 March 2008).

Anon. (2006b) Valuing the crew. Available at: www.worldcruise-network.com/features/feature679 (accessed 30 January 2008).

Anon. (2007) Costa unveils new hotel personnel training school. Available at: www.cruiseindustrynews.com/ index.php?option=com_content&task=view&id=807&Itemid=58 (accessed 29 October 2008).

Boella, M. and Goss-Turner, S. (2005) *Human Resource Management in the Hospitality Industry: An Introductory Guide*. Butterworth-Heinemann, Oxford.

Briscoe, D. and Schuler, R. (2004) *International Human Resource Management: Policies and Practices for the Global Enterprise*. Routledge, New York.

Brotherton, B. (1999) Towards a definitive view of the nature of hospitality and hospitality management. *International Journal of Contemporary Hospitality Management* 11(4), 165–173.

Carnival Corporation (2007) Corporate profiles. Available at: www.carnivalcorp.com (accessed February 2007).

Charlier, J.J. and McCalla, R.J. (2006) A geographical overview of the world cruise market and its seasonal complementarities. In: Dowling, R.K. (ed.) *Cruise Ship Tourism*. CABI, Wallingford, pp. 18–30.

CLIA (2006) Cruise industry overview. Available at: www.cruising.org/press/overview%202006/ind_overview. cfm (accessed 6 January 2007).

Cohen, W. and Levinthal, D. (1990) Absorptive capacity: a new perspective on learning and innovation. *Administrative Science Quarterly* 35(1), 128–152.

Colton, T. (2007) Ship Building History. Available at: www.shipbuildinghistory.com/ (accessed April 2008).

Fleet Maritime Services India (2008) Cruise careers website. Available at: www.cruisecareers.in (accessed 1 April 2008).

Foss, N. and Pedersen, T. (2004) Organizing knowledge processes in the multinational corporation: an introduction. *Journal of International Business Studies* 35(5), 340–349.

Gibson, P. (2005) Communities of practice: employment on cruise ships. Paper presented at the CHME Research Conference, Bournemouth.

Gibson, P. (2006a) Cruise communities: constructivism and internships. Paper presented at the 24th EUROCHRIE Congress, Thessaloniki.

Gibson, P. (2006b) *Cruise Operations Management*. Butterworth-Heinemann, Burlington.

Gibson, P. (2007) Credible careers: tomorrow's cruise hotel managers. Paper presented at the Cruise Shipping Opportunities and Challenges conference, Naples, Italy.

Gibson, P. (2008) Cruising in the 21st century: who works while others play? *International Journal of Hospitality Management* 27(1), 42–52.

IMO (2007) Shipping and world trade. Available at: www.marisec.org/shippingfacts//worldtrade/index.php (accessed January 2008).

International Labour Office (2007) Global employment trends brief, January 2007. Available at: www.ilo.org/ empelm/what/pubs/lang--en/docName--WCMS_114295/index.htm (accessed July 2007).

Jones, P. (1996) *Introduction to Hospitality Operations*. Cassell, New York.

LaLopa, J. (1997) Commitment and turnover in resort jobs. *Journal of Hospitality & Tourism Research* 21(2), 11–26.

Lave, J. and Wenger, E. (1991) *Situated Learning: Legitimate Peripheral Participation*. Cambridge University Press, Cambridge.

Lundy, O. (1994) From personnel management to strategic human resource management. *The International Journal of Human Resource Management* 5(3), 687–720.

Mabey, C., Salaman, G. and Storey, J. (1998) *Human Resource Management: A Strategic Introduction*. Blackwell Publishers, London.

Schneider, S. and Barsoux, J. (2003) *Managing Across Cultures*. Prentice Hall, Harlow.

Seaview (2008) New cruise ships. Available at: http://seaview.co.uk/newships/newships2007.html (accessed 25 January 2008).

Tayeb, M. (2005) *International Human Resource Management a Multinational Company Perspective*. Oxford University Press, Oxford.

Part III

Cruise Line Marketing Management

_____

9 Marketing Communications in the Cruise Industry

Robert Kwortnik and Joe Rand

Introduction

This chapter introduces the reader to marketing-communications strategies and tactics used by cruise lines to build brands, generate brand awareness and promote brand propositions to target customers. Much like the rapid growth and evolution of the cruise industry itself, cruise marketing communication has evolved dramatically during the past 40 years. Cruise lines in the 21st century still use tried and true marketing tactics such as indirect sales through travel agents and print advertising to generate demand, but also new media such as web-based direct sales and social networking via the internet. The practice of cruise marketing communication has become more complex, dynamic and exciting both because the cruise market is more sophisticated and because the variety of communication tools available for cruise promotion has increased. Without a doubt, marketing is one of the most important areas of cruise management today.

After reading this chapter, you will:

- gain a perspective of the changing role of marketing communications in the cruise industry;
- recognize the need to identify and understand target markets for cruise marketing communications;
- understand the challenges associated with consumer perceptions of cruising and with communicating cruise-product value;
- identify main channels of cruise sales and marketing communications;
- distinguish between communication that drives primary (category) versus selective (brand) demand;
- learn how cruise marketers use a mix of communications tools to reach and influence target markets; and
- develop insight about the vital role played by brand marketing in the cruise industry.

Marketing Communications in the Cruise Industry: a Look Back

In 2010, Celebrity Cruises is on Facebook, Disney Cruise Line is on Twitter and Norwegian Cruise Line (NCL) is on YouTube with the Freestyle Channel. If the cruise industry's marketers in the 1970s could see how their field has changed, they would be amazed (a few of these pioneers are still in the business as cruise line presidents or chief marketing officers!). Marketing in the cruise industry's formative years served a very different purpose than it does today, namely to educate travellers about this new leisure product and to get them to give the experience a try. While these objectives remain part of cruise marketing today, new communications objectives have emerged – and for some companies, become predominant, such as to build the cruise line brand, to foster customer loyalty by developing cruise communities, and, of course, to increase sales, revenues and profits.

From shipping to cruising

The cruise industry of the early 1970s was a travel sector in transition. Whereas the core product of passenger shipping companies, as cruise lines were called in the mid-20th century, was transportation, the advent of jet aircraft as a more efficient means of transport demanded a new focus on the core product of leisure travel.[1] Early cruise marketing tended to focus on the destinations served and not the cruise itself, based on the belief that travellers were most interested in where they were going, not how they were getting there (Dickinson and Vladimir, 2008). This marketing perspective was a holdover from the era of transatlantic crossings, journeys that could be unpleasant if not harrowing experiences because of the rough weather and waters of the North Atlantic. Many of the ships plying the new cruise waters were former transatlantic liners that were not designed for pleasure, unless one was travelling first class. For example, most ships did not have air conditioning, which was a comfort must for Caribbean cruises, and leisure facilities such as pools, gyms, show rooms, theatres, etc., were small – if they existed at all. Luxury cruise offerings were by no means spartan, including pampered service, black-tie dining and musical entertainment. However, the cruise experience was really just a stylized form of transportation for a sightseeing holiday (Kwortnik, 2008).

Cruising as a luxury product

Another marketing remnant from cruising's past was a focus on the high end of the market and the glamour of cruising. In fact, cruises were relatively expensive holidays, with voyages of 7–14 days or longer being the norm in the 1970s. Brochures and print advertisements for cruises showed society-types dressed in the latest fashions and enjoying cocktail parties, fine dining, ballroom dancing and deck-top shuffleboard. One of the industry's founding marketers, the former president and CEO of Carnival Cruise Lines, Bob Dickinson, long lamented the elitist imagery of cruise marketing – even the naming of cruise lines and ships using royal labels (Royal Caribbean Cruise Lines, Regal Cruises, Crown Cruise Line, Grand Princess, Majesty of the Seas). He argued that such symbolism, while showcasing the high quality of cruise holidays, also suggested an experience that did not match the lifestyle and comfort level of most potential cruisers (Dickinson and Vladimir, 2008). Consequently, the number of people who chose cruising as a holiday was very modest – approximately 500,000 in the mid-1970s (CLIA, 2005).

The selling concept of cruising

Because the cruise product in its pure leisure form was new and unknown to the public, early marketing efforts used a selling model of promotion as opposed to a more customer-focused marketing concept. That is, cruise marketers needed to sell the ships they had and primarily to regional markets (e.g. New York, Miami or Los Angeles going to Bermuda, the Bahamas or the Mexican Riviera, respectively). Commonly used marketing channels were tour operators and newspaper advertising. To expand the market, some innovative cruise salesmen began to bundle airfare, pre- and post-cruise hotel, and the cruise fare into a package price and promote to regions beyond the main feeder cities (Dickinson and Vladimir, 2008). This sales-oriented approach persists today, though the dozen or so cruise lines that survived the shake-out of the industry as it matured – when some 70 cruise brands disappeared – have adopted a far more market-centred model of product development and market communication.

Cruising and Cruise Marketing Change Course

Initial demand for leisure cruise holidays, though small when compared with the resort-holiday market, showed clear potential. The industry began to tap that potential by, first, introducing new vessels that were purpose-built for pleasure cruising. These ships featured a greater variety of amenities, more comfortable cabins, more lavish entertainment (e.g. Las Vegas-style reviews and casinos) and more public space (e.g. lounges, deck space, pools and theatres), all to enhance the 'sun and fun', pleasure and recreational dimensions of the experience (Kwortnik, 2008). A second market-moving strategy involved focusing marketing efforts on a large external sale force – travel agents. The complexity and cost of the cruise product, coupled with the travel market's lack of familiarity with cruising, meant that the purchase process was difficult for would-be cruisers. Travel agents with connections in local markets could provide the personal attention needed to overcome purchase barriers to cruising and to match customers to the right product; however, these agents, most of whom had never been on a cruise themselves, needed training on the product. A third market-development strategy was greater availability and promotion of shorter itineraries – the 2–5-day cruises that now comprise 30% of all sailings. Shorter cruises permitted travellers to sample the experience at a lower opportunity cost, both in terms of price and holiday days. Furthermore, the lower price point made the product accessible to more than just the affluent market. Finally, the power marketing punch for the industry came about serendipitously when the *Love Boat* television series appeared in 1977 and popularized the idea of cruising as a holiday to millions of consumers. By 1980, an estimated 1.5 million people took a cruise; each new decade has seen the number of cruisers double, with more than 14 million people expected to cruise in 2010, for an average annual growth rate of 7.4%, making cruising the fastest-growing sector of the travel industry (CLIA, 2010).

Driving primary demand to attract first-timers

The *Love Boat* offered travellers the first good picture of the cruising experience. Still, to change cruising from a niche product to one with mainstream appeal would require converting non-cruisers into first-timers – consumers who would become advocates for cruising and tell others about it. Growing the first-timer pool was a challenge and continues to be one today, as suggested by one estimate that only one in five people in the main cruise market of North America has ever taken a cruise. One way to persuade more first-timers to cruise is to focus marketing efforts on building primary demand for the cruise-holiday category as opposed to selective demand for specific cruise brands (Kwortnik, 2006). Cruise lines have taken steps toward building primary demand for cruising by, for example, investing in Cruise Lines International Association (CLIA), the trade organization dedicated to the promotion and growth of the overall industry. CLIA-member cruise lines, which include 25 major brands, financially support CLIA's efforts: education programmes designed to teach travel agents about the cruise product and how to sell it; sales-promotion programmes such as cruise conventions and trade shows; and consumer media campaigns such as the National Cruise Vacation Month (CLIA, 2005).

Overcoming misperceptions about cruising and barriers to buying

One of the biggest challenges facing cruise marketers even today is a set of misperceptions about the cruise experience that create barriers to buying (Maucini, 2004). Dealing with these misperceptions requires an ongoing education campaign targeting travel agents (to give them the tools for countering the misperceptions) and the travelling public (to change attitudes toward cruising by first altering specific beliefs about the experience). Among the common misperceptions are:

- Cruising is for old people. While some cruise lines do appeal to an older clientele, the median age of the cruisermarket is now 45 (CLIA, 2010). Cruising is a particularly popular holiday for multigenerational families travelling with children, parents and grandparents.
- Cruising is expensive. Cruises are not cheap holidays especially when compared with holidays that use budget lodging and fast-food dining. On the holiday spectrum from visiting-friends-and-family trips to high-end resort holidays, most cruises fall in the middle (Kwortnik, 2006). However, the price-value of a cruise has improved significantly over time. For example, a 7-day cruise priced at US$1200 in 1980 would cost US$3120 today if adjusting for changes in the consumer price index. Yet, cruise fares have increased little in 30 years. In fact, according Ward (2009), the base fare for cruising was as low in 2008 as in 1980! The perception of cruising as expensive is attributable to two sources. First is the fact that cruise fares include multiple days and travel elements (e.g. transportation, dining, entertainment, lodging), so that US$1200 per-person base price for a 7-day cruise can induce sticker shock for the shopper who is more used to the per-day prices quoted by hotels and resorts. In addition, cruises used to be promoted in brochures that featured high rack rates, even though the price of the cruise often was discounted at the point of sale. Recently, cruise marketers altered how fares were stated by using 'lead-in' pricing that described 'prices starting at...' and promoted the lowest-price cabin categories.
- I will get seasick. The advent of ship stabilizers – wings attached to the ship's hull below the water line that reduce the left-right roll of the ship – as well as the trend toward ever-larger vessels has largely mitigated the rocking motion that causes seasickness. Some cruisers also use Dramamine and similar drugs that combat motion sickness. Finally, cruise ships usually sail in calm coastal waters. In sum, though some people may become seasick, the vast majority do not, and often say they can barely feel the motion of a cruise ship.
- I will feel confined on the boat. A common concern of non-cruisers is that a cruise ship at sea will start to feel restricted. However, modern cruise ships, especially the mega ships of 100,000 to 220,000 t, were designed with ample public space, outdoor decks, high-ceiling dining rooms and theatres, multi-storey lobbies, and cabins with verandas, all of which create a feeling of openness (Kwortnik, 2008). Moreover, most cruise itineraries do not include consecutive sea days and instead visit a port of call nearly every day.
- There won't be anything to do. Years ago, the main activities on board a cruise ship were reading, socializing, promenading, listening to music, dancing and sunning. While there were games and activities, these tended toward shuffleboard, bingo, trivia games and poolside horse racing (with wooden horses and dice). Today's cruises feature activities that run the gamut – from rock climbing and zip lining to wine tasting and hot-rock spa treatments. In fact, a bigger problem than not having anything to do is having too many choices for what to do – and too little time. A quick glance at the daily itinerary of almost any cruise (often posted online) highlights the considerable array of activities that can suit most any interest and lifestyle.
- Cruising is dangerous. Though the occasional emergency – fire, rogue wave, on-board crime, intestinal illness (norovirus) and even ship sinking – has happened, these instances are rare. Cruising is actually a very safe way to travel, especially to see multiple foreign

cities in one trip (one of the most appealing benefits of a cruise holiday to both cruisers and non-cruisers) – and to return each evening to the security of one's floating hotel. Cruise lines have also implemented a range of precautions to enhance traveller safety, such as metal-detectors at boarding gangways, on-board security personnel, video surveillance systems throughout the ship and hand-sanitizer stations outside dining and ship-boarding areas.

- I'll get fat – all people do is eat. Dining is definitely a major activity on a cruise, and for some people, the main attraction of cruising is the food-and-beverage experience. Many cruise ships feature 24-h complementary dining, a dozen or more restaurants and bars, and higher-end speciality restaurants that charge a nominal fee. Dinners are usually lavish, multi-course affairs, and 'all-you-can-eat' buffets are often available for each meal. The quality and variety of the food is typically excellent and certainly better than what one might experience at a land-based banquet, which is remarkable considering that cruise lines prepare fresh meals for several thousand people every day. New cruise ships feature open-air walking promenades and running tracks, as well as large fitness facilities with the latest exercise equipment. Cruise lines also offer fitness classes (e.g. yoga, Pilates, strength training) and healthy menu items for cruisers who are most concerned about watching their weight while on holiday.

Addressing these misperceptions through image-based marketing communications, travel agent training and consumer education (e.g. website FAQs) are a significant component of cruise marketing. Still, industry research shows that misperceptions remain. Furthermore, non-cruisers find it difficult to anticipate the benefits of a cruise holiday. Research by CLIA (2008, 2009, 2010) found that more than half of cruisers consider cruising better than other holidays in terms of the chance to visit several different locations, being pampered, fine dining and being luxurious. Even more revealing is that cruisers versus non-cruisers consider cruising better in terms of the chance to explore a holiday area to return to later (62% versus 30%); good value for the money (53% versus 22%); offering something for everyone (59% versus 31%); being reliable (49% versus 22%); being safe (45% versus 18%); the chance to relax/get away from it all (63% versus 37%); being hassle-free (58% versus 32%); and being a fun holiday (53% versus 28%). What is notable in these data is the gap between those who have cruised before and those who have not in terms of these beliefs, which indicates that the cruise industry must continue to focus marketing education efforts on non-cruisers to change their perceptions and build primary demand for cruising as a holiday alternative.

The Changing Cruise Customer

Successful marketing communications are less about creativity and more about reality, i.e. an effective marketing message is one that resonates with target customers by making a promise to deliver a desired experience. This means that communications design should begin with systematic analysis of potential target markets and their needs and wants. Marketers must have a grasp of the underlying motivations for cruise travel as well as the existing positive and negative attitudes in order to create a communications campaign that taps into these motivations. For example, some cruisers just want to escape and get away from it all; other cruisers want to learn and experience new things; others want to enjoy time with family and make new friends; still others want to feel pampered and cared for in a highly personal way. It is critical for cruise marketers to study cruisers and potential cruisers closely to bring these motivations to the surface.

The cruise customer has changed dramatically during the past 40 years. Much of this change is a simple result of

Fig. 9.1.   Disney villain Captain Hook and his junior crew. Source: Disney Cruise Line.

demographics: as more cruisers have entered the fold, there has been greater diversity of ages, nationalities, income levels, family structures, lifestyles, etc. For example, children were a rare sight on cruise ships in the 1970s. Today, the family market is booming – and sought after – by such mainstream cruise lines as Carnival, Royal Caribbean, NCL and Disney (Fig. 9.1). Each of these companies has adapted the cruise product to appeal to families, such as by creating children's and teen play areas, lounges and swimming pools, with dedicated activities coordinators. The marketing communications of these cruise lines often features families.

In addition, the 'sweet spot' of the market – the 50-ish empty nester or newly retired couple – has changed over time. Thirty years ago, this person was a product of the Great Depression who came of age during the Second World War era. Their taste in food (meat and potatoes), drink (spirits and cocktails), music (big band) and activities (bingo and dance contests) – especially their willingness to join in group games and mixers – is quite different from the Baby Boomer target of today. The Boomers, who came of age in the turbulent 1960s

and 1970s, though a diverse cohort, exhibit lifestyles that require a cruise product based on independence, variety, experimentation and choice. Boomers show a greater preference for nouveau cuisine, wine, eclectic music (from the Beatles to 1980s punk), and active adventure or education-based activities. Above all, the Boomer cruiser seeks freedom of choice to do everything or nothing at all in an environment that is invigorating and unstructured. For attracting the Boomer market, marketing communications must emphasize these benefits. For example, a commercial featured in Royal Caribbean's award-winning 'Get Out There' brand campaign (2000–2008) showed little of the ship – instead focusing on a variety of activities seen in quick-cut images and supported by a voiceover saying, 'somewhere between the Mayan ruins, the ice rink, the horseback riding, and the rock wall, it hits you – this is way more than a cruise'. With the first wave of Baby Boomers retiring in 2011, it will be imperative for cruise marketers to track the needs and wants of this segment over time, as well as to study the upcoming Generation X – the 30/40-somethings of today who are the next wave of cruise prospects.

Reaching Cruisers through Travel Agents

An important target for cruise marketing communications is the travel trade, in particular, travel agents. For some cruise lines, especially the luxury lines like Cunard, Seabourn, Crystal and Silversea, or the speciality lines like Windstar Cruises, little marketing communications (especially paid media such as advertising) targets the consumer; instead communications are focused on travel agents. The reason for this is simple – three out of four cruisers book their holiday with a travel agent. Even two out of three internet-savvy Generation X customers book through travel agents. Luxury cruise customers (76%) use travel agents most often, and mass-market (contemporary) cruise customers (60%) use agents least often (CLIA, 2008).

The travel agent channel, though important, is also expensive. Agents are paid a commission on the cruise fare of 12–14% and sometimes higher depending upon override incentives based, for example, on sales volume. Travel agent commissions are one of the largest line items on cruise line income statements, which is one reason Wall Street analysts continually call for cuts in agent commissions to boost profits – and stock prices.

The cost of the agent channel and the changing way in which consumers shop for travel are reasons why direct sales to consumers are a growing distribution channel for cruise lines. These sales agents in the US often called 'personal vacation planners' (PVPs), work out of call centres that receive inbound inquiries from potential cruisers and that make outbound sales calls to consumers who have registered on the cruise lines' websites or otherwise expressed interest in a cruise (Kwortnik, 2006). Large cruise lines employ several hundred PVPs because this channel offers brand-specific expertise and often lower costs per sale. However, cruise lines are very careful to avoid channel conflict between PVPs and travel agents. For example, in consumer advertising and even on cruise line websites, there is almost always a call to action that says 'call your travel agent'. Further-more, PVPs generally avoid making sales calls to past cruisers who may have previously booked through a travel agent. Despite the growing importance of direct-marketing channels, travel agents remain indispensable to the cruise industry. Consequently, cruise lines support the sales efforts of travel agents in two main ways: travel agent training and agency co-marketing.

Travel agent training

To be effective in matching travel products to customers, travel agents need considerable knowledge about myriad travel providers. Developing this knowledge on one's own can be difficult. Therefore, cruise lines use a variety of training programmes to teach travel agents about the brand, different products/itineraries, target customers, and how best to sell the experience. One such endeavour is run by CLIA, which offers one of the most successful education certification programmes (live seminars, trade shows, ship visits and online training) that is credited with training hundreds of thousands of travel agents (CLIA, 2008). Cruise lines also provide their own brand education through the following:

- Sales calls to travel agencies. The oldest and most reliable of cruise line marketing communications is the agency sales call performed by a cruise salesperson – what cruise lines call a 'business development manager' (BDM). The BDMs visit agents to promote new ships, itineraries, price promotions, etc., and generally to teach agents about the brand. BDMs will provide brochures or other sale support, such as speaking at a 'cruise night' sales event. BDMs will also help agents with specific customer bookings and problem resolution.
- Online training. Many of the major cruise lines have their own online training programmes (e.g. Carnival's CCL University or Holland America Academy) where agents can learn more about the brand. Upon completing the training, agents can earn a variety of benefits, such as

personalized certificates, credits toward CLIA Cruise Counsellor certification, shipboard credits (US$ to be spent on board), access to sales support and more.

- Promotion in trade media. Cruise lines also educate travel agents by buying advertising and placing publicity stories (e.g. articles that describe new ships, itineraries and marketing efforts) in travel-trade media (websites, magazines and newsletters) that target the agent community, such as *Travel Weekly*, *Travel Agent*, *Vacation Agent Magazine*, *Cruise Industry News*, Cruisemates.com, CruiseCritic.com, Agent@Home, as well as consumer travel magazines.

- Trade shows. Cruise lines support and participate in conventions and trade shows that feature the industry (e.g. CLIA Cruise3Sixty) or broader holiday-travel trade shows (e.g. The Trade Show (Travel Retailing and Destination Expo), Luxury Travel Expo or the National Tour Association Annual Convention). By sponsoring trade show booths, serving as event speakers and presenters, and joining panel discussions, cruise management and marketers have the opportunity to communicate directly with travel sellers.

Travel agent co-marketing

Cruise lines also recognize that many travel agencies are small operations with limited marketing budgets. To help agencies promote and sell cruises, cruise lines often provide cooperative marketing support. This might come in the form of cooperative advertising dollars, such as sharing the cost of newspaper advertising if the travel agency features the cruise brand in the advertisement. Most agencies also have group sales departments and similar reservations staff whose specific function it is to help travel agents with cruise bookings. And several cruise lines have designed internet marketing support, such as templates for customer newsletters, advertising, public relations and the like, that travel agents can customize with the agency's

name, logo and contact information for distribution to the agent's own mailing list.

Reaching Cruisers through Consumer Media

Only a handful of cruise lines make regular use of paid consumer media, especially national broadcast television (TV/cable) and print advertising. This is in part related to the cost of consumer-media channels but also because the mass-market reach of broadcast media is far wider, and therefore less efficient, than the more narrow markets pursued by luxury and niche cruise lines. If these lines do use paid consumer media, this will tend to be paid print advertising in travel magazines such as *Conde Nast Traveler*. The following are some examples of traditional media that cruise lines use to communicate marketing messages to cruisers.

- Television advertising. Carnival was the first cruise line (in 1984) to use broadcast television as part of a national marketing campaign for the brand. The company has continued to use limited TV advertising with new campaigns every few years. Royal Caribbean and NCL are two other contemporary cruise lines that use broadcast television.

- Print advertising. A few mainstream cruise lines place image-based brand advertising in general interest magazines such as *Newsweek* or *People*. A more common target is lifestyle and travel magazines such as *Wine Spectator*, *Vanity Fair* or *Travel + Leisure*. Cruise lines also use newspaper advertising, but mostly for tactical ads designed to stimulate sales from key feeder markets.

- Public relations. One of the most powerful communications tools in the cruise lines' marketing portfolio is public relations. Most cruise lines have in-house PR departments or contracted PR firms who generate press releases and answer press inquiries with the goal of placing stories about the cruise line in consumer and travel-trade media. The most common types of story are announcements about new ships, features and itineraries, that are provided to the travel media for hopeful publication (the risk of a PR-based communication strategy is that there is no guarantee that an editor will publish the story, which has to be newsworthy and of interest to the editor's audience). An example of a creative PR effort was a Carnival Cruise Lines event in support of the Fun Ships brand during which the company dropped two giant (36-foot) beach balls into crowds of onlookers in downtown Dallas. The event was acknowledged by the Guinness Book of World Records and received considerable press coverage – with videos of the event played on YouTube. Cruise line PR departments often work with entertainment media, such as Discovery Channel, The Travel Channel and National Geographic, to produce long-form video about the cruise experience. For example, Disney Cruise Line was the focus of a 1-h Discovery Channel programme in 2006 that was repeated often in subsequent years.

- Direct mail. Though used less in the internet age, direct mail is still a communications tool employed by cruise lines, especially smaller lines that target niche markets. Access to mail lists that contain certain types of prospects (e.g. North Americans living on the east coast who have travelled to Europe and who subscribe to wine magazines) permits efficient use of marketing dollars to convey specific, timely messages, such as to announce discounts or sales on itineraries that have unsold capacity.
- Collateral. Full-colour promotional brochures, once a mainstay of cruise line marketing communication that filled the brochure racks of travel agencies, are still available and provided to agents along with advertising specialities (e.g. pens, key chains, bottle openers, hats, stress balls, etc.) as promotional giveaways. More often, brochures come in DVD format for less expensive

shipping, or are electronic and can be downloaded from suppliers' websites.

Reaching Cruisers through New Consumer Media

As in many other sectors of the travel field, the revolution in marketing communication has been electronic, though cruise lines were late in coming to the party because of the reliance on travel agents. Within the past few years, though, internet marketing has boomed and will likely continue to play an ever-more important role for cruise lines for two main reasons: (i) the ability to efficiently and effectively convey the cruise experience through video, interactive web pages (e.g. virtual tours of ships) and consumer-generated content; (ii) the timeliness of the electronic channel for reaching potential cruisers with last-minute promotions to stimulate demand.

Below is a sample of new media tools used by cruise lines:

- Internet database marketing. Cruise lines possess detailed information about past cruisers and their behaviour, such as past cabin levels booked and on-board spending. However, most cruise lines were reluctant to mine this data for outbound direct marketing to avoid conflict with travel agents who view cruisers they booked for the line as their own customers. As a result, database marketing has largely used email blasts to announce discounts on select itineraries, and usually featuring the call to action, 'Contact your travel agent'. More recently, though, cruise lines have begun to analyse their databases for the development of new products, marketing promotions and loyalty programmes. Communicating via email newsletters to past cruisers who opt into loyalty programmes is a particular focus for promotional announcements about new itineraries and sales.
- Cruise line websites. The cruise industry's initial foray into the online space was largely limited to simple promotion

(e.g. descriptions of itineraries and photos of ships) in part to avoid conflict with travel agents who feared the direct-booking capability of the internet. Today, cruise line websites are dynamic sources of rich content – and a channel through which cruisers can book their holiday. Cruise line websites serve many purposes, both for the consumer and for travel agents, who have their own portal for information and reservations. Most important is provision of basic cruise information about itineraries, destinations served, departure ports, ships, accommodations, dining options, entertainment, activities, shore excursions and FAQs about how to pack, what to wear, how to pay, etc. Images of the cruise experience are still typically conveyed by photographs and text. However, some cruise lines have used innovative interactive formats to encourage site visitors to explore and play. For example, Royal Caribbean developed a fascinating application much like a video game to enable cruise shoppers to see the *Freedom of the Seas* ship before the vessel was even built. The site allowed visitors to scroll over a computer-generated image of the ship and click on links that showed how rooms would look or how activities could be enjoyed. Actors were matted over computer-animated elements of the ship to explain in greater depth about the experience. Similarly, Carnival created a Fun Ship Island section of the company's site that featured videos shot from the cruiser's perspective of, for example, the company's signature deck-top water slide and the rider enjoying the experience. A newer section of Carnival's site, Welcome to Funville, offers visitors games to play, commercials and videos to watch, and a variety of ways to customize the page for future visits such as by creating one's own fish to swim in Carnival's virtual aquarium.

- Web advertising. As the travel space on the internet becomes more connected, cruise lines continue to experiment with banner advertisements on popular websites to encourage click-through to the cruise line site. Behavioural-based online advertising allows cruise lines to target consumers engaging in a particular behaviour online (searching for cruises or broader holiday destinations, for example) and serve up an advertising message based on this observed behaviour. Cruise lines also engage in search engine optimization, key word bidding and sponsored advertising on search engines to ensure that consumer word searches (e.g. Caribbean cruise) return via a link to the cruise line's site, preferably high on the first page.

- Social media. Some of the leading communication platforms of today did not exist 2–5 years ago. This is especially true in the social media space. Cruise marketers have caught the social media wave. Many cruise lines now have pages on Facebook, where fans can post photos and videos, as well as view the photos, videos and stories posted by other cruisers – and posted by the cruise line itself. Some cruise lines use Twitter to send 'tweets' to followers about cruise events and promotions. Another social media site used by cruise lines is Flickr, where cruisers and cruise companies post photos for sharing. Cruise marketers also buy advertising on these social media outlets to encourage participants to visit the company's own site. Social media will continue to be a key marketing platform, not a passing fad.

- Broadcast marketing/product integration. Some cruise lines are using media buying power and entertainment connections to integrate their cruise brands into television programming and to develop dedicated content. An example of product integration is including Disney Cruise Line as a holiday experience for the families featured on the popular television programme *Extreme Make-Over Home Edition*. Although this product integration does not often offer deep product messaging opportunities, it does allow the brand to leverage a hit programme to extend topmost awareness. Combining that with dedicated content, such as a 1 hour special on Travel Channel, and the result is stronger message reach and depth during a programme viewing, when consumers are paying attention and not fast-forwarding through ads.

The Importance of Branding in the Cruise Industry

As cruising continues to evolve from the sales-based model that propelled many companies into the forefront of the industry, to a more market-centric model focused on creating and delivering a holiday experience desired by target customers, a marketing strategy that grows in importance is branding. A brand is, in essence, a set of meanings and associations in the consumer's mind about a company and its product (Kwortnik, 2011). Brands include company/product names, logos, designs, features, perceived quality, typical customers and similar concepts. Strong brands offer a promise to customers about the experience and how it will satisfy customers' needs and wants. Brands are vital in product categories where market offers are similar, the purchase process is difficult and consumers use the brand as a signal of how the product fits one's self-identity – all dimensions that describe the cruise industry.

Key to brand-based marketing strategy is that the brand resonates with target customers, and that marketing communications (as well as product design) are aligned with the brand promise. For example, Carnival Cruise Lines is, arguably, the power brand in the industry with its Fun Ships brand promise (Fig. 9.2). Created in 1973, the Fun Ships theme has changed messages with the times, but has never changed the basic promise that cruisers on Carnival ships will have a fun experience – one typified by excitement, novelty, games, dancing, drinking, parties and a vibrant atmosphere (Kwortnik, 2006). Such a brand promise was quite different from the staid image of cruising that had long characterized the industry. The Fun Ships brand pervades the company's decisions about ship design, which features 'entertainment architecture'; service delivery, with such features as towel animals in the ship's cabins, pool-side games and dancing waiters; and marketing messages, which focus on cruisers having a great time on their holiday. When Carnival has deviated from the brand message, such as the more sophisticated 'Million Ways to Have Fun' advertising campaign in the mid-2000s, the brand's marketers are quick to return to the core message, even by developing irreverent concepts (e.g. the world's largest beach ball promotion and a web video series featuring talking towel animals) (Kwortnik, 2006).

Fig. 9.2.   Cruise line brands and claims: Carnival, Royal Caribbean, Holland America, Norwegian Cruise Line (NCL).

In contrast, Carnival's two main competitors developed highly distinctive brands in early in 2000 to take some of the wind from Carnival's sails. The aforementioned 'Get Out There' brand campaign for Royal Caribbean defined a different version of fun for the mainstream cruiser – one that offered active adventure more than a party atmosphere. Key to the brand was a signature element on the ships – a rock climbing wall that traversed the back of one of the ship's funnels. For most of the past decade, Royal Caribbean's marketing communications revolved around this active adventure theme, showing cruisers enjoying physical activities both on and off the ships. The cruise line's new brand campaign, the 'Nation of Why Not', takes the theme in a different direction by suggesting 'why not be able to do X activity' (e.g. ride a zip line or play in a water park) on board a ship.

NCL, which was a distant third in market share in the contemporary cruise segment, opted for a particularly bold brand strategy when the company introduced 'Freestyle Cruising' in 2000. This brand promised cruisers an unstructured experience with no set dining times, unlike other cruises, which required diners to choose either early or late seating. The Freestyle concept is especially appealing to cruisers who are more comfortable with a resort-casual type of holiday. Despite operational challenges with implementing Freestyle, such as occasional queues during peak dining times, NCL has advanced the brand with the new *Epic* ship that features more dining and entertainment venues to increases cruisers' freedom of choice (Kwortnik and Thompson, 2009).

Compared with the contemporary cruise lines, brands in the premium segment, in particular Holland America, Celebrity and Princess, have found brand differentiation more difficult, though equally important, as each of these brands delivers an excellent product with similar features. Lacking distinguishing brand promises, consumers will use price as a main choice characteristic – a situation that will tend to depress prices and devalue the brand proposition. Both Celebrity and Princess have experimented with different brand promises and slogans since 2000, and continue to work towards a brand that will resonate with target customers and become the focus of marketing communications. Holland America, on the other hand, has successfully communicated an image of cruising tradition through the 'Signature of Excellence' brand campaign. The strategy focused on brand touch points that symbolized excellence in the cruise experience, such as upgraded bedding, more extensive wine lists, new restaurant tableware, new menus, fresh flowers and enhanced service training to reinforce personal attention.

Even though there are fewer cruise lines in 2010 than when the industry emerged from the passenger-shipping era in 1970, the emphasis on branding as a marketing strategy will no doubt continue in the future. Building brand equity by creating a clear brand identity that connects with target customers and fosters loyalty to the brand provides a line of defence against marketing challenges, such as the issues discussed next in the closing section of this chapter.

Cruise Marketing Challenges Today and Tomorrow

Cruising has faced a variety of challenges in the industry's relatively young life as a hospitality product. These include the transition to a leisure product, corporate consolidation of the 1990s, the fall-off in demand following the dot-com bust and the 9/11 tragedy at the turn of the century, and the more recent fuel-price spikes and economic recession that deflated prices and squeezed profit margins. Through it all, though, cruising has grown and delivered value to customers and shareholders.

The cruise industry will continue to face marketing challenges such as those described above – changing customer markets, misperceptions about cruising, converting non-cruisers to first-timers to satisfy growing cruise line capacity, and distribution-channel conflict between travel agents and direct marketing. However, cruise-marketing managers will surely face new challenges in developing and delivering on brand promises. These include:

- Emerging video platforms. The media world continues to be highly fragmented. In the area of television alone, the average household today has 118 TV channels to choose from compared with an average of 11 TV channels in 1980. And the adoption of digital video recording (DVR) devices makes time shifting more prevalent than live television viewing. In addition to the explosion of 'traditional' channel options, consumers have even more choice with the emergence of new video platforms like network websites and partnerships such as Hulu.com enable online viewing of content from a computer screen. All of this makes it increasingly difficult to leverage mass media to build reach and frequency, and will require better consumer research and greater focus from marketers to develop content that is relevant for these micro-media markets.

- Managing content on consumer generated sites. Social media is a double-edged sword. Although social-networking sites such as Facebook or community sites such as CruiseCritic provide another, more personal, channel for communicating brand messages, consumer-generated content may include negative messages about bad product experiences or simply negative attitudes toward the brand. Social media give consumers a public forum to express their opinions and rate service providers. The unanswered question for marketing managers is whether it is better to ignore online criticism or to confront it head on. Regardless, as social media gains strength as a means for communication between consumers and as an information source for cruise shoppers, marketers will need to develop a systematic approach for managing the channel.

- Home-based agents. Another channel that has changed is the travel trade. As more travel shopping moved online, traditional travel agencies have either disappeared or been forced to change business models. One result of this dynamic is the shift of agents to home-based operations. Whereas in the past, home-based agents were often low-volume producers who just dabbled in travel sales, a new breed of professional home-based agents has captured a growing share of travel sales. Reaching these independent agents efficiently is problematic, especially having BDMs call on agents. While some cruise lines do call on home-based agents, it will be necessary to develop new, more efficient marketing communications and sales-support systems for this channel.

- Brand innovation – product and message. Cruise lines have successfully redefined the cruise experience from transportation to leisure holiday. In the 21st century, cruise lines have pushed the experience line even further, with ever-larger ships with more fantastic entertainment, activities and amenities. The result is ships that are floating theme parks, resorts, showplaces, casinos, shopping centres and restaurant complexes, rolled into one. Each new innovation sets the bar higher for the next generation of ship and challenges cruise marketers to create a compelling message that will cut through the clutter. As cruise lines that compete within market segments offer more similar products, the pressure will be on the brand to stand apart.

If the past is any indication of the future, cruise line marketing 40 years from now will look dramatically different from the way it looks today. Perhaps the travel agent channel will be supplanted by consumer-direct sales. Perhaps social media will dominate marketing communications. Perhaps brand messaging will no longer be slow-changing commercials and websites, but will be co-created live, in real time, by on-board marketing managers and cruisers. Regardless of the dynamics, cruise marketing will surely offer an exciting journey for the industry's future communications professionals.

Note

[1]It is notable that the industry's main trade association, CLIA, was born in 1975 out of a predecessor organization, International Passenger Shipping Association. The name change was a direct reflection of the new marketing focus on leisure cruising as opposed to the shipping of passengers.

References

CLIA (2005) *Cruise Thirty*. Cruise Lines International Association, New York.

CLIA (2008) *2008 Cruise Market Profile Study*. Available at: http://www.cruising.org/sites/default/files/pressroom/Market_Profile_2008.pdf (accessed 16 June 2010).

CLIA (2009) *2010 Cruise Industry Media Update*. Available at: www.cruising.org/pressroom-research/2010-cruise-industry-media-update (accessed 16 June 2010).

CLIA (2010) *2010 CLIA Cruise Market Overview*. Available at: www.cruising.org/sites/default/files/misc/2010FINALOV.pdf (accessed 16 June 2010).

Dickinson, B. and Vladimir, A. (2008) *Selling the Sea: An Inside Look at the Cruise Industry*, 2nd ed. John Wiley & Sons, Hoboken, New Jersey.

Kwortnik, R.J. (2006) Carnival Cruise Lines: Burnishing the Brand. *Cornell Hotel and Restaurant Administration Quarterly* 47 (August), 286-300.

Kwortnik, R.J. (2008) Shipscape Influence on the Leisure Cruise Experience. *International Journal of Culture, Tourism, and Hospitality Research*, 2(4) 289-311.

Kwortnik, R.J. (2011) Building and Managing Your Brand. In: Sturman, M.C., Corgel, J.B. and Verma, R. (eds.) *The Cornell School of Hotel Administration on Hospitality*. John Wiley & Sons, Hoboken, New Jersey, pp. 388-404.

Kwortnik, R.J. and Thompson, G.M. (2009) Unifying Service Marketing and Operations with Service Experience Management. *Journal of Service Research* 11(4), 389-406.

Mancini, M. (2004) *Cruising: A Guide to the Cruise Industry*, 2nd ed. Thomson Learning, Clifton Park, New York.

Ward, D. (2009) *Complete Guide to Cruising & Cruise Ships 2009*, 18th ed. Berlitz, London

10   Pricing and Revenue Management for Cruises

Michael Vogel

Introduction

Over two decades ago, Mentzer (1989, p. 43) noted that

> In the past, a cruise ship journey was a relatively unique luxury service patronized only by the very wealthy, who were relatively insensitive to small differences in pricing. [… However,] cruise ship travel is evolving from a one-of-a-kind product into a mass commodity. The anticipated overcapacity in cruise ships, especially in the Caribbean, will force cruise operators to pay increasing attention to the details of fare-setting with an eye toward attaining the optimal financial return.

This quote provides the justification for a chapter on cruise pricing and on the management of cruise line revenue in the present book. Cruises may still not be commodities in the strict sense of the term, yet Mentzer was right with his prediction, in that declining market growth rates and signs of market satiation, especially in North America, have been fuelling price competition among cruise lines for new and existing customers. The continuous arrival of ever larger new builds in the market is exacerbating the pressure on cruise fares. In response, cruise lines have been fine-tuning their price models and developing sophisticated computer-based information, decision-making and communication systems enabling them to implement thousands of price adjustments per day, subject to changes in demand and ship occupancy.

The aim of this chapter is to explain the economic principles of pricing and revenue management as applied in the cruise sector in an accessible, non-technical way. The chapter is divided into two main sections. The first one addresses aspects of cruise brochure pricing, including the concept of economic value and its estimation; segmented pricing; the role of customer information; and the influence of costs on prices. Since brochure prices are set long before the departure of a cruise and under significant uncertainty about the future demand, competition and costs, they can only be approximations of the prices that would be set if perfect information were available.

For this reason, many cruise lines have departed from the model of static brochure prices and instead adopted dynamic prices, which are adjusted during the booking period as more information becomes available. Dynamic pricing is an instrument of revenue management, which is the focus of the second main section. This section also looks at other revenue management approaches, at the management of on-board revenue and at the important influence of on-board revenue on cruise fares.

Brochure Pricing

In his early contribution to the literature on cruise pricing, Mentzer (1989) used multiple regression analysis to explore the influence of different ship and itinerary-specific variables on cruise brochure prices. On the basis of a sample of 605 cruises in all parts of the world, he found that:

- The price of a cruise was increasing with the ratio of crew members to passengers. On cruise ships for 1000 passengers, each additional crew member was associated with a price increase of US$2.67. On smaller ships for 100 passengers, each additional crew member warranted a fare increase of US$26.69.
- A large dining room able to hold all passengers at once was worth US$490.10 more than a dining room of only half that size.
- Ticket prices of cruise ships flying flags of convenience were lower than those of ships registered in the USA.
- Shorter cruises and older ships led to lower prices, whereas seasons, ship size, speed or successfully passed US coast guard health inspections seemed to have no impact.

One may be tempted to blame the costs of a higher crew ratio, of a larger dining room, of a longer cruise etc. for the higher cruise prices. However, this view is misleading. If high crew ratios, large dining rooms and long cruises had only been cost drivers without adding value, the passengers would not have been willing to pay higher prices. The value of a higher crew ratio consists of a better service. The value of a dining room with enough seating capacity lies in the freedom it offers to all passengers to have dinner whenever they want. And the value of a longer cruise may be seen in the additional or more remote destinations that can be visited or in the greater emotional distance from everyday life it creates. As a general rule, value to the customer and not cost should determine prices. If costs are higher than that which customers are willing to pay, raising prices to a 'cost-covering' level would only kill demand and boost costs per remaining passenger. Products must be worth their price.

Price and economic value

The kind of value that is relevant for pricing is the *economic value* of a product. Economic value arises from comparison and is defined as 'the price of the customer's best alternative (called the reference value) plus the value of whatever differentiates the offering from the alternative (called the differentiation value)' (Nagle and Holden, 2002, p. 75; original emphasis removed). In Mentzer's study, for instance, the passengers' willingness to pay US$490.10 extra for a large dining room on a cruise ship represents a differentiation value.

Thus, for the brochure pricing of a cruise, marketing or product managers need to estimate the economic value that their planned cruise product will offer to their target customers. This comprises four steps. In a first step, the price of another cruise, which the target customers consider the best alternative, is selected as the reference value. Market research can provide the necessary information about the customers' perception of alternatives. In a second step, differences in hardware, service, itinerary, on-board entertainment etc. between the two cruises are identified and documented. In the third step, the (positive or negative) value to the target customers of each differentiating factor is determined through market research. The statistical method of conjoint analysis is often used for this purpose. In the fourth and final step, the reference value and the various differentiation values are added up to yield the economic value.

Ideally, this economic value estimation is repeated for every major market segment, which is to be targeted with the cruise product. Segment-specific value estimates can provide clues as to how different cabin types (inside, outside, balcony, suite etc.) should be priced. Moreover, as cruise lines have significant capacities to fill, and any pricing strategy needs to take this into account, it is not enough to have an idea of the economic value that a particular cabin on a particular cruise may represent to different target customers. Also the size of each segment must be estimated, as the following example will show.

An example of applied economic value estimation

The new cruise ship X will be introduced to the market under a new brand in next year's summer season. The product manager has asked a market research firm to estimate the economic value to a passenger of a particular cabin type, double occupancy, on a specific Baltic itinerary. She has also asked the firm to estimate the market potential of each segment. The market researchers return the following results per cruise day (Tables 10.1, 10.2).

This information, combined with market potential estimates, is depicted in Fig. 10.1 as economic value profile (Nagle and Holden, 2002).

Figure 10.1 shows that the economic value of a cruise day to the first group of target customers is higher than to the second group and that the lower economic value is associated with a much larger market potential. Note that to both groups the economic value of a cruise day is US$205 or more. The product manager now has to decide which price should be printed in the brochure. If the higher price is chosen, fewer cruises can be sold, since US$235 per passenger cruise day may be prohibitive for the second group. If the market potential of the first group is sufficiently large in relation to the ship's capacity, the higher price will still be appropriate. On the other hand, if the capacity of ship X is large in relation to the market potential of the first group and/or if the passengers of the first group need an extra incentive to switch from ship A to the new ship X, the lower price should be chosen.

Table 10.1. Economic value analysis for a first target segment.

Target segment	Couples aged 55+ seeking romantic and relaxing holidays		
Best alternative	Ship A		
	Reference value		US$250
Differentiation	Ship X and its brand are unknown	−US$40	
	Ship X is new	+US$15	
	Ship X has more speciality restaurants	+US$10	
	Differentiation value		−US$15
Result	Economic value		US$235

Table 10.2. Economic value analysis for a second target segment.

Target segment	Groups of friends aged 55+, active, feeling young at heart		
Best alternative	Ship B		
	Reference value		US$190
Differentiation	Ship X and its brand are unknown	−US$12	
	Ship X has state-of-the-art facilities	+US$12	
	Ship X offers a wider range of activities	+US$15	
	Differentiation value		+US$15
Result	Economic value		US$205

Economic value per passenger and cruise day

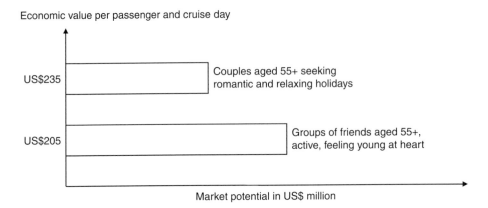

Fig. 10.1. Economic value profile for ship X.

As the cost of an occupied cabin does not depend on who stays in it (passengers of the first or second target segment), it is enough to compare expected revenues in order to make the pricing decision. Whichever price leads to a higher expected revenue is the better one. Let $s(US\$235)$ denote the number of cabins that are expected to be sold if the ticket price per cruise day equals US\$235. The expected revenue is then given by $US\$235 \times s(US\$235)$. So if $US\$235 \times s(US\$235) > US\$205 \times s(US\$205)$, the higher price can be expected to maximize revenue and is therefore preferable. Otherwise, the lower price represents the better choice.

Segmented pricing

In the above example, a combination of both prices is also possible. For example, the lower price could be reserved exclusively for groups of friends aged 55+ that comprise at least three persons booking together. The practice of offering the same product to different customers at different prices is called price discrimination or segmented pricing. If potential buyers value the same product differently, segmented pricing is generally superior to a single-price strategy (see Vogel, 2009a for a discussion of Carnival and Royal Caribbean's segmented pricing strategies), provided that effective rate fences between the segments

are established. With a brochure price of US\$235 per cruise day and a group discount of US\$30 per cruise day and person, the economic potential of both segments in the above example can be fully exploited.

In cruise brochures, it is common to find a variety of segment-specific prices. For children in the company of their parents, cruises are offered for less to make them more attractive for the parents. Groups with a defined minimum size have access to special group rates. Repeat cruisers may qualify for loyalty discounts. Customers booking a fly-cruise package are likely to pay less than those who purchase the flight and the cruise separately. Further examples of segmented pricing include the negotiated fares for participants of conferences taking place on board and the special rates for travel agents undertaking a familiarization cruise.

A particularly important case of segmented pricing in cruise brochures is seasonal pricing. Customers are segmented on the basis of their departure dates, as the demand for cruises is time-variable. Holiday times in the source markets, special events in the cruise destinations, weather conditions and other factors determine the variability of cruise demand. The segments are often referred to as high season, shoulder season, low season or A/B/C/D/E seasons. Time-variable demand implies a time-variable economic valuation of cruises by their passengers. In terms of the economic value concept, one can say that many cruisers attribute a positive differentiation value to a Mediterranean cruise during the warm summer months compared with one in stormy autumn. They are therefore willing to pay more for the summer cruise.

In the cruise sector, time-variable demand meets invariable supply. Since cruises cannot be stored, supply equals fixed capacity at any given moment. Cruise ship capacity is expressed in available passenger cruise days (APCD) per year. US cruise lines typically calculate their APCD by multiplying the number of cabins on a ship by two, assuming double occupancy, and by the number of cruise days per year. In Europe, it has been more common to base the APCD calculation on the actual number of lower berths. In either case, APCD is largely fixed for a given cruise ship.

The way cruise lines respond to time-variable demand is by trying to set their prices at the highest level that still maintains full occupancy. High prices in the high season serve a double purpose: they skim the passengers' greater willingness to pay and shift part of the demand to less popular and less expensive cruising periods. Seasonal pricing thus leads to a more even distribution of demand across the year, reducing cruise lines' capacity requirements and capacity costs in the high seasons, enhancing their occupancy rates in the low seasons, and thus contributing significantly to more affordable cruises.

Economic value and information

The economic value concept makes two fundamental assumptions: (i) alternatives are available and potential buyers are aware of them and their prices; (ii) potential buyers are able to identify and evaluate the differences between the alternative offerings. In the cruise sector, the variety of products has increased enormously over the past decades. For practically any cruise line, cruise ship and itinerary, alternatives are available and potential buyers can find information about them on the internet or in travel agencies.

Thus assumption (i) can be considered fulfilled. With assumption (ii), however, the situation is less clear. The variety of available cruise products and the large number of product features make it difficult, especially for inexperienced cruisers, to find out what the relevant differences between the alternative offers are. Moreover, brochures and advertisements present all cruises as unique and of outstanding value, clouding the differences between them and rendering comparisons even more difficult. One consequence is that differentiation values estimated by market research often deviate from the price differentials that are actually realized in the market. Another consequence of lacking market transparency is the risk that even highly differentiated cruise products may be drawn into price battles if their distinguishing features are not communicated properly or credibly. Since customers evaluate offers on the basis of the information they are given, it follows that any pricing strategy must be supported by a consistent communication strategy.

Pricing and costs

So far, cost as a factor influencing cruise prices has only been mentioned in passing. This has to do with the particular cost structure of cruises: cruising is effectively a fixed-cost business, and even more so as the departure date of a cruise approaches. Two weeks before departure, the only costs that will vary with the number of passengers are the food cost and passenger-based port and handling fees. Sales commissions payable to travel agencies are also variable but tend to be excluded from cost considerations, since cruise lines regard net revenue (sales minus commission payments and other costs of revenue) as their relevant revenue. All other costs are fixed: the ship is there anyway, causing significant operating, maintenance and financing costs. Crew and staff numbers cannot be adjusted at short notice. And overhead costs for product development, marketing, administration etc. have already incurred and cannot be revoked.

A pricing approach, which was widely used in the hospitality and cruise sectors at least until the early 1990s, is the so-called cost-plus pricing (Ladany and Arbel, 1991). Its underlying idea is that prices should cover costs and earn the producer a reasonable profit. So prices are set equal to the sum of all costs directly and indirectly attributable to individual passengers, plus a profit margin. This approach, however, is flawed for several reasons. First of all, a cost-based pricing ignores economic value and therefore ultimately the potential customer. Second, the allocation of fixed costs to individual passengers involves an assumption as to the total number of passengers. The total number of passengers, in turn, is influenced by the price, which, at this stage of the calculation, is unknown. Thus, cost-plus pricing is based on a logical error. Third, if cruise demand is expected to be strong and occupancy high, the total cost share allocated to each individual cruise passenger will be low, resulting in a particularly low price in a market situation that actually calls for high prices. Thus 'Cost-plus pricing leads to overpricing in weak markets and underpricing in strong ones – exactly the opposite direction of a prudent strategy' (Nagle and Holden, 2002, p. 3).

So how should costs influence prices? While the upper limit to the price of a cruise is the economic value that the cruise represents to a passenger, the lower limit is given by the variable (or, more precisely, the marginal) cost of this passenger. Charging a price that does not even cover the variable cost would mean that the cruise line is economically worse off with every additional passenger. Given the very low variable costs of cruises, there is a tremendous bandwidth within which cruise prices can be set.

Revenue (or Yield) Management

While the costs of a cruise hardly vary with occupancy, net revenue does. Every additional passenger means substantial additional revenue for a cruise line. The main sources of cruise revenue are ticket sales, passenger transportation to and from the ships, on-board sales, cancellation fees, as well as sales of insurance and of pre- and post-tours. Figure 10.2 gives an overview of the main revenue and cost components of a cruise business.

Economically speaking, not every passenger is equally attractive for a cruise line. Some passengers book more expensive cabins than others, spend more in the on-board casino, in the bars or on shore excursions. Yet, to simplify matters, assume for the moment that every passenger contributes exactly the same amount to cruise line net revenue. The resulting stylized revenue and cost structure is depicted by Fig. 10.3.

By definition, fixed costs are independent of the ship's occupancy. The fixed cost curve is therefore horizontal. Variable costs are added to fixed costs to obtain total costs. Without any passengers, no variable costs incur, and hence fixed costs equal total costs. On a fully booked ship, on the other hand, variable costs might represent around 10% of total costs. Revenues are depicted by a relatively steep upward-sloping straight line, reflecting the assumption of constant net revenue per passenger. At full occupancy, the net revenue curve is well above the total cost curve. The vertical distance between both curves represents profit. At low occupancy levels, however, total costs exceed net revenues by far, indicating a loss. The point where both curves intersect marks the break-even occupancy rate.

The most important message of Fig. 10.3 is that due to the high fixed costs, cruise line profits and losses depend crucially on net revenue. Maximizing profits is therefore largely equivalent to maximizing net revenue, which is why the function of revenue management is so central for cruise lines. Moreover, since revenue is so closely tied to passenger numbers, Fig. 10.3 emphasizes the importance of selling even the last cabin on a cruise ship: 70–90% of the cruise fare contributes to fixed cost coverage and profit.

It was mentioned earlier that brochure prices are set up to two years before the

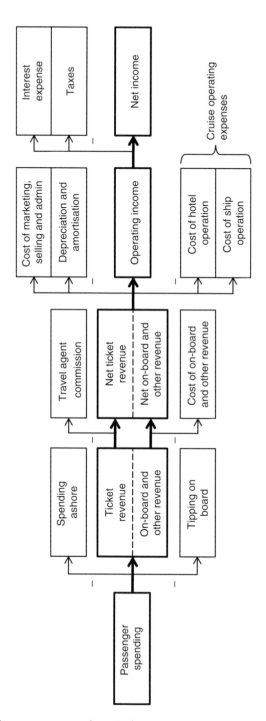

Fig. 10.2. Revenue and cost components of a cruise business.

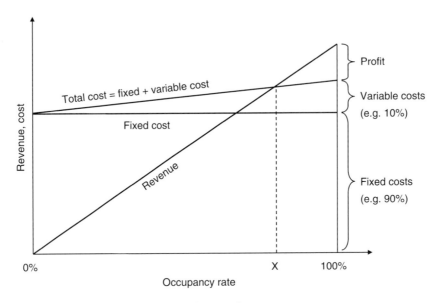

Fig. 10.3. Stylized revenue and cost structure of a cruise business.

departure date of a cruise. The reason is that many cruise lines want to give their customers at least 18 months time to book their cruise. Before the beginning of a booking period, the brochures need to be produced and distributed to travel agencies, product data entered into the reservation systems, and travel agents informed and trained. And before all this, the products must be designed, itineraries planned, services contracted, costs computed and prices calculated (see Papathanassis, Chapter 6, this volume).

Two years are a long time during which much can happen. Cruise regions may become more or less fashionable, their political or security situation may change, currency exchange rates can make them more or less expensive etc. At best, brochure prices are based on informed expectations about the future developments of demand, competition and costs, but they are unlikely to anticipate all of these developments correctly years in advance. Therefore, many cruise lines have introduced systems of dynamic pricing, either to complement or to replace their static brochure prices. Dynamic pricing is a revenue or yield management instrument.

Revenue management and yield management are technically equivalent, since revenue and yield only differ by a (largely) constant factor, namely capacity. This can be shown as follows:

$$\text{revenue} = \text{price per diem} \times \text{passenger cruise days sold}$$

$$= \text{price per diem} \times \text{occupancy rate} \times \text{capacity}$$

$$\Leftrightarrow \text{revenue/capacity} = \text{price per diem} \times \text{occupancy rate}$$

$$= \text{yield}$$

Hence yield can be expressed as revenue per unit of available capacity or as price multiplied by the occupancy rate. It can be calculated for a particular cabin type, itinerary, ship or even an entire cruise line. With constant capacity, maximizing yield means maximizing revenue.

According to Kimes (2000), revenue management is applied most effectively if there is relatively fixed capacity, high fixed cost, low variable cost, perishable inventory and time-variable but predictable demand. All of these conditions apply to cruises.

Revenue management is a forward-looking activity with the objective of maximizing future revenues. Since the future is unknown, hypotheses guide much of the revenue managers' decisions. These hypotheses are largely derived from historical booking data through statistical analyses, assuming that the past has something to say about the future.

Booking curve

A widely employed tool of revenue management, which makes use of historical data, is the booking curve. It is simply the plot of cumulative bookings or occupancy over the booking period. Figure 10.4 depicts the booking curve for a hypothetical cruise. It differs from the booking curve in Fig. 1.2 (Vogel and Oschmann, Chapter 1, this volume) in that it is cumulative. The cruise is opened for sale at time S, for instance 18 months before departure. During a first phase, bookings come in quickly from customers who know exactly which cabins they want, and who book early to secure them. These tend to be loyal repeat buyers. The curve slopes steeply upwards, indicating several new bookings per day. In a second phase, the booking curve becomes flatter as the best cabins have been taken and there is no more need for customers to decide quickly. The final phase of the booking period is again marked by a rise in

bookings per day and in the booking curve. Usually this is when the undecided realize they have to make up their mind if they want to go on a cruise at all, and the bargain hunters look for last minute deals.

Booking curves may also take very different shapes than the one in Fig. 10.4. It is important to understand what drives bookings over time in order to identify the respective revenue-maximizing booking curve. By means of historical booking data, statistical demand estimation and mathematical optimization, approximations of optimal, i.e. revenue-maximizing, booking curves can be derived. The purpose of such quasi-ideal booking curves is to provide a benchmark for operational revenue management.

Dynamic pricing

Suppose that Fig. 10.4 represents the planned (possibly quasi-optimal) bookings. It is then the revenue manager's job to ensure that actual bookings follow the time path of planned bookings sufficiently closely, meaning that the actual booking curve should stay within a defined tolerance interval around the planned booking curve. In Fig. 10.5, the tolerance interval is indicated by the shaded area, which is bounded from above and below.

As long as actual bookings stay inside the tolerance interval, there is no need for the revenue manager to act. However, at point A in Fig. 10.5, the actual booking curve crosses the upper threshold of the tolerance interval. This means that demand for the cruise is stronger than anticipated. Without an intervention, actual bookings might follow the steep dashed line, and the cruise would already be booked out halfway through the booking period. What looks like a good thing turns out to be an opportunity loss on closer inspection. By filling its ship more quickly, the cruise line gains nothing, but foregoes the opportunity of fully capturing the customers' willingness to pay. To benefit economically from the unexpectedly strong demand, the cruise line raises the price. The price increase is depicted in Fig. 10.5 below the booking curve. It reduces

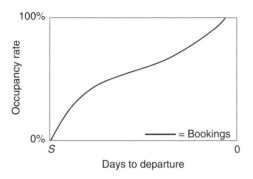

Fig. 10.4. Cumulative booking curve of a hypothetical cruise.

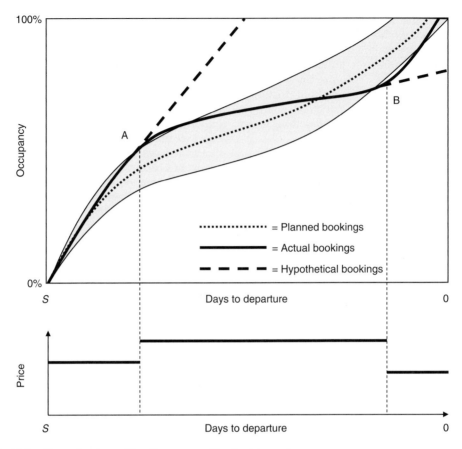

Fig. 10.5. Planned and actual booking curves with price interventions.

the demand for the cruise, inducing a decline in the number of bookings per day. The actual booking curve levels off and returns into the tolerance interval.

At point B, the booking curve crosses the lower threshold. If no countermeasures are taken by the revenue manager, at the current booking rate the cruise will not be fully sold by the end of the booking period. Therefore, potential customers must be given an additional incentive to book: a price discount. This is the moment the bargain hunters have been waiting for, and quickly they book the remaining empty cabins.

In practice, dynamic pricing is a highly automated process. Computerized pricing systems operate on the basis of algorithms and decision rules. Only the decision

parameters are set by the revenue manager, whilst the monitoring of actual bookings, their comparison with the relevant thresholds, the adjustment of prices and their communication to distribution partners and buyers is taken care of by machines. This allows cruise lines to manage simultaneously thousands of prices relating to different cabin types on different ships sailing different itineraries and being offered in different source markets.

Other revenue management approaches

Dynamic pricing can be a very effective tool for managing ticket revenue. Its downside is, however, that it cultivates a passenger fixation on price rather than value. Cruises are fairly complex products, which are not easily explained. The economic value concept emphasizes the role of value differentials, but differences between two cruises or ships are hard to communicate, and even more so in an emotionally appealing way, if potential customers have been sensitized for price differentials. It is therefore in the cruise sector's own best interest not to rely on price-centred revenue management but rather make full use of value-centred approaches.

Value-centred revenue management (or 'silent' yield management; see Papathanassis, Chapter 6, this volume) tries to stabilize prices by responding to time-variable demand with the inclusion or exclusion of selected product features. For instance, to generate additional bookings for certain departure dates, cruise lines can tempt potential customers with cabin upgrades, vouchers for restaurants or the spa on board, with fruit and champagne served in the cabin, free internet access or US$100 on-board credit per person. Each of these extras represents a differentiation value if communicated properly, and makes the cruise better value for money. For the cruise line, the marginal cost of such offers is typically much smaller than the value they represent to passengers. In periods of weak demand when ship occupancy is low, upgrading passengers costs nothing at all if the more expensive cabin category is not fully booked anyway.

A further, more strategic approach to revenue management that avoids turning customers into keen bargain-hunters is based on geographical segmentation. Experience shows that different geographical markets display quite different demand characteristics and booking patterns, which may reflect the local culture, the climate, institutional factors such as school holidays or the competitive situation. Internationally operating cruise lines can anticipate these differences in their pricing and capacity allocation strategies. Two examples (based on Vogel, 2009a):

- A cruise line can sell its products in two markets, A and B. Market A is able to absorb 60–70% of its capacity at very good prices and the remaining capacity with a significant discount. In market B, the same products can only be sold at the discounted price of market A (competition might be tougher in market B, or the cruise products might not be well adapted to local preferences, or the currency exchange rate might be unfavourable). Under these conditions, it makes sense for the cruise line not to discount in market A, but to use market B for 'capacity dumping'. This way, the cruise line preserves its pricing image in market A, avoids the risk of habituating passengers in market A to discounting, develops its presence in market B and retains full flexibility to react to fluctuations in demand in either market.

- A cruise line can sell its products in two markets, C and D. In market C, customers book early, whereas in market D, demand sets in only 8 weeks before departure. Market D is only small but offers very high prices for balcony cabins. Market C is much larger, yet the customers' willingness to pay is not as high. One option for the cruise line is to offer the same cabins for the same prices in both markets. But one price for two heterogeneous markets will not do: a high price will deter potential passengers in market C, and a lower price will leave no cabins for market D. Instead, the cruise line needs to protect a certain allotment of balcony cabins for the later-booking market D by making them unavailable for market C in the reservation system. In case the demand from market D turns out weaker than expected, and not all protected balcony cabins can be sold at the high price, the remaining cabins can still be offered at the lower price in market C.

Managing on-board revenue

Revenue management in the cruise sector is not limited to the management of ticket revenue. At Carnival Corporation, net on-board revenue contributed 22% to total net revenue in 2010. And at Royal Caribbean Cruises, this share amounted to 26%. While these percentages may not look particularly impressive, a comparison of the companies' net on-board revenues with their operating profits surely does. In 2010, Carnival's net on-board revenue exceeded its operating profit by 12%, and at Royal Caribbean, net on-board revenue was even 69% higher than its operating profit (Carnival, 2011; RCL, 2011; author's calculations). What does this mean? It means that even though net on-board revenue only represents about a quarter of total net revenue, the margins earned on board pay for the companies' entire operating profits and also contribute to the coverage of their fixed costs.

There are many ways, some very sophisticated and subtle, in which cruise lines influence their passengers' spending behaviour once they have booked a cruise. The most important incentive for passengers to spend money is an attractive offer. Over the past 30 years, the cruise sector has become very proficient in this domain. It is the reason why cruise ships today look the way they do. Most of them have been designed to accommodate a large number of revenue-generating businesses and to capture a maximum share of the passengers' wallets.

The layout of decks and staircases ensures that passengers pass the shopping area and casinos several times a day. To increase passenger traffic further in shopping areas, small events and presentations may be held there. Bars and à la carte restaurants are frequently located near the ship's theatre to attract passengers after the end of a show. Shore excursions, art auctions, spa and beauty treatments etc. are advertised round the clock on the in-cabin entertainment system as well as on screens in public areas. Shops, casinos, photo service, art auctions, beauty parlour, shore excursions etc. are either organized as separate businesses, which are operated by concessionaires, or they are run as profit centres by the cruise line itself.

Their power has allowed some cruise lines even to extend their revenue generating networks to certain destinations, where they recommend particular shops to their passengers in order to receive 'recommendation fees' or commission payments.

To facilitate payments on board and to prevent theft and fraud, cashless on-board expense accounts are commonly used. Equally important, however, are their functions to lower the passengers' emotional barriers to spending money and to provide statistical data on purchasing behaviour. Data collection is particularly simple on cruise ships where all passengers are uniquely identifiable and where all points of sale are under cruise line control. By matching booking data to spending data for millions of passengers and analysing the resulting enormous dataset, cruise lines learn more about their customers than almost any other kind of business. Insights thus gained are fed back into the processes of product development, ship design, service delivery and, of course, into the refinement of revenue management.

Managing cruise line revenue holistically

Even though operationally, ticket revenue and on-board revenue are managed separately, there is a close relationship between them, which cruise lines know very well: if ticket prices are set too high and ship occupancy rates turn out low, on-board revenue is also low. On the other hand, if ticket prices are set too low, so that customers must be turned away, ship occupancy rates, as well as on-board revenue, are high. In other words, overpricing is punished twice, whereas underpricing is punished only once. This asymmetric relationship induces especially those cruise lines that generate a large share of their net revenue on board to price their cruise tickets rather more than less aggressively. It is therefore no surprise that over the last 10 years, the occupancy rates of Carnival and Royal Caribbean's cruise ship fleets never fell below 105% (Carnival and RCL's annual reports of 2001–2010) despite the terrorist attacks of 9/11 and the financial crisis of 2008/2009.

Of more strategic significance is another relationship between ticket revenue and on-board revenue. At least since 2001, three tendencies have been identifiable in Carnival and Royal Caribbean's annual reports: (i) real ticket prices tend to decline; (ii) ticket prices are no longer cost-covering; and (iii) net on-board revenue is outgrowing ticket revenue (Vogel, 2009b, 2011). These three stylized facts suggest that a gradual shift has been taking place in the major cruise companies' business models, a shift towards a greater reliance on on-board revenue for business success. As pointed out earlier, operating profits do not come from operating cruises but from using cruises as a platform for selling ancillary products. Just as McDonald's is said not to be in the hamburger business but in the cola and fries business because this is where their profits come from, the big cruise lines can be said to be in the shopping, casino and shore excursion business, rather than in the passenger shipping business.

The reason for this development seems to lie in the increasing commoditization of cruises, just as Mentzer predicted in his quote at the outset of this chapter. Strictly speaking, commodities are standardized goods without any qualitative differentiation. Commodity buyers base their purchasing decision only on price. Clearly, cruises are no commodities, but mainstream cruise products all have close substitutes of which the more experienced cruisers are aware. According to the economic value concept, if the differentiation value of a cruise is close to zero, the only selling argument that remains is a lower price. Hence competition on the market for mainstream cruises is becoming more and more price driven.

Fortunately for the cruise lines, the cruise sector consists of two markets, not one. The second market is much less competitive because it consists of many small monopolies: it is the market for the goods and services offered to passengers. With the booking of a cruise, passengers turn into a captive clientele and, especially after embarkation, have little other choice than to spend their money with the only supplier there is: their cruise line and its partners.

Each ship represents a fragment of the 'on-board market' and is monopolized by the respective cruise line. Since monopolists can charge higher prices and earn higher margins than suppliers facing competition, the cruise lines' real profit zone is on board. Most passengers are willing to pay higher prices than ashore, although occasional angry messages on internet forums show that this is not always the case.

Through the passengers' on-board spending, their value to the cruise lines increases. In order to capture more of this value, cruise lines attract additional passengers by subsidizing ticket prices with the net on-board revenue they expect to earn. In doing so, they exploit the passengers' low price elasticity of demand on board to compensate their more price elastic demand for cruise tickets. Over time, this process has driven down ticket prices to levels where they are no longer cost-covering (see the above stylized fact (ii)). Thus, as Klein (2005) points out, 'The cruise fare is the "loss leader" while on-board revenue generates sizeable profits' (p. 127). As shown in Vogel (2011), the practice of subsidizing ticket prices with expected net on-board revenue is an important, if not the most important, driver of cruise sector growth.

Concluding Remarks

This chapter touches but the tip of the iceberg of cruise pricing. This is related both to the limited length of a book chapter and the large number of cruise brands and products, all of which require their own specific pricing solutions. Price is part of the marketing mix and needs to match the respective product, promotion and distribution strategies. All-inclusive cruises where all extras and tips are calculated into the brochure prices may work in the luxury segment, whilst in the budget segment the opposite makes more sense. Market entry strategies may require aggressive pricing, potentially triggering defensive reactions from the established players and leading to price wars. Large, internationally active multi-ship cruise lines are confronted with very different pricing challenges than single-ship cruise companies serving a local market only.

However, despite these differences, there is a common ticket price trend, and it points downwards. In real terms, cruise products today cost less per cruise day than they used to (see Fig. 1.1 in Vogel and Oschmann, Chapter 1, this volume). This trend has permitted the cruise sector to expand its base of actual and potential customers enormously and enabled it to grow substantially. Growth, in turn, has driven down costs through scale effects and opened up further potential for ticket price cuts. Even unprofitably low ticket prices have become economically acceptable, as long as the overall cruise ship economics, including the on-board business, work out fine.

It would be an oversimplification to reduce the cruise sector's growth story to a pricing story. Cruising has also benefitted greatly from macro social developments (Vogel and Oschmann, Chapter 1, this volume) and from very successful product diversification (Spiegel, Chapter 12, this volume). Yet without its sophisticated pricing and revenue management practices, the cruise sector would not have evolved to what it is now. Mentzer's (1989) prediction is probably still valid: 'cruise ship travel is evolving from a one-of-a-kind product into a mass commodity. The anticipated overcapacity in cruise ships [...] will force cruise operators to pay increasing attention to the details of fare-setting with an eye toward attaining the optimal financial return' (p. 43).

References

Carnival (2011) *2010 Annual Report*. Carnival Corporation & plc, Miami, Florida.

Kimes, S.E. (2000) A strategic approach to yield management. In: Ingold, A., McMahon-Beattie, U. and Yeoman, I. (eds) *Yield Management. Strategies for the Service Industries*, 2nd edn. Continuum, London, pp. 3–14.

Klein, R.A. (2005) *Cruise Ship Squeeze: The New Pirates of the Seven Seas*. New Society Publishers, Gabriola Island.

Ladany, S.P. and Arbel, A. (1991) Optimal cruise-liner cabin pricing policy. *European Journal of Operational Research* 55(2), 136–147.

Mentzer, M.S. (1989) Factors affecting cruise ship fares. *Transportation Journal* 29(1), 38–43.

Nagle, T.T. and Holden, R.K. (2002) *The Strategy and Tactics of Pricing*, 3rd edn. Prentice Hall, Upper Saddle River, New Jersey.

RCL (2011) *2010 Annual Report*. Royal Caribbean Cruises Ltd, Miami, Florida.

Vogel, M. (2009a) The economics of U.S. cruise companies' European brand strategies. *Tourism Economic* 15(4), 735–751.

Vogel, M. (2009b) Onboard revenue: the secret of the cruise industry's success? In: Papathanassis, A. (ed.) *Cruise Sector Growth*. Gabler, Wiesbaden, pp. 3–15.

Vogel, M. (2011) Monopolies at sea: the role of onboard sales for the cruise industry's growth and profitability. In: Matias, A., Nijkamp, P. and Sarmento, M. (eds) *Tourism Economics: Impact Analysis*. Physica, Heidelberg, p. 211–229.

11   Cruise Packages

Grenville Cartledge

Introduction

Even including a few challenging years, the cruise industry has seen phenomenal overall growth since the late 1970s. Admittedly, throughout this time there has been much consolidation aligned with smaller operator casualties; however, the year-on-year patterns for the industry have shown consistently better growth rates than the tourism industry generally, and the industry continues to flourish. Its success is related to the attractive product offering and its relative value compared with land-based resort holiday options. Furthermore, it is related to a number of complementary factors driving the passenger carry numbers.

Yet the cruise industry's growth is largely supply-driven, rather than demand-led, in spite of what many within the industry may say. It is this supply paradigm on which the present chapter will focus. Its guiding question is how tour operators, through cruise packages and fly cruise options, have significantly influenced the development of the industry. It will look to take into account some of the principal factors affecting cruise industry and tour operator executives when planning operations, acquisition and deployment of vessels, product offering and fleet composition. Real life examples will be used whenever possible as reference points or short case studies.

Early Days of the Cruise Industry

Although pleasure cruises were offered as early as the 19th century, the current cruise industry has its roots in the creation, and development, of the US-based cruise lines from the late 1960s and early 1970s. These early beginnings are referred to in Bjelicic (Chapter 2, this volume), and they are well documented in other publications.

Prior to these early days, ship travel, as a means of getting from A to B, had been much cheaper and more comfortable than the alternative offered by the airlines. However, these advantages were severely challenged with the appearance of the jet aircraft, and in particular the introduction of the Boeing 747.

The success of these new jumbo jets made passenger liners virtually redundant and, as a result, many lines went under and ships were sold for a fraction of their previous value or simply scrapped. Companies had to change their strategy simply to survive and, in addition to line voyages, e.g. transatlantic crossings, they introduced cruises to the sun. The Caribbean quickly became   the   preferred,   and   popular, destination for both the cruise lines and the passengers, and an entire new industry was effectively born.

This shift in the supply paradigm spawned the forming of new companies dedicated to operating ships as cruise vessels. Norwegian Caribbean Lines (NCL) had been set up in 1966, Royal Caribbean Cruise Line in 1968 and Royal Viking Line in 1970, but it was Ted Arison, a true pioneer of modern-day cruising, who laid the real foundations of the industry we know today. Famously, he had been instrumental in forming NCL in 1966, with colleague Knut Kloster, but he established Carnival Cruise Lines in 1972 with a personal vision, and passion, of making cruising accessible to the average holidaymaker and not just the affluent. It is no overstatement to say that without the creation, and development, of this North American market there would be no modern cruise industry of any consequence.

Although NCL had begun the development of the modern cruise industry, particularly in the Caribbean, it was Carnival's launch of a converted transatlantic liner – TSS Mardi Gras – that gave the industry growth real impetus. Despite a shaky start with their first ship, the company continued to expand by successfully offering shorter and more affordable cruises than those offered by the more traditional and established lines.

In a parallel move, which itself contributed to the revolutionizing of the cruise product, Arison sought to cut costs of the Mardi Gras by reducing the operating speed and, thereby, fuel consumption and the number of port calls. These simple economizing measures were to change the face of the cruise industry forever. In addition, Arison introduced further on-board entertainment features such as disco, casino, movie theatre and nightclubs. The Mardi Gras was labelled 'The Fun Ship' by the marketers, a label that has remained to this day, and other cruise lines quickly followed Arison and Carnival's lead.

Carnival and other operators also became much more aggressive with generating on-board revenue. These days most

cruise lines, certainly the non-luxury brands, will leave no stone unturned in their desire to maximize the passenger per diem (ppd) spend on non-inclusive elements of the cruise holiday. It can be one of the more negative elements of a cruise experience, and many passengers (particularly first timers) are less than enamoured by the approach of some of the cruise lines. In mitigation, it is difficult for the cruise lines to get the balance right between the need to generate revenue to support lower ticket rates, but not to affect the total experience negatively. This is especially true, as many of the revenue generating areas on board ships are concessions operated by companies other than the cruise lines, and clearly their success, and indeed survival, is bound by the ability to maximize revenue at every opportunity.

More cruise companies established their headquarters and offices in Florida, which also rapidly became the main cruising hub. This meant that ships did not have to sail from more northerly ports, such as New York, which had many advantages for the cruise line. It avoided colder weather, rougher seas, fuel costs, and more expensive port and office overhead costs amongst others. California became the base on the West Coast for cruises to the Mexican Riviera, and Vancouver in Canada became a turnaround port for summer cruising to Alaska.

In a somewhat ironic twist, and as an example of the increasing symbiotic nature of the global tourist industry, aircraft and their operators turned out to be indispensable partners in the growth of the cruise industry. Clearly many of the cruise passengers had to travel long distances to the embarkation ports, with many of them opting to fly to their destination. Very soon, working relationships were formed to offer cruise, hotel and airlift packages for one all-inclusive price. In principle, these were the precursors of the fly cruise, air/sea cruise packages, which are predominant in the industry today.

At this stage, the supply paradigm began to shift inexorably as increasing passenger numbers allowed for the commissioning, and building, of larger ships. These ships, with their economies of scale, technological advancements and on-board revenue generating opportunities, could be operated at significantly lower costs per passenger. This allowed more aggressive pricing, which in turn fuelled further demand – and so the cycle began.

The 1980s and Innovative Marketing

This decade brought the cruise industry massive expansion. Between 1981 and 1991, the number of berths on North American ships more than doubled from 41,000 to 82,000 – with Carnival Cruise Lines being the main driving force, and beneficiary, of this boom. In 1982, the Carnival fleet carried around 200,000 passengers and during the recessionary years of the early 1980s, they ordered three more new ships. This made them the largest cruise line in the world with seven ships. To help consistently fill these ships, Carnival adopted aggressive marketing and advertising strategies – something that had not really been done previously to promote the cruise industry.

In 1984, the Fun Ship advertising campaign was implemented. This US$10m campaign featured high profile TV personalities enjoying the facilities on board ship together with advertising during prime time TV slots – in particular during the ad breaks of the famous 1980s cruise-based TV series *Love Boat*.

As a unique, and effective, way of getting travel agents to support and promote their product, Carnival sent representatives to enquire directly about cruise holiday options. If a cruise holiday was recommended first, then the agent concerned would receive US$10; if this was a Carnival cruise then this amount would be US$1000. Clearly, this focused the mind of many travel agents and helped drive impressive sales and growth figures. By the end of the campaign, Carnival had given away over US$500,000.

Arison had recognized that, to fuel growth, the industry had to attract younger,

more middle-class customers to cruise, which traditionally had been the preserve of older, upper-class and wealthier clientele. Carnival, therefore, offered cheaper and shorter cruises packaged together with flights and hotels. In 1988, the company's low-priced air and sea packages were at least 20% below industry average.

Advertising also included, in 1988, an Independence Day party held on board a Carnival Ship, which was broadcast live by MTV – a TV music channel targeted at the younger audience. These strategies, which had far-reaching implications on the future development of the cruise industry, were successful, as 30% of Carnival passengers, in the early 1990s, were between the ages of 25 and 39. In addition, Carnival ships were consistently sailing at full capacity.

Tour Operators and the Growth of the UK and European Market

Although, compared with the North American market, developments in Europe are lagging behind, there has been phenomenal growth of the cruise industry in the UK market since the early 1990s. It is also widely accepted that there is still enormous potential for the growth of the UK market, and that Europe is showing signs of attaining and sustaining significant growth in the next few years. Further afield, Asia and Australasia are still in the very early stages of market development but, again, rapid market expansion is expected in the coming years.

It is the growth in the UK and, to a lesser extent, Europe that this section will look at in context of the aforementioned symbiotic nature of the relationship between tour operators and the cruise industry. It will consider, and seek to answer, some of the rationale behind this growth and in particular the significant relevance of the vertically integrated model, and the fly cruise and cruise and stay packages. Many of the references will therefore be fairly UK-centric; however, it is felt that the principles involved have enduring global relevance.

In the early 1990s, the growth rate of the UK cruise market was reasonable, if unspectacular, and by no means comparative to the buoyancy of the US-based, and predominantly Caribbean-focused, cruise industry. However, there was an increasing awareness of the burgeoning US-industry, and selling cruise holidays on behalf of the established cruise lines of the times started to become popular and, more significantly, profitable for travel agents.

Around this time, the major tour operators had set out on the acquisition trail, seeking to build vertically integrated holiday conglomerates. It was a time of acquisitions and mergers (see Bjelicic, Chapter 2, this volume) and, in particular, the tour operators began to operate and control the travel agency network.

The cruise industry has traditionally and historically been able to pay relatively high commissions to travel agents because of the high margins that cruise holidays attract in comparison with land-based resort alternatives. Cruise holidays were also a relatively easy sell for the travel agents, as most customers, at the time, had already decided they wanted to book a cruise, and booking through a travel agent was still the way this was done by the majority.

The cruise lines, therefore, had to offer suitable financial incentives for the agent to support their product or brand against others. In addition, the cruise bookings were still small in number in relation to land-based resort holidays, and the cruise lines had to pay high commission rates for the travel agents to keep their product at the forefront of any sales drives. These higher commission rates, paid to the travel agency companies, were invariably passed down the line in the form of increased earnings to the travel consultants, which itself continued to fuel the growth and growing awareness of the cruise holiday.

Although we now see US-based cruise lines, and others, well established in the UK and European markets, at the time they were somewhat slow to react to the growing awareness of cruise in UK and Europe. This was probably for a number of reasons; however, they already had very healthy occupancy levels for the capacity of their fleets and they did not need to look further afield to fill these ships.

In any case, the tour operators were quick to recognize the huge commercial benefits available if they were able to increase the number of customers to which they sold cruises. Therefore, in 1993, one of the leading tour operators of the time, Airtours (re-named MyTravel 2002, merged with Thomas Cook 2007), approached some of the major cruise lines, including Cunard and NCL, with a view to developing a business relationship similar to the allocation model adopted with their airline and hotel partners. Simply put, they were looking for a guaranteed allotment of cabins on certain cruises, which they would bundle and sell on with airlift and, often, hotel stay. For this they were, of course, also looking for advantageous per diem rates from the cruise lines.

Again for many reasons, most of which we can only surmise, the cruise lines rejected the proposition. The popular assumption is that the cruise lines did not wish for the tour operators to be so directly involved, as it would devolve some of the control to them, it would dilute the product offering, it would somehow 'cheapen' the 'aspirational' image of cruise and, of course, affect their yield.

This was like the proverbial red rag to a bull as far as Airtours, and their entrepreneurial chairman – David Crossland – were concerned. This setback only seemed to increase his desire and resolve to gain a bigger share of the cruise market for his company. Although a hugely significant one, he also saw this as just another challenge that he had thrived on when building the Airtours business. In 1995, less than 2 years after committing to set up their own cruise operation, Airtours introduced two ships, *Seawing* and *Carousel*, to the UK market. By 1999, a further two ships were acquired from Royal Caribbean, and added to the Airtours fleet – *Sundream* (ex-*Song of Norway*) and *Sunbird* (ex-*Song of America*).

The US industry had been started using older or redundant ships. In another ironic and symbiotic twist, it was now similar tonnage, no longer required for the US market, that Airtours acquired from NCL (*Southward* re-named *Seawing*) and Royal Caribbean (*Nordic Prince* re-named *Carousel*) that was responsible for kick-starting the UK market. Other major tour operators were quick to seize upon this new opportunity – in particular Thomson, which had, incidentally, chartered cruise ships for a short time as long ago as the mid-1970s; however, the oil crisis of the time caused an early abandonment of this early foray in the sector.

With the emergence of the Airtours cruise product and its immediate success in creating mainstream market demand, Thomson re-entered the market in 1996 with fervour. Like the Airtours brand, Sun Cruises, it introduced a recognizable face and name to millions who before may not have, realistically, considered heading to sea for their holidays. In 1999, cruise holidays were responsible for one in every 26 UK package holidays; this had increased to one in every 12 by 2008 (PSA, 2008).

Since the mid-1990s, the Thomson Cruises brand has grown considerably to offer a hugely diverse, and accessible, product offering. It has continued to develop the product in a successful bid to grow market share. Thomson has, for instance, introduced multi-regional UK port departures (e.g. Newcastle, Leith, Liverpool, Harwich), implemented Red Sea cruising, being the first company to use Sharm-el-Sheikh as a turnaround port, introduced 24-h flexible dining on board budget ships, promoted adults-only cruising on *Calypso*, amongst many other initiatives.

Initially, the Thomson strategy was to charter their vessels rather than purchase – as Airtours had done – with ships like *Island Breeze*, *Topaz*, *Sapphire*, *Emerald*. This meant, basically, that their exposure to risk was limited to selling their charter allocation, and that they could concentrate all efforts on doing just that. The operation and management of the ships was left to the owners and management companies. Another major advantage of this approach was that the charters' risk was further limited to the commercially more advantageous 'spring and summer' seasonal cruising without the challenge of 'winter' cruising capacity.

There is, however, a recent change in this strategy, which may, or may not, indicate a longer-term change and commitment. The more recently acquired tonnage – *Thomson Celebration* (ex-*Noordam*) and *Thomson Dream* (ex-*Costa Europa*) are both on long-term bare-boat leases with options to purchase. This has meant that Thomson has a much greater control of the product, and, of course, the vessel itself. Thomson is now very much a cruise line, as they now appoint and manage the operational aspect of vessels directly, albeit through third party management companies.

Thomson also benefitted greatly from the demise of Sun Cruises in 2004/05, which had been caused by the commercial failure of the parent company MyTravel. At the time, the management of the Sun Cruises fleet passed over to Louis Cruise Lines, as did the ownership of the ships apart from *Sundream*. Thomson seized the opportunity presented by this withdrawal of their main competitor and, in 2005, added *Thomson Destiny* (ex-Sun Cruises ship *Sunbird*) to the fleet, which was chartered from Louis Cruise Lines.

Vertical Integration

Another significant development at this time was the push by the major travel companies to create the all-encompassing, vertically integrated, conglomerates mentioned earlier. In addition to the development of their respective travel agency networks, the major UK tour operators, e.g. Airtours, Thomson and Thomas Cook, were busily acquiring, and operating, their own aircraft. They already had healthy land-based resort programmes based, primarily, on the chartering of aircraft and guaranteed allocations.

Entering the cruise industry directly was a logical extension of what was already well underway. The increased returns on the cruise ticket sales, and the control of allocation, were key decision points; however, it was the development of in-house airlines that provided the ultimate raison d'être.

Operating their own airlines gave them a significant extra dimension in terms of control, as it allowed them completely to dictate the regional flying programme, and yields, in support of the cruise operation. At the peak of their fly cruise operation, in 1997/98 Airtours had up to 26 regional flights arriving into Palma, Majorca, every weekend on turnaround day. By implementing this extensive regional airlift, it meant that very few passengers, and potential passengers, were any more than an hour and a half away from a departure airport. At the time of writing (2010), Thomson are scheduled to operate three ships out of Palma, Majorca and will have 22 regional departures to support this operation.

Fly Cruising and First Time Cruisers

As Majorca was already a popular package-holiday destination, and it was only a relatively short flight from the UK, Palma was a perfect first turnaround port for Airtours to use for their ground-breaking fly cruise, and cruise and stay products. Its location in the Mediterranean meant that the company could offer different week-long butterfly cruise itineraries. These itineraries included shore-excursion in rich destinations, e.g. Civitavecchia (Rome), Livorno (for Pisa), Barcelona, Nice etc.

The week-long nature of the itineraries, combined with the regular weekly airlift, and the popularity of Majorca as a package holiday destination led to the phenomenal take-up of the cruise and stay option. Usually this was a 2-week holiday to include a 1-week hotel or resort stay and 1-week cruise. However, because of the butterfly cruise concept, the options were available for 1-, 2- or 3-week cruises only, and increased cruise (or even resort) periods within a cruise and stay package.

For much the same reasons that Palma became the default summer cruise hub for Airtours, Tenerife became the winter season choice, although winter capacity was much more challenging to sell, as the traditional package holidaymakers still primarily took their holidays in the summer months, and there was and is market resistance to flights longer than 3 or 4 h.

Where and how to deploy ships in the winter months was a big challenge for the tour operators as, in addition to winter not being a traditional time for package holidays, operating costs were much higher and any airlift was, relatively, much more expensive. Indeed, if tour operators were able to operate their ships at break-even, this was considered a success.

Fly cruising (or air/sea as it is commonly known in the USA) was one of the main drivers of the growth in the early days of the US market. Regional airlift meant that the market catchment area extended well beyond the embarkation states (California and Florida) and seemingly free air travel was a hugely effective marketing tool in creating demand.

As an aside, although fly cruising was instrumental in driving the early growth of the US industry, an interesting development in the market (which was later mirrored in the UK for somewhat different reasons) took place in the mid-late 1990s when there was a discernible shift back towards cruise-only bookings. In the USA, one reason for this change was that many passengers utilized air miles they had accumulated on frequent flyer programmes with the domestic airlines. In the UK, it was more about repeat passengers becoming more mature and sophisticated, regarding their expectations of the product (see below for more on this).

In these early days of the tour operator fly cruise market, the vast majority of customers opted for the cruise and stay option – around 80% booked 1-week cruise with 1-week hotel stay, which led to an interesting and unexpected challenge for the tour operator. Namely, the hotel or resort facilities used, historically with good customer satisfaction levels, were quickly seen as poor, and often unacceptable, in relation to the standards of product delivery on board the cruise ships. The level of service, food, entertainment and overall standards on board far exceeded those of the land-based options, and it soon became apparent that the stay part of the package needed urgent re-vamping. As a result, better quality hotels were contracted for cruise passengers, and many cruise-only hotels were created. Also, as a result of the cruise product far exceeding most customers' expectation, there was a rapid shift in the cruise and stay percentage, i.e. soon 80% of customers were booking cruise only, many for 2 weeks, instead of cruise and stay.

Younger Market and Repeater Customers Challenge

Since the 1970s, it has been universally accepted that, to expand the market, a younger, less affluent customer needed to be attracted to the cruise product. While this has been done to some degree of success by the cruise operators, it is a challenge that remains to this day. However, to some observers, the success claimed would itself be challenged, and countered, as demographic statistics point to a relatively poor job done by the industry in marketing the cruise holiday concept to a younger clientele.

There was a relative slump in the North American market in the mid-1990s. This was concluded to be related to the cruise lines and agents concentrating efforts and resources, marketing to past customers. The sell was easier to the past customers, but it soon became apparent that the prime target for marketing purposes should be the first-time cruiser.

A market profile undertaken by the Cruise Lines International Association (CLIA) in 1998 (Peisley, 1999) showed that 78% of past cruisers, who had cruised in the previous 5 years, were 'interested in cruising', whereas among those who had not previously cruised the share was only 55%. The difference in these figures was even more marked when the target groups were asked if they would 'definitely/probably take a cruise in the next 5 years' – the responses were 67% and 31%, respectively. Ten years later, CLIA (2008) undertook a

similar profile and the percentages of those 'interested in cruising' were virtually the same at 77% and 55%, respectively. However, interestingly, there was quite a significant drop to 53% and 26%, respectively, when the groups were asked if they would 'definitely/probably take a cruise in the next 3 years' (see also Oschmann and Vogel, Chapter 1, this volume). So while the cruise industry has made important strides and carries more passengers than ever before, it is still faced with certain challenges to convince large percentages of people that cruise holidaying is a holiday option for them.

It is a seemingly obvious statement perhaps, but the biggest challenge is getting new customers, in particular the younger age group, to experience a cruise in the first place. It is, of course, only then they can genuinely understand the concept of a cruise holiday. Because of the degree of uncertainty they may have, a high proportion of first-timers are attracted to shorter cruises. This factor alone significantly helped fuel the boom of short fly cruise and cruise and stay markets promoted by the tour operators.

As the UK market discovered later, as the market matures, and repeat customers become more familiar with the cruise offer and market conditions, this leads to pressure on yields as passengers look to book smarter, e.g. leaving booking later for extra discounts. This maturity, or familiarity, also puts pressure on the generation of on-board revenue, as an increasing number of passengers are reluctant to spend on shore excursions in ports they have previously visited, on souvenirs they have previously bought etc. They also become comfortable with cruising as a means to an end, i.e. the experience is treated more as a means of relaxation rather than a more frenetic see, buy, eat and drink as much as possible, which the less experienced cruisers have a tendency to do.

These factors also put pressure on itinerary planning as the repeat customers also look for new destination experiences. This is one of the prime reasons that the fly cruise model, while enduring, is challenged and why, after a few years of fly cruise only, the tour operators switched some tonnage to ex-UK sailing. The development of the market, built on the foundation of fly cruising, has also encouraged most of the major cruise lines to operate significant ex-UK programmes, and many of the UK ports are now well used to welcoming big, new ships to their facilities. Although, in spite of the relative success of UK port departures for the tour operators, their core business is still fly cruise because of the margin made on the airlift element of the package.

Capacity Planning, Packaging and Pricing

The vertically integrated tour operators have a distinct advantage when it comes to assistance with airlift – although any pricing advantage is being challenged in more recent times, as companies create stand-alone profit centres creating pressure on internal cross-company rate transfers that perhaps was not relevant before. However, it is fair to say the vertically integrated tour operator is better placed in terms of flight planning and the packaging of a cruise holiday because of group access to flights, hotels and ground handling infrastructure.

There is clearly an ongoing commercial challenge for cruise and tour operators to sell cruise berths – particularly in view of the increasing level of competition and numbers of berths now available – but that challenge is increased in both terms of scale and complexity when the issue of packaging the cruise holiday is added.

The biggest challenge faced is one of capacity planning, which is tackled somewhat differently by cruise lines and tour operators. The most significant challenge to meet is to ensure that no flight seat and no cruise berth goes empty. The flight element of the package is the biggest factor to take into account when packaging the cruise holiday. To be able to sell a fly cruise package successfully, the operator has to arrange the necessary flight(s), airport transfers etc. and to pass this cost on to the customer within a competitively priced package. Not altogether a challenge in itself perhaps, but there are, in fact, multiple challenges faced by the operator in doing this.

The first is that most flight seats will need commitment both to secure them at all and also to secure them at a cost that allows competitive pricing. The logistical planning of flights from international and regional departure points is critical to the success of the operation. This is one area where the vertically integrated tour operator has a distinct advantage as manager and operator of their own airlines, giving them much more flexibility with regional departures. Also they will usually be utilizing aircraft that are being used for land-based resort operations so that capacity planning and risk can be shared across the group.

This regional flexibility is one of the greatest selling points for the tour operator – for instance, in 2010, Thomson Cruises in the UK operated from 21 regional airports into Palma, Majorca, for the cruise ships based there. This is possible as the company also has a large number of customers for its land-based programmes in Majorca. The seats associated with the cruise berths were also not necessarily on an allocated basis, meaning they were sold on a first come, first served basis depending on from where the cruise passenger wished to fly. Clearly this would be dependent upon seats being available on the preferred flights, and not being used by land-based customers, but it gives a much more flexible approach to the selling of cruise holidays than being fixed to, say, the two main London airports as departure points.

Not every tour operator will work to exactly the same system as Thomson/TUI, and each will meet the challenges of airlift planning slightly differently. Within some tour operators, there will be internal mechanisms and systems for dealing with regional departures but not necessarily to the same degree of flexibility. Airtours/MyTravel certainly had significant capacity planning issues, as their Sun Cruise product was sold within the group to the Scandinavian, North

American and European markets at the same time.

The challenge for the non-tour operator (and indeed also the tour operator when chartering externally) is to plan accurately not only the airlift capacity but also the departure points and their own individual respective capacities. It is known that the major cruise operators will contract a number of air seats to be used in conjunction with their cruise programme, but travel agents may decide to source alternative flights and package themselves. This can lead to significant issues with unused and committed airlift capacity.

Overall, the groups will look at yield management and endeavour to have systems in place to maximize the yield (see Vogel, Chapter 10, this volume) when combining cruise and land-based operations. It is essential that the commercial operational departments work together and monitor closely the dynamics of yield to the point of release. Even if it means leaving cabins unsold, it may be better overall to release a flight seat for use by a land-based customer.

The yield management process and system should also consider an overall view of margin and contribution and constantly track sales volumes to ensure the optimum selling prices. Each operator will determine price points in a different way, but most will include some element of market comparison and tracking to ensure competitiveness.

Another major element of a cruise holiday package to consider is the hotel for cruise and stay options. Again, this is an area where the tour operators have a distinct advantage, as they are already usually contracting significant numbers of hotel rooms for their land-based operations and so will generally enjoy better commercial deals. They will even own many of their own properties in some of the more popular destinations. Any hotel choice, however, is critical to the overall success of the cruise holiday, and it is imperative that the appropriate and requisite standard is offered as part of the package.

Concluding Remarks

The cruise industry certainly appears to be on a relentless upward drive with its continuing introduction of new, bigger ships with on-board product and facilities that were virtually unimaginable until very recently. It has been remarkably successful in increasing its market share of the global holiday and tourism market year-on-year and expanding its awareness and appeal across the world, which it continues to do. However, with this success comes the ever-increasing challenge of sustaining the growth and interest in the product while at the same time controlling operational costs to maintain the relative value of cruising as a holiday of choice.

The competition between the cruise operators is intense and, while it is an industry that enjoys relatively healthy levels of collaboration between companies, it is likely that there will be further consolidation of the major operators and, sadly, commercial casualties amongst the smaller cruise lines. At the time of writing, there is huge pressure on cruise pricing and an increasing trend for customers to book later and later in order to get the best deals. With the major US operators positioning a lot of their vessels in Europe (and beyond), this inevitably has a significant competitive and commercial impact on the European operators. Where these European operators, in particular the tour operators, have some distinct advantage is in being able to offer logistically flexible and price-advantageous cruise packages, and this remains the key commercial lever they hold.

It is going to be extremely interesting to see what the next few years will bring in the changing landscape of the cruise industry and whether the phenomenal growth in the industry seen until now is sustainable. Whilst they still focus on growing current markets, the major cruise operators are already well advanced in their search for new and emerging markets, with Asia currently seen as the next prime, and virtually untapped, growth area.

References

PSA (2008) *UK and European Cruise Market 2008 – Ocean Cruise Holidays vs. Foreign Inclusive Holidays.* Passenger Shipping Association, London.
Peisley, T. (1999) *World Cruise Market: Analysis, Trends and Opportunities.* Informa Publishing, London.
CLIA (2008) *Cruise Market Profile Study.* Cruise Lines International Association, Fort Lauderdale, Florida.

Part IV

Cruise Product Management

_____

12   Cruise Product Development

Steffen Spiegel

Introduction

The cruise industry's growth rests in part on its ability to offer products for an ever more diverse group of customers. Product diversity is the result of development processes, which unite two opposite poles. On the one hand, there is the systematic, rational, research-based dimension of product development. On the other hand, novelty requires a portion of intuition, inspiration and creativity. The challenge of product development is to balance the tension between these two poles in such a way that the end product is different from existing products yet still similar enough to be understood by the customers.

The term product development has more than one meaning in the relevant literature. In Ansoff's product-market matrix in Table 12.1, which links a company's marketing strategy with its general strategic direction, product development represents a growth strategy for an existing market. For Kotler *et al.* (2010), product development is the stage of the product creation process where a prototype of a new product is created to test it and present it to target audiences. Hüttel (1998) distinguishes between product development as the variation or modification of an existing product and product development as the creation of a completely new product.

In this chapter, I adopt a rather comprehensive definition. Product development shall refer to an integrated process that starts with the collection of ideas and ends with the introduction of a new or significantly modified product to a current or new market.

In tourism, a product can be a visitor service, an activity, an attraction or an experience (France, 2009). A cruise product, however, is always a bundle of basic tourism, hospitality and event products, framed and linked by tangible (cruise ship hardware) and intangible (itinerary, overall service concept) attributes. Product development can refer to the development of individual components of the cruise product (e.g. a new catering system) or the development of the entire bundle. Different cabin types on a particular cruise, and package holidays consisting of a particular cruise and different flights, airport transfers and/or additional hotel stays (see Cartledge, Chapter 11, this volume) are not considered as separate cruise products in this chapter.

This chapter outlines the product development process for service products in general, before suggesting a framework suitable to describe product development in the cruise industry. According to Papathanassis and Beckmann (2011), the majority of published research papers on cruising focus on environmental and economic impacts of cruise tourism on destinations,

Table 12.1. Product-market matrix.

	Current products	New products
Current markets	Market penetration	**Product development**
New markets	Market development	Diversification

Source: Ansoff (1965).

on medical issues, and on financial aspects of the cruise planning process. Their extensive literature review does not mention a single paper that addresses product development in the cruise industry. Thus, many ideas and concepts presented in this chapter are drawn from my own working experience in different positions in the cruise business, ashore and on aboard.

The chapter starts with the description of a prototypical product development process in services from which a customized cruise product development process will be derived. This is followed by a look at the information required by and the departments involved in this process. The discussion of the practical example of Royal Caribbean's 'Project Genesis' illustrates the concepts that are detailed in the last section.

Is Product Development Art or Science?

Product development is nowadays a systematic, rational, research-based process, which makes sure that all available information is taken into account and the uncertainties of the development process are reduced to an acceptable level. This has not always been the case. Product development used to be more intuitive and creative. But the shift from a seller's market to a buyer's market (Weiermair, 2001) in many industries, including leisure travel, has forced companies to consider consumer preferences and their competitive situations more seriously than before. In the cruise industry, for instance, such changes have included:

- market concentration, i.e. growing market shares are controlled by fewer players (see Bjelicic, Chapter 2, this volume);
- a cruise ship capacity race among the main players, leading to more and larger numerous ships;

- overcrowding of certain key cruise destinations, resulting in cruise ship capacity being deployed elsewhere;
- decreasing passenger growth rates in North America, the cruise industry's core market (see Vogel and Oschmann, Chapter 1, this volume); and
- declining cruise fares and rising pressure to generate on-board revenue (see Vogel, Chapter 10, this volume).

Cruise lines face strong competition. They see the need to attract new customers and keep existing customers either by frequently introducing new product lines to the market or by adding new features to existing products. Innovation cycles have shortened substantially. The core question is: how can a cruise product be developed so that its market success is no mere coincidence? Many employees in the cruise business today still sense a certain air of creativity and holiday feeling while working on their products. For them, product development might be an art. For others, with a background that is influenced more by thinking in business and management terms, the creation of a new product is a process that follows a strict, almost scientifically rigorous pattern. If all stages of the process are completed correctly, a successful product will – to their way of thinking – be the likely outcome. As mentioned before, a shift from intuitive product development towards a systematic and standardized product development process has taken place in the major cruise lines.

Prototypical Service Product Development Process

The prototypical service product development process can be divided into six to eight different stages (e.g. Hüttel 1998; Kotler *et al.*, 2010). Pikkemaat and Peters (2006) point out that the process is not necessarily sequential, as the elements often overlap. And Smith (2007), whose concept explicitly deals with flexible processes, suggests that processes are emergent, i.e. processes are created whilst being applied.

Based on my own work experience, I agree with these authors and see their approaches largely reflected by the actual product development processes in the cruise sector. As a synthesis, I propose a model of the product development process with overlapping stages (Fig. 12.1) which, by and large, represents the reality of cruise product development.

The concept development and testing stage is especially demanding in the service sector, because of the immaterial nature of services. Developers are faced with the challenge to test a product that often can only be properly perceived and evaluated when consumed in its real-life context. It is very difficult to pre-test passengers' reaction to a new layout of the pool deck before it is realized and used on aboard.

Smith (2007) suggests approaching the design of the product development process bottom-up: add items to the process as you feel the need for additional stages, instead of using an existing process and deleting unnecessary parts. But he points out that well-trained managers are needed for this more flexible approach. He seems to agree with Servi (1990), who points out that a 'mechanical' methodology of product development does not guarantee success.

The first stage of the basic product development process is the search for product ideas (idea generation). It is important to focus on the company's core competences which will be relevant in the future, and which are in line with the company's mission and vision. Hüttel (1998) differentiates between two sources of ideas:

- market-generated ideas (from customers, suppliers, fairs, literature, etc.);
- company-generated ideas (from experience or intuition).

At this initial stage, many companies face the problem of the sheer quantity of new product ideas. This is where the second stage starts: idea screening. The ideas generated in the first phase are now checked for their economic potential, .i.e. their likely value to customers and cost implications.

In order to develop a product concept and test the product idea (stage three of the process), Hüttel (1998) proposes the following core questions:

- Which image shall the new product create/foster?
- How shall the product idea be realized?
- Who are the potential customers?
- Which added value shall the product transport?
- What shall the product be used for?

Concept development and testing is a recursive, iterative process during which the initial ideas are gradually refined, worked out in detail, integrated with one

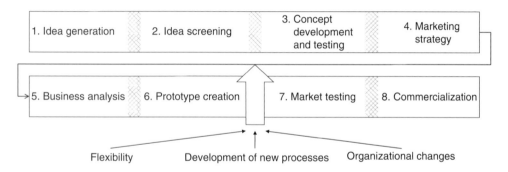

Fig. 12.1. Basic product development process with overlapping stages.

another, evaluated for feasibility and documented for further use and decision making.

In the fourth stage, the product development team has to create and decide on a marketing strategy for the new product (design, name, communication, product-related services, price, etc.). Now, the business analysis (stage five) overlaps with the marketing strategy: developers undertake an in-depth analysis of the current market situation (e.g. the market potential for the new product, reaction expected from competitors, the needs of retailers and environmental aspects). This task is of utmost importance in order to avoid failure of the new product at its launch. Furthermore, the economic feasibility of the new product has to be checked once more.

If these checks for feasibility and the market analyses deliver positive results, stage six follows with the creation of physical prototypes of manufactured products or of service prototypes including the hardware and software needed for service delivery.

In stage seven, a test market is defined and the product prototype is tried out in this limited environment. If the product has to be altered, this is the last chance to do so before it is finally launched on to the market (stage eight).

Smith (2007) underlines the importance of flexibility in areas where a company has to be innovative. But flexibility can only be expected at the higher levels of R&D management, while at the lower levels standardization is regarded as speeding up the process. This general approach can be very well applied in the service sector: on the one hand, checking the potential for improvements on a regular basis (e.g. by analysing customer questionnaires) is a standardized process; on the other hand gathering and developing ideas for innovation (e.g. a new product line) should be a flexible undertaking. Depending on the kind of product being developed, a certain amount of flexibility in the development process might foster future success in sales.

The Consumer-driven Cruise Product Development Process

As just described, the basic product development process consists of different and partly overlapping stages. In this section, I apply this general model to the cruise sector.

The international cruise market is dominated by oligopolistic structures (three big international players). This model appears suitable. Walder's (2006) dynamic competition model suggests that companies in an oligopoly tend to be more innovative than companies in monopolistic or competitive markets, because of higher profit expectations from innovation in oligopolies. The so-called pioneer company that launches a new product bears high innovation cost and high risk. But at the same time, it benefits from its competitive advantage and higher market shares. When Aida Cruises was launched in the German market in 1996, the company was a pioneer for a lifestyle-oriented cruise concept. It gained a high market share in a short period. After the start of TUI Cruises, a competitor imitating parts of the Aida product (but also introducing new features), Aida Cruises responded by launching further innovations such as a new show concept, in order not to lose market share.

Bieger and Weinert (2006) underline the importance of the consumer in the product development process: either the consumers are the ones to initiate innovation (pull pattern), or the developing company wants the consumers to absorb a new product (push pattern). In the first case, a new idea is brought into the company by the consumers (for example by means of customer feedback). In the second case, the idea for a new product is created within the company, and the marketing department tries to persuade the consumers to buy the new product. In cruise product development the driving force for innovation is mostly the consumers – be it as initiators or as the target of innovation. Through questionnaires and detailed market research, cruise companies can identify the needs and desires of their existing and potential customers. Sometimes, the customers might not be aware of their desires (latent desires), but they will be happy to consume a service that meets their lifestyle.

Still following Bieger and Weinert's (2006) pull pattern, the first stage of the innovation process (after the initial idea by the customer) consists of extensive research. In the cruise industry, trends in tourism, leisure and lifestyle, in demographics, social life and the economy should be identified and checked for relevance. Also customer expectations and feedback as well as employees' experiences and suggestions need to be collected. All of this can be valuable input into the development of a new product.

An important difference between product development in manufacturing and product development in the service sector lies in the timeframe of the decision-making process (Bieger and Weinert, 2006). Because of significant investments in research and development, managers in manufacturing have to decide at an early stage on the fate of the new idea, whereas managers in services usually only face high costs at the end of the development process (marketing, launch). They can decide at a later stage if the product should reach the market. For the cruise sector, this means that new product ideas can be pursued without much investment and risk – unless, of course, the service prototype requires the building of a whole new cruise ship. Thus, the potential for innovation is high.

But before the final stage, when major investments (e.g. in hardware) are inevitable, thorough market research ought to be undertaken to ensure that decisions are made on the basis of the best available information. If, for example, a new restaurant concept is to be implemented, the vessel in question has to be refitted in dry dock, requiring a substantial investment. If this new catering concept proves not to be successful in the market, the company will face further investments for changing the hardware of the vessel again (apart from an opportunity loss and a potential loss of reputation).

Hapag-Lloyd Cruises' CEO, Sebastian Ahrens, recently stated that in his company, many aspects of a major new cruise product under development emerged in a creative environment. Intensive dialogue was used in the development process (von Pilar, 2011). This underlines the importance of soft skills of the personnel involved – and it defines the main tasks for product development managers: to design an environment that supports the creative development of ideas.

Summing up, with its oligopolistic structure the cruise industry offers good conditions for innovation. The product development process in the cruise industry has to focus on the customers as the driving force. Either they inject ideas into the cruise companies or the cruise companies analyse the market and demand trends to identify the potential for innovations that will be welcomed by the customers. The decision in favour of or against the launch of a new product can be taken rather late in the development process. The cruise company becomes a 'creative melting pot' by providing the creative environment and the forum for intensive dialogue with internal and external stakeholders, especially customers. This results in a consumer-driven cruise product development process, as depicted in Fig. 12.2.

Within the product portfolio of an existing cruise company, product development can have different objectives: modernization, expansion, diversification, targeting new customer groups within an existing market, entry into a new market, and the prolongation of a product life cycle. The proposed model can be used for any of these objectives, although slight modifications might be needed in order to meet the needs of a specific project. Every stage of the model is actually a process of its own.

Departments and Functions Involved

After having discussed the general product development process, and pointed out the particularities of the cruise sector, I will now take a short look at the departments

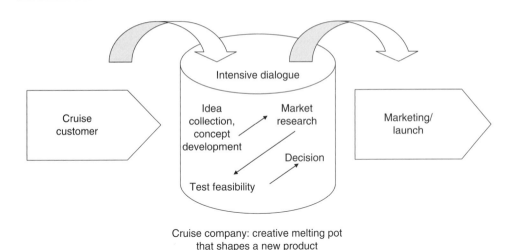

Cruise company: creative melting pot
that shapes a new product

Fig. 12.2. Customer-driven cruise product development process.

and functions involved in cruise product development.

The sales department is one of the main generators of ideas for product development. By using certain techniques of sales analysis with existing products, areas with a potential for a new product can be identified. Marketing is also a department that creates ideas by following general trends in lifestyle, tourism and cruising. Marketing will be involved in the launch process of the newly developed product, as well.

The technical department can be a driving force in the idea-generating stage, especially if ship design is involved. In river cruising, tests were made with catamaran-style river cruise vessels (e.g. the *Mozart* on the Danube). The designers were the source of inspiration in this example. Another way of involving the technical department was used when Aida Cruises' marketing department decided to create a new form of on-board entertainment. Instead of hosting traditional shows in the ship's theatre every evening, with *AIDAdiva* the so-called 'Theatrium' was introduced in 2007. This open space, which covers three decks in the middle of the ship, combines the main show facility and an atrium. Here, artists stage their smaller acts and bigger shows throughout the day. After the idea was born in the marketing department, the technical

department had to design the rest of the vessel around the Theatrium. The result can be seen in Fig. 12.3 where the dark glass façade in the centre of the *AIDAdiva* indicates the position of the Theatrium and contributes to the ship's distinctive exterior.

Also suppliers (and the cruise lines' procurement departments as their main points of contact) are part of the product development process (Liao *et al.*, 2010). Their own ideas and innovations may trigger cruise line product development processes. Suppliers can also be invited to participate in cruise product development and to contribute their particular expertise and experience. When the technology for TV on demand became available, for example, cruise lines responded by redesigning cabins and adjusting their overall on-board entertainment concepts to integrate this new form of en-suite entertainment in their products.

Project Genesis

One of the most ambitious new cruise products in recent years was Royal Caribbean's *Oasis of the Seas* and the other *Oasis* Class ships, initially code named 'Project Genesis'. It is an interesting example that illustrates the theoretical principles that I have discussed so far.

Fig. 12.3. *AIDAdiva* with the three-deck-high, glass-enclosed Theatrium. Source: M. Vogel.

Product development is a process that needs time. In this case, 6 years passed between the first plans in 2003 (RCI, 2009b) and delivery in October 2009. The order was placed early in 2006, but by then the details of many on-board features still had to be finalized (MSNBC.com, 2006). This shows how the different stages of the product development process overlap.

When *Oasis of the Seas* was ordered, she was the biggest and most expensive cruise ship ever built, featuring 'daring innovations' (RCI, 2009b). Securing capital for the payment of such an expensive vessel was a major task for the company's financial department. Its completion was celebrated with a special press release in 2009. Royal Caribbean had already been known in the past as an innovative company, but Project Genesis was exceptionally innovative even by the company's own standards.

Seven so called Neighbourhoods (themed areas) are located in the open space between the two hotel blocks (RCL, 2010). This new layout enables the construction of a large number of outside cabins with either sea view or view to the park and the open spaces inside the vessel (Fig. 12.4). The increase in outside cabin numbers enhances yield as those cabins can be sold at higher prices. Furthermore, the vessel enables Royal Caribbean to capture cost savings through economies of scale and lower fuel consumption per passenger.

The seven neighbourhoods and some of their new features are:

- Central Park (featuring the first living park at sea and a bar that moves vertically);
- The Pool and Sports Zone;
- Vitality at Sea Spa and Fitness Centre;
- Boardwalk (featuring an outdoor aquatic amphitheatre with the deepest pool on board a cruise vessel);
- Royal Promenade (including the first handcrafted carousel at sea);
- Youth Zone; and
- Entertainment Place.

Even the lifeboats (referred to as 'life ships' because of their size) feature a lavatory. 'Innovation' is a term generously used in Royal Caribbean's publications about the *Oasis* class and emphasizes the company's credo of creativity. In the case of the *Oasis of the Seas* and her sister ships, product development as a marriage of art and science seems to have been perfectly realized, sparing not one part of the design and the ship-side organization.

Ports had to adapt to the size of the new vessel by dredging the approaches and by enlarging their facilities (RCI, 2008). The company itself had to invest significantly in

Fig. 12.4. Aft view of Royal Caribbean's *Allure of the Seas*. Source: E.W. Manning, Tourisk Inc.

their private bay at Labadee/Haiti: a pier that can accommodate the *Oasis*-class vessels was constructed in order to avoid a long and probably nerve-wrecking tender operation (RCL, 2010). Still today, only a limited number of ports in the Caribbean are able to accommodate the vessel. Furthermore, the check-in and check-out procedure as well as the catering and procurement concept had to be altered in order to cope with a maximum of more than 6000 passengers at the same time. And finally, as the high number of press releases related to the launch of the new product show, the marketing department had to develop a dedicated strategy to keep the public aware of the new product throughout the building stage, during the launch and even post-launch.

But even the 6-year intensive product development process like Project Genesis could not entirely avoid problematic side-effects: passengers are 'encouraged' to pre-book their shows online up to 3 months in advance (RCI, 2009a). Marketing tries to communicate this as an advantage, but it is obvious that the large number of passengers cannot be hosted in the traditional way of two consecutive shows every evening. For some passengers, the need to reserve tickets might transfer the stress of working life to their holidays. Another example of unwanted side-effects of innovation are the queues that inevitably build – the vision of developing a completely new product is taken to a tough test here. The operational area of the vessel is quite limited because of its size. The company thus loses flexibility in the deployment of its vessel. In case of environmental or political disturbances, it will be difficult to find another geographic area where ports are equipped for the handling of such a large vessel.

Challenges to Product Development

Minderhoud and Fraser (2005) suggest that product development is confronted with three main challenges today:

- Multiple players and companies (subcontractors) operate in product development where there used to be only one single development unit within the company. This leads to a more complex and error-prone communication process between the participants in product development.

- There is a growing pressure for cycle-time reduction to improve time-to-market.
- The reception for first-of-a-kind products is uncertain in a dynamic market environment.

In the context of the cruise industry, the first of these challenges seems less significant. Although many cruise lines outsource ship design and technological problem solving, the product development process as a whole is still very closely controlled in-house.

The second challenge, however, is becoming increasingly serious for cruise lines, since product life cycles seem to be getting shorter and innovation rates higher. The innovation race in the cruise industry is fostered by the oligopolistic market structure and the possibility of each cruise company to observe what the others are doing. With every new mega-liner launched, at least one new feature is marketed (e.g. surfing on board the *Freedom of the Seas*, glass blowing and natural lawn on the *Celebrity Eclipse*, a brewery on the *AIDAblu*) and also expected by the media and the cruising community. In this competitive environment, short time-to-market allows cruise companies to react to, and even to pre-empt, each other's moves.

The imperative to market new products and to maximize ship occupancy represents a barrier to ever shorter product lead times in the cruise industry. Brochures are normally published up to 2 years in advance. By that time, the product development must be completed.

The third challenge to product development mentioned above, namely the uncertainty associated with the dynamic market environment, follows partly from the competitive dynamics of the cruise industry, partly from the long lead times of new products, and partly from external influences, such as economic and geo-political uncertainty. The way cruise companies tend to minimize the uncertainty of their products' success is by spreading risks. For instance, Glover and Prideaux

(2009) advise companies to 'develop products and services that have the capability to appeal to multi-generation markets rather than focusing only on one generation' (pp. 30–31). Indeed, many of the new mega-liners feature attractions for children, their parents and even the grandparents, as well as for couples without children and for single travellers. The spatial segmentation of the *Oasis of the Seas* fulfils a similar function: different passenger types may feel at home in different 'Neighbourhoods'.

The third challenge, product success in times of global economic instabilities and accelerating change in the conditions of life (see Vogel and Oschmann, Chapter 1, this volume), is most relevant for the cruise sector in the light of the long time-to-market of new cruise ships and their expected useful life of several decades. Pikkemaat and Peters (2006) stress the importance of the market research stage in the product development process. Product development, especially if it involves major investments and/or long-term consequences, should only be based on very robust research, in order to avoid failure of the new products because of misjudged market potential or deficient product positioning.

Information flows within organizations are essential indicators of the quality of the development processes (Minderhoud and Fraser, 2005). In the cruise industry, the most critical and sensitive information flows connect vessels and the shore-side organizations. However, since cruise ship crew and head office staff tend to set different priorities in their work and often do not share the same knowhow and experience, communication breakdowns between both sides are no exception, posing threats to product development and innovation processes even in absence of the three aforementioned challenges.

Conclusion

At the beginning of this chapter, I asked the question: is cruise product development art or science? From the findings of the literature review, the message seems to be clear: the more industrialized a trade, the more systematic the process becomes. But how industrialized is the cruise industry today? Bigger cruise companies have formed during the last 20 years. This development was accompanied by process rationalization and standardization, and also by greater professionalism. Professionalism is good for the companies involved, good for the customers and good for the industry as a whole. Now the cruise industry needs to make sure that the intuitive and creative component of product development is preserved, e.g. by making it an integral part of its concept of professionalism.

References

Ansoff, H.I. (1965) *Checklist for Competitive and Competence Profiles; Corporate Strategy.* McGraw-Hill, New York.

Bieger, T. and Weinert, R. (2006) On the nature of the innovative organization in tourism: structure, process and results. In: Weiermair, K., Peters, M. and Reiger, E. (eds) *Vom alten zum neuenTourismus.* Studia Universitätsverlag, Innsbruck, pp. 87–102.

France, M. (2009) Developing tourism products and services. Available at: www.tourismbusinesstoolkit.co.uk/xsdbimgs/TK1.aDOC%20-%20Developing%20Tourism%20Products.pdf (accessed 27 February 2011).

Glover, P. and Prideaux, B. (2009) Implications of population ageing for the development of tourism products and destinations. *Journal of Vacation Marketing* 15(1), 25–38.

Hüttel, K. (1998) Produktpolitik. 3. Aufl. Kiehl, Ludwigshafen.

Kotler, P., Bowen, J.T. and Makens, J.C. (2010) *Marketing for Hospitality and Tourism.* Pearson, Upper Saddle River, New Jersey.

Liao, S., Chen, Y. and Deng, M. (2010) Mining customer knowledge for tourism new product development and customer relationship management. *Expert Systems with Applications* 37(1), 4212–4223.

Minderhoud, F. and Fraser, P. (2005) Shifting paradigms of product development in fast and dynamic markets. *Reliability Engineering and System Safety* 88(1), 127–135.

MSNBC.com (2006) Royal Caribbean orders largest-ever cruise ship. Available at: www.msnbc.msn.com/id/11199685/ns/business-world_business/# (accessed 1 March 2011).

Papathanassis, A. and Beckmann, I. (2011) Assessing the 'poverty of cruise theory' hypothesis. *Annals of Tourism Research* 38(1), 153–174.

Pikkemaat, P. and Peters, M. (2006) Market information – a key success factor in the new product development process in tourism? In: Weiermair, K. and Brunner-Sperdin, A. (eds) *Erlebnisinszenierung imTourismus.* Erich Schmidt Verlag, Berlin, pp. 81–96.

RCI (2008) Royal Caribbean announces Oasis of the Seas itineraries. Available at: www.royalcaribbean.com/ourCompany/pressCenter/pressReleases/info.do?prDate=06-20-2008&prCode=A (accessed 5 March 2011).

RCI (2009a) Now that's entertainment! Available at:www.oasisoftheseas.com/downloadRelease.php?id=39 (accessed 5 March 2011).

RCI (2009b) Royal Caribbean International takes delivery of much anticipated Oasis of the Seas. Available at: www.oasisoftheseas.com/downloadRelease.php?id=45 (accessed 5 March 2011).

RCL (2010) *Annual Report 2009.* Royal Caribbean Cruises, Miami, Florida.

Servi, I. (1990) *New Product Development and Marketing. A Practical Guide.* Praeger, New York.

Smith, P. (2007) *Flexible Product Development.* Jossey-Bass, San Francisco, California.

Von Pilar, C. (2011) Kreativer Akt. *Fvw* 2(4), 8–9.

Walder, B. (2006) Sources and determinants of innovations – the role of market forces. In: Walder, B., Weiermair, K. and Pérez, A. (eds) *Innovation and Product Development in Tourism.* Erich Schmidt Verlag, Berlin, pp. 7–21.

Weiermair, K. (2001) Neue Organisations-, Koordinations- und Führungsprinzipien im alpinenTourismus. In: Weiermair, K., Peters, M. and Reiger, E. (eds) *Vom alten zum neuen Tourismus.* Studia Universitätsverlag, Innsbruck, pp. 108–117.

13   Itinerary Planning

James Henry

Introduction

The cruise ship's itinerary is at the heart of passenger expectations along with the actual shipboard experience. This chapter explores the parameters that go into the planning of such itineraries. For planners, the market has become well segmented, and there is now a need to find and develop new and exciting ports of call to attract and retain a loyal customer base.

As such, itinerary planning seeks to provide a particular cruise with a 'point of difference' for passengers and to give that cruise an edge over that offered by a competing cruise line or brand. From a cruise ship company's perspective, planning takes place some 2–3 years prior to an actual voyage. This timeframe is necessary to ensure that all is in place to provide passengers with a seamless product experience, alongside the logistical and operational requirements of the particular cruise ship.

Selected criteria for making such decisions are summarized in Table 13.1. Each of these factors will be discussed in turn. A case study at the end of the chapter is used to illustrate many of the concepts discussed within the chapter.

In addition to the above criteria, a number of stakeholders have an influencing role to play and can significantly influence the itinerary planning process. The main ones to be aware of are:

- The *inbound tour operators*, also known as incoming agents or ground handlers, are the local tourism specialists who design suitable tours by packaging a range of products designed to be attractive to passengers. These products are then on-sold to the cruise ship operators who sell these tours to passengers prior to the ship's arrival in port. Inbound tour operators arrange all the supporting infrastructure and service requirements to ensure that passengers have a positive experience. They are typically responsible for the entire package offering. In addition to these services, they may be the primary organization responsible for organizing the transfers to and from the ship for disembarking and embarking passengers.
- *Local customs and emigration officials* will be involved whenever a ship's voyage goes outside the departure port country's territorial waters and is calling at another country's port. Depending on the country visited, there may also be agriculture surveillance measures in place.
- The *cruise ship's agent* has a number of responsibilities for all matters relating to

Table 13.1. Selected itinerary planning criteria.

Categories	Sub-categories
Cruise ship type	Large resort ships
	Mid-sized ships
	Small or boutique ships
Cruise duration	<7 days
	8–15 days
	>15 days
Cruise style	Lifestyle
	Speciality
Port locations	Turnaround ports
	Provisioning and
	bunkering ports
	Destination ports
Destinations	Distance between
	destinations
	Attractiveness
	Access
	Infrastructure
	Yield management
	Passenger feedback
Passenger	Target markets
characteristics	

the ship's call, from both a passenger and operational perspective. These include the organization of passengers who are both disembarking and embarking. They also arrange for the berthing of the ship and for any stores and supplies that could be required. They are the go-between for the ship and the local authorities.

• The *port authorities and berthing operators* are the organizations that look after getting a ship safely into harbour and for berthing at the wharf. The control of the wharf and the associated facilities is the responsibility of the port authority or the berth operator. They work closely with the ship's agent once it has berthed. Environmental and security aspects of a cruise ship's visit are strictly controlled according to the status of the berth and any local and international requirements.

Cruise Ship Types

The physical size and passenger capacity of a ship heavily influence the content of the

itinerary and passenger characteristics. Generally, the ships that have recently been commissioned and are currently under construction are bigger than ever, thus creating a mass market product and allowing companies to achieve economies of scale (Weaver, 2005). In addition to this market segment, there has been a growth in niche markets catered to by smaller luxury and specialist ships.

Typically, cruises can be classified according to the following three types.

Large resort ships

These ships typically carry between 1600 and 3000 passengers. There are now new mega-cruise ships that can carry over 6000 passengers, such as the recently launched *Oasis of the Seas* and her sister ships that have a 6300 passenger capacity. Large resort ships are now the most common size of cruise ship in operation. They are designed for those passengers who are sociable and typically enjoy an urban environment, so an itinerary needs to match their specific requirements. As these ships are able to take advantage of economies of scale, they can offer a more budget type cruise to appeal to that segment of the market.

Their large physical size places a number of constraints on their destinations. First, they need to be based at a turnaround port that can handle large volumes of passengers quickly and efficiently, such as Port Everglades in Florida. Second, they require ports that can physically handle such large ships and where there are no impediments to berthing. The mega-size cruise ships such as the *Oasis of the Seas* require an air draught or height (up to 72 m) and water draught or depth (9.5 m), excluding them from many ports and waterways where there are bridges that prevent the passage of such large ships as the city of Bergen and the Baltic region. Their width, at 47 m, excludes them from transiting the Panama Canal (max size of 32×294 m) or the Suez Canal (40-m beam). More typical of this size of ship is the Princess Cruises' *Grand Class* that docks at Phu My instead of the destination port of Ho Chi Minh City (Saigon) because of its draught restrictions. Similar restrictions apply to Brisbane, where larger ships cannot go under the city's bridge and have to dock at the container terminal some distance away.

However, these ships tend to have a shallower draught and less air draught. This enables them to berth at traditional city wharves or ports closer to main centres of attractions. An example of this is Darling Harbour in Sydney that is not available to larger ships, as they cannot pass under the Sydney Harbour Bridge.

Mid-sized ships

These ships typically carry between 600 and 1600 passengers. Figure 13.1, for example, shows Oceania Cruises' *Regatta* with a berth capacity for 684 passengers. With fewer passengers on board the cost per passenger rises, particularly if it is a newer ship. Depending on the ship in question, this does tend to attract a highly differentiated group of passengers and may target a specific segment of the industry, such as the over 60s patronage of Saga Cruises. Because these ships are smaller, they are able to berth at places not available to the larger ships. Typical of this size of vessel is the Fred Olsen ship *Balmoral*, which has a length of 190 m. On the smaller ships the entertainment is usually restricted, and there may be fewer lectures by experts.

Small or boutique ships

These ships typically provide the passengers with an intimate cruise experience. This has been a market that has seen a rapid increase in numbers because of increasing demand from those who want to venture away from the crowds, journey to some of the more remote places on earth and have the opportunity to experience some 'soft adventure' activities such as kayaking.

The ships range from an Antarctic cruise aboard a no-frills research ship such as the *Professor Khromov* (aka *Spirit of Enderby*) to the five star expedition ship *Orion* of Expedition Cruises that has been described by Ward (2008) as 'the latest in the quest to build the perfect expedition

Fig. 13.1.   Oceania Cruises' mid-sized *Regatta* in Milford Sound, New Zealand. Source: Oceania Cruises.

vessel'. Ships specially designed for this expedition type cruising are suitable for an itinerary that is unavailable to the larger mass-market type ships with environmental or logistical constraints. Such places as the Amazon, Antarctic, small islands or places with shallow draught and limited space are unavailable for the larger ships. The hull may be ice-strengthened, or they have waterline access for inflatable boats to tender small groups of passengers into otherwise inaccessible places. These types of ship may offer a higher class of accommodation and food.

Cruise Duration

Itineraries are based around the following types of cruise ship product:

- short holiday or party cruises where the itinerary may not be a major consideration from a passenger's viewpoint (under 7 days length);
- destination specific cruises (8–15 days) where passengers have specific expectations about where they go and what they see; and
- sector or world cruises (longer than 15 days) where the ship itself plays a greater part in the overall passenger satisfaction.

Another important factor, in addition to the above points, is the length of holiday the passengers have available to them, i.e. short week, 2-week holiday period or extended time available (see Vogel and Oschmann, Chapter 1, this volume). Examples of this include P&O's *Ventura* 2-night weekend cruise from Southampton to Belgium, the 'casino' cruises based out of Singapore and the party cruises out of Florida.

Consideration also has to be given to the travelling time from the passengers' home base to the points of departure and arrival for a cruise. Where there is a strong home base market there are no major passenger travelling times to the port of embarkation. Southampton for the UK market and Florida for the North American market are prime examples of this. At the other end of the spectrum are the destinations of Asia and the South Pacific for both Americans and Europeans. Here the travelling time to reach a departure port may involve two days of travel before embarking upon a ship.

Itineraries are best organized in such a way that they are grouped within a region in a pattern that enables the major attractions to be visited within the specified length of the cruise. The Baltic and Eastern Mediterranean are prime examples of this, where a different port and set of attractions can be reached overnight. Therefore, it is desirable to review what a specific destination can offer in relation to those nearby.

Sector or world cruises generally involve a cruise of 15 days or longer and may or may not have a home port as the departure or arrival port. Thus some degree of air travel will be involved. The exception to this is the Atlantic crossing. Generally, these cruises have a higher proportion of sea days in comparison to shore excursion days and are an attraction for those passengers who enjoy being on board the ship as much as at ports of call. Specific ports may be chosen such as Kota Kinabalu in Borneo, so that passengers can see endangered wildlife such as orang-utans.

Cruise Style

The itinerary needs to match the overall style of a cruise and reflect the specific needs and preferences of the customer segments to be targeted by the cruise. Cruise style is a slightly ambiguous term, which can refer to a range of different characteristics. For example, it may relate to a particular passenger lifestyle or to special passenger interests.

Lifestyle

Family: With great kids' programmes, rock-climbing walls, the latest video games and even teen-only discos, family cruises have something for everyone, from the tiniest infant to the gregarious teenager. A cruise line can provide special family-friendly cabins with separate rooms or more than one bathroom, such as Disney Cruises.

Seniors: Celebrations, birthdays and anniversaries can be a feature of a cruise. Some cruise lines, such as Saga, specifically target the golden-years passengers and cater for senior-friendly activities, and P&O have *Arcadia* as a child-free ship.

Other lifestyle-oriented cruises may cater especially for the needs and preferences of gay and lesbian customers, luxury lovers, honeymooners and romantics, singles or people with disabilities.

Speciality cruising

Expedition: An expedition cruise is all about the destination. Passengers are seeking places that are remote or not easily accessed and therefore less visited. This type of cruise caters for those who want 'soft adventure', such as snorkelling at the Great Barrier Reef, viewing natural attractions such as the unique fauna on the Galapagos Islands, or a southern ocean voyage to the glaciers and penguins of Antarctica. Alongside the adventure and exploration ashore are all the comforts of the ship's amenities and facilities.

Transatlantic and repositioning: Ocean crossings allow plenty of time at sea to enjoy a ship's many amenities, such as spa treatments and varied cuisine. Popular routes sail from the UK or the Mediterranean to New York or Florida, and vice versa. These voyages suit those passengers who prefer sea days to shore-based activities. They may even provide a means of transport from point to point for those who prefer not to travel by air.

World cruises: World cruises can last more than 100 days or can be broken down into 15-day sectors. The majority of the time on these voyages will be spent at sea. When considering sector cruises, the starting and stopping point for each sector is critical to enable high capacity ratios to be achieved. Destinations such as Los Angeles, Sydney,

Singapore and Hong Kong are chosen for their attractiveness, based on the turnaround port selection criteria discussed.

Other specialities include fitness and recreation cruises, gourmet cruises, theme and special interest cruises as well as exclusive cruises for groups (e.g. incentives and conferences).

Port Locations

Ports need to be classified according to a number of criteria, because there are implications for both the operation of the cruise ship and the requirements of passengers and the local authorities.

Turnaround ports

Turnaround ports are the ports where a cruise starts and ends. If the port has a large number of cruise ship visits and a high volume of passengers to be managed, there are massive logistical demands. Major ports such as Miami and Vancouver are equipped to handle the large volumes, but other ports that receive few turnarounds, such as Oslo or Edinburgh, do not have the ability to cater for large passenger volumes.

Turnaround ports need to have both a wharf and infrastructure that supports the arrival and departure of a large number of passengers over a short period of 7–9 h. For turnaround ports where there is not a large home market, there need to be sufficient airline connections and airlift capacity to enable passengers to arrive and depart. With the average number of passengers on the newer cruise ships approaching 2000–3000 passengers, this is a significant number of people to transport and process in such a timeframe. Remember that the current passengers have to first disembark before new passengers are embarked (on board) for the next cruise.

To achieve an even flow of passengers and to accomplish such a task within a suitable time, it is necessary for a ship to arrive early in the morning before 09:00 h and to begin disembarking passengers as soon as possible. This allows sufficient time to reorganize the ship for the incoming passengers, who generally board from mid-afternoon onwards prior to an early evening departure.

From a ship's perspective, it is necessary to process a large amount of documentation in respect of passenger movements. On board the ship, all cabins and facilities have to be prepared for the incoming passengers.

Ports have to fulfil a number of regulatory requirements for security and waste product disposal, as well as provided a high level of service. As the ships are operating according to a fixed schedule, they have to be able to arrive at and enter a port regardless of the tide, and be able to berth safely. Because of this schedule, they require a guaranteed berthing preference before all other shipping at a port. In addition to this, modern cruise ships of 2000 passenger capacity need to be able to navigate to a berth with a safe draught of 11 m. They also have a requirement for a 600-m minimum turning basin and require a berthing length of 300 m.

In terms of a passenger terminal facility, the requirement is to be able to process the disembarking passengers within 1–2 h and the embarking passengers within 2–3 h. Terminal facilities are an important feature of the cruise ship industry, as they are the interface between land-based and the sea-based experience. Any disruption to this passenger flow reflects upon the total experience. Terminals need to be similar to what one now expects at an airport, with air bridges connecting the ship to the terminal and any customs and immigration requirements to be speedily handled. In addition to this, there needs to be adequate passenger transportation services to support such a large number of passenger movements at any one time. There is also the requirement to have the necessary government agencies such as Customs and Immigration and Agriculture.

Another important consideration is the supporting infrastructure, which includes passenger reception facilities, airlift capacity and passenger transport. Without this infrastructure, potential passenger numbers will be limited. The supporting infrastructure will depend to some extent upon where the potential passengers are drawn from and the ease with which they can get to the cruise ship terminal. If all the potential passengers live within close proximity to the terminal, then the infrastructure requirements are likely to be minimal. If, on the other hand, you are dealing with large numbers of people arriving or leaving from a departure/arrival port, then a number of things have to be in place. Therefore, the access to sufficient hotels and air connections is extremely important, as is the ability to provision with fresh water and some stores.

Consider the case of a cruise ship turning around in Singapore with predominantly North American or European passengers. The disembarking passengers will either want to fly back to their home country the day they disembark, or they will stay on in a local hotel for a period (typically 1–5 days). The embarking passengers will generally have arrived the night before departure and stayed at a local hotel or will have arrived by air on the morning of departure. Therefore, there is a requirement for up to 750 hotel rooms and aircraft capacity of the equivalent of six jumbo jets to fly these people back to their home country. If these aspects cannot be accomplished, then a ship will not be able to sail at full capacity, or will have to find enough locals to take up the unfilled berths.

Provisioning and bunkering ports

Provisioning and bunkering are not always undertaken at the turnaround port, although this would be the ideal situation. These ports provide the life-blood for any cruise ship and are the critical component in the operation of the ship. It is often the case that top-ups will be made at intermediate ports to provide fresh produce and urgent supplies, or where a good price has been negotiated. It may also be more economic to carry less fuel and top-up more often, because a ship uses less fuel and therefore costs less to run when it is lighter. It is also not uncommon for some turnaround ports to lack provisioning capabilities, such as Sydney in Australia.

Provisioning is the taking on of supplies and services necessary for the daily running of the ship and includes such items as food, beverages, consumables, fresh flowers, items for the various shops on board and even currency. It is not unusual for a ship to consume the equivalent of 15 standard and refrigerated 40-ft containers at any one time. In addition to this, there is a need to dispose of waste and recyclable products such as cooking oils, wine bottles and cardboard, etc.

Bunkering is the taking on of fuel to run a ship. This is a major exercise in itself and can take many hours to complete. It is also an expensive item to purchase because of the large volumes used, when one considers a ship could burn 6–10 t per hour when travelling. This figure is very dependent on both the size of the ship and the speed with which it is travelling. Therefore, consideration has to be given to the most economic speed used to cover any particular route or distance. At 18 knots, you achieve 420 nautical miles in a 24-h period, as opposed to travelling at 22 knots and achieving a distance of 520 nautical miles but at a considerably higher operating cost.

Destination ports

These are the ports or places where the ship either stops nearby (tender ports) or berths so that passengers can go ashore. Tender ports or destinations without landing facilities typically make use of the ship's own craft to ferry passengers to a particular location of interest. This does slow down the transfer of passengers and may be more weather dependent than berthing at a port. The tendering process often takes place so that passengers can go ashore to beaches or places where no port facilities exist or the ship itself is too large to be accommodated.

A normal transit port does not have the infrastructure requirements of a turnaround port, and often the berth is at a general ship berth with no dedicated passenger facilities. This aspect in itself can be a major issue, both in terms of passenger comfort and accessibility to local attractions. It is not uncommon in this instance to be berthed at a container terminal some distance from a place of interest, as is the case in Singapore for larger cruise ships.

Transit ports provide access to shore attractions and as such are a feeder to the activity undertaken ashore. Some of these ports provide a gateway to a specific attraction or destination which may be located far away. Examples of this and the requirement for an integrated transport/transfer system can be seen at places such as Rome, where the port of Civitavecchia is about 1.5–2 h from the city by bus or train; Ho Chi Minh City (Saigon), where the port of Phu My is a 2-h bus trip away; and Berlin, which is a 2.5-h train ride from the port of Warnemünde.

Popular destination ports are often called by several cruise ships simultaneously, which may cause congestion in port, in a nearby town centre and at the main tourist attractions. Figure 13.2 shows three cruise ships and cruise ferries leaving the port of Stockholm. The picture has been taken from a fourth ship. Itinerary planners need to consider carefully whether calling at popular but congested ports will suit their respective cruise products.

Destinations

Distance between destinations

The distance between ports is one of the main variables that go into an itinerary planning exercise along with the desired cruising speed of the ship (18 knots). Distance here refers not only to the distance between ports, but also to the distance from a home port to the destination port. A cruise line also needs to take into account the distance from where passengers originate, and the ship's departure and final destination

Fig. 13.2.   Popular destination: cruise ship race in the Stockholm archipelago, Sweden. Source: E.W. Manning, Tourisk Inc.

port, as these may not be the same. Itinerary planners need to consider whether passengers are able to get to the departure port within 8 h of their home town, or does it take 2 days to reach the other side of the world? This is an important consideration, as passengers may not want to travel a great distance to join a voyage. It also adds to the duration of a cruise holiday. The extra cost of airfares and accommodation will add to the total holiday cost, and capacity constraints may limit the ability of a passenger to arrive at or leave a destination port.

In addition to this, the desired time to be spent at a destination port needs to be carefully considered. Generally passengers wish to arrive at a port by 08:00 h (in the morning) and leave before 18:00 h (in the early evening). This enables maximum daylight hours ashore and the ability to leave after breakfast and return for an evening meal.

The desired voyage length in terms of days influences the potential number of ports or destinations that can be visited. With longer voyages, it may be possible to have a greater number of port calls. With some of the shorter voyages, a critical

distance may be the distance to the first port of call and the distance to the last port of call, to enable an early arrival to speed up disembarkation of passengers at the end of a voyage. The number of sea days is an interesting topic. Some passengers like sea days, while others hate them and want to visit a new destination every day. Therefore, a balance needs to be found between choosing attractive destinations and yet having a voyage that fits with passengers' available timeframes for holidays.

It has been found that there appears to be a difference between first-time cruisers, who tend to demand more intensive port itineraries, and more experienced cruisers, who appear to prefer a more relaxed itinerary with more days at sea (Cartwight and Baird, 1999; Lingard, 2002; Haller, 2005). Thus these opposite desires will influence the cruise planning philosophy (Marti, 1992), and itinerary planners need to consider the target market for a particular cruise in order to achieve the correct balance between the number of ports visited and the number of days at sea. A typical cruise ship may be comprised of over 70% of passengers who have already cruised before.

There does exist the opportunity for planners to promote to the first-time cruise passenger market through the use of short cruises to give passengers a taste of cruising. Such cruises are generally of less than 4 days duration and operate out of a home port, thus segmenting the market and leading to higher levels of passenger satisfaction.

From an operational perspective, the distance between the turnaround port, bunkering port and provisioning port, plus the duration of the voyage, require careful consideration.

Attractiveness

For a destination to be attractive, it has to offer the cruise company a desirable package, whether with port facilities or as a gateway for passengers to have a memorable and enjoyable experience ashore and the required infrastructure to support such a ship visit.

Where a destination port is a turnaround port, the ability to handle foreign or interstate passengers provides an opportunity for add-on services, either before or after a cruise, for example hotel accommodation, excursions, shopping and sightseeing. These complementary experiences may be sold to prospective passengers and have become another opportunity for cruise companies to extend their product offering. This is especially true when passengers either have to travel a long distance to join a cruise or to return home from where a cruise ends. A destination such as Sydney in Australia has the ability to offer a package holiday either prior to or at the end of a cruise for those people from the northern hemisphere.

The shore-based attractions and activities need to be packaged in such a way that they can be sold to passengers prior to arrival at a destination, and then this activity will generate a positive financial return to the cruise line.

The ability of a cruise line to offer an attractive and varied itinerary attracts new passengers and encourages past passengers to cruise again. Many cruise lines have a choice of ship size to deploy on any given itinerary, so it is possible to build up with a small ship and then move to a larger ship, should that particular itinerary become popular with passengers. It is also possible to replace a larger ship with a smaller one, should problems occur in any particular segment. Therefore, allowing for a larger ship to fit into an existing itinerary is an important consideration when developing a new destination. Such an entry strategy has been employed by Princess Cruises in developing its Asian destinations.

Passenger feedback plays an important part in measuring the attractiveness of a port or destination, and most cruise lines carry out intensive surveys of passengers' experiences. This research is then fed back into the itinerary planning process for future voyages. For new or potential destinations, port inspections will often take place. When determining the factors that influenced the passengers' choice of cruise, it was found that the selection of ports of call ranked second only to the cost (Marti, 1991).

For many passengers, there can be a feeling of fear and apprehension when visiting countries or places with which they are unfamiliar. To overcome this, itinerary planning needs to choose locations and attractions that offer similar standards to either that of the passenger's home country or that of the ship. When it comes to the type of attractions that can be undertaken at a destination, two views can be taken. If it is a speciality cruise type, then common type attractions may suffice. An example of this would be a cruise to the fjords of Norway. If not, then destinations that offer different but balanced complimentary attractions may be the best choice, and examples of this include cruises around the Mediterranean visiting places of historical interest.

Port access for both ships and passengers

From a ship's operational perspective, basic facilities such as berthing or anchorage and jetty facilities are required, while from a passenger perspective a base level of infrastructure in terms of reception, transport and activities is expected. Figure 13.3

Fig. 13.3.   Sint Maarten's dedicated cruise port offers direct access to Philipsburg. Source: E.W. Manning, Tourisk Inc.

depicts Sint Maarten's extensive dedicated cruise port which meets cruise lines' as well as passengers' infrastructure requirements.

With the predominance of the larger resort ships, shore facilities have not universally matched this change. This has resulted in access being limited or relocated to distant facilities at many ports. The use of tendering, while possible, is not preferred by some passengers and is not an option for passengers with limited mobility. It is a slower transfer process from ship to shore and is also more weather dependent.

In terms of a access to facilities at ports, cruise ships are competing in many cases with cargo shipping for berth space (Fig. 13.4). This is particularly the case at smaller ports or for the larger cruise ships that require considerable wharf space. When a cruise line is not a regular visitor or the cruise ship visits are infrequent, then they may be seen by the port as a disruption to its operations and will not get the priority access to shore facilities that they would prefer. Therefore, an understanding of the local situation will help when advanced

planning is being undertaken. It may also mean that to gain port access, berths have to be booked many years in advance to ensure access is guaranteed.

At ports that receive simultaneous ship calls on any one day, congestion may occur, both at the port and ashore. This can cause both delays and confusion in terms of what attractions to provide for passengers. It may also mean that passengers have limited or crowded access at attractions and become dissatisfied with the destination. Such a situation occurs for the attractions at Athens, Rome and at ports in the Caribbean and Alaska. To overcome these issues, ports can play an active role in managing cruise ship traffic and preventing congestion.

Infrastructure

Infrastructures are in two forms: the port facilities and the supporting facilities at the destination. The appropriateness of port facilities is important when planning an itinerary. Berthing facilities are the first

Fig. 13.4.   Cruise ships sharing piers with containers in Port Chalmers, New Zealand. Source: J. Henry.

consideration, followed by shore facilities. If it is a turnaround port, then shore facilities for passenger movements are crucial for disembarking and embarking passengers.

Much has been said in respect of the role passenger terminals play in satisfying both the cruise line and passengers' expectations and perceived level of service (Singh, 1999; Jugovic´ et al., 2006; Miotke-Dziegiel, 2007). As the cruise industry has grown, so has the provision of facilities, yet they have lagged behind the growth mainly because of the high capital costs involved and the seasonal nature of the industry.

To overcome some of these issues, many ports are now provided with or planning to provide dedicated cruise ship terminals such as Miami and Bremerhaven. Some of the smaller ports are already doing this in conjunction with local government assistance in places such as Darwin, Edinburgh and Cobh (Cork). Carnival, the leading operator, has its own dedicated facility at Long Beach. Much of this development is being driven by the perceived economic impact of a cruise ship visit on a destination.

The importance of supporting infrastructure cannot be overemphasized. Passengers may need hotel accommodation prior to and after a cruise. Suitable buses may be needed to transport passengers to shore attractions, and a local service sector is necessary to ensure passengers have an enjoyable time at a destination.

Yield management

Yield management provides an opportunity for time customization of prices (see Vogel, Chapter 10, this volume). Time customization is the offering of variable prices to encourage demand. An example is the 'future cruise' special prices and benefits available to passengers who book their next cruise while on board the existing cruise. According to Austin (2009), the Senior Vice-President of Planning, Yield Management and Customer Service for Princess

Cruises, 'At the end of the day, the formula is simple: How to generate high demand and high revenues, that focuses on "delivering" both from on-board and ashore.' If information on demand is initially limited, time customizing of prices can be used to respond to demand. Any business that has a fixed capacity, perishable inventory, demand fluctuations and high fixed costs will benefit from yield management, and this will make the operation more profitable. The cruise industry fits all of these criteria. The task, then, from a planning viewpoint, is to price and manage the availability and demand for a particular product offering. It is the product offering that itinerary planning can help create. This can be achieved through offering different ports of call and sought-after attractions at a destination. If this offering is very attractive, then demand will be higher, and the prices do not need to be discounted as much, if at all, to the different segments of the cruises' potential passenger base. The object of the exercise is to fill all the berths at the maximum possible price and to capitalize on the revenue from shore excursions.

Passenger feedback

Passenger feedback assists the planner in developing and enhancing an itinerary. Customer preferences and levels of satisfaction and enjoyment may be particularly strong, and this leads to word-of-mouth being passed on in respect of a particular cruise line or voyage. According to Chris Allen (2009), Director of Deployment and Itinerary Planning for Royal Caribbean, Celebrity and Azamara Cruises, 'Consumer preferences and internal feedback (from ships and travel agents) are also considered' and, 'The itineraries must have a fit for the target markets.'

Such feedback can be used to inform and influence destinations' attractiveness and lead to a win-win situation for both the cruise line and the destination involved.

Passenger Characteristics

Passenger characteristics can be described in many ways. Country of origin has been the most common form of classification to date. Passengers originating from the USA account for up to 90% of the cruise ship passengers worldwide. Hence the influence of this market is tremendous. The UK, Germany, Italy and Spain make up the bulk of the European-based passengers. The growth markets are seen as coming from Asia and Australasia.

Passenger supply and demand characteristics since the economic downturn of 2008 have impacted the cruise industry in a number of ways. There has been a noticeable decline in a significant number of American passengers' willingness to travel on long haul flights to distance locations. This has meant that the American-based passengers want to go on their more traditional Caribbean cruises. Another consequence of this recession is the demand from passengers for shorter cruises, which come at a lower personal cost.

An increase in the volume of berths available on cruise ships and the downturn in the economic situation has seen many of the cruise lines focusing on attracting 'first time' cruisers through the use of localized short cruises. This can be seen in the new itineraries of lines such as P&O and Royal Caribbean, who are offering mini cruises of under 7 days' duration. A characteristic of some of the 'first time' cruisers is their limited budget and unwillingness to pay for additional services or tours that are profitable for the cruise line.

To balance the winter deployment of ships from the northern hemisphere many of the cruise lines have sent their ships to South America, South-east Asia, and 'Down Under' to Australia and New Zealand. However, with the lack of American patronage passengers are being sought from both the local and international markets. Traditionally these local markets have not been accustomed to taking cruise ship holidays. An example of this is Princess Cruises who have recent deployment of three ships to the Australian and New

Zealand market. This is driven in part from their existing customer base, which is also looking for new experiences. Those passengers from North America and Europe are inclined to spend more for a cruise that is perceived to be more exotic. This combination will drive alternative deployments of ships and itineraries.

As markets change and the existing passenger base that has grown wants to experience new destinations, new markets need to be developed. This is also necessary in order both to attract first-time passengers and to convince previous passengers to voyage again to a different destination.

While the North American market dominates the cruise industry, the European and Asian markets are presently growing faster than the US (Butler, 2003; Vogel and Oschmann, chapter 1 this volume). This expansion is not only geographic, it is also socio-demographic with, for example, cruise organizations targeting new age groups, families, and population segments with lower and higher levels of income. Overall, the demographic profile of the average person taking a cruise is: over 55 years old, earns an annual income over US$75,000, has a university degree, is married and employed (CLIA, 2004; PSA, 2004).

Lingard (2002) observed that the more affluent and experienced sea tourists have the desire for first-hand knowledge of less-visited parts of the world. It has been estimated that two-thirds of people taking a cruise are repeaters (Dickinson and Vladimir, 2007). The assumption is that repeat passengers wish to visit new and different destinations.

Conclusions

First, there is the need to consider the port of embarkation and disembarkation as an integral part of the itinerary planning process. The supporting infrastructure needs to be in place to maximize the attractiveness of these ports for a cruise ship. Second, passengers' views and experiences impact the viability or otherwise of a destination and

may indeed help shape it for future visits. The need to develop new destinations and activities ashore is necessary to attract new passengers and to retain past customers. While the shipboard experience is important, the itinerary and destination attractiveness is what encourages many passengers to take a voyage in the first place. Operational issues such as port access, berthing, bunkering and provisioning, and a ship's characteristics act as modifiers to any itinerary. Also included in these issues are the nature of the voyage and the distances between ports.

Case Study: Australia and New Zealand Summer Cruise

For the larger brand cruise lines planning itineraries for their large fleets of ships, there are two issues for consideration. First, the planners need to find new and exciting destinations for their loyal customer base and second, to utilize the available ship capacity.

Planners need to cater for the needs of the majority of passengers who are mainly from the USA and the UK. During the northern hemisphere summer, the focus for these passengers is cruising the main geographic destinations of the Caribbean, Alaska, Northern Europe and the Mediterranean. During winter the attractiveness and viability of cruising Alaska, Northern Europe and the Mediterranean is severely diminished. Therefore, alternative destinations are sought. To provide a summer break, the available destinations shift either to the Caribbean and Panama or to the southern hemisphere. The southern hemisphere areas include South America, South-east Asia and Australia/New Zealand. The advantage of these cruise regions is that few North Americans and Europeans have visited them, which represents a significant potential.

To demonstrate the influence of different criteria (Table 13.1) and restrictions influence the planning of an itinerary, an example will now be given in form of a short case study. The cruise itinerary around New Zealand and Australia depicted in Fig. 13.5 and outlined below allows passengers from North America and Europe to see some of the major attractions of both countries within a 12-day period.

When not dealing with a home market, and there are considerable distances involved in travelling between major attractions, there is an opportunity to start and end a cruise at a different port, provided the required conditions can be met. The major cities of both Australia and New Zealand can provide both a start port and end port. Therefore, a cruise of this nature can operate as a separate cruise in either direction (yo-yo cruise).

From a planning perspective, the following physical facilities and constraints are important and must be considered carefully:

- The major bunkering ports are Auckland, Melbourne and Sydney.
- The major provisioning ports are Melbourne and Tauranga, with limited facilities available at Auckland and restricted facilities (ship size dependent) in Sydney.
- Some ports have limited berths and associated facilities – Auckland and Lyttelton – and need to be booked well in advance (2 years).

- The ports must be able to accept ships of the intended physical size in terms of length and draught, regardless of tidal constraints.
- Container terminals are at Auckland, Tauranga, Christchurch, Dunedin, Melbourne, Hobart and Sydney, the bulk of the provisioning being supplied in containers from North America.
- The major international airports are Auckland and Sydney.
- The ship can reach the destinations within an acceptable speed range (16–18 knots) for economic fuel consumption and still give passengers sufficient time ashore.

From a passenger perspective, the following are important requirements:

- the ability for international passengers to fly to the departure port and depart from the arrival port;
- good hotels at both departure and arrival ports;
- potential to arrive at a destination prior to a cruise and stay at a destination after a cruise;
- the cruise length will fit into a holiday break period of 14 days;
- each of the ports to be visited has attractions that will appeal to the major target group of passengers;

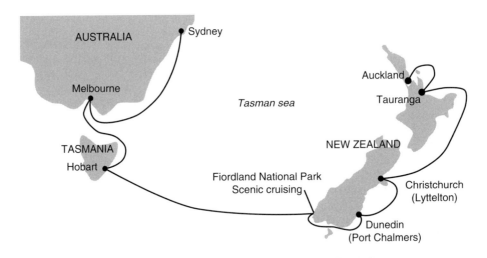

Fig. 13.5.   An exemplary 12-day cruise itinerary around New Zealand and Australia.

- some sea days are acceptable; and
- the destinations are seen as safe for passengers.

The starting port for the Australia and New Zealand summer cruise can be either Auckland or Sydney. When beginning in Auckland the itinerary includes major visitor attractions of Geyserland or a native Maori show from Tauranga, calling at several ports along the New Zealand coast and ending in a scenic cruise of the New Zealand fjords. After crossing the Tasman Sea, the major attractions include the indigenous animals of Australia, such as the koalas and kangaroos, the penal colony remains at Port Arthur near Hobart and the attractive city of Melbourne. The voyage ends in the beautiful harbour at Sydney.

Given all the above considerations and suitable visitor attractions, an itinerary was planned and is detailed in Table 13.2. Travelling distances and time have to be consistent both with the requirements of passengers and from a ship's operational perspective. The itinerary, once finalized, was fed into the intended ship's schedule, port and associated facilities were booked, and company promotional material was prepared.

Once these steps had been carried out, the cruise company was committed to undertaking the voyage. However, because of the 2-year lag from planning the itinerary to the actual departure, a number of changes occurred either before or during the cruise, which affected the itinerary. A cruise that left Auckland in the summer of 2009 is used to illustrate many of the issues raised within this chapter.

The first major changes that occurred were within the international financial markets and increased security regulations at airports and ports. The major airlines that serve the North American market (Qantas and Air New Zealand) cut back on flights to/from USA because fewer North Americans travelled, because of financial constraints arising as a result of the world financial crisis. Passengers from Australia and New Zealand tended to choose to fly to Europe via Southeast Asia instead of via the USA, because of

perceived delays at the American border. Consequently, the airlift capacity to reach and depart New Zealand and Australia from North America was severely depleted.

To make up the deficit in passenger numbers, the cruise line decided to promote heavily to the home market of New Zealand and Australia with a planned itinerary not specifically designed for these passengers. The itinerary was originally planned around the preferences of passengers from North America, who have different spending characteristics and preferences to those from the home market. This promotion decision had some financial implications for the cruise company. The home market passengers often travelled independently on their on-shore sightseeing tours and did not book through the cruise company in the same numbers as the North Americans, so the yield per passenger earned by the company was lower.

With the reduced airlift capacity and the length of flight from the northern hemisphere, many of the passengers booked both a pre- or post-cruise tour of between 2 and 7 days from the cruise line, which increased the yield associated with the cruise.

Following the itinerary as detailed in Table 13.2, the ship departed from Auckland. There are several considerations for itinerary planning at this port because it has only a single berth for cruise ships, and 10 h are needed to accomplish a turnaround. Sufficient time must be allowed for the processing of several thousand passengers embarking and disembarking the ship, clearing customs and immigration. There are space constraints here, so it is difficult to take on provisions. The next port of call is Tauranga, where more than one cruise ship may be berthed at any one time. There is sufficient area here for provisioning. The Port of Lyttelton can accommodate only one large cruise ship at a time. A rival cruise line that had not booked well ahead had to anchor in the alternative port of Akaroa and tender passengers ashore, with an associated extra 1.5-h drive to reach any of the desired attractions.

After leaving the last port of call in New Zealand at Dunedin, the ship headed

Table 13.2. Itinerary for cruise around New Zealand and Australia.

Day	Port	Distance (nautical miles)	Avg. speed (knots)	Arrive	Depart
1	Auckland				18:00
2	Tauranga	147	15	07:00	19:00
3	Cruising the South Pacific Ocean				
4	Christchurch (Lyttelton)	577	18	08:00	18:00
5	Dunedin (Port Chalmers)	188	16	08:00	18:00
6	Cruising Fiordland				
7	Cruising the Tasman Sea				
8	Cruising the Tasman Sea				
9	Hobart	927	16	08:00	18:00
10	Cruising the Tasman Sea				
11	Melbourne	469	15	08:00	18:00
12	Cruising the Tasman Sea				
13	Sydney	568	18	08:00	

overnight for a day of scenic cruising in the New Zealand fjords. At the end of that cruising day, the weather deteriorated markedly. The Tasman Sea changed from a 1-m swell to a 5-m swell with strong winds. In the interests of passenger comfort, the ship altered course and reduced speed. After some period of travelling along this course, the Captain made the decision to abandon making the planned call at Hobart, Australia, and to head for an early arrival in Melbourne.

Altering course and reducing speed changed the characteristics of the voyage. While it was possible to reach Hobart in time, it would have come at a cost to passenger comfort and a reduced time in port.

To increase speed to make up for lost time would have caused additional passenger discomfort and increased the ship's fuel usage, as it went to the top end of its cruising speed. From a passenger perspective, this was a major disappointment for the Australian home-based passengers, who would have preferred still to call at Hobart and not Melbourne. From an operational perspective (that overrides in most situations), Melbourne was a critical port, and it was there that full provisions and bunkering were to be undertaken. Thus Hobart was sacrificed for operational reasons, and passengers gained an extra day in Melbourne with an unplanned overnight stay.

References

Allen, C. (2009) Itinerary Planning and Demand Revenues. Available at: www.cruiseindustrynews.com/cruise-news-articles/67-articles/2448-spring-09-itinerary-planning-demand-and-revenues.html (accessed 20 July 2010).

Austin, D. (2009) Itinerary Planning and Demand Revenues. Available at: www.cruiseindustrynews.com/cruise-news-articles/67-articles/2448-spring-09-itinerary-planning-demand-and-revenues.html (accessed 20 July 2010).

Butler, M. (2003) *Worldwide Cruise Ship Activity*. World Tourism Organization, Madrid.

Cartwright, R. and Baird, C. (1999) *The Development and Growth of the Cruise Industry*. Butterworth Heinemann, Oxford.

Cruise Lines International Association (CLIA) (2004) *The Overview – Spring 2004*. Cruise Lines International Association Inc., Fort Lauderdale, Florida.

Dickinson, B. and Vladimir, A. (2007) *Selling the Sea: an Inside Look at the Cruise Industry*, 2nd edn. Wiley, New York.

Haller, A. (2005) Setting Different Courses for Royal Caribbean and Celebrity. Available at: www.cruise
industrynews.com/cruise-news-articles/67-articles/44-spring-05-setting-different-courses-for-royal-
caribbean-and-celebrity.html (accessed 18 March 2005).

Jugović, A., Mezak, V. and Lončar, S. (2006) *Organisation of Maritime Passenger Ports. Pomorski zbornik*
44(1), 93–104.

Lingard, N. (2002) The route less travelled: Fred Olsen Lines keeps it interesting. *International Cruise & Ferry
Review* 6(2), 193.

Marti, B.E. (1991) Cruise ship market segmentation: a 'non-traditional' port case study. *Maritime Policy
Management* 18(2), 93–103.

Marti, B.E. (1992) Passenger perceptions of cruise itineraries. *Marine Policy* 16(5), 360–70.

Miotke-Dziegiel, J. (2007) Ports in development of maritime tourism, problems and challenges – the case of
the Pomeranian region. *Tourism and Hospitality Management* 13(2), 483–492.

PSA (2004) *Annual Cruise Review*. Passenger Shipping Association, London.

Singh, A. (1999) Growth and development of the cruise line industry in South East Asia. *Asia Pacific Journal
of Tourism Research* 3(2), 24–31.

Ward, D. (2008) *Complete Guide to Cruising & Cruise Ships 2008*, 17th edn. Berlitz, London.

Weaver, A. (2005) Spaces of containment and revenue capture: 'super-sized' cruise ships as mobile tourism
enclaves. *Tourism Geographies* 7(2), 165–184.

14 Shore-side Activities

Wendy R. London

Introduction

People cruise for different reasons. They may want to visit as many ports as possible, use the ship as a comfortable means of transport between two or more destinations or transform their cruise holiday into a resort holiday and remain on board. The profile of cruise passengers is equally varied, including their nationality, age, economic status and whether they are travelling alone, as a couple or with a large family group.

However, getting as many passengers as possible off the ship, no matter what their age, income or number of travel companions, needs to be the objective of port destination communities because of the economic contribution that passengers make to those communities. Passenger spend can be made up of micro-payments for bus rides, entry fees or a quick sandwich or more substantial payments for a full day shore excursion, which includes lunch and a visit to an upmarket jewellery shop or the purchase of expensive 'souvenirs'. In other words, port destinations must be able to capture as much of the cruise visitors' consumer surplus as possible, i.e. making sure that there are sufficient opportunities for the cruise visitor to spend what they are willing or prepared to spend and not end up repatriating their left-over holiday money at the end of their cruise. For a discussion about tourists' consumer surplus, see Wells (1997).

Given the limited time that cruise passengers have in port, the shore excursion is the most effective way of capturing that consumer surplus because, largely, passenger behaviour during the shore excursion can be managed. Attractions, activities and retail outlets, which have been groomed to appeal to generally well-off cruise passengers, can successfully capture that surplus. However, the design, development and supply of shore excursions are an increasingly complex exercise as both the motivations and profiles of cruise visitors become more varied. Port destination communities, shore excursion operators and other product providers, who do not understand the nature of cruise tourism, will be less successful. Therefore, they must understand both their role in the development and design of shore excursions (supply) as well as cruise passenger behaviour in relation to shore excursion preferences (demand). Only when these two variables tally will the port destination be able to capture the available consumer surplus. Both supply and demand are discussed in this chapter.

It should be noted that while the topics presented in this chapter are relevant to cruise destinations worldwide, most of the examples derive from New Zealand where the cruise industry continues to experience substantial growth. During the 1996/97 cruise season, New Zealand hosted 19,400 passengers on 27 cruises, with a total direct expenditure of NZ$42 million. During the 2009/10 season, these figures increased to 109,951 passengers on 81 cruises, with a total direct expenditure of NZ$271 million. Passenger numbers are expected to increase to 199,943 passengers during the 2011/12 season (Market Economics, 2010). New Zealand poses an interesting context for a discussion of shore excursions, not only because this growth has led to continuing investment in the further development of onshore activities for visiting passengers, but also to a heightened awareness of the value of cruising to the New Zealand economy and a growing interest amongst New Zealanders in cruising.

Supply: Making an Impression on Ships and their Passengers

Capturing passenger spend through shore excursions is a proposition that involves not only the passengers themselves but also the ships that transport them. In that sense, both the passenger and the ship are the destination's customers. The ships must be lured to the destination while passengers must be attracted not only to the destination but also to the ship which will take them there. In addition, the destination's onshore attractions and activities must compete against each other for passenger spend whether the passenger books through the ship's shore excursion office or the local visitors centres, or wishes just to wander and discover the essence of the destination independently. It is therefore important for destinations to understand how they can attract ships and their passengers.

Commitment to cruise tourism

The decision by a port community to become a cruise destination requires a long lead-in time to ensure that all relevant stakeholders (e.g. port representatives, attraction operators, retail owners, safety and security personnel and transport providers) can become 'cruise ready'. Cruise ready means that these stakeholders understand the nature of cruise tourism and perhaps more importantly, the behaviour and expectations of cruise passengers. It means also that destination communities must comprehend and be able to respond to the differences between land-based and cruise tourism. Many if not most attractions have been designed primarily for land-based tourists, thereby giving rise to a host of problems when attempting to cater to a distinctly different group.

For example, visitor numbers for most land-based attractions on any given day are low and spread over a longer period, whereas cruise tourism places significant pressures on attractions in a limited time. Usage, revenue streams and management techniques differ as to whether an attraction is geared to land or to cruise visitors:

> The cruise sector has opened up an opportunity for heavy use and instantaneous cash flow from short term but intense use. Unfortunately, in some cases, this had added pressure onto land-based facilities, resulting in congestion, scheduling and control problems, which have affected visitor satisfaction. Ironically, [cruise] Lines complain about the quality of attractions in some of the traditional stomping grounds, calling them stale and overworked. By inference, one has to question whether the term stale is used when Lines experience reduced ship yields from an attraction.
> (Atherley, 2003, p. 9)

The situation described by Atherley is illustrated by Figs 14.1 and 14.2. It is directly applicable to any cruise destination where land tourism prevails, in both practice and policy, as the predominant form of tourism. For example, it is likely that the operators of a scenic railway never envisaged accommodating hundreds of passengers from a large cruise liner on a single day, or at times even from two large cruise liners on the same day. Cruise tourism can place unanticipated and sometimes unwelcome capacity pressures

Fig. 14.1.   Cruise tour traffic jam in Charlotte Amalie, US Virgin Islands. Source: E.W. Manning, Tourisk Inc.

Fig. 14.2.   Cruise buses and tours all arrive at the same time at the Acropolis, Athens. Source: E.W. Manning, Tourisk Inc.

on a community's attractions and services, thereby alienating both residents and land-based tourists and causing dissatisfaction amongst cruise passengers (e.g. Key West, Florida, Hritz and Cecil, 2008; and Charleston, South Carolina, Harris, 2003, B1).

However, if a community is serious about attracting ships and their passengers, there must be careful consideration given to the process of determining which attractions and services will appeal to and can be transformed to fulfil the needs of cruise passengers, or at least provide the level of service required by these passengers during their visit. It should be noted, though, that when compiling an inventory of potential attractions, activities and services for shore excursions that 'the number of excursions is not necessarily the deciding factor for cruise companies in selecting ports of call' and that the 'quality and variety of available excursions is much more important than pure quantity' (Northern Economics, 2002, p. 1-5). The key to successful shore excursions, therefore, is not quantity but instead, understanding the nature of cruise tourism and the expectations of cruise passengers.

Designer shore excursions

The traditional, or at least stereotypical, shore excursion consists of 50 or 60 fellow cruise passengers being ferried around by coach to the scenic and cultural highlights of the port city, stopping for photo opportunities, lunch and a late afternoon visit to the recommended jewellery or craft shop. However, passengers' tastes as well as their sophistication are changing. Shore excursion operators must re-design the cookie-cutter coach tour in order to respond to changing learning styles, passenger preferences and passenger demographics.

For example, operators must respond to passenger feedback such as a preference for more shopping time. More importantly, though, the design of the sightseeing component itself needs also to change to accommodate different learning styles and attention spans. The older generation of

cruise passengers may well be content remaining in their coach bubble (Jaakson, 2004), being driven around to all of the battle sites within a 50-km radius and given 10 min for each photo opportunity high on the hills above the port, but the younger generation requires constant stimulation and an ever-changing landscape of attractions and activities.

Younger passengers, often the children of the Baby Boomers, who increasingly cruise in family groups or with their coterie of friends, will seek out shore excursions that not only satisfy their interests (which are likely to include food, wine, fashion and sport) but are also visually active, consistent with their propensity to multi-task and most importantly, are perceived to be authentic. Authenticity is a notoriously problematic concept, but is used here in its everyday sense of 'being honest'. For a discussion of authenticity and the authentic tourist, see Hall (2007).

Authenticity for these passengers is not just about experiencing cultural or ethnic authenticity but also about meeting the locals and experiencing their way of life, sharing their food, shopping in their local shops and playing a round of golf at the local golf course. Their reliance on the guide on their bus is less; they prefer more to find things out for themselves and get 'stuck in' to the local scene. Combining such authenticity and interactivity, many cruise passengers are interested in attending workshops and demonstrations where they meet the artist or craftsperson, find out how their favourite food or beverage is made or harvested and take home a souvenir of something they made.

Passengers expressed an interest in attending workshops and learning more about the maker during the author's own market research for the development of an e-commerce website, which promotes authentic New Zealand goods and experiences to visiting cruise passengers. Also, as outlined below, as from the 2010/11 cruise season Princess Cruises are offering cultural workshops on board their ships in selected New Zealand ports (Princess Cruises, 2010).

Additionally, many cruise passengers will seek to purchase (or make) something to use, consume or wear and not just something that endlessly gathers dust displayed on a shelf in a mementos cabinet. This propensity to interact with local craftspeople and learn more about their crafts was signalled by Littrell *et al.* (1994) in their discussion about travel styles and shopping characteristics in the broader tourism sector.

and more sophisticated and discerning in their tastes and choices, shore excursions that were popular 5, or even 2 years ago, may lose their interest as tastes change. Therefore, there is a continuing need to refresh the inventory, based on accurate and up-to-date information about passenger interests, travel styles, demographics and other relevant factors (see Vogel and Oschmann, Chapter 1, this volume).

Repeat and refresh

In addition to offering a selection of quality, proven shore excursions, operators must also constantly refresh their offerings, generally by continuing to offer new shore excursions. While the industry continues to attract a high proportion of new cruisers (45% according to CLIA, 2008) repeat cruisers predominate, therefore making it necessary to add new shore excursion offerings on a regular basis. Also, as cruise passengers become more

The independent shore excursion

The design of the shore excursion product must also take into account a growing preference by cruisers for independent or self-organized tours. Many cruise lines have reacted by offering a range of more individual, semi-independent excursions such as quad bike or jeep safaris (Fig. 14.3), bicycle tours or sea kayaking.

The trend towards more independent shore-side activities is being experienced by many destinations including New Zealand

Fig. 14.3.   The jeep safari, a semi-independent form of shore excursion. Source: E.W. Manning, Tourisk Inc.

and Australia. Destination Victoria observes that:

> [T]here are also some tentative signs of a move away from packaged shore excursions to unique independent and personalised tours. At least two of the major cruise lines have acknowledged this trend at a global level. There are a number of possible reasons for this apparent trend, but to some extent, it may be symptomatic of a need to review tour product, particularly given the high incidence of repeat patronage for cruise ships.
>
> (Destination Victoria, 2002, p. 41)

This view was confirmed by a former cruise line Commercial Director who stated that:

> this is a worldwide trend that the cruise lines are beginning to address; the world has moved in terms of available information and direct booking ability and the cruise lines have not. I think over the next few years we will see an inverse of this trend and passengers reconsidering tours offered by cruise lines.
>
> (Personal communication, 15 December 2010)

In New Zealand, visitor centres report a significant increase in independent passengers seeking something different, something affordable and something fun. For example, one port has conducted a survey that revealed that increasing numbers of passengers are making use of the shuttle buses between the port and the city, thereby indicating that fewer passengers are opting for organized tours. A similar pattern is being observed in another New Zealand port (Tauranga/Mt Maunganui) where the pressure being placed on the visitors' information centre just outside the port gates has led to the placement of a large, permanent second information centre facility on the wharf itself.[1]

A reduction in the number of shore excursions sold by the ship has also been acutely observed on those Australia/New Zealand itineraries where there are significant numbers of 'home cruisers', i.e. passengers who live in Australia or New Zealand. In those cases, passengers seek to organize their own shore excursions based on their own knowledge of the area or, in many cases, meet up with friends and relatives en route. For example, an unexpectedly high number of Australian and New Zealand passengers on a March 2009 voyage of Holland America's *Volendam* resulted in unforeseen demand in the Port of Burnie (Tasmania) for the port's shuttle bus, at the expense of organized shore excursions. Normally, 800 passengers would sign up for tours, but on this particular voyage, only 400 signed up for tours, with the result that all other passengers wishing to go ashore could do so only by taking the shuttle through the port precinct. The port's well-managed transportation providers were able to redeploy the coaches originally earmarked for shore excursions to shuttle duty at very short notice.

Given this trend towards more independent tours, visitor centres are finding that they need to make changes to the way they provide information about and market local attractions and tours. For example, more staff needs to be available in visitor centres to respond to hundreds of passengers all seeking to plan their day within a half-hour of disembarking. This shift is also being felt by the local excursion and activity providers. Local providers must be able to meet the demands of increasing numbers of independent passengers whilst visitor centres must have both adequate staff and systems, including online capability, to answer all of their questions and book tours efficiently and quickly. In addition, local businesses must acquire an understanding of and be prepared to accommodate passengers who prefer merely to wander, shop and have a meal.

Multi-generational shore excursions

Any analysis of passengers' interests and styles in respect of shore excursions, and indeed of the shore excursions themselves, cannot, however, be restricted to the traditional, stereotypical cruise passenger – the well-heeled retiree. The cruise holiday is becoming increasingly popular amongst multi-generational family groups whose interests, even within that group, may range from the passive viewing of scenery to sport fanatics who want to try the local danger sport. Cruising appeals to family groups because it provides excellent value for families.

However, the presence of children can act as a barrier to participation in various activities. While cruise ships themselves are perceived to provide a fun and safe component of the cruise holiday for younger passengers, onshore activities may not be as suitable for them. For example, shore excursions generally are designed with the adult passenger in mind, both in content and how they are conducted. Whilst city tours on coaches are functionally suitable for children (i.e. there are no major barriers that would militate against a child joining the tour), commentary will be targeted at adults and the seats may prove to be too low for children who wish to look out of the window. Also, visits to wineries may not be suitable for children. Therefore, tour operators need to design tours that can be offered by the ships, while locals need be able to suggest activities that are suitable for all ages and interests of children. Finally, the marketing and promotion of cruise destinations and shore excursions needs to promote their child friendliness.

The accommodation of impaired or elderly passengers on tours also raises a host of potential issues for shore excursion providers, including the ships. While the online booking of shore excursions – either through the ship or independently through local tour operators – is an increasing practice amongst passengers, there are pitfalls that need to be considered. The Shore Excursion Manager on one ship noted that he welcomes the 50% of bookings made online so that tickets can be printed off and left in passengers' staterooms as they embark, but because those passengers no longer call at the ship's shore excursion desk, his staff has no way of knowing whether individual shore excursions are appropriate for the passengers who have booked them. For example, a shore excursion listed as 'low activity' may still pose difficulties for an elderly person who has some difficulty in walking, as was the case when such a passenger was observed having difficulty walking through a city's cobblestone streets, even though the streets were on flat land and the shore excursion was designated as 'easy'.

The un-shore excursion

Many passengers choose to stay on board or spend the day with friends and relatives and as a result, do not spend money in the port destination community. Therefore, the author submits that port destinations should consider bringing local product to the ship. The 'un-shore excursion' can provide valuable exposure and considerable revenues for local businesses through the promotion and sale of local goods by bringing those goods on board the ships in port or at a previous port in anticipation of calling into the port represented by those goods. Moving goods, and attractions, on board is suggested by Nilsson et al. (2005) to address such issues as a suspicion by passengers that the souvenirs and other goods they may purchase in local markets or shops are fake and to overcome passengers' reluctance to venture off the beaten track either because of fear or their limited time in port. Having the convenience of on-board access to local wine, art, crafts and books, and an opportunity to meet and talk to the producer of those goods can be attractive to both passenger and producer.

In fact, given the increasing popularity of the activity-based shore experience, which focuses more on adventure rather than shopping, on-board promotion and sales of local products may prove the best way to promote local products to cruise passengers. The opportunity to browse through on-board promotional displays, watch short videos on the production of the goods being displayed and make purchases of goods available on board or which can be shipped directly to passengers' homes would be particularly welcomed by independent passengers at the start of their day to see what is available in and around the port destination and also from mid-afternoon, as many passengers begin to drift back to the ship in time for an afternoon drink.

Princess Cruises may in fact be taking the first step towards the un-shore excursion on their New Zealand itineraries. In 2010, Princess announced that their New Zealand-themed cruises will include not only New Zealand food, wine and entertainment (including 'New Zealand Island Night' and a 'Chef and Bartender Challenge') but also in port cultural programmes. During these afternoon presentations, passengers will have the opportunity to partake in workshops in Maori dance traditions, rituals and language (Princess Cruises, 2010).

The cost of shore excursions

The cost of shore excursions is a perennial source of dissatisfaction amongst cruise passengers and often acts as a deterrent to their purchase through the cruise line. The perception is that the cruise lines unjustifiably add a considerable mark-up to the price of shore excursions. However, there is little appreciation by cruise passengers of costs, both direct and indirect, involved in their supply. For example, the cost of tickets for entry, lunch, coach hire and the driver are not the only costs involved in pricing shore excursions. Indirect costs, such as the insurance coverage required to protect both passengers and local guides, drivers and other actors, are also factored into the price paid by passengers, as is a contingency margin for delays, ensuring that the tour will arrive back in time or that if not, the added costs of the ship remaining in its berth can be met.

Other costs are incurred by the cruise line to pay for the features that differentiate ship-organized shore excursions from independently organized ones. For example, cruise passengers who book an excursion on Dunedin's (New Zealand) Taieri Gorge Railway need not travel for 20 min in a coach to get to the railway station to board their train. Instead, they can join the train, which is brought on to the pier, so that passengers can board it immediately adjacent to their berthed ship. Another cost that sometimes needs to be factored into the cost of shore excursions is the perceived premium value that some onshore providers attach to their attraction or event. In other words, there is a risk that onshore providers may take advantage of cruise passengers and charge far in excess of what the tour may be worth.

Foreign exchange fluctuations also affect the cost as well as the perceived value of shore excursions for cruise passengers. For example, it has been observed that American cruise passengers are more reluctant to purchase shore excursions, which appear to be more expensive from year to year because of currency fluctuations. Much of the basis for this apparent increase in costs can be traced to the industry practice where the cruise lines contract for shore excursions up to 3 years before the season in which they are offered, and then find that they need to make up for any intervening currency fluctuations by, in this case, charging more for tickets to protect their margin. Thus, shore excursions purchased wholesale by the cruise lines in the currency of the destination but sold by them to passengers in US$ (in the vast majority of cases) can often result in significantly higher prices for passengers.

One industry representative reported that during the 2008/09 season, there was a 15–20% decrease in the number of shore excursions being sold through the cruise lines in New Zealand, but that there was a concomitant increase in tours sold through the local visitor centres (personal communication, 17 June 2009).

Another factor that affects passenger take-up of shore excursions is the cost of the cruise itself, a factor that appears to be directly linked to the national profile of passengers on board as well as their sensitivity to the prevailing foreign exchange rates. Similarly, fewer shore excursions are likely to be purchased where a particular cruise voyage is heavily discounted. In other words, because discounted cruises attract the budget conscious cruiser passenger, those passengers are less likely to purchase shore excursions from the ship because of their perceived high cost. Another factor that has an effect on the uptake of shore excursions is the number of passengers who use the cruise only as a means of transportation to visit friends and relatives.

The human capital of shore excursions

The personality and expertise of tour guides is another significant issue that needs to be considered. Unresponsive, ill-trained coach drivers and guides will result in wholesale disappointment for the passengers, because the personality and knowledge of the tour guide can be determinative as to whether shore excursions and other local tours are considered a success or not. All actors involved in the provision of tour services to cruise passengers should be required to undergo pre-employment screening, training and continuous vetting to ensure that they can meet and ideally exceed cruise passengers' high expectations. These requirements form the core of what would be expected of service providers who are governed by a recognized external or self-regulating quality standard. For example, a self-regulating quality scheme has been implemented by the Port of Tauranga (New Zealand). Fears of shoddy coaches, poor drivers, ill-trained guides and aggressive tour operators galvanized the port into developing regulations that ensure the safety and enjoyment of cruise passengers and that consistently result in Tauranga being voted the most popular New Zealand port amongst cruise passengers.

Another component crucial to increasing cruise passengers' enjoyment of them is the presence of knowledgeable and personable port lecturers and experts on board the ships. A good lecturer or expert will produce increased bookings for shore excursions for the cruise line as well as increased local interest and demand. However, the placement of port lecturers on board ships and the organization of lectures is not consistent throughout the industry. For example, local experts (i.e. from the destination itself) may travel with the ship for much of its itinerary, giving a series of lectures, whilst other voyages rely on their own staff

or contractors for most of the lectures. Both arrangements can be problematical for a variety of reasons.

First, the local expert may carry with him or her a particular bias, borne of his or her own interests or willingness to talk about certain subjects and not others. Also, whilst the port lecturer may be an expert on local culture or current politics and deliver detailed lectures about those subjects, passengers are for the most part eager to find out which local tours will provide them with the best experience, how to dress, what things cost, shop opening hours and where they can find nearby amenities and services. Much of this information can be found in the port notes distributed to passengers by the ship's shore excursion office or passenger services desk, but often this information is inaccurate or out-of-date. Given that port lecturers can yield either huge benefits or a negative feeling about a region, ports should exert more pressure to place properly trained lecturers on board, whether those lecturers are port ambassadors, university lecturers or tourism representatives. Thus, approaches should be made to the cruise lines or the agencies from which they source speakers to consider appropriately qualified local speakers for placement on board ships.

A decision by Holland America Line to combine the roles of port lecturer and travel guide has proven to be successful because, in that role, the lecturer combines the scenic and historical highlights of the destination with the practical information required by the passengers, thereby supplementing what is otherwise available on the Internet. In addition, the travel guide is perceived to be independent, so whilst he or she helps to promote the ship's tours, passengers do not feel compelled to purchase those tours and instead, consider also independent options.

Demand: Push Marketing

As discussed earlier in this chapter, there appears to be a trend towards fewer shore excursions being purchased by cruise passengers. Where shore excursions are purchased, that decision often is made a few days before calling into any given port, based on conversations with fellow passengers, attendance at port lectures and research on the internet. While it is clear that this pattern reflects a general change in consumer purchasing behaviour, it exposes also a weakness in cruise ship marketing, i.e. the lack of systems that not only capture passenger likes, dislikes and preferences, but that also target those passengers with shore excursions or other shore activities that will be of interest to them.

Targeting passengers – the Amazon.com effect

Individuals who have purchased books from Amazon.com will be familiar with the page that they first see when they log on, displaying suggestions for future purchases based on past purchasing and browsing behaviour. This process, push marketing, can work in any consumer-based sector, including, especially, the cruise sector. Over the past several years, cruise lines have recognized the importance of and made investments in, their loyalty programmes and past passenger databases. Millions of passenger names now populate cruise line databases. However, the information collected by the cruise lines is for the most part perfunctory. Questions of regions already visited, household income and number of cruises taken are common, but questions relating to specific port cities visited, activities undertaken while there, activity preferences and any physical limitations that could affect passengers' enjoyment of shore excursions are all but absent.

The question invariably arises at this point as to whether the cruise lines' objective is to sell their ship, specific itineraries or shore excursions, but the argument can then be made: 'How do you sell the ship or the itinerary unless there are attractions or activities of interest to do once you get there?' The challenge for the cruise lines, then, is not only to improve their customer

relationship marketing vis-à-vis the cruise line itself, but also the individual products it sells as part of the total cruise experience, including shore excursions.

For example, a comprehensive and detailed customer database will reveal that over their past three cruises, Mr and Mrs Jones from Dubuque, Iowa, purchased three shore excursions involving food and wine, two shore excursions aboard great train journeys and one consisting of a museum sampler in a large city. Therefore, instead of leaving to chance that Mr and Mrs Jones will book any shore excursions for their next cruise, their booking dialogue should include suggestions of the kinds of attractions and activities that might be of interest to them. Because their next cruise is to New Zealand, Mr and Mrs Jones will undoubtedly enjoy the full-day Marlborough wine tour when their ship calls into Picton at the top of the South Island and a half-day each experiencing Dunedin's Taieri Gorge Railway and a tour of the city's museums.

Another aspect of collecting information relating to passengers' interests and limitations is to ensure that all shore-side providers have sufficient information about passenger preferences and their motivations for cruising, to be able to provide the kinds of products and services that would appeal to them. Inbound tour operators need to know which tours will appeal to the 600 passengers aboard the luxury, niche cruise ship, which is scheduled to make ten port calls during the next season, whilst the local visitors centres must have on hand a range of tours and other suggestions for ships that might carry a thousand North American passengers and an equal number of passengers with varying language skills. Local service and amenity providers must also be prepared to welcome a large number of passengers with different preferences and expectations. For example, the arrival of a large cruise ship at a South Pacific island propelled local restaurant owners to prepare expensive, elaborate lunches but were disappointed with the low number of customers. The next time the ship called into that port, passengers found plain, ordinary meat pies. They were sold out in an hour.

Information management

Matching passengers to shore excursions and other shore activities is dependent on one, important, key component: information. Information about onshore activities must be accurate, detailed, current and available in the languages represented on any given voyage. Armed with more accurate, detailed and current information, tour operators can tailor their offerings and realize significant revenues from tours that are specifically geared to passengers whether they are able-bodied, young, independent, impaired or elderly.

The discussion in this chapter militates in favour of ensuring that information is managed in a systematic and structured way and that the right information gets to passengers in a timely, useful and attractive way. More information must be provided to passengers on board, both in the form of printed information and communicated through local tourism representatives who board the ship and make themselves available to passengers with questions and who wish to book tours. However, onshore visitor centres must also make better use of the new technologies capable of collecting and distributing electronic information. Wireless (WiFi) enabled devices allow visitor centres to push local information out to visiting cruise passengers, whilst smart mobiles can enable passengers to make micro-payments for transactions such as snacks, attraction entry fees and transportation, thereby removing problems associated with passengers handling unfamiliar currency.

The bottom line for attraction and event providers, tour operators and the cruise lines is that more research, investment and development need to be undertaken into the ever-changing travel preferences of cruisers. For the foreseeable future, there will still be those cruisers who seek out the security of coaches and their guides, who wish to see the magnificence of the Tuscan hills through the plate glass window of their luxury coach and who are content with a mediocre lunch at an abnormally large cafe catering to large groups of tourists. On the other hand, there is an increasing number of cruise passengers who prefer to be transported in smaller vehicles such as mini-buses or vans in which they can explore the local environment, meet the locals, choose a small winery or café for lunch, play a few holes of golf, spend an hour on the beach and return to the ship feeling as if they have compressed a whole lifetime living in that region into their 8- or 9-h port call.

Conclusion

Whatever the case, port destination communities must understand passengers' motivations, expectations and preferences in order to enable them to offer a memorable experience on shore so that they can capture as much of the cruise passengers' consumer surplus as possible, retain their competitive edge against other destinations and ensure that the ships continue to return, based on favourable passenger comments and exemplary service to the ship itself. No longer can port destinations merely sit back and wait for the ships to turn up. They must first develop an attractive inventory of excursions and activities, convey that those excursions and activities are operated in a professional and safe way, and find ways in which they can be marketed effectively and intelligently to both the cruise lines and their passengers.

Note

[1]Whilst almost every port in New Zealand has a visitor centre presence dockside, they tend to be smaller, often temporary structures, which enable local tourism representatives to store and distribute local information and operate from an identifiable, sheltered location on the wharf. In contrast, the Tauranga facility is a fully operational information centre and, as at the time of this writing, has plans to grow.

References

Atherley, K. (2003) Cruise industry-related challenges facing Caribbean destinations. Available at: www.linkbc.ca/torc/downs1/CaribbeanCruiseIndustry.pdf (accessed 16 March 2011).

CLIA (2008) *Cruise Market Profile Study*. Cruise Lines International Association, Fort Lauderdale, Florida.

Destination Victoria (2002) Cruise ship strategy 2002-2005. Available at: www.transport.vic.gov.au/doi/doi-elect.nsf/2a6bd98dee287482ca256915001cff0c/92bc0f88997414c3ca256cd4001c9af5/$FILE/Cruise%20Ship%20Strat%20Dest%20Victoria.pdf (accessed 25 May 2009).

Hall, C.M. (2007) Response to Yeoman et al: the fakery of 'the authentic tourist'. *Tourism Management* 28(4), 1139–1140.

Harris, N. (2003) Big cruise ships cause traffic jams in ports. *The Wall Street Journal*, 20 August, pp. B1, B6.

Hritz, N. and Cecil, A. (2008) Investigating the sustainability of cruise tourism: a case study of Key West. *Journal of Sustainable Tourism* 16(2), 168–181.

Jaakson, R. (2004) Beyond the tourist bubble? Cruise ship passengers in port. *Annals of Tourism Research* 31(1), 44–60.

Littrell, M.A., Baizerman, S., Kean, R., Gahring, S., Niemeyer, S., Reilly, R. and Stout, J.A. (1994) Souvenirs and tourism styles. *Journal of Travel Research* 33(1), 3–11.

Market Economics (2010) *New Zealand Cruise Industry Study*. Available at: www.tourismresearch.govt.nz/Documents/Research%20Reports/Cruise/New%20Zealand%20Cruise%20Industry%20Study.pdf (accessed 16 March 2011).

Nilsson, P., Marcussen, C., Pedersen, J. and Pedersen, K. (2005) Cruise tourism in the Baltic and Bothnian Sea – a pilot study on maritime tourism. Available at: www.crt.dk/media/WP%2024%20Seagull.pdf (accessed 16 March 2011).

Northern Economics (2002) Benefits of Valdez city dock improvements. Available at: www.ci.valdez.ak.us/clerk/documents/Rep2110308.pdf (accessed 17 May 2009).

Princess Cruises (2010) Princess Cruises adds a Kiwi flavor to New Zealand voyages. Available at: www.princess.com/news/article.jsp?newsArticleId=na1099 (accessed 16 March 2011).

Wells, M.P. (1997) Economic perspectives on nature tourism, conservation and development. Environment Department Paper no. 55. World Bank, Washington, DC. Available at: www-wds.worldbank.org/external/default/WDSContentServer/WDSP/IB/1999/09/14/000178830_98101912354394/Rendered/PDF/multi_page.pdf (accessed 16 March 2011).

15   Service Quality and the Cruise Industry

Mandy Aggett and Wai Mun Lim

Introduction

Customers deciding on a holiday seek a hassle- and stress-free time regardless of whether the holiday is in the form of a short city break, a luxurious resort break or a cruise. Unlike most other travel companies, cruise lines possess the upper hand when it comes to controlling and ensuring quality service delivery from the time a customer searches for a holiday mode to the time they complete their holiday. Customer satisfaction can only be achieved if quality has been achieved throughout the service process. But what is quality? This chapter reviews the concept of quality management within the context of service, by examining specific quality improvement programmes, which can be applied to the cruise industry. It includes the consideration of several interrelated issues, beginning with the evaluation of service quality via five broad approaches as discussed by Garvin (1988).

The chapter thus highlights established concepts of service quality that have often been applied by practitioners and discusses the recent development of the newer service concept known as the co-creation of value. The relevance and significance of understanding these service concepts is illustrated in the following case study, depicting how Princess Cruises improved their passengers' service experience through making a simple change to their disembarkation process.

Case Study

Princess Cruises, one of the leading brands of the Carnival Corporation, sum up their quest for excellent customer service in their C.R.U.I.S.E. credo: Courtesy, Respect, Unfailing in Service Excellence. The C.R.U.I.S.E. programme began as a shipboard effort in 1996, and has since been extended throughout Princess Cruise's shore-side operations. The extension of the programme was anticipated to bring on shore the high level of service experienced by passengers on board.

Providing passengers with a seamless pleasurable cruise experience in the rapidly expanding cruise industry is an essential business requirement. Cruise companies are challenged to deliver quality services that are second to none. To improve the quality of the service delivered, Princess Cruises sought to benchmark its performance with respect to service delivery, ensuring that their cruise teams are committed to unfailing compliance to quality by developing the all encompassing customer service credo.

The C.R.U.I.S.E. programme is observed by all members of the ships, although officers and management staff are responsible for driving the C.R.U.I.S.E. message forward. The programme is reinforced by seven key values that clearly spell out the ethos of all crew members; they are:

- always be friendly and welcoming;
- go the extra mile;
- share what you know with others;
- keep your promises;
- make it happen;
- learn today, to do better tomorrow; and
- remember, everyone's an individual.

Led by the Captain and the Executive Committee, the programme develops and empowers teams to embrace the values. All new members of staff and re-joiners receive induction training, and are issued with a C.R.U.I.S.E. pack, which outlines the programme, what it means to the organization and how it works. C.R.U.I.S.E. 'joggers' (training and briefing sessions) are carried out on a fortnightly basis, and meetings are held once a month, where officers of all levels are invited to brief the Executive Committee on their efforts to reinforce C.R.U.I.S.E. Other 'cues' include a C.R.U.I.S.E. newspaper, which is circulated to staff to update them on developments, and posters displaying the results of the Customer Service Questionnaires (CSQs), collected at the end of every cruise.

Staff members' committed acceptance of the programme ensures that the C.R.U.I.S.E. programme is not only a central topic in one of the executive committee's meetings every month but also encourages officers to share their C.R.U.I.S.E. programme initiatives and good practices. This concerted commitment to the programme was undoubtedly the key to two recent service improvements. First, Princess Cruises introduced earlier embarkation as a result of negative feedback, obtained from their CSQs, on previous policy. On making this change, passengers' perception of the quality of the embarkation procedure increased dramatically. More recently, changes have been made to the disembarkation procedure.

The traditional 'hurry and wait' disembarkation process of cruises has long been subjected to frequent criticisms from passengers, who would otherwise have enjoyed the entire cruise experience. The 'hurry and wait' process required passengers to wait (on their final morning of the cruise) and listen to the public address system for their luggage tag colour to be called out. This would then signal the staggered times they would disembark. This process of disembarkation did not allow passengers to plan their final morning on board, since they were not told their disembarkation time. This practice also resulted in unnecessary strains over other facilities, such as rapid turnover at breakfast service, and the congregation of passengers in the ship's atrium nearest to the gangway.

In accordance with the service credo of 'unfailing in service excellence', cruise management and crew designed 'a more gracious send-off on their [passengers'] final morning with us' (in the words of Jan Swartz, Princess' senior vice president of customer service). The new disembarkation process (rolled out from early 2008) sees that passengers are sent letters on the night before disembarkation, detailing the assigned time and place for them to assemble on the final morning, where they will have a crew member escorting them to the gangway, making the end-of-cruise departure system more efficient and passenger friendly.

This complements the new early embarkation policy, and bears testament to the cruise managers' appreciation of the value of seamless quality service delivery – from embarkation to passengers' experience on-board to disembarkation. The attention cruise managers pay to ensure customer satisfaction and to advance quality improvement programmes, have contributed greatly to the high levels of customer satisfaction achieved by the company.

It is vital for service managers to be aware of the core approaches of service quality, because each can be evaluated against various service delivery encounters, so that managers can effectively implement quality policies. The following section, therefore, outlines some generic approaches.

Generic Approaches to Service Quality

This section demonstrates that the analysis of service quality could be examined from the standpoint of the customers (obtaining customer satisfaction) and/or the service deliverer (achieving service excellence). Theories have often suggested and focused on how manufacturers/service deliverers could follow through a conceptual model's process of achieving service excellence or ensuring customer satisfaction. However, when examining quality, many approaches that have been developed look squarely at customers' perceptions, expectations and experiences. Garvin (1988) presents five approaches to quality that could be applied to the cruise industry, they are:

- transcendent-based;
- attribute-based;
- user-based;
- manufacturing-based; and
- value-based.

The *transcendent-based approach* to quality recognizes that quality cannot be easily defined because the ensuing result of it is highly dependent on the individual. For example, a person who enjoys going on cruises may feel that his first cruise experience was better than his second cruise experience but may not be able to explain why. The passenger may have no complaints on both sailings with the same cruise liner. The transcendental nature of service provision makes it impossible to explain accurately why the passenger's first cruise experience was better than the second. Was it because the cabin steward always had a ready smile? Was it because the passenger did not have to queue to settle his on-board account at the purser's desk? Or was it the bartender who remembered he preferred to have his cocktails shaken and not stirred? Therefore, on the basis of this approach, there are no clear-cut definitions of quality, as it is an attribute that can only be learned through experience, which may not be noticed, but makes a difference to a passenger's perception of service quality.

The *attribute-based approach* takes a more tangible stance as it recognizes that quality can only be a result of an amalgamation of factors and antecedents of a service. It is implied that quality can be assessed with this approach by way of the number of positive attributes experienced. A cruise liner with more appealing attributes such as having a wide selection of themed restaurants and entertainment may be perceived as being of a higher quality than a liner with a limited number of restaurants and organized activities.

The *user-based approach* to quality on the other hand, is highly subjective as the term implies. Quality is determined by the passenger who may have a very different opinion of quality from the next passenger. This approach can be a problem because it is based on the premise of customer perceptions, where organizations solicit for customers' notions of quality but do not bolster the provision of quality outcomes.

The *manufacturing-based approach* to quality is considered in quantifiable terms, where every service must be met by a finite number of specifications in order to achieve a positive quality outcome. For example, passengers should wait for no more than 8 min before they are seated at the main restaurant, invoices for final account settlement should be error free, or requests for cabin items should be delivered within the hour. This approach relies on the organization's management and service deliverers to assess the specifications required in order to attain quality.

Finally, the *value-based approach* to assessing quality is derived solely from the customer's perspective. In simple terms, the approach measures the difference between what the customer paid for a service/product and the satisfaction, benefit or contentment derived from its consumption. For example, every passenger visits the same ports of call on a specific cruise with similar access to entertainment, facilities and food, but service levels vary on Cunard between Caronia Staterooms, Mauretania Staterooms and the Queen's Grill passengers. The intrinsic value derived from the cruise by all cruise passengers regardless of class may be the same, but some passengers may perceive that by paying as Queen's Grill passengers, the satisfaction and gratification provides value for money.

Garvin's (1988) five approaches to quality neatly encapsulate the various schools of thought in service quality. In fact, almost all conceptual descriptions of service quality are explored via either the context of customers or organizations, but rarely both. We will now explore the key challenges to, and conceptual paradigms of, service quality before introducing a model that calls for both customers and organizations to participate in the value creation process of service quality.

The Challenges

Carlzon (1991, p. vii) states that service quality is concerned with 'knowing your customers, designing services to meet customers' needs, and finally managing the service production and delivery process to the customer's satisfaction.' There are, however, a number of challenges that must be overcome in meeting these specifications. As Czepiel et al. (1985, p. ix) explain, encounters between service employees and customers are 'intertwined with a complex of managerial issues, ranging from marketing and consumer behaviour to employee relations and organizational behaviour,' while Ghobadian et al. (1994, p. 44) attribute impacts pertaining to 'certain inherent characteristics of the service sector [which] increase the complexity of "quality control" and "improvement efforts".' These characteristics are identified (Ghobadian et al., 1994; Gabbot and Hogg, 1997; Hoffman and Bateson, 2006) as the inseparability of service production and consumption, and the intangibility, perishability and heterogeneity of services.

Drawing upon Carlzon's statement above, it is clear that service quality is dependent upon two distinct conditions:

- identifying and meeting customers' (passengers') needs and expectations; and
- managing service production and delivery effectively.

If we refer back to the case study here, it may be seen that the changes made to the embarkation policy and disembarkation process came as a result of consideration of these concepts, and relate to Garvin's (1988) user-based and value-based approaches.

Identifying and meeting passengers' needs and expectations

In order to provide a quality product and services, cruise industry organizations need to identify and meet passengers' needs and expectations. It is therefore essential that these are identified, understood and provided for. Teare (1998), however, stresses that this is not an easy task, owing to difficulties in assuring consistency in service delivery, and because customers' expectations differ from one another (as highlighted in the discussion of the user-based approach). Growth, and the resulting competitiveness within the cruise industry, has led to the diversification of passengers, as cruises are now available to a wider audience (Gibson, 2006; Petrick et al., 2006), which implies there is a diverse range of needs and expectations to be identified and met. This is further exacerbated because the expectations of individuals themselves change over time, depending upon experience and the context (transcendent-based). The intricate and multi-faceted nature of the construct of expectations therefore, represents the first challenge for service providers.

Managing service production and delivery effectively

As outlined earlier, the service sector is affected by inherent characteristics, which impact upon the quality of the service provided. Two of the most challenging of these, for the cruise industry, are the heterogeneity of service production and delivery and the inseparability of service production and consumption.

In the cruise industry, front-line employees are on show to passengers for long periods, particularly on days at sea, and therefore the number of opportunities for mistakes, unsatisfactory service outcomes and substandard performance or behaviour of employees is high. Hence, in high-contact service systems, the prevalence of inconsistency is higher than in low-contact systems, and refers to the *heterogeneity of service production and delivery*.

Consistency in service quality is essential for an organization's success. However, as Gabbot and Hogg (1997, p. 138) identify, 'services are delivered by individuals to individuals and therefore each service encounter will be different by virtue of the participants or time of performance.' In the cruise industry in particular, problems with consistency may arise as a result of staff turnover and a multinational crew, who may differ in their perceptions of service quality. The heterogeneity of service production and delivery is thus a cause for concern. One of the main challenges lies in assuring uniformity in the behaviour and performance of service employees (Ghobadian *et al.*, 1994). This is particularly challenging for HR managers and on-board trainers in the cruise industry because of the nature of leave programming, where crew members are replaced by new staff at the end of each contract. Staff 'turnover' created by leave programmes can lead to a lack of continuity, and changes in management cause a particular problem. For example, on Princess Cruises' ships, the more senior a member of staff, the fewer number of months they are required to work. As a result, a crew member, on a 9-month contract, may have two or three different managers during that time. Although standard operating manuals are in use, each manager will bring their own expectations and ideas on how best to achieve the required outcomes of these.

The *inseparability of service production and consumption* is concerned with the inability to separate service production and delivery from the customer (Parasuraman *et al.*, 1985; Ghobadian *et al.*, 1994). The customer participates in the production of service, 'by making choices and interacting with service staff' (Teare, 1998, p. 78),

which lowers the opportunity for standardization as their behaviour impacts the way in which the service is delivered. Therefore, the customer has been identified as a co-producer of the service (Vargo and Lusch, 2004), and may consequently affect the level of quality, and hence their own (and others') satisfaction. However, the alternative concept of viewing the customer as a co-creator of value is of significance here and is outlined later in the chapter.

The participation of cruise-ship passengers in service production and delivery is fairly high because the nature of cruise-ship operations necessitates high-contact systems. Chase (1978, pp. 139–140) identifies three effects of this on operations: less control, 'since the customer can always make an input to (or cause a disruption in) the production process'; difficulties in matching capacity with demand on the system at any given time; and the need for employees with public relations skills, as 'any interaction with the customer makes the direct worker in fact part of the product and therefore his attitude can affect the customer's view of the service provided' (Chase, 1978). The following section identifies some of the approaches that managers may take to tackle the challenges.

Tackling the Challenges

Identifying and meeting passengers' needs and expectations

Managers often find it difficult to integrate conceptual models into their pursuit of excellence in service quality. The difficulty is often fuelled by limited consideration of what customer satisfaction is and what it entails. For example, in the cruise industry, management may stipulate that the average waiting time for a passenger waiting to be served at the purser's desk should be no longer than 15 min (a manufacturing-based approach). This stipulation is redundant, however, if passengers believe that a wait of more than 5 min equates to poor service. It is therefore essential that customer expectations are identified.

These expectations are shaped by a number of factors, which may include the media, previous experience, word-of-mouth communications, promotional materials, price and corporate image. A common method employed in the cruise industry for identifying passenger expectations is the measurement of satisfaction using CSQs. As outlined earlier in the chapter, these are completed by passengers and collected at the end of every cruise. The responses are then analysed and used as a basis for improving the products and services offered.

Often, however, a cruise organization's policies will conflict with the expectations of a passenger. This is because each passenger is an individual, possessing a unique set of needs and expectations, which require a response from the service provider. Cruise organizations tackle this problem to some extent through market segmentation (a user-based approach). Where there are no existing procedures for dealing with an unforeseen request or situation, a service-oriented climate or culture is required to guide employees' behaviour (Chung and Schneider, 2002). A positive service climate may be created through consistent messages obtained from human resources practices, such as service-focused training and development, and performance appraisals that are linked to the provision of service quality (Chung and Schneider, 2002). Princess Cruise's customer service programme, C.R.U.I.S.E., has ensured a positive service climate on board each of their ships.

Managing service production and delivery effectively

To facilitate a reduction in *the heterogeneity of service production and delivery*, standard operating manuals must be in place and communicated to all members of staff. In instances where managers are frequently replaced, procedures should remain consistent with those outlined in the standard operating manuals, and everyone should be informed of any changes immediately. The variability of passenger expectations and their individual behavioural influences on service systems, however, cannot all be considered and accounted for in standard operating manuals. Hence, these tools may only contain standards for day-to-day operational procedures, and guidelines for dealing with frequently occurring requests and complaints.

A more valuable contributor to consistency in service organizations is the communication of a clear service quality vision to all members of staff. Ghobadian *et al.* (1994, p. 47) suggest that 'in the absence of a clear vision and definition [of quality] employees are likely to have their own interpretation of service quality' and a 'lack of common vision will inevitably increase the variability experienced by the customer'. Princess Cruises' C.R.U.I.S.E. programme ensures that every one of its employees is aware of the company's focus on service quality and the seven values at the core of this. The programme directs behaviour and ensures that everyone understands and can contribute to meeting its objectives. The training element of C.R.U.I.S.E. allows for messages relating to the values and the aims of the programme to be reinforced. Even with the difficulties imposed by leave programming, every member of staff receives the same induction training and fortnightly briefing sessions to promote consistency.

As identified earlier, the *inseparability of service production and consumption* means that passengers may influence the quality of service provided, and their influence on service production and delivery implies they are actually co-producers of the service. Bitner *et al.* (1997) recognize that some believe customers should be separated from service production and delivery processes wherever possible, by reducing direct contact between the customer and the service production system (through the use of automated services for example). This should ensure that the influence customers have on the service system is reduced. Others, however, suggest that customers should be viewed as 'partial employees' and their levels of participation increased (with the use of full self-service for example), in the hope of improving productivity (Bitner et al., 1997), and perhaps reducing the number of opportunities for conflict with service employees.

The nature of the cruise product demands that passengers may not be separated from the service production system, and are in fact interacting with its component parts for extended periods. This is of benefit to the providers of service on cruise ships, as service relationships may be developed throughout the course of a cruise, as opportunities arise for value fulfilment through customer/employee interactions. Chase (1978) argues that, ultimately, the attitude of the service employee and customer, and the environment in which the system exists will determine the quality of service. Therefore, cruise ship organizations should concentrate their efforts on managing employees' performance and passengers' behaviour while in the service production system, through well-designed processes, systems and routines, and environmental planning and design.

Grönroos (1990, p. 210) advises that inefficient operational or administrative systems may act as a hindrance to service and can impact service quality in two ways. First, they may impact upon the employees' ability to provide a quality service ('if a certain system is considered old-fashioned, complicated, or in some way not service oriented, the employees who will have to live with the system will get frustrated'). Second, they may also influence the customer's perception of the quality of service offered, as they must also interact with the system.

A useful model that highlights customers' perspectives and focuses on improving the service delivery process is the concept of the co-creation of value.

The Co-creation of Value

To put it simply, the co-creation of value is one of the founding propositions that form the basis of the service dominant (S-D) logic developed by Vargo and Lusch (2006). Moving away from the goods-dominant logic

(G-D logic), Vargo and Lusch (2008) recognize that the customer is always a co-creator of value, rather than a co-producer, and S-D logic is 'primarily about value creation, rather than "production," making units of output' (p. 7). They add, however, that co-production has a place in S-D logic, as a component of the co-creation of value.

The co-creation of value is viewed as 'a desirable goal as it can assist firms in highlighting the customer's or consumer's point of view and in improving the front-end process of identifying customers' needs and wants' (Payne et al., 2007, p. 84). The concept of co-creation can be understood from a few angles, but here we will focus on how the service supplier (i.e. organization) can manage the co-creation of value. As depicted in Fig. 15.1, the co-creation of value framework consists of three main components, they are:

- customer value-creating processes;
- supplier value-creating processes; and
- encounter processes.

Critically, the framework highlights the different encounters between customers and suppliers as a result of the value-creating processes developed. In the context of the cruise industry, the arrows found between customer (passenger) processes indicate that their learning process is based on the experience that they have had during service encounters. These encounters take into consideration the emotional, cognitive and behavioural dimensions in the relationship experience. In turn, what the passenger learns will have an effect on how the passenger will participate in future co-creation of value with the cruise liner.

In the same way, the arrows found between supplier processes (cruise liner) indicate that the organization's learning process is based on their experience with the passengers. Opportunities to improve the service delivery increase as they learn more about their passengers, further enhancing their relationship and improving the co-creation of value with passengers. An example of how the co-creation of value framework can be adopted in the context of a cruise liner is illustrated in Fig. 15.2.

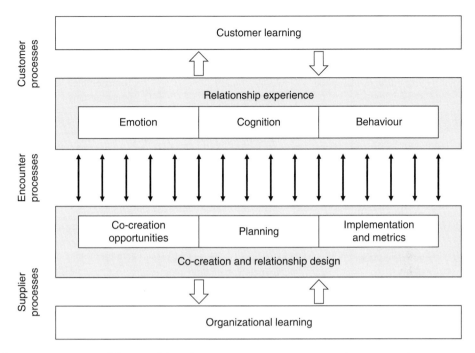

Fig. 15.1.   A conceptual framework for value co-creation. Source: Payne *et al.* (2007, p. 86).

The changes to Princess Cruises' embarkation and disembarkation procedures were introduced as a direct response to learning from passengers during on-board service encounters. It was found that an otherwise enjoyable cruise was marred by previous policy. The new procedures, having been co-created by passengers, have improved the quality of the on-board cruise experience for both passengers and the crew involved in embarkation and disembarkation.

Summary and Conclusions

The chapter began by introducing Garvin's (1988) five approaches to quality. Critically, each of the approaches can be evaluated against various service delivery encounters which can be mapped in a service process. Service quality provision in the cruise industry is dependent upon identifying, understanding and meeting passengers' needs and expectations, and the effective management of service production and

delivery systems. The complexity of service systems and interactions between service employees and passengers, however, presents a number of challenges. The varying needs and expectations of the growing and diverse market in the industry, along with fluctuations in individual's needs and expectations, the inseparability of service production and delivery and the heterogeneity of service delivery, have been identified in this chapter as particular problems.

Ghobadian *et al.* (1994) identify a number of practices that may address these challenges and improve the quality of service provided, the basis of which is that organizations must focus on the market and the customer. CSQs are used in the industry to measure satisfaction and identify areas in need of improvement. However, because of the individuality of passengers, and their diverse range of expectations, it is not easy to satisfy all of these people all of the time, and standard operating manuals, although useful, cannot account for every eventuality. In order to deal with this challenge, a

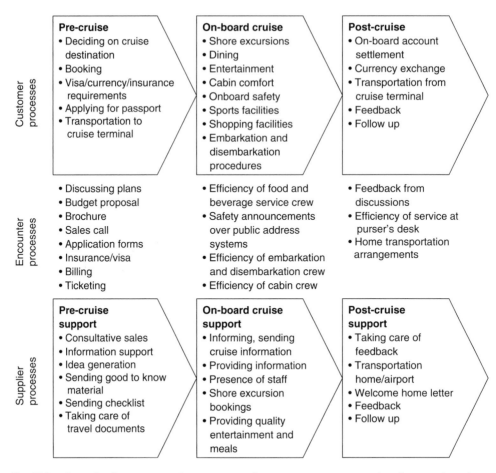

Fig. 15.2. Example of passenger, cruise company and encounter processes mapping. Source: adapted from Vargo and Lusch (2006).

positive service-oriented climate or culture is required to guide employees' behaviour in response to passengers' demands.

As passengers may not be separated from the service production and delivery system, it is important that employees' performance and passengers' behaviour be managed effectively. This may be achieved through well-designed processes, systems and routines, and environmental planning and design. Systems, and the environment (or servicescape) in which they exist, should consider the needs of both employees and passengers. It must be noted, however, that no matter

how well designed these are, they will become ineffective if employees are not adequately trained, motivated and empowered to respond to the impacts that passengers may have on the system through their behaviour and unique needs and expectations.

The co-creation of value framework creates opportunities for the organization to plan and implement better service delivery systems by understanding and learning more about customers' experiences. In this way, cruise organizations benefit from such an approach, as evidenced in the case study.

References

Bitner, M., Faranda, W.T., Hubbert, A.R. and Zeithaml, V.A. (1997) Customer contributions and roles in service delivery. *International Journal of Service Industry Management* 8(3), 193–205.

Carlzon, J. (1991) Foreword. In: Brown, S.W., Gummesson, E., Edvardsson, B. and Gustavsson, B. (eds) *Service Quality: Multidisciplinary and Multinational Perspectives*. Lexington Books, New York, pp. ix–x.

Chase, R.B. (1978) Where does the customer fit in a service operation? *Harvard Business Review* 56(6), 137–142.

Chung, B.G. and Schneider, B. (2002) Serving multiple masters: role conflict experienced by service employees. *Journal of Services Marketing* 16(1), 70–87.

Czepiel, J.A., Solomon, M.R., Surprenant, C.F. and Gutman, E.G. (1985) Service encounters: An overview. In: Czepiel, J.A., Solomon, M.R. and Surprenant, C.F. (eds) *The Service Encounter. Managing Employee/Customer Interaction in Service Businesses*. Lexington Books, Lanham, Maryland, pp. 3–15.

Gabbot, M. and Hogg, G. (1997) Consumer behaviour and services. In: Gabbot, M. and Hogg, G. (eds) *Contemporary Services Marketing Management*. The Dryden Press, London, pp. 136–148.

Garvin, D. (1988) *Managing Quality: 'The Strategic and Competitive Edge'*. Free Press, New York.

Ghobadian, A., Speller, S. and Jones, M. (1994) Service quality concepts and models. *International Journal of Quality & Reliability Management* 11(9), 43–66.

Gibson, P. (2006) *Cruise Operations Management*. Butterworth-Heinemann, Oxford.

Grönroos, C. (1990) *Service Management and Marketing*. Lexington Books, Lanham, Maryland.

Hoffman, K.D. and Bateson, J.E.G. (2006) *Services Marketing. Concepts, Strategies, & Cases,* 3rd edn. Cengage South-Western, Mason, Ohio.

Parasuraman, A., Zeithaml, V.A. and Berry, L.L. (1985) A conceptual model of service quality and its implications. *Journal of Marketing* 49, 41–50.

Payne, A.F., Storbacka, K. and Frow, P. (2007) Managing the co-creation of value. *Journal of the Academy of Marketing Science* 36(1), 83–96.

Petrick, J.F., Tonner, C. and Quinn, C. (2006) The utilization of critical incident technique to examine cruise passengers' repurchase intentions. *Journal of Travel Research* 44, 273–280.

Teare, R. (1998) Interpreting and responding to customer needs. *Journal of Workplace Learning* 10(2), 76–94.

Vargo, S.L. and Lusch, R.F. (2004) Evolving to a new dominant logic for marketing. *Journal of Marketing* 68, 1–17.

Vargo, S.L. and Lusch, R.P. (2006) Service-dominant logic: What it is, what it is not, what it might be. In: Lusch, R.P. and Vargo, S.L. (eds) *The Service Dominant Logic of Marketing: Dialog, Debate and Directions*. M.E. Sharpe, Armonk, New York, pp. 43–56.

Vargo, S.L. and Lusch, R.F. (2008) Service-dominant logic: Continuing the evolution. *Journal of the Academy of Marketing Science* 36, 1–10.

Part V

Cruise Operations Management

_____

16 Hotel Operations Management on Cruise Ships

Ben Wolber

Introduction

A cruise […] offers you a chance to relax and unwind in comfortable surroundings, with attentive service, good food and a ship that changes the scenery for you.

(Ward, 2009, p. 8)

Cruise ships can be regarded as floating hotels. The 'hotel service team usually dominates in terms of numbers of employees' (Gibson, 2006, p. 94) on board a cruise ship, and the expectations of cruise guests largely refer to hotel services – they will rate the cruise experience mainly based on service, food and accommodation.

The management of hotel operations in the cruise industry, however, presents very different challenges than hotel management ashore. There are many cruise products available, catering for very different demographics and budgets – but no matter what brand or vessel classification, hotel operations on board are multifaceted and demanding.

The challenges start with the multinational and multilingual crew working in confined surroundings and living at their workplace. Cruise ships frequently operate in remote parts of the world. The shore-side infrastructure is often either insufficient or unavailable. Constantly changing and sometimes contradictory regulations apply in many ports of call. Passengers spend much more time on board a cruise ship than they normally would in a hotel ashore, and not only because an average cruise length of 7.2 days (CLIA, 2010) is longer than the normal duration of stay in most hotels. Each of these challenges distinguishes hotel operations on cruise ships from hotel operations ashore.

A clear chain of command, standardization and strong support from shore-side management are answers to the above challenges. While the interaction with guests and therefore the actual creation of the product happens on board, the hotel operations department in head office must be more than just a think tank for new concepts. Properly managed and with a clear division of functionalities, numerous potential problems can be solved before the guest even steps aboard. Streamlined communications and clearly defined responsibilities are the key to a successful operation.

While hotel operations in the cruise industry are divided between ship and shore, the focus of this chapter will be on the former. However, as part of the case study further below, aspects of the planning and pre-opening of a new vessel, which are taken care of in head office, are also discussed.

An Integrated Approach to Hotel Operations: the General Manager

> Hotel managers in today's rapidly changing technological world hold some of the most complex, yet rewarding, job in the hospitality industry.
>
> (Hayes and Ninemeier, 2004, p. xi)

While in some cruise companies the hierarchical structure on board still reflects more traditional nautical lines (Gibson, 2006), there is a clear tendency today to adopt a more modern approach. Instead of the Captain being ultimately responsible for the entire operation on board the ship – including guest services – a General Manager reporting directly to head office is the person to oversee hotel operations.

With this approach, companies ensure that professionals with hotel background and a career path in the respective field handle the essential aspects of the product provided to the guests. This includes discipline and budget control. The 'General Managers run the ship [...] Whereas captains must be experts in many technical and engineering operations, the general manager is an expert in the overall product' (Rumbarger, 2008). In short, the General Manager's job is to

> orchestrate the vacation experience that the cruise line has promised to deliver to its

passengers. To do this requires coordination of all passenger services and ensuring the line's standards are maintained. Everything that has to do with guest satisfaction is his [i.e. the Manager's] bailiwick. If a vessel has a low guest satisfaction rate, he is held accountable long before the Captain unless problems are due to mechanical failures or marine operations.

> (Dickinson and Vladimir, 2008, p. 80)

In the organizational structure described above, the General Manager oversees all departments related to guest services. This includes food and beverage (F&B), housekeeping, administration, shore excursions and often also entertainment (Fig. 16.1). Besides being overall accountable for the guests' experience – and to a great extent also for the crew's well-being – in many cruise lines, the General Manager will also be the company's representative on board for all matters concerning the coordination with and the revenue of concessionaires. Also the medical department (as a revenue centre with direct impact on the guest experience) may be under the General Manager's supervision.

Looking at the extent of responsibility of this function, it is clear why only individuals with vast experience in the various fields of the hospitality industry will be able

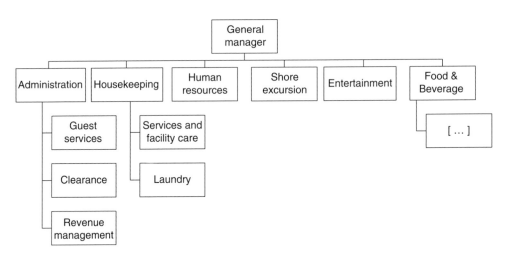

Fig. 16.1. Organization of the hotel department, headed by a General Manager.

to handle the numerous challenges coming up every day. '[...] General Managers routinely face unique problems and situations that require outstanding decision making skills' (Hayes and Ninemeier, 2004, p. xiv).

While a large part of the planning and staffing is done in head office, leadership, control and evaluation can only take place on board. The coordination of the different departments performing to create one seamless and well integrated product requires management skills and expertise. In this respect, the General Manager 'is also responsible for the human resources function for all of the departments that report to him. This includes everything from mundane tasks like scheduling work (or approving schedules) to communication and morale' (Dickinson and Vladimir, 2008, p. 80).

All functions on board have to be performed in a framework of compliance with environmental and USPH regulations, as well as the ISM Code (see Neumann and Ullrich, Chapter 18, this volume), requiring not only the General Manager to be thoroughly familiar with those regulations, but the entire hotel management team. To ensure this, is again the General Manager's responsibility.

While the General Manager needs to keep the hotel operations staff working together, he or she is also the one to coordinate relevant issues with other main departments on board – the deck, engine, shore excursion and entertainment teams, and also with concessionaires. No department on a cruise ship can perform their task independently from the others.

Product delivery depends on the orchestration of all services and backstage processes. Routines need to be established to create a balanced workload that is fair to all departments. Standard operational procedures need to cover all eventualities and be kept in an easily retrievable manner for all managers, the best form being a vessel operations manual or in an electronic form.

Administration

The caduceus is sometimes found on the epaulettes of the purser staff – symbolizing

mercury as god of trade, profit and commerce (author's aphorism).

The Chief Purser or Finance Officer, who reports to the General Manager, is normally in charge of the entire front office and administration department. This includes reception and Concierge services, as well as revenue management and the ship's clearance with customs and immigration authorities in the ports of call. All communications with the local port agent, as the company's partner at the destination, should be routed through the Chief Purser. The purser department also handles the disbursement account – relating to the administration of services ordered in the port of call and verification of respective charges. Among other things, this includes tug, stevedoring and terminal services, water and lubricating oil deliveries as well as sludge removal.

Guest services

In general, guest services offered by the front office team will differ according to the ship's and company's standards. However, everywhere, the main hub for information and guest requests is the reception or front office, also called the guest relations desk. This is the first line of support for all inquiries. It is therefore important that the reception staff is copied on all communication related to guest services to enable them to answer guest queries. Also in this department, currency exchange is handled and safety deposit boxes are available.

The management of the front office on board a ship is not much different from that of a regular hotel. However, while in hotels the main task is to check guests in and out on a daily basis, this happens only once per cruise. The focus of the guest relations desk on a cruise ship is on providing help with questions regarding on-board services. The reception team has a major influence on the guests' overall cruise experience.

Obviously, the challenge in this area is communication. Only when guest requests or complaints are forwarded in a timely manner to the responsible party on board, can appropriate action be taken. For this purpose, a reception log is kept and entries are communicated (electronically or by phone) to the managers in charge. Most incidents are dealt with on a first come, first served basis.

The Concierge is part of the front office team and, depending on the ship's standard, will handle out-of-the-ordinary guest requests, such as special arrangements in a port of call, flight changes that need to be coordinated with head office or follow-up on lost luggage.

Clearance

Normally, the Second Purser or Clearance Officer – reporting to the Chief Purser – is the person in contact with the port agent to prepare all necessary documents for the clearance of the ship at destination. Authorities will require guest and crew lists, check and stamp the passports and call for copies of relevant ship and officers' certificates. Special requirements of certain destinations need to be communicated by head office – Brazilian authorities might, for example, go as far as demanding a crew cabin inspection by their officials.

Although being a mere 'back of house' functionality in most cases (apart from the rare circumstances in which authorities at a certain destination would require a so-called 'face check' of guests and their passports), clearance can have a tremendous impact on the guest experience. A clearance delay can cause late tour departures. Moreover, if important information regarding local requirements such as vaccinations or visa conditions is not communicated to guests before their departure, they might even be denied shore access.

Revenue management

The purser and front office team on board a cruise ship are more than just a mere administrative department. Here, the

financial results of all on-board activities are recorded and analysed.

Most financial transactions of guests on board a cruise ship are cashless. The room key card serves as means of payment, and unless guests collect their guest check copies (if provided) or ask for intermediate updates at reception, they will only see their folio at the end of the cruise. Most companies print a copy on the last evening of the cruise and provide it to the guests the night before disembarkation, after all revenue operations have closed. This way guests have the possibility to verify their folio before checking out, and unless disputable charges are found, there is no need to return to reception. A credit card imprint is already taken and authorized at the beginning of the cruise. Depending on the cruise line's revenue structure and cruise length, credit card files are replicated either twice a cruise or daily from ship to shore for charging.

The revenue from bars and surcharge speciality restaurants has to be recorded and analysed, in the same way as for shore excursions. Several concessionaires have to report revenue from shops and the spa, as well as the cash from the casino on a daily basis. As the medical centre is a revenue centre, the income from medical services provided to guests is often used to offset the cost for crew medical treatment.

Revenue is reviewed by senior management both on board and in head office on an ongoing basis to enable immediate reaction to below-target results. Special offer promotions, increased advertisement in daily programme inserts and even increased PA announcements can help to achieve higher revenue.

In general, on-board revenue policies and targets depend mainly on the business model of the cruise line. While some companies (e.g. Regent Seven Seas) market themselves as a true 'all inclusive' experience without charging for drinks and even shore excursions, they will still work on achieving high spa and casino returns. Other companies (e.g. Royal Caribbean) are highly dependent on adequate on-board spending to offset their fixed costs (Vogel, 2009).

Housekeeping

Undeniably, housekeeping is one of the most important departments within any hotel operation. 'Guests want, first and foremost, a clean room' (Hayes and Ninemeier, 2006, p. 223). Since room attendants also have numerous direct contacts with the guests in their staterooms, their impact on guest satisfaction with the cruise product as a whole is immense. Because of the numerous tasks to be handled, the housekeeping department is one of the largest departments within the hotel operation.

Obviously, this is more than just keeping clean – the housekeeping department has a direct impact on maintaining the biggest asset of the company: the staterooms. This is normally 'the most heavily used area and [...] is likely to be critically examined more frequently and in more detail than any other area of the ship' (Gibson, 2006, p. 131).

Services and facility care

The Executive Housekeeper – reporting to the General Manager – is the individual on board who oversees a wide variety of services provided to the guests, from turndown to laundry. Reporting to the Executive Housekeeper are room attendants, public area cleaners (often working during the night time) and the laundry team.

Unlike in other 'back-of-house' departments, the quality of the housekeeping work is immediately visible to all guests. Depending on the vessel's standard and accommodation category, the room attendant will visit the stateroom numerous times a day to maintain cleanliness and serve as first point of contact for special requests. It is not surprising that ratings in this area are normally the best. Guests do appreciate the personal contact, and housekeeping has a tremendous impact on the holiday experience.

The housekeeping team also plays a critical role in maintenance. Non-routine work, which may be needed, is reported frequently through an AVO system. AVO stands for 'Avoid Verbal Orders', a system found on many cruise ships to report maintenance issues or deficiencies to the hotel engineering or electrician team, to track and document actions taken, and to allow the identification of frequently recurring problems.

Besides maintenance of the staterooms, also the cleanliness and maintenance of public areas and the crew area normally fall under the responsibility of the housekeeping team. An exception to this is the galley area, where the team of the Chief Steward (reporting to the Executive Chef) is in charge. The provision area and the laundry are also maintained by the staff of the respective departments.

Laundry

Unlike hotels ashore, cruise ships have no possibility to outsource the laundry operation. Depending on the standard of the cruise line and the extent of 'free laundry' perquisites offered, the volume to be handled will vary. On an average sized cruise ship, depending on the climate, the laundry has to process several tons of linen and terry towelling daily. A full linen change on a turnaround (cruise end/start) presents a workload by which a lot of shore-side laundries would be overwhelmed.

Given both space and manpower restrictions, the laundry facility must be designed for utmost efficiency. Receiving areas for dirty linen, washing machines with sufficient capacity and extraction, matching drying facilities and a professional ironing machine have to be positioned in such a way that a clear and uninterrupted workflow is guaranteed. This set up is an essential part of the planning for a new ship – to be discussed at a later point within this chapter – and can hardly be changed later, as the machines not only require connections for water and steam, but are simply too large to be re-positioned. Also sufficient dry cleaning capacity is needed for the guests' garments and the crew's uniforms.

Spot removal and ironing tables, as well as presses and sufficient storage for clean laundry and uniforms, need to be laid out in a way that facilitates the workflow and guarantees operational efficiency. Many older ships have still been designed without capitalizing on expertise of laundry operations personnel – often causing the laundry to be spread out over various watertight sections (watertight doors must be closed during manoeuvring), causing downtime and constant problems. Today, cruise companies and shipyards alike have realized the importance of this area, and planning is based on workload forecasts.

Food and Beverage (F&B) Management

F&B management is not only an integral part of the overall guest experience – and therefore falls into the domain of hotel department – but also one of the most challenging areas within hotel operations on cruise ships. The F&B Manager reports to the General Manager. Cartledge (Chapter 17, this volume) provides a more extensive account of the F&B function on cruise ships.

Information Systems

Information systems suitable for hotel operations on cruise ships are quite different from systems for regular hotels. Crew management, for instance, plays a vital role in the cruise industry. Contract and deployment management, the administration of required certificates and the tracking of promotions and disciplinary actions cannot be processed by using off-the-shelf human resource management software for hotels.

As vessels operate detached from head office (and one another), frequent replication of data is necessary. With the vast amount of information collected, automatic data consolidation is needed for management control.

Today, various providers of specialized cruise operations software systems exist, offering single modules or complete, integrated systems. Besides payroll administration and human resource management, property management is usually supported by a special information management system. Property management systems are connected to all points of sale on the ship and host the guests' folios for billing (see also Papathanassis, Chapter 6, this volume). At the same time, property management systems have to be able to provide access control at the gangway and show in real time, which guest is on board and who is ashore. Safety information, as well as all guest details for lists required by local authorities – see clearance – must be available at a keystroke.

Supply chain management can be seen as the backbone of the hotel operations (see Véronneau and Roy, Chapter 7, this volume). Not only will a functioning inventory and purchasing system enable the company to keep costs low, but unreliable stockholding management can potentially have a major impact on the guest experience – especially when essential items run out in the middle of the cruise.

For technical management, the supply chain is normally connected to a separate maintenance cycle system to ensure compliant handling of overhaul and servicing of machinery. This applies also to galley and laundry equipment where numerous different appliances and equipment are vital for continued operation.

Closely connected to the supply chain management system in hotel operations are meal count systems (providing a planning tool for food ordering) and restaurant reservation modules. The latter has become increasingly important with growing ship size and the number of outlets open to the guests. On the *Oasis of the Seas* – the Royal Caribbean vessel introduced to the market in 2009 – guests have the choice between 24 food outlets and 37 bars. With up to 6000 passengers on board, it becomes obvious that not everyone can go to the same speciality restaurant at the same time.

For proper revenue management, a shore excursion system must support the sales of tours on board, but also help to make invoice control for the respective tour operator's charges easy and transparent. This should be connected to the shore-side booking engine for pre-cruise sales, and ideally also to an online reservation portal allowing guests to pre-arrange their excursions before stepping aboard. Revenue from bars and other sales outlets – also concessionaires – should be recorded in a cashless point-of-sale solution, enabling automated budget/actual comparison.

Ideally, all modules are linked to a proper port and itinerary planning module, providing seamless integration of cruise and regional information.

Performance Indicators

The key to ascertain quality is to understand customer needs and wishes.

(Gibson, 2006, p. 103)

Main performance categories for the hotel operations are costs (especially food cost, but also costs of beverages, amenities and other items sold), revenues made in the various outlets and, of course, the outcome of the guests' cruise evaluation. As described above, information systems must support management by providing key figures and ratios in an easily retrievable way.

More difficult to measure are the 'soft' factors. 'The effective performance of any cruise ship is underpinned by the quality of service' (Gibson, 2006, p. 95), and many guests will base their booking decision on word-of-mouth or on previous experience on board. With the importance of guest satisfaction in mind, the cruise industry today has better quality control systems in place than most hotel companies ashore.

The so-called 'ratings' play a huge role in the day-to-day operation, and many companies do not only send out a guest questionnaire at the end of the cruise, but also have a mid-cruise form for longer voyages. Cruise questionnaires are normally forwarded to the shore-side part of the operation; this systematic quality control procedure ensures that trends are discovered early and appropriate action can be

taken for the entire fleet, not only on a single ship. As challenges might also sometimes be related to the personnel on board, response from shore-side management is essential.

Outsourcing and Management Contracts

While part of the guest service department and even the entire F&B operations can be outsourced to third-party contractors, cruise operators should avoid giving up their control of the management of the overall guest experience. As part of the contractual agreement, third-party contractors should commit themselves to a detailed catalogue of services that meet the cruise operator's requirements and standards. This should also include clear guidelines regarding the product to be provided and conditions for crew members on board.

A general management decision with vast consequences is the outsourcing of key functions, guest-facing or not, to third parties. This obviously depends not only on expertise of the in-house management, but also on financial considerations and the possibility to partly convert fixed costs into variables.

Whether a company only contracts certain services like shop or spa to an outside party or outsources an entire department, the impact on the on-board operations – and the job description of the key personnel as the company's representative on the ship – will be tremendous. What do companies need to consider before taking this step?

The first step should be a qualitative evaluation – can the contractor provide products and services according to desired standards, which are equal to, if not better than those that could be produced in house?

Only if this is confirmed can the next step follow – the quantitative evaluation, dealing with relative costs. Does it make sense in financial terms to outsource?

When it comes to outsourcing the F&B operations or even the entire hotel operations, there are only a handful of experienced providers available. Experience in the specific market segment of the cruise operator is essential.

For smaller parts of the operation, the general opinion in the industry is that specialized providers will be able not only to provide a better product for the guest, but to do so in a way that is financially favourable for the cruise operator. This applies especially to beauty, spa and hairdresser or shops. There is also a marketing aspect to the brand name of certain spa providers, which might be seen as an upgrade and underlines the exclusivity of a cruise company. For casino operation, licences and specialized expertise are required.

Photography used to be a significant revenue outlet on board ships; however, with the development of simpler and cheap digital cameras, many operators have seen a decrease of revenue in this area. On many ships today, the services of a photographer who takes (and sells) pictures of special occasions are discontinued. In their place, guests often find an art gallery on board cruise ships today. This provides an opportunity for the cruise operators to utilize their walls for additional revenue generation (and not having to pay for their 'own' artwork) as guests seem to be quite willing to purchase paintings while in a relaxed holiday mood.

From Planning to Practice – a New Ship

> The events that contribute to the success or failure [...] begin with an idea or concept and end with effective implementation and performance.
>
> (Katz, 1997, p. 3)

In 2011 alone, the North American cruise market is expected to grow by 14,554 lower berths with 16 new ships to be introduced, after an increase by 23 new ships with a total of 21,624 lower berths in 2010 (CLIA, 2010). While some of these new ships are the second or the third of their class and operations on board are largely identical to those on existing vessels, others will represent a further development of an existing product or even an entirely new concept. The creation of a new product entails manifold aspects that require diligent consideration (see Spiegel, Chapter 12, this volume). This applies to the hotel department as much as to any other department on the ship, or any part of it.

As an example, consider the planning associated with an F&B concept. Today, on many new ships, dining facilities are no longer planned for fixed seating arrangements. Restaurants have 'open seating', meaning that guests can sit where and with whom they want. This adds significant complexity to the job of the maître d' (short for maître d'hôtel, the person in charge of the dining room operations) who now has to assign available tables flexibly and with a maximum of efficiency during mealtimes. In the planning process, a balance needs to be struck between available seats and opening hours, which in turn has important implications for the planning of the required manpower. And since every additional staff member requires a cabin and berth, the F&B concept has ramifications for the size and design of the crew area.

Another part of the F&B concept is the design of buffet restaurants. No matter what standard of ship, long buffet queues are to be avoided. Facilities need to be arranged to maximize 'guest throughput' subject to the specific demands of the F&B concept. Coffee machine capacity has to be designed to cope with peak times during breakfast, without requiring more space than absolutely necessary.

When developing the F&B concept, menu cycles constitute the basis for a standard items list and future requisitioning and purchasing. Provision rooms need to be designed in such a way that they allow for sufficient stockholding – if too small, permanent re-ordering (if not running out of items) will result in high operational costs.

Another example is housekeeping: staterooms should be optimized for easy cleaning to save manpower, i.e. labour costs and expensive accommodation space. Architects' ideas are often attractive in respect of visual effects and a matching, pleasant composition of the staterooms and public areas – but operational imperatives and practical considerations need to be given priority. Will the same bathroom fixtures still be available in a few years' time? Were safe and mini bar customized for the new ship and (when broken) must be manufactured on demand at high costs and with minimum order quantities? Is there sufficient washing and drying capacity, and how can the internal logistics be organized?

Furniture needs to be selected to match standard and décor and enable an easy workflow. It also needs to be durable and easy to re-upholster on board. The specification and pile depth of carpets influence not only the guests' comfort and the ship's aesthetics, but also the necessary height of fire doors and low-level lighting installation.

In all these respects, the relevant maritime regulations must be obeyed. For instance, balcony furniture is required to be fireproof according to IMO standards (unless fixed fire detection and extinguishing systems are installed for the balconies). And last but not least, crew must be recruited, selected and trained for the operation. A new coffee station requires a barista with sufficient skills to prepare speciality coffees, and for the authentic Asian restaurant, a sushi chef needs to be found.

What is the answer to these challenges? As the examples suggest:

- a clear idea and concept;
- the involvement of hands-on and experienced operations personnel; and
- the early consideration of hotel operations requirements

are essential ingredients if a new cruise ship is not only to be beautiful but also functional.

Moreover, it needs to be understood that the ship should match what the guests know and like about other vessels of the same brand. 'I believe great companies are great because they build *brands*, not products' (Del Rio, 2010; original emphasis).

Not the smallest part of this branding is a unique hotel experience for the guests, consisting of a balanced array of services, which are performed in a seemingly easy and uncomplicated way.

Concluding Remarks

Hotel operations in the cruise industry differ in various ways from land-based hotel operations. In one way, the operation is more complex and includes additional functions that apply only to the unique environment cruise ships present. On the other hand, hotel operations on cruise ships are in some ways simpler than in many hotels ashore, as the sales and yield management functions are taken care of by the head office.

Cruise operations are a very people-driven discipline; and the different requirements result in diverse and distinctive career paths for the individuals working in this field. A large part of the cruise experience is created by interaction of crew and guests. Baron and Kreps (1999) emphasize that 'Human resources are key to organizational success or failure' (p. 4), and this is nowhere more true than in a confined atmosphere in which crew from numerous different nations work together for many months without a break in between. One focus of hotel operations therefore has to be on human resources.

Another priority should be the standardization of services. Regardless of market segment or category of ship: only with a clear idea of the kind of experience or product that the company wants to provide to their guests, can on-board operations succeed. Here, the shore-side team comes into play – while the general direction has to be planned in agreement with Sales, Marketing and other departments, the plan needs to be translated into workable terms and clearly communicated to the shipboard players.

Designed as a framework of company policies, the hotel services concept will be filled with life by the on-board team.

References

Baron, J.N. and Kreps, D.M. (1999) *Strategic Human Resources: Framework for General Managers.* John Wiley & Sons, Hoboken, New Jersey.

CLIA (2010) *2010 Cruise Market Overview.* Cruise Lines International Association, Fort Lauderdale, Florida.

Del Rio, F. (2010) Oceania Cruises on fast growth track. *The Miami Herald*, 13 May. Available at: www.miamiherald.com/2010/05/13/1626701/oceania-cruises-is-on-fast-growth.html (accessed 29 April 2011).

Dickinson, B. and Vladimir, A. (2008) *Selling the Sea: an Inside Look at the Cruise Industry*, 2nd edn. John Wiley & Sons, Hoboken, New Jersey.

Gibson, P. (2006) *Cruise Operations Management.* Butterworth-Heinemann, Oxford.

Hayes, D.K. and Ninemeier, J.D. (2004) *Hotel Operations Management.* Pearson Education, Upper Saddle River, New Jersey.

Hayes, D.K. and Ninemeier, J.D. (2006) *Restaurant Operations Management.* Pearson Education, Upper Saddle River, New Jersey.

Katz, J.B. (1997) *Restaurant Planning, Design, and Construction.* John Wiley & Sons, Hoboken, New Jersey.

Rumbarger, M. (2008) Getting to the Top. Interview with the Director Hotel Operations of Oceania Cruises. *Cruise Industry News*, Winter 2008/2009.

Vogel, M. (2009) Onboard revenue: the secret of the cruise industry's success? In: Papathanassis, A. (ed.) *Cruise Sector Growth.* Gabler, Wiesbaden, pp. 3–15.

Ward, D. (2009) *Complete Guide to Cruising & Cruise Ships 2009*, 18th edn. Berlitz, London.

17 Food and Beverage Operations

Grenville Cartledge

Introduction

This chapter will look at some of the broader elements of food and beverage (F&B) operations on board cruise ships. The focus will be on the huge changes that have taken place over the last 10–15 years or so in terms of food service. The chapter will also consider some of the contributing factors that have come together to bring about these changes and some of the key issues and challenges in delivering the level of service standards now expected by cruise passengers.

Importance of Food and Beverage Operations

Since the earliest days of cruise ship operations, F&B service has been one of the most significant factors in determining the success of the ship, the brand, the operator and the industry as a whole. Opulence, indulgence and quality have been keywords throughout the history of the industry and, even to this day, cruise ships are still largely recognized as offering some of the best quality, most varied and plentiful food available anywhere.

F&B service, therefore, has been one of the main cornerstones of cruise ship operations to the present day, and this is not expected to change in the future – on the contrary, the development of this element of the industry is seen as one of the key differentials between brands and operators going forward.

The Traditional Service Model

The 'traditional' service model retains its place within the industry, with many passengers still choosing to cruise with brands and ships offering more limited F&B options. However, the biggest change has seen the shift from two-sitting dining to complete freedom of choice of dining time and venue. As a result, there is currently significant competition between cruise lines to create defining differentials in product and service and, since the late 1990s, the industry has seen quantum shifts to the myriad choice now offered across the brands.

This more traditional model is based upon a two-sitting dinner with assigned dinner seating augmented by a standard 'Lido' buffet operation at breakfast and lunch time, with limited 'alternative' (and generally more informal) dining options some evenings. In addition, there would generally be a good quality Afternoon Tea option, together with Midnight Buffets and regular Gala Buffets – the latter usually on a week-by-week or cruise-by-cruise basis. The trend, though, has been, and continues to be, away from this more traditional service to one of greater choice and freedom with, very often, dining options available around the clock, 24 h per day.

The Change from the Traditional Model

The early Carnival Cruise Lines, and other US-based cruise lines in the 1970s/80s, had begun to change the industry approach of the more traditional service model for many different reasons, partly to compete with the more informal offerings of hotels and resorts, but also to attract passengers to cruising, which was still perceived as being 'traditional' and somewhat elitist, which put many people off considering a cruise holiday. However, it was not until the late 1990s and the early 2000s that the revolutionary changes happened, and they happened very quickly indeed.

Norwegian Caribbean Line (NCL, later Norwegian Cruise Line) was the first cruise line to challenge fundamentally the accepted standard food service options on board with their introduction of 'Freestyle Dining' in 2001. This dining concept was initially met with trepidation, doubt and even disdain by many within the industry. However, some 10 years on, nearly every single cruise operator has since adopted some, if not all, of this freedom of choice across all brands from super-luxury to mass-market.

Freestyle dining

In 2001, NCL introduced *Norwegian Sun* and *Norwegian Star* – the first purpose-built Freestyle Cruising vessels to the market. The key elements were that the ships would offer a much more relaxed resort-style approach to open seating, together with

extended dining hours, thereby allowing passengers to dine at their chosen time and to dress as they please. Another hugely significant innovation was in the scale and variety of dining choices available – these new ships included some 13 different restaurants and dining options on board.

The other major operators were very quick to adapt their own product offering and have since developed, and continue to develop, their own versions of this freedom of choice and product variety to virtually unimaginable magnitude.

Open seating dining continues to grow in popularity and is virtually fleet-wide amongst the large cruise lines. Royal Caribbean International recently introduced a slightly different concept called MyTime Dining in 2009, where passengers can opt to dine at any time in the main dining room. 'The innovation with our system is to preserve what guests can experience in the traditional seating model, where the permanent waiter will remember and deliver guest's preferences every night after the first night' (Frey, 2009, p. 24).

Also Carnival now have fleet-wide open-seating options, and Celebrity launched the Celebrity Select dining programme in 2009, one that is similar to MyTime Dining. However, Celebrity claim a point of difference in that the guests can select their preferred dining time and be guaranteed a table.

Challenges to the concept of open or casual dining

It has not been all 'plain sailing' in this change from the traditional model to one of more informality and choice, and some cruise operators continue to baulk the trend for various reasons. This may be because of limitations of the ships themselves, with much of the older tonnage not having the necessary space and/or facilities; however, it is also true that there is still a significant and (currently at least) sustainable market for the more traditional cruise product.

There were also a number of challenges for the cruise operators in the early days of 'freestyle'. In addition to hardware and cost challenges, there was significant operational challenge, the main one being overcoming a lot of negativity from the on-board management and staff themselves. This resistance is generally true of any change within any working environment, but it was exacerbated in this case by the experienced F&B management teams genuinely believing this concept to be flawed and, in many cases, simply unworkable.

Some negativity towards the more informal style was also experienced by some of the passengers who were used to, and enjoyed, the more regimented traditional approach. In particular, they liked to know their table reservation, and a positive part of the cruise experience for many was enjoying the company of the same table companions at each dinner time. Also, many enjoyed the dress code element of the cruise, especially the formal nights with the traditions that went with that, e.g. formal dress code, Captain's Cocktail party, Gala Dinner, Chef's Parade etc. It is true that some, if not all, of these elements still exist as part of the product offering; however, in a much more disjointed and divisive way – for instance, you will now see formal nights on board with some passengers dressed in their finery mixing with fellow passengers dressed in various modes of 'casual' or 'smart casual'. This was unheard of on many cruise ships until Freestyle Cruising, and even to this day appears extremely incongruous to many.

So the new approach was not welcomed by everyone, and initially there was definitely some market resistance. However, with the advent of a whole new generation of cruisers, together with distinct product differentiation that is almost universally understood, this situation does not really exist any longer, and passengers can make their brand and ship choices according to their tastes. However, it is fair to say that the majority of the mainstream cruise operators do offer a variance of the freestyle concept and it is only the smaller, or niche, operators now offering the traditional experience.

This freedom of choice also brought with it many other operational challenges, not just in relation to the actual service of food.

One distinct advantage of the more 'regulated' and controlled traditional service model, with set dining times, was that passenger flow was much easier to predict and manage – this being particularly true at dinner time when the ship's entertainment programme would be built around the times of the two sittings. The implementation of the more informal approach to dining, compounded by the development of multi-embarkation and disembarkation ports, has led to a distinct loss of 'structure' to many cruises. The traditional two-sitting model, with one main embarkation and disembarkation port, meant that the ships would offer a fairly standard programme of events on particular days and times throughout the cruise, so the freestyle product brought about many fresh planning challenges in terms of controlling passenger flow and provision of entertainment accessible to all.

The two challenges are, of course, interrelated, as the entertainment programme helps to drive and control passenger flow, yet the timing and provision of food service also determines the entertainment timings. For John Bywater, Head of Food & Beverage Services at Carnival Group UK, 'The key thing is managing the flow' of passengers to make the Freestyle Cruising product work (2010, personal communication). So the provision of the entertainment programme and dining options has to be managed to ensure that the flow is as steady, orderly and predictable as possible, because it is often impossible for everyone on board to dine, or be entertained, at the same time.

Choice is the Keyword

'Choice' is now the keyword in F&B service, and it is this that has seen the most significant change and development in recent times, in terms of choice of the service style, choice of time and choice of seating. It would not be an exaggeration to suggest that this, together with the variety of F&B options now available, has seen the industry transformed in the last 10 years or so. John Bywater of Carnival Group UK claims that 'the greatest development over the last ten years is choice' and that 'choice is the key driver of cruise F&B operations' (2010, personal communication).

There are many reasons that have influenced these changes, some of which will be considered in this chapter. Some relate to things such as new tonnage, new technology, reaction to hotel and resort competition, industry innovation and global availability of product; however, perhaps the most significant driving factor has been the increased awareness and expectations of cruise passengers.

Passenger and public awareness

One of the key drivers of change within the cruise industry, and indeed the hospitality industry generally, is increased public awareness and sophistication of food (and beverage) and its trends. This has been related to many influences including increased foreign travel, media coverage, access to information on the internet and 'celebrity' chef culture, to name but a few.

People are generally much more adventurous in their tastes, yet are also much more aware of health issues related to diet. This has drastically changed their perception and expectations of what is a good product offering.

The huge increase of media coverage has led to people wanting to know the provenance of their food and has greatly increased their knowledge, and awareness, of food quality. There is an ever growing and significant awareness of sustainable and 'Fairtrade' products and cruise operators are constantly striving to satisfy demands and expectations within often extremely constraining budgets.

Perversely though, much of the marketing material for the cruise industry, and indeed still the appeal to many for a cruise holiday, centres around the opportunity for indulgence and perhaps to enjoy foods that are a little different to their usual diet and, in most cases, probably richer in content. So, whilst the health-conscious element is important, it should all still be tempered with the underlying desire for the cruise passenger to enjoy an indulgent experience, and this continues to be a key challenge to the corporate F&B teams in their planning.

Special dietary requirements

Cruise ship operators have always prided themselves on being willing and able to provide for passengers on special diets, and that is still as true today as it always was; however, the challenge is now – what is a special diet as opposed to a personal preference?

With the growing awareness of healthier living and the vast array of healthier products available to the consumer, the distinction between special diet and personal preference is now often quite blurred. This leads to extra challenges for the cruise operator with increasing requests from passengers for food items that do not necessarily fit into the genuine special diet requirement.

The operators must decide what the ship(s) will provide as standard, i.e. what range of products they will carry and offer as part of the regular food offering. For instance, the range of dairy items now offered as standard by most, if not all, cruise ships would include full fat, semi-skimmed, skimmed and soya milk. Is it too much to expect the ships to also offer, as standard (standard can also mean available on request), sheep, rice, oat, goat and, say, almond milk? This conundrum for the cruise line also extends to other dairy products, in particular with regard to the boom in the pro-biotic yoghurt market. Should this relatively expensive, yet increasingly popular, product be offered as standard? Clearly, the issue covers a whole range of other foodstuffs and not just dairy products, the example of which is used simply to illustrate the point.

The cruise operator must decide what else will be offered as standard and what will be provided on request at no extra cost to the passenger. This will largely be dependent upon passenger nationalities, demographics and market sector (e.g. luxury or mass-market) and how much the operator sees the importance of the differentiation of how they treat the question of special diets and special requests.

At some point, there has to be a trade-off between giving the passenger service and the practicality or cost of offering it on board. Factors such as cost itself, world-wide availability, shelf life, storage and operational constraints all have to be taken into account by the F&B teams.

However a cruise line decides to tackle the issues of special diets and preferences, there is no doubt that the growing awareness of healthier living, and change in lifestyle habits, continues to influence significantly the decision-making of F&B management teams in its planning.

Global Food Supply

The supply and availability of F&B products around the world has significantly influenced some of the dramatic changes the industry has seen in the last 10–15 years. The development and cost of shipping dry and refrigerated containers has led to a previously unthinkable range of options for the supply of such products. This, together with the shift to consolidated supply chains and sophisticated stock control and ordering systems, has meant that many cruise operators are now able to provide a complete range of standard products worldwide.

Apart from some local purchases, procurement for the ships is now largely controlled by purchasing and logistics teams based in head office. The purchasing team liaise with the on-board management and, dependent upon the sophistication of the computerized stock control and ordering system and the size and style of operation, will plan the purchasing and logistics

accordingly. This will often mean that orders need to be placed several weeks in advance of delivery to the ship to ensure that there is a consistent supply of the correct products. In some cases, particularly for the major operators, this ordering may be automatically generated, such is the strength and capability of the electronic systems used. These orders/requests are generated by continuous automatic analysis of consumption, forecast consumption and stockholding of products.

Most cruise operators now implement some element of 'corporate' (standardized) menu cycles that are designed by culinary teams working in head office. As mentioned above, the size and style of the operation will influence the degree of this corporatization with the large mainstream cruise lines operating virtually 100% corporate menu cycles.

This centralized control gives an operator many advantages, including factors such as greater control of supply chain, consistency of product, reduced requirement for skilled and creative production personnel and an overall reduction in product costs. However, one of the main disadvantages of corporate menu planning is that senior chefs are generally motivated by a desire to control, or at the very least, influence menu composition. The challenge for the corporate F&B management team is how they balance this need for their senior chefs to find creative satisfaction whilst working with centrally controlled menu planning. The recent development of speciality restaurants has helped a little, with chefs being allowed some freedom to develop their own menus, allowing signature dishes to be included on menu choice has also helped, and most cruise lines will involve their senior chefs to a lesser or greater degree in the menu planning process.

Many chefs do feel professionally constrained by working with corporate menus, and some will seek to work with some of the smaller or niche cruise operators where there is generally much greater freedom, or look to opportunities in land-based hotels, resorts or restaurants.

Corporate Culinary Support

The scale of corporate culinary support is largely determined by the size of the cruise operation and, of course, by the extent of the corporate planning that takes place. Apart from some small or niche operators, there will be a culinary person, or persons, based centrally to support the operational fleet. The range of their roles will be dependent upon the scale of the operation, but will include such things as menu planning, dish development, training, quality assurance, standard writing, technical support and trend analysis.

The corporate team will often consist of senior chefs who fulfil an executive travelling role. They will usually be on sea-going contracts and will spend most of their time working alongside the ship-based teams in a menu implementation, training and development, mentoring and operational support capacity. Some of these 'travelling' chefs will also spend a certain part of their time fulfilling the relief role of Executive Chef on board to assist in work schedule planning and to cover emergency periods. They will also contribute greatly to the assessment and development of on-board personnel and to the menu planning and implementation process.

De-skilling of the Culinary Operation

As stated earlier, the last 10–15 years have seen a remarkable transformation in the provision of F&B services on board ship and there are many contributory factors. One of the less palatable developments for some has been the de-skilling of the culinary operation. This de-skilling has partly happened because of external influences outside the control of the industry and partly because it has been driven by the industry itself.

One of the key challenges of the cruise industry and, indeed, the hospitality industry as a whole, is the availability of qualified, experienced personnel. This is particularly true of the global availability of skilled culinary personnel. John Bywater of Carnival Group UK says, 'Whatever you may want to offer food-wise, it is the people to actually

produce it, and deliver it, consistently on board that is still the most important consideration'. He also adds, 'It [the availability of qualified crew] is a challenge across the industry and not just in food preparation and service' (2010, personal communication).

The main contributory factors to this reduction in availability of suitable crew is the enormous growth and demand of the industry itself, the competition from five-star hotel and resort operations, particularly in the Middle Eastern countries, and the technological advances in food preparation, both in terms of equipment and worldwide availability, and competitive cost, of quality frozen and vacuum-packed pre-prepared foods.

The emergence of the large, luxury hotel and resort operations in the oil-rich countries of the Middle East has had a particularly significant impact on the availability of qualified personnel for the cruise industry. They are now offering comparative terms and conditions, in many cases preferable ones, and are therefore able to attract personnel from the traditional cruise-recruiting areas of the developing countries, e.g. India. The Philippines and other parts of the world have also seen a huge growth of these hotel and resort operations, which are now offering viable employment opportunities to many who, in the past, would have chosen a career on board.

This has all contributed to another significant development, over recent years, in the growth of cruise line sponsored food preparation (and service) training schools. The larger operators will have their own training schools or work in liaison with local colleges, academies and recruitment partners in the key recruiting countries, e.g. India, the Philippines. These training schools are primarily to give students a basic grounding in food preparation and service, so that at least the cruise line has a steady, yet limited, source of part-qualified and competent crew.

Internationalization of Cruising

The growth of the cruise industry has been phenomenal. This growth has not only seen huge increases in the numbers of ships and passengers carried, but also the virtual internationalization of the industry. This has driven a constant search by the operators for new markets, for ways to increase market share and for new destinations and itineraries. The major operators now have a number of international brands to cater for passenger preference, from mainstream to luxury and niche operations, but they also own, operate or partner many country-specific or regional brands.

This internationalization in the cruise market has had, and continues to have, significant impact on the F&B operations on board. The challenge of operating ships that serve several heterogeneous markets is not just limited to the F&B provision; there are many others including language, entertainment, crewing etc., and it is important that this aspect of the cruise product is planned and implemented correctly to ensure that the tastes and preferences of an increasingly diverse mix of passengers are satisfied.

A good example of this internationalization in recent years is the increasing presence of the major US operators in Europe. Until relatively recently, typically these cruise ships would reposition to Europe following their Caribbean season, but would still be mainly sold out of the USA and, therefore, the majority of passengers on board would still be American. This meant that the product offer did not necessarily have to change to take into account any change in the passenger mix. Now increasing numbers of these ships are home-ported in Europe and are being sold through newly developed distribution channels to British and other European passengers.

This means that not only has the passenger mix drastically changed but tastes, preferences, perceptions, cultural needs and expectations are also significantly different to the predominantly American product. As a counter and reversal to this trend, there are some European operators and brands selling a significant quantity of cruises through US distribution channels, leading to a need to offer a product to satisfy these passenger needs, and some brands are selling to a mix of different European,

US and other international passengers. All in all, there is generally a hugely diverse mix of passenger nationalities across all brands, giving the operators challenges at all levels – not least within F&B operations.

Not all operators meet these challenges in the same way, and the F&B (and wider programme) planning is largely dependent upon the anticipated passenger nationality breakdown. Going back to the US operators' move to Europe as an example, some make wholesale changes to the American product to take into account British and European tastes, whilst others will make relatively minor changes to their operation and market the product as an American one, thereby negating the need to make any wholesale changes.

The changes necessary from an American to British operation will not only relate to product changes but also to things such as the formality and speed of service – British passengers, in the main, prefer a slower and more formal style of service. Other alterations or adaptations to the operation would include the provision of hot plates and hot(ter) food that the British tend to favour over Americans, the interaction of the service personnel (again the British tend to expect and prefer less informality than Americans), dining times themselves may need to be adapted, the introduction of a more formal Afternoon Tea, and changes to the pricing and tipping policy. These and many other aspects of the operation need to be considered by the operators as they strive to serve and satisfy an ever increasing international passenger base.

The above is only one example of a product change and of the challenges faced with passengers of different nationalities – there are obviously many other examples where the operators must take into account the passenger mix in product planning, dependent upon the specific nationalities involved.

The universal development and acceptance of international buffet-style dining has helped enormously in the provision of a wide range of foods to satisfy most tastes. With the range of foods now available globally as standard, it has become more straightforward – if the ship has the necessary space, equipment and labour resource – to cater for an international passenger base.

The Influence of the High Street

As ship's F&B operations develop and as new ships are constructed, it is extremely noticeable that the tastes and trends of the High Street are greatly influencing the on-board cruise product. There is an ever-increasing expectation that cruise ships will provide the wide range of products, services and even the popular brands that are found on the High Street, in the shopping malls and cafés and restaurants ashore.

This development has changed the face of the public spaces found on the modern, larger cruise ship, with ships such as *Oasis* and *Allure of the Seas* – both recent Royal Caribbean International tonnage – devoting swathes of space, in some cases whole decks, to create so-called neighbourhood areas. These neighbourhoods are brilliantly conceived, designed and then constructed to incorporate myriad dining options (24 according to Royal Caribbean International website) with options to satisfy all tastes, from the most discerning palate in an upscale restaurant to a Johnny Rockets diner. Other options include a speciality steak house, pizzeria, Italian and Asian cuisine, ice cream parlour, doughnut shop, seafood shack and coffee shops, as well as a private dining experience. The fundamental point being that, while many of these offerings will be complimentary, many of them will have some element of additional cost or applicable cover charge.

For a perfect example of the influence of the High Street on cruise ship F&B operations, one needs to look no further than Royal Caribbean International's *Allure of the Seas*, which, when it began operations in November 2010, introduced the Starbucks brand to the cruise line with the opening of Starbucks at sea. There are many other examples of High Street brands within cruise F&B operations, but the collaboration of two global brands such as Royal Caribbean International

and Starbucks is particularly significant and indicative of the trend. Another recent trend heavily influenced by the High Street is in-cabin delivery service of take-away foods such as pizza.

Celebrity Chefs

The boom of the 'celebrity chef' culture in recent years has had significant impact on public awareness of food and eating habits – and to a lesser extent that of wine and other beverages. It is true that TV and celebrity chefs have been around for four or five decades, but the last 10 years or so have seen a major increase in their coverage in the media and their influence on societal change to dining – both in and out. There is no doubt that the unprecedented media coverage given to F&B programmes in the TV schedules, magazines, books etc. has led to a greatly enhanced public awareness and expectation of F&B preparation, service and quality.

The cruise industry has recognized the strategic and commercial value of association with famous chefs for many years, for example in the 1990s P&O Cruises (UK) contracted the Swiss Chef, Anton Mosimann, who was one of the pioneers of the nouvelle cuisine culinary style of the 1990s. Mosimann was only contracted to design and endorse menus, to help in the training of ship culinary personnel and to assist with the implementation of such menus. The relationship was obviously seen as an important one for both parties, but was much more low-key than many of the relationships now in place between celebrity chefs and the cruise lines.

There are now many different associations between celebrity chefs and the cruise operators, and there is conflicting opinion, which is clearly difficult to substantiate, of their commercial overall worth to the operation. There is no doubt that such associations do add value to the operation, though the ongoing questions are how much value do they add, how sustainable are these associations and the biggest question of all is, does the benefit versus cost continue to be viable? As is often the case, the sales and marketing departments will not always perceive and answer these questions in the same way as the operational departments. The association of celebrity chefs with a brand is primarily about giving that brand certain kudos, and the choice of chef will largely be dependent on the target market, and brands will choose chefs that suit their own passenger profile.

There would also seem to be conflicting opinions about the value of celebrity chefs amongst the passengers themselves – although there is no freely available information or data currently to hand to substantiate this. However, anecdotally some passengers are not happy about having to pay extra for the privilege of a special menu or dining experience, and many feel they do not necessarily need to. Of course, to counter the latter point the simple fact is that the extra dining opportunity is an option of personal choice.

Another counter argument of the worth of celebrity chefs is that only a very small percentage of passengers are able to, or choose to, experience the dining experience offered. However, it has undoubtedly opened up a world of opportunities for many to such experiences. One small example would be the chance for P&O Cruises passengers to enjoy a Marco Pierre White meal for around £15 (US$25), as opposed to paying at least four or five times that amount for a similar meal ashore.

In addition to the celebrity chefs, and often to complement them, many of the major cruise lines have introduced demonstration kitchens that feature specific culinary programmes throughout the day. These programmes are a fusion of entertainment, education and dining option and seem to be very popular with passengers. Cunard Line has been associated with the famous American chef Todd English for a number of years. This association was initially based on the endorsement and compiling of menus but has since developed to the point where QM2 includes the Todd English restaurant as a dining option.

Crystal Cruises has had an association with Japanese Master Chef Nobu since 2003, and continues to value the relationship in terms of it being a point of brand difference and one that is greatly appreciated by their guests. As part of the association, Nobu regularly cruises with the line and provides a number of his chefs to replicate the Nobu menus served in one of his restaurants worldwide. The trend certainly does not show any signs of abating at the time of writing, and it will be interesting to note the developments over the next few years.

On-board Revenue

The recent development of High Street brands, speciality restaurants, celebrity chefs etc. has also led to a growing awareness and understanding amongst the cruise line operators that food operations themselves, and not just beverage operations, are significant on-board revenue streams that were largely untapped until relatively recently.

This is also because the traditional cruise model was one where the food operation was much more limited and it was marketed that the cruise itself was all-inclusive (AI) with regard to food service, i.e. all meals and hot beverages were included. The move to a more informal style of operation, and the introduction and creation of a plethora of extras, means that most cruise ships now offer a wholly different product and one that is now generating necessary on-board revenue. This revenue stream is critical to supporting the rest of the operational costs and to enable the cruise lines to remain competitive with land-based hotels and resorts.

Using the example of the recent Royal Caribbean International new builds, the majority of modern cruise ships are designed to maximize these revenue opportunities with a combination of extremely clever design concepts, management of passenger flow and the provision of a wide range of F&B options – as stated earlier, many of which are mirroring what is available on the High Street.

Other Challenges

The cruise F&B and operational management teams have different challenges to overcome in their quest to deliver the best possible on-board experiences and to continue to exceed passenger expectations wherever possible. Some of these have been touched upon previously in the chapter, e.g. internationalism, crewing and public awareness, though there are many others that cannot really be covered in the scope of this overview of F&B operations – such things as rising commodity costs versus the corporate requirement for cost control, satisfying the quickly changing tastes and trends of the public, food supply itself and the public demand for choice.

One of the key and continuing challenges, though, is the need to comply with an ever-increasing range of legislation covering such things as training, garbage disposal, health and hygiene, International Labour Organization (ILO) working hours, food sourcing, menu description etc. On the question of hygiene legislation alone, the industry has predominantly worked for several decades using the United States Public Health (USPH) Vessel Sanitation Program as the benchmark for health and hygiene practices and procedures. These are a very stringent set of regulations that are regularly updated and put great emphasis not only on hygienic practices but also on the correct equipment design and structure. The standards have largely been accepted globally for well over 30 years but, at the time of writing, there is new European-wide legislation being implemented, which, although similar in many ways, will present even further challenges to operational teams.

Also, F&B executives realize that while innovation is a big factor, it is just as important not to alienate past passengers who are still looking for the familiar and to balance individual expectation. 'Innovation is good, but familiarity is key for many of our guests. So, in many cases, we evolve our programs rather than radically revolutionize' (Frey, 2009, p. 24).

Beverage Operations

This chapter has primarily focused on the development of cruise ship food operations simply because the industry has experienced such a huge change in its nature. Although on a relatively smaller and perhaps less noticeable scale, cruise ship beverage operations have also seen significant change and development over the same period.

Some of this change has been as a direct result of the same factors influencing the development of food operations and is related, primarily, to the demand and expectation for choice coupled with hugely increased public knowledge and awareness. Enhanced global product availability is a key factor that has also impacted greatly on beverage operations, and the influence of the High Street can also clearly be seen.

Generally speaking, the public are much more confident in their choices of wine in particular, and most passengers will know what they want to drink because of their greater knowledge and awareness. This has led to greater emphasis on wine sales and a much wider selection available in recent years. There has been a significant development in the promotion of wines, with many ships now having public space dedicated to wine bars themselves, a recent example being The Glasshouse on P&O Cruises *Azura*, where tapas style food is served to complement the wines being served.

There has also been a huge increase in the number, variety and quality of wines now available for sale by-the-glass. This has been to meet demand and general acceptability for wines to be served in this way, but the growth has also much to do with technological advances in wine dispense itself. Such machines are now able to preserve even the better quality and more expensive wines for at least 2–3 weeks at the correct temperatures and with no loss of quality. Cunard Line has recently installed several of the Enomatic range of wine dispensers and some of the wines are selling at as much as US$60–70 per glass. John Bywater of Carnival UK says,

This type of dispensing system allows us to offer a much enhanced selection of wines by-the-glass, including some of our more expensive wines. This would not have been feasible until we installed these dispensers which are proving to be extremely popular. As a result we are selling far more bottles of many more wines than we previously did when selling by the bottle only and these represent significant incremental sales.

(2010, personal communication)

Also in recent years, the cruise industry has placed much greater emphasis on the importance and relevance of beverage sales in relation to on-board revenue and its contribution to overall revenue, and, therefore, the profitability/viability of the cruise operation itself. With ever-increasing pressure on ticket pricing, most cruise lines are looking to maximize their on-board revenues, and beverage operations is one of the key areas for these sales opportunities.

As with food operations, choice is seen as the key aspect of beverage service on board. Dependent upon the brand and style of service, the cruise lines will offer the most comprehensive range of products and beverage experiences they are able. There has been a steady introduction of private wine labels across the industry and this has not been limited to only the luxury operators, with some mainstream brands successfully promoting and selling 'own-label' wines. There are many examples within the industry; however, one example of an upmarket operator's private label would be Cunard's partnership with Rothschild. This cross-exposure fits with both of the luxury brands and helps to give Cunard another point of difference against the competition. Cunard also have their Churchill own-label reserve port.

As stated earlier in the chapter, the internationalization of the cruise industry has meant that the range of products and services offered by many cruise lines and brands has had to be adapted to meet the demands of the eclectic mix of passengers. This is just as true for beverage options as it is for food, and the management teams have to be mindful of the different tastes of their passengers. This may be anything from simply making available particular beverage options, e.g. German beer, to completely amending the type and style of service.

Depending upon the passenger mix, brand, style of cruise etc., many cruise lines have adopted and implemented various sales initiatives to increase beverage revenues, including soda and wine package options and AI derivatives. Few brands now offer a full AI option, although it has been used with success by both the mainstream and luxury operators, but some offer a more limited form of AI that will, for instance, allow certain wines, beers and soft drinks to be consumed at meal times. The soda packages offered by the major cruise lines are extremely popular with younger cruisers – in particular families – where a fixed price is paid for virtually unlimited consumption. This is possible, of course, because of the extremely low unit cost of the sodas. In the case of wine packages, the premise is that the passenger will enjoy relatively high discounts on pre-paid wines, thereby ensuring consumption of wine and increased revenue from sales. Of course, the passenger still benefits from the discounted pricing but, in many cases, the wine package purchase is reflective of incremental spend.

Summary

F&B service has been one of the cornerstones of the cruise industry since its very inception. It is still of key importance to the continued appeal and success of the industry overall, and equally so to the individual operators and their respective brands.

Although the provision of these services has seen monumental operational and delivery changes over the last 10–15 years, in particular within food operations, the cruise lines continue in their aim to exceed the ever-increasing expectations and demands of passengers. F&B management teams are working under very tight cost constraints to satisfy both corporate and passenger needs, which are often conflicting in relation to the service required against budgets set.

Aside from the cost issues of providing such a range of services, operational management teams also have a plethora of other challenges to meet, e.g. increasing legislation, human resource, food supply, rapidly changing tastes and trends, to name but a few. Each cruise line will meet these challenges in different ways and much will be dependent upon their target market segment and brand values; however, the challenges are common to all.

Growing public awareness, fuelled largely by the media, has also increased pressure on cruise lines to provide food (and beverage) service options that would have seemed unlikely until recent years. Choice and informality are probably the two keywords that would sum up the prime developments in recent years, and the operational boundaries continue to be pushed, particularly by the major operators.

It is difficult to envisage how much further F&B operations will develop; however, cruise management teams are continually working on such developments and initiatives that will help give them the edge in the battle for the paying passenger. Perhaps the last word should be given by an industry senior executive – Frank Weber, Royal Caribbean International VP Food & Beverage, when asked about the future of the industry's F&B offerings, said, 'Innovation for us is a continuous process of improvement. What was great last year may no longer be good enough today. We are never finished' (Frey, 2009, p. 29).

Reference

Frey, L. (2009) Balanced innovation. *Cruise Industry News*, Summer, 24–29.

18   Safety and Security Management

Sarah Neumann and Andreas Ullrich

Introduction

According to the International Maritime Organization (IMO), 'Shipping is perhaps the most international of all the world's great industries – and one of the most dangerous' (IMO, 2011b). There is, because of its nature, the need for safety regulations in shipping, as became dramatically obvious in 1912 when the *Titanic* disaster happened. Safety is more than a sufficient number of lifeboats hanging on the sides of a ship, though. A broad variety of factors contributes to the safety of a ship and thus its passengers. This includes the construction of safe ships, the installation of life-saving appliances, the carriage of personal protective equipment, the enforcement of collision regulations, the proper training of crews and the safe management of ships, to name only a few.

All of the above are internationally regulated and have to be enforced by flag states, as outlined by Boy and Neumann (Chapter 3, this volume). In addition to the safety of life, security, or in other words the protection from any criminal activity, has also increased in importance over the past decades. Although safety always comes first, both issues are closely linked to each other and implementation often goes hand in hand.

The concern about safety in shipping is considerable, and the public focus on this topic is especially high in the cruise industry. It is therefore essential to understand the basic principles underlying maritime safety and security in order to realize further the impact of safety and security issues on the operational management of cruise ships. This chapter shall provide a general overview on how and why regulations are being developed, and shall furthermore outline the contents of major regulations and the role of classification societies in this regard.

Background on Regulations

Was shipping regulated some 500 years ago? Based on historical evidence, the answer is basically no. Regulation was initiated by insurance companies in Europe in the course of the industrialization and the related shipping of goods in large amounts. Regulations at that time had a regional character, i.e. they were valid only in the waters controlled by local or regional powers. The development of international regulations started with the first SOLAS Conference, which took place in January 1914, as a result of the sinking of the passenger ship *Titanic*.

The first stage was the setting up of ship safety regulations, followed by environmental regulations and, more recently, by security regulations. Until some years ago, rule development was always the result of accidents in shipping, combined with the loss of human life or damage to the environment. Nowadays, rule development is more goal oriented and makes use of risk management methods.

IMO Conventions and Codes

Conventions established by the IMO can be grouped in three major categories, depending on their concern:

- maritime safety;
- prevention of marine pollution; and
- liability and compensation.

The following conventions are aimed at enhancing maritime safety:

- The International Load Line Convention of 1969 is concerned with draught limitations in the form of freeboards, which determine the amount of cargo a ship can load, depending on water density and temperature.
- The Convention on the International Regulations for Preventing Collisions at Sea (COLREGS) of 1972 defines standards with regard to lights and signals to be carried on board in order to prevent collision. It also introduced traffic separation schemes.
- Safety of Life at Sea (SOLAS) of 1974 – see below.
- The International Convention on Standards for the Training and Certification of Watchkeeping for Seafarers (STCW) of 1978 established international basic requirements on training, certification and watchkeeping for seafarers.
- The Convention on Search and Rescue (SAR) of 1979 was aimed at developing an international SAR plan to ensure the coordination of SAR operations worldwide.

Where necessary, the conventions have been specified in greater detail in codes, which can be either binding or recommending. Linking a code to one of the conventions is advantageous, as in case of amendments or adjustments, not the whole convention but only the code needs to be changed. For the process of adopting conventions and ratification by flag states, see Boy and Neumann, Chapter 3, this volume.

SOLAS Convention

The SOLAS convention adopted by the IMO is generally understood to be the most important of all treaties in respect of maritime safety. Many of today's life-saving appliances on board and procedures concerned with the safety of life go back to the event that caused SOLAS to come alive: the *Titanic* disaster of 1912. SOLAS has been amended several times and is continuously being improved as regards minimum safety standards. Flag states bear the responsibility to ensure the compliance with the provisions given under SOLAS.

Compliance with SOLAS standards is proven through different certificates cargo ships have to hold:

- Cargo Ship Safety Construction Certificate;
- Cargo Ship Safety Equipment Certificate;
- Cargo Ship Safety Radio Certificate.

The above certificates are valid for 5 years and require annual endorsements. Passenger ships have to follow even stricter rules and regulations than cargo ships. A passenger ship in compliance with SOLAS will hold a Passenger Ship Safety Certificate, which is valid only for 1 year.

Several binding codes concerned with safety have been established under SOLAS. The following codes are applicable to passenger ships:

- The *Intact Stability Code* presents mandatory and recommendatory stability criteria and other measures for ensuring the safe operation of ships.
- The *Fire Test Procedure Code* provides international requirements for laboratory

testing, type approval and fire test procedures.

- The *Fire Safety Systems Code* defines technical specifications for fire safety equipment and systems.
- The *International Life-Saving Appliances Code* defines technical requirements for life-saving appliances.
- The *International Safety Management Code (ISM)* – see below.
- The *International Ship and Port Facility Security Code (ISPS)* – see below.

The International Safety Management (ISM) Code

The ISM Code became mandatory in 1998. It was developed as a result of the sinking of the *Herald of Free Enterprise* in 1987, which was caused by human error. Human errors in shipping are no exceptional cases; on the contrary, they account for 80% of shipping accidents (van Dokkum, 2007). This illustrates the need for regulations of safety management. Unlike other codes before, mostly concerned with technical aspects, the ISM Code regulates the organization of a ship and the company operating it as well as the ship–shore-relation.

> The cornerstone of good safety management is commitment from the top. In matters of safety and pollution prevention it is the commitment, competence, attitudes and motivation of individuals at all levels that determines the end result.
>
> (Excerpt from the preamble of the ISM Code, IMO, 2010)

So to prevent accidents and environmental damage, the ISM Code's preamble emphasizes the importance of leadership and individual behaviour. Implicitly, its reference to the competence of individuals points to the need for training and preparation. To comply with the code, shipping companies must establish and maintain a Safety Management System (SMS). Minimum requirements for the SMS include:

- a safety and environmental protection policy, which specifies how the objectives of the ISM Code shall be achieved.

The policy has to be implemented and brought to the attention of all personnel concerned;
- procedures for safe on-board operations, such as checklists for bridge operations, bunkering or under-keel clearance;
- a designated person (DP), acting as a link between ship and shore with direct access to the management level. In 2007, the IMO agreed upon qualifications a DP should have. Before this date, basically anyone could take on this role. The DP has to have either seagoing experience or education and experience recognized as relevant. Furthermore, the DP will undergo relevant training in regard of safety management under the ISM code. In accordance with the code the DP is amongst others responsible to ensure adequate shore-based support to the ships;
- emergency preparedness through contingency plans and drills; and
- procedures for internal audits and management reviews (external and internal).

The SMS can also be referred to as a manual, in hardcopy and/or electronic form, which each company has to develop individually using the guidelines provided by the ISM code. All of the above, such as procedures, checklists, responsibilities etc. may be found in this manual. The extensiveness of included information will always depend on the company itself.

Once the system is in place it is audited internally and externally on a regular basis. Both the ship and the shipping company have to go through this verification process and will then, if compliant, be granted the relevant certificates. The shipping company receives a Document of Compliance (DOC), which is issued by the flag state and therefore only valid for the respective flag. Companies with vessels registered under different flags will need several DOCs. Safety Management Certificates are issued for a single vessel of the fleet and will lose their validity immediately if the DOC of the company is withdrawn.

With effect 1 July 2010, the amended ISM Code came into force. As a major change, ship operators are now required to carry out proper risk assessment and establish procedures for it.

The International Ship and Port Facility Security (ISPS) Code

With increasing terrorist activity, there was a need for security regulations concerning the international shipping industry. The IMO and its member states responded to this need by developing a new set of regulations. These do not only determine duties and responsibilities of ships and crew but also of other parties involved in shipping. The code requires close cooperation with flag states, which again hold the responsibility of ensuring compliance.

The ISPS Code came into force in 2004. It was triggered by several terrorist attacks, some of them involving ships. Before and after the 9/11 attacks on the World Trade Center in New York, two ships, the USS *Cole* and the MV *Limburg* were attacked by small boats carrying explosives, causing fatalities and pollution.

The intention of the ISPS Code is to collect and exchange security relevant data within an international framework in order to be able to recognize potential security threats, to take preventive action and thus to minimize the risk of terrorism and piracy.

A security assessment is to be carried out on board vessels and within port facilities, based on which a Ship Security Plan (SSP) or a Port Facility Security Plan (PFSP) is prepared. This plan contains procedures for reacting to different security levels and sets out roles and responsibilities. Depending on their nature, companies are required to appoint a Company Security Officer (CSO), a Port Facility Security Officer (PFSO) or a Ship Security Officer (SSO) on board each ship of a fleet. Besides carrying out security assessments and preparing and updating the SSP, the CSO is responsible to provide the SSO on board the vessel with all relevant information released by the flag states or other authorities. The CSO will support the SSO in security relevant questions.

Under the ISPS Code, ships operate on different MARSEC (maritime security) levels, MARSEC level 1 being the regular level of operation and MARSEC level 3 meaning highest alert. Flag states determine or recommend for which countries or ports higher MARSEC levels apply. These settings are obligatory for vessels, but the master has the right to increase the security level further whenever deemed necessary.

Additionally, the United States Coast Guard (USCG) issues a list of countries or ports for which they require measures equivalent to a higher security level on those vessels intending to call at a US port afterwards (USCG, 2010).

The Role of Classification Societies

Originally, classification societies were established as supervisory organizations for the construction and safety of ships. Classification means the categorization of ships according to their structural reliability and the condition of the ship's hull; later also machinery installations have been included.

The impulse for classification came from insurance companies, which published the first register of shipping as early as 1764. The categorization of ships into classes required the development of criteria and of standards for their application. Since ship classification was in the common interest of all insurance companies, neutral dedicated service providers – the classification societies – were created for this purpose.

Functions of classification societies

Until today, classification societies are strictly impartial. They do not provide expert opinions on behalf of an interested party; their role is limited to the verification and documentation, for the benefit of all interested circles (owners, insurers, yards, etc.), of a ship's compliance with defined and commonly accepted technical standards. Compliance will be verified during design, construction, building and operation of a ship, right up to the end of her useful life.

Classification societies may act as Recognized Organizations (RO) for flag states. In this capacity, they control the compliance of ships, flying their respective flag, with statutory class requirements, such as SOLAS, MARPOL, Load Line, but always within the scope of authorization by contracting governments. Classification societies, both in their role as RO and as members of International Association of Classification Societies (IACS), act as consultants for the IMO, providing technical expertise and capabilities.

Moreover, their role extends to the development, in close cooperation with other parties concerned, of new appraisal and verification processes and methods. For instance, as IMO seeks to define goal-based construction standards for new ships (IMO, 2011a), it depends on the expertise of the classification societies. '"Goal-based regulation" does not specify the means of achieving compliance but sets goals that allow alternative ways of achieving compliance' (Hoppe, 2005).

Construction of cruise ships

In the past, new requirements have been developed mostly as a consequence of accidents, in part involving the loss of human life. Since the mid-1990s, IMO has changed this practice by playing a more proactive role in the specification of new and stricter safety requirements. A reason for this was the new generation of giant cruise ships being built.

One implication is that cruise ships constructed on or after 1 July 2010, with a length of more than 120 m have to comply with the 'safe return to port' regulations. Since a ship is its own best lifeboat, these regulations require essential ship systems to remain operational following certain fire and flooding damages (Safety at Sea, 2011).

Among many others, the following factors have to be considered in the construction of cruise ships:

- *Large glass portions:* Because of increased demand from architects, owners and even passengers the amount of glass partitions on cruise ships is steadily increasing, which for example, requires special attention to strength and ability to withstand pressure from water. Suites nowadays have windows extending nearly from deck to deck so that passengers have an unrestricted view of the sea.
- *Application of lightweight materials:* Because of the increase of size and subsequent stability issues, and in order to decrease weight, aluminium or even FRP (fibre-reinforced composite) constructions are more and more being used, especially in the upper part of superstructure. When applying such materials special attention needs to be paid, for example, to their resistance against fire. Here additional insulation or even dedicated sprinkler systems will be fitted, which limits the weight savings.
- *Areas extending over several decks:* Special attention from a strength point of view is to be paid to the construction of atriums connecting several decks, to theatres, the atriums and large wellness areas. The opening grade of decks to each other is large and requires additional stiffeners based on a finite element analysis.

Cruise Lines International Association

In 1975, the Cruise Lines International Association (CLIA) was formed in order to promote a 'safe, healthy, and secure shipboard environment for both passengers and crew' (CLIA, 2010). CLIA is a non-governmental organization that consists of 25 cruise line members, 16,000 North American travel agencies and around 100 businesses providing services to the cruise sector. Through its consultative function to the IMO, it participates in the development of policies and regulations.

In the cruise sector, with steadily increasing numbers of passengers and a continuous enlargement of the market, highest priority is given to the safety and security of people on board. CLIA members closely cooperate with the USCG and other maritime states, always seeking for improvement of safety and ensuring the compliance with international standards. In addition to international regulations, CLIA issues industry standards applicable to its members. These include for example personal flotation devices for infants on board cruise ships, local sounding smoke alarms and helicopter pick-up areas.

Piracy

The International Maritime Bureau defines piracy as 'An act of boarding or attempting to board any ship with the apparent intent to commit theft or the intent or capability to use force in the furtherance of that act' (IMB, 2010, p. 3). Piracy has been a concern for the shipping industry for a very long time, if not to say since the earliest days of shipping. Piracy attacks are most likely to occur in sheltered areas with a high traffic density, such as in straits or transit areas, bordered by countries with economic and/ or political instability. Figure 18.1 shows the geographical distribution of the 406 reported incidents of 2009.

In 2008, Somalia showed an exceptionally high piracy activity with a total of 135 attacks, resulting in 44 ships having been seized by pirates and more than 600 seafarers kidnapped and held for ransom (IMB, 2010). The situation apparently improved in 2009, when only 27 actual attacks (26 vessels hijacked) and 53 attempted attacks in Somali waters were reported.

Within the Gulf of Aden, 20 vessels were actually attacked; another 96 attacks have been attempted in 2009. In two-thirds of these cases, vessels were fired upon (IMB, 2010). The Gulf of Aden is considered a bottleneck for the shipping industry. Transiting the Suez Canal on the way to or from

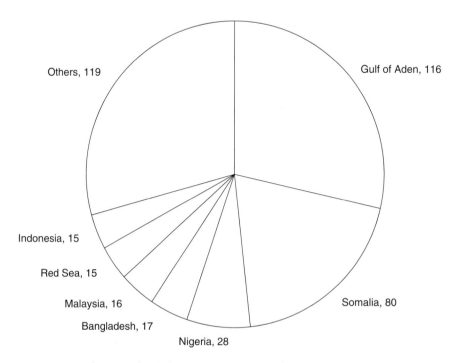

Fig. 18.1.   Piracy attacks reported 2009 by country. Source: based on IMB (2010, pp. 5–6).

Table 18.1. Types of vessels attacked 2005–2009.

Type	2005	2006	2007	2008	2009
Bulk carrier	81	57	32	48	109
Container	30	49	53	49	63
General cargo	46	30	36	38	53
Passenger	1	2	1	3	1
RoRo	5	2	3	1	8
Tanker	70	48	83	91	115
Others	43	51	55	63	57
Total	276	239	263	293	406

Source: based on IMB (2010).

Asia is much faster and less expensive than going around the Cape of Good Hope, which is why it is an area of immense traffic volume. For cruise lines, it furthermore links attractive destinations and thus is included in several itineraries.

Considering the high number of cruise ship passengers and the public interest in cruise ships, they seem to be an attractive target to both pirates and terrorists, although the actual threat of pirate attacks on passenger ships is low (Table 18.1). As Herbert-Burns *et al.* (2009) states, 'Piracy is committed for private ends', meaning that pirates, unlike terrorists, intend to make money by hijacking a vessel, rather than making a political statement through the publicity they receive upon an attack. They are furthermore usually equipped with small boats or fishing vessels, which make cruise ships with their high freeboards and fast speed a not very vulnerable target.

Terrorism

Terrorism can be defined as 'violence, or the threat of violence, committed to create an atmosphere of fear and alarm' (Herbert-Burns *et al.*, 2009, p. 76) through which it aims at enforcing political objectives.

As outlined in the previous paragraph, the threat of pirate attacks on cruise ships is relatively low. For terrorist attacks, they do form an attractive target, though. Because of the large number of passengers on board and public interest in passenger shipping, a terrorist attack on a cruise ship would surely result in immense media coverage, thus ensuring terrorists greatest attention (Herbert-Burns *et al.*, 2009).

To ensure the security of passengers on board a vessel, cruise lines strictly follow international security regulations. Access to cruise vessels is controlled through passenger screening, which is similar to screening procedures at airports. Embarking or disembarking requires passing through defined security checkpoints and the entry on an official manifest. Personnel on board cruise ships are trained in security matters. The implemented security measures partly remain invisible to the passengers on board (CLIA, 2010).

References

CLIA (2010) Personal Safety and Security. Available at: www2.cruising.org/industry/personal_safety_security. cfm (accessed 19 April 2010).

Herbert-Burns, R., Bateman, S. and Lehr, P. (2009) *Lloyd's MIU Handbook of Maritime Security.* CRC Press, Boca Raton, Florida.

Hoppe, H. (2005) Goal-based standards – a new approach to the international regulation of ship construction. *WMU Journal of Maritime Affairs* 4(2), 169–180.

IMB (2010) *Annual IMB Piracy Report 2009*. ICC International Maritime Bureau, London.

IMO (2010) ISM Code and Guidelines on Implementation of the ISM Code 2010. Available at: www.imo.org/OurWork/HumanElement/SafetyManagement/Pages/ISMCode.aspx (accessed 30 April 2011).

IMO (2011a) Goal-based construction standards for new ships. Available at: www.imo.org/OurWork/Safety/SafetyTopics/Pages/Goal-BasedStandards.aspx (accessed 30 April 2011).

IMO (2011b) Maritime Safety. Available at: www.imo.org/OurWork/Safety/Pages/Default.aspx (accessed 30 April 2011)

Safety at Sea (2011) Approval and Systems Availability Analysis – A ship is its own best lifeboat. Available at: www.safety-at-sea.co.uk/ship_concept_design-9.html (accessed 30 April 2011).

USCG (2010) Port Security Advisory (3–10). Available at: www.apl.com/security/documents/security_advisory_anti_terrorism.pdf (accessed 30 April 2011).

Van Dokkum, K. (2007) *Ship Knowledge*. AJ Enkhuizen, Dokmar.

19 Cruise Ship Marine Operations

Simon Véronneau

Introduction

Marine operations of cruise ships are seldom reported on. Even on board the many cruise ships currently sailing, few crew members fully understand the complexity and the liability involved in being a marine officer on such vessels. Perhaps marine personnel bear some of the responsibility for the depreciation of their own representations, for in the pride they evince in the technical advancement of their ships – joystick control, automatic positioning and even the ability to dock themselves – they downplay their crucial roles. Though technological marvels can perform the aforementioned feats, marine officers more than earn their living in nonroutine operations. When machinery fails or emergencies arise, their mettle is truly tested. The goal of this chapter is to explain the role of the marine operations for a cruise company by examining both the shore-side support component and the on-board organization, with a focus on the latter.

Transient perspective versus long-term perspective

One fundamental characteristic differentiating the marine department personnel from their management is the long-term perspective held by most officers. Marine department personnel choose a career at sea early in life. That they end up on cruise ships is a matter of preference and/or opportunity, for they are all trained to work on a variety of ships. In contrast, though some hotel personnel may log years of service at sea, the majority tend to maintain a short-term perspective, viewing their on-ship work as transient, an attractive stepping stone in a larger career in the hospitality field. After their time on board, they might return to shore to work in some other function connected to the tourism industry.

The fundamental character traits distinguishing these two types of personnel are reflected in differences in their respective management strategies. In their decision-making, marine officers consider a ship's life cycle, planning maintenance years in advance to ensure that problems are solved and not passed on to the relieving crew. The overwhelming sentiment among officers is proprietary: the ships are theirs, and they therefore bear the responsibility for maintaining their grace and seaworthiness. The number of ship specifics and the concomitant investment in a single ship further entrench their sense of ownership and, perhaps, for good reason.

Unlike the management of galleys, casinos and spas, which can count on similar operating characteristics from ship to ship, the marine management of one ship varies greatly from class to class. Therefore, while the hotel department manages very much from season to season or even voyage to voyage, the marine department takes a multiyear perspective in both planning and decision-making. It is also worth noting that only licensed marine officers can be personally held criminally liable for their decisions.

Educational background

As mentioned above, the decision to work in a marine department is often made at a fairly young age, typically 17. At that age, aspiring seamen go to a seamen's school, and officers go to a college or university to obtain a bachelor's degree in nautical science or its equivalent. Today's training standards are upheld by STCW 1995, to be discussed in more detail below. For a prospective seafarer to be seen as globally employable, he or she must train in programmes that meet these standards and that will earn him or her an STCW 1995-endorsed licence (McCarter, 1999).

Shore-side Support

The shore-side department of marine operations is responsible for the safe manning and operations of the fleet. It establishes policies and standard operating procedures (SOP) to be followed on board by the captain and his officers. Typically, a ship superintendant will be tasked with managing a handful of ships and act as the main point of contact for the captain and chief engineer. The ship superintendant is responsible for his ships' budgets and ensuring proper life cycle management of assets.

Flag of registry

One of the most important decisions an international shipping company must make is under which nation it will register its flag.

Though the popular press often suggests the only relevant factors in such a decision are a country's lax safety requirements and potential for fiscal advantage, the choice is a little more complicated (Goulielmos, 1998; Thanopoulou, 1998; see also Boy and Neumann, Chapter 3, this volume) and informed by concrete operational advantage perspectives.

A company will choose to register under a friendly nation knowledgeable in the operations of cruise companies and able to offer proper services. Some nations, for example, have strict restrictions on the nationality of the crew members who can serve on board. For an industry that relies on leveraging an international workforce to offer a quality experience, it is therefore imperative that the flag of registry allows maximum hiring flexibility. Furthermore, each registry has its own specifications in terms of marine crew certification requirements. Though almost every registry requirement is based on the STCW 1995 convention (IMO, 1996), a shipping company can minimize paperwork and interference if it ensures a registry allows foreign national licence holders to sail with their home licence, or recognizes their licence equivalent.

The flag of registry will also determine itinerary planning, as nations protect their respective domestic markets through various forms of legislation, or cabotage laws (US Customs and Border Protection, 2010), which prohibit domestic service by unregistered ships. A case in point is Norwegian Cruise Line (NCL), which flagged some of its ships to the American registry to allow it to service the Hawaiian domestic market. The effort ended in failure, however; many US workers could not perform to the international standard of other ships in the NCL fleet and yet demanded higher than average market wages. At the height of the crisis, cruises were cancelled as the crew claimed exhaustion, prompting NCL to reconsider their strategies and return to international flags and crews.

Staffing

Marine personnel can make or break a cruise line. Because the marine department is responsible for the upkeep of vital parts of the ships, as well as its safety, employing people without the right skills could be very costly. Furthermore, a single major incident can send a company's stock plummeting, even to bankruptcy, as it loses its brand equity, as well as overall consumer and shareholder confidence. In order to obviate problems resulting from poor hiring, a company typically works with a few specific nations to fill certain positions, establishing links with local hiring partners and more or less hiring only those nationals. From time to time, a hiring policy must be reviewed in response to market realignment.

As such, the marine department has not been immune to globalization trends and downward pressure, which have meant few salary rises compared to other, protected markets. Of course, the goal of the companies is to get the best officers and crew for a certain price. When this price does not suffice any more, there are two possible outcomes: the hiring of new nationals or the raising of wages. Often a dual strategy is employed, causing a gradual shift in a crew's national mix, as well as pressure on wages to stay below the inflationary level.

Marine operations company policies

The marine department within a given company establishes fleet-wide policies to ensure a certain degree of conformity from ship to ship on a variety of operations. These include setting standard operating procedure policies and training requirements for the continued proficiency of the marine personnel, as well as their socialization to norms.

Standard operating procedures

Standard operating procedures are the day-to-day guidelines for a company's normal operations (Véronneau and Cimon, 2007). A standard is established for an entire fleet, serving as both policy and guidance as to

best practice in such matters as anchoring the vessel or picking up the pilot.

Training

Training is an important part of any quality programme, especially for companies striving to improve. While it is typical that all personnel on board ships must attend company training on matters of policy and improving guest experience, the marine department must complete regulatory training mandated by international law.

This training involves a broad range of knowledge that must be maintained by licensed officers. Topics include bridge resource management or engine resource management, first aid, crowd management and firefighting. Because these mandatory training programmes are typically valid for only 5 years, administering, managing and updating them are taxing both for the personnel and for the company.

For a ship or a fleet of ships to be in compliance with classification societies, all regulatory training must be up to date, and a system of tracking training and scheduling must be in place. Training is mostly mandated under various regulations of the IMO, either from STCW 95 or SOLAS. Further training, beyond the regular international standard, might be required by the seafarers' respective states.

Beside these international training requirements, most cruise companies require company-specific training in various facilities around the world. These include advanced seminars and training on technology specific to the company or to its own internal policies governing the handling of various situations. Such training may, for example, take the form of special engineering training at the manufacturer of engines or navigation training at the facility of the company supplying the radar and other navigation systems. While some of these trainings are not mandated, they are part of a company's internal policies designed to ensure proper knowledge is available on board.

Lastly, a fair bit of training occurs on board, with many companies employing full-time instructors dedicated to that purpose. This training can range from ship-specific safety training to guest experience improvement seminars.

Environmental protection

Environmental protection is high on every seagoing officer's list of priorities. Both engineers and navigation officers are personally liable for the protection of the environment and, if negligent, can face criminal charges resulting in hefty fines, loss of licences, and even imprisonment (Ketkar, 1995). Consequently, marine personnel take compliance very seriously and consider their stewardship of the environment of utmost importance. Currently, the strictest regulations for marine pollution from passenger vessels are found in the state of Alaska, which has passed stringent guidelines that even the most eco-friendly and forward-thinking companies are struggling to meet.

Main regulations and acts

While there are a number of vital regulations that officers must take into account, only the most important to non-marine personnel will be examined here. These regulations and acts are mainly pushed by various nations into the IMO for adoption by member countries. Once a new IMO act is adopted by the member country, the entailed regulations need to be ratified into the country's laws and statutes. For more details, see Boy and Neumann, Chapter 3, this volume.

International regulations

In this section, we will briefly discuss some significant regulations adopted at the IMO level. Because of the international focus of this chapter, country-specific regulations and acts will not be discussed.

The International Convention on Load Lines has been established to prevent overloading vessels and imposes strict stability guidelines for the seaworthiness of ships (IMO, 1989). Based on these guidelines, ships are assigned a load line from a classification society. Unfortunately, we still see cases of capsized passenger ferries in emerging economies, because of overloading.

STCW 95, short for the international Standards of Training, Certification and Watchkeeping Convention 1995 (IMO, 1996), is an international regulation that dictates the standard for proficiency for the safe manning of competent marine officers.

SOLAS, short for the convention on the Safety of Life at Sea (IMO, 2005), was introduced after the *Titanic* disaster to ensure better safety standards on ships. SOLAS regulates in precise detail many safety standards, including those involving lifejackets, the water integrity of vessels and, of course, lifeboats.

The latest international convention to be passed, the International Ship and Port Facility Security code (ISPS), deals with maritime security (IMO, 2002). It was pushed forward with great speed following the 9/11 terrorist attack in the USA (King, 2005). Such a measure was deemed a priority, given the new found vulnerability of the transportation system to possible terrorist attacks or misuse for terrorist purposes. ISPS provides a set of guidelines for ships and ports to codified threat levels, but does not prescribe ship-specific or port-specific security plans. These are redacted for each ship and port by its respective governance body: ship plans are created by ship owners and approved by local government; port plans are created by port authorities and approved by local agencies. ISPS is designed to facilitate communication about threat level, or maritime security (MARSEC) level, between a port and a ship, thereby enabling either party to adjust its threat level accordingly: a ship operating at MARSEC Level 1 calling to a port operating at Level 2 must adjust to Level 2 and vice versa.

Classification societies

Since the middle of the 18th century, classification societies have provided insurance companies a way to rate the risk of insuring a vessel and its cargo (Boisson, 1994). The purpose of the classification society was to guarantee that a ship was seaworthy and built to an acceptable standard. Modern classification societies have a similar role in establishing best practices in ship construction and maintenance. It is common today for port state inspectors and classification society inspectors to work hand in hand and exchange information in order to facilitate inspections.

The two main classification societies today are Lloyd's Register (not to be confused with Lloyd's of London) and Det Norske Veritas (DNV) from Norway. The choice of classification is a business in and of itself, a managerial one; classification societies have similar rules, but small differences can prove advantageous in certain trades.

On-board Operations

The marine department's primary goal is the safe function and longevity of its operating system. Therefore, great emphasis is placed on prevention and proactive maintenance, with planning done years in advance. However, the marine department's practice of assessing the short-term impact of a given voyage in light of its long-term effect on a ship's functional life often results in friction with the hotel side of operations, concerned as the latter is with the short-term efficacy of an actual voyage. The marine department may wish to take a guest amenity offline, for example, closing a pool for maintenance for a few days, thereby risking a negative short-term impact on guest satisfaction for the positive long-term impact on the longevity of the pool.

Most marine personnel trained among the pocket-sized crew of a general merchant ship, but employed on a cruise ship, encounter for the first time a vast decision-making structure complicated by the sheer number of personnel in the on-board management. On-board emailing, for example, is the norm, with officers receiving dozens of emails on any given day. The illustration below sketches the contrasts between the organizational structures of merchant and cruise ships.

Working hours

A typical work schedule for marine personnel is 7 days a week, 12 h a day, with on-call, emergency availability during off-hours. Watchkeepers spend 8 h of their 12-h shift on watch and the remaining on paperwork or on inspections, in accordance with regulation.

Holiday time system

While holiday systems vary greatly from one company to another, the competitive currently offer a 1:1 system: for each month at sea you accrue 1 month of holiday. The other prevalent system is 2:1: for every 2 months at sea you accrue 1 month of holiday. In common practice, this translates to about 2 months on board and 2 months ashore in the former system, and 4 months on board and 2 months ashore in the latter. The current best system is offered by the oil and gas industry, the norm of which is 2 weeks on, 2 weeks off, or 1 month on, 1 month off. Regardless of the holiday system, officers are looking at the same monthly salaries. For the company, the only advantage of longer rotations is minor savings in transportation expenses and simplification of their scheduling.

The deck department

The deck department is responsible for the safety and general upkeep of the ship, as well as for safe navigation. Because the range of tasks on a cruise ship greatly exceeds that on traditional cargo vessels, officers choosing the cruise trade must learn to manage a very large department. On a typical merchant ship, the department will be composed of anywhere between half a dozen to a dozen officers and crew. On a modern cruise ship, however, this number is closer to 60 deck officers and crew, with as many as 2200 officers, staff and crew members on the bigger ships. Below is a brief description of all the key actors in the deck department.

While each company may have a slightly different structure, the following generic definitions capture most current companies' standard operations. The officers working in the deck department and possessing a navigation licence are also known as bridge officers or mates.

Commodore and captain

To the author's knowledge, only the Cunard line employs an officer of the commodore rank. Currently, the captain on Cunard's flagship, the *Queen Mary 2*, holds the rank of commodore and is seen as the fleet's senior captain. As ships get bigger, this practice might be adopted by other companies looking at adapting their rank structure to the growing size of their operations.

The captain, also known as the master, is the highest-ranking person on board any ship and commands the ship at all times. He is criminally liable for the actions of his officers and crew. While some companies entertained the idea of ranking the hotel director higher on board, international law stating that a marine licensed master is the most senior person in charge on board a ship precluded such a move. Though a common misconception has it that a captain spends most of his time on the bridge, the reality is that the captain spends only 2–3 h a day on average on the bridge during critical navigation moments, such as heavy fog or transit in and out of port. The majority of his time is spent tending to the business operations of the ship and entertaining guests on board. A modern cruise ship, with its large crew complement and numerous passengers, is a complex operation; as the highest ranking manager on board, the captain always has plenty of responsibilities to tend to.

Staff captain

The staff captain is the second in command on board and holder of the licence of master

mariner. As the name suggests, he is in charge of the staff, discipline and security, the equivalent of the executive officer (XO) in most navies. Like the captain, he also spends 2–3 h a day on the bridge, devoting the rest of his time to tending to business, with a special emphasis on human resources issues.

Chief officer, chief mate

The chief officer is a senior marine officer, holding the licence of chief mate foreign going. Typically, chief officers do not have regular watchkeeping duty but are on-call to the watchkeeping officer, should he need guidance. Their normal duty is typically that of a 'day man', working from morning arrival until the end of deck operations at 20:00 h. They are typically in charge of the deck department, ensuring that all on-board upkeep is carried out to the specifications of a ship's classification and the international standard set forth in the regulations.

Chief officer, safety officer

The chief officer safety, also known as chief officer or safety officer, is responsible for the overall safety on board the ship. Responsibilities include enforcing workplace safety, investigating accidents and conducting safety training for all crew members. He is typically assisted by other watchkeeping officers, as well as able-bodied seamen (AB), in his duties and regular checks of all on-board safety equipment.

Watchkeeping officers, mates

The watchkeeping officers are in charge of ship safety and proper navigation on behalf of the ship's captain. Whereas the captain is in charge of the ship 24 h a day, 7 days a week, the watchkeeping officer is in charge of the ship for only his watch, which typically lasts 8 h. On most of today's large cruise ships, two bridge officers, a senior and a junior officer, will man a watch with one to two AB to assist. Though the number of officers at a given rank varies from company to company, the following is a list of typical ranks in the order from most senior to most junior: Senior 1st officer, 1st officer, Senior 2nd officer, 2nd officer, 3rd officer, 4th officer. A typical combination of two officers on watch pairs a 1st officer with a 2nd officer, or a Senior 2nd officer with a 3rd officer. Designated the officer of the watch (OOW), the senior officer of any pairing carries the bulk of the responsibility, with liability resting on his licence, while the junior officer assists, shares some duties and provides crucial double-checking on many decisions.

Deck cadet, apprentice officer

On many of today's ships, it is common to find an apprentice officer usually bearing the title of deck cadet. These officers are not typically licensed and spend time at sea intermittently, often between semesters at college, in order to garner the experience and mandatory sea time sufficient to earn their licence in their own country. Hence, these cadets are supernumerary, their primary purpose being to learn as much as possible in the 12 months of sea time typically required for examinations.

Quartermaster, petty officer

As mentioned above, watchkeeping officers are helped by senior seamen who can bear many titles, e.g. quartermaster, petty officer and able seaman, whose primary duty is typically to maintain a lookout and assist with general bridge duties assigned by the OOW. It is not uncommon, however, for some senior seamen to assume extra duties in line with their abilities, such as manning the radar, answering phones, or performing navigation duties. These senior seamen may also be in charge of safety equipment maintenance under the supervision of the safety officer or a watchkeeping officer.

Boatswain, bosun

The boatswain, also known as the bosun or bos'n, is the most senior unlicensed seaman, acting as supervisor of the other seamen. Though boatswains are most often unlicensed, some do hold a junior watchkeeping licence. They work under the chief officer to ensure the ship is well maintained and enforce basic supervisory discipline of the seamen in the deck department.

Deckhands

The deckhands are unlicensed seamen who typically hold one of three ranks: junior seaman (JS), ordinary seaman (OS) and able-bodied seaman (AB). They work under the direct supervision of the bosun, performing routine maintenance of the ship, and are ultimately accountable to the chief officer. The jobs assigned to them are based on their individual skill sets, as well as their seniority. It is also common for seamen to work in pairs, e.g. AB with an OS, or OS with a JS, so that the more experienced seaman can act as both coach and teacher to the junior during on-the-job learning opportunities.

Carpenters

Lastly, carpenters are specialist tradesmen charged with the upkeep of certain inside structures of the ship. For example, they will repair wall panelling, doorways, latches and removable sailings, as well as seeing to locksmithing. Because of the wide range of equipment they have to maintain, they are typically quite busy throughout the ship.

Engine department

The engine department is responsible for maintaining and managing all the machinery and technical equipment on board ships. On normal cargo ships, the systems are relatively small and simple, but given the size of cruise ships and the number of passengers on board, many more engineers and specialists are needed to ensure smooth operation. The following non-exhaustive list details the tasks and duties of key members of the engine department, which numbers around 60 engine officers and crew.

The engine department on board a cruise ship is quite extensive. It is responsible for the long-term health of all on-board systems and for the cost, consumption and waste management on these ever-growing ships.

Chief engineer

The chief engineer is responsible for the engine room and the structural aspects of the ship. He reports to the captain for on-board operation and to the shore-side ship superintendant for budget and long-term operations decisions. He is assisted in the daily management of the engine room by a number of other senior engineers and by specialists for certain systems such as refrigeration and electronics.

Chief engineer junior

The chief engineer junior, the executive assistant to the chief engineer, is responsible for daily operations and good order. He works a normal day schedule but remains on call for special needs, such as coming into ports or other emergencies. He works closely with the chief engineer to ensure operations stay within budget.

1st engineer

The first engineer, the engine equivalent to the deck side chief officer, is responsible for maintenance projects occurring in the engine room during the day and supervises the mechanical assistant in planned maintenance and overhaul projects. He also works a normal day schedule but remains on call for watchkeeping engineers needing assistance during their watch.

Watchkeeping engineers

The watchkeeping engineers are licensed engineers responsible for the safe operations of all ship systems on behalf of the chief engineers. Like bridge officers, they maintain a typical 8-h daily watch divided into two 4-h duty turns. They are also responsible for the good health of individual systems, which they oversee in their overtime hours. The rank of the engineer on

watch differs from one company to another, but the most senior to most junior ranks are as follows: 2nd engineer, 3rd engineer, 4th engineer.

Environmental engineer

With increased government oversight, regulations and complexity of environmental protection systems, many companies have created the position of environmental engineer, whose sole job is to look after environmentally sensitive systems, such as incinerators, oil–water separators and sewage plants.

Chief electrician

Because cruise ships' electric and electronic systems have grown in complexity and number, it is common on all ships to have a number of electricians and electronic specialists. Responsibility for shipboard electrical delivery and electronic apparatus falls to the chief electrician, who manages a number of electricians and electronics specialists. In the usual order of seniority, they are 1st, 2nd and 3rd electrician.

Chief refrigeration engineer

In response to the increasing size of ships and the variable climates within which they operate, refrigeration or climate control systems on board cruise ships have grown bigger and more sophisticated. Typically, every ship has a chief refrigeration engineer, also known as the chief reefer, who oversees the refrigeration system and who will seek mechanical assistance from the 1st engineer when jobs warrant.

Engine cadet, apprentice engineer

Like the deck cadet, the engine room cadet is typically a college student completing his sea time with a hands-on training component. He too is a supernumerary functioning as a helping hand on various projects when required and working under the direction of the 1st engineer.

Engine foreman

The engine foreman, the most senior unlicensed mechanical assistant (the equivalent to the bosun on the deck side), oversees all mechanical assistants and works directly under the first engineer, as well as for the chief engineer junior. While some may have a 4th engineer licence, most are unlicensed but with decades of seafaring experience.

Mechanical assistants, oilers

Each watchkeeping engineer will typically be assigned a mechanical assistant who carries out tasks in the engine room while the engineer remains in the engine control room. These mechanical assistants work the same watch as the engineer on watch, assisting him in routine maintenance of the specialized system he is assigned to. Along with the mechanical assistant assigned to a watch, a number of day men mechanical assistants work directly under the supervision of the engine foreman, carrying out routine maintenance and planned major overhauls. The number of assistants varies with ship size, levels of automation and company policies.

Incinerator personnel

The incinerator room, where recyclables are separated from the waste that is to be incinerated, has dedicated engine room personnel, often simply called 'incinerator men', performing the necessary tasks. The number of personnel allocated to these tasks varies with ship size, but will usually include a supervisor and some regular workers.

Medical

Historically, the medical department has been part of the marine department. While its place in the overall organizational structure moves between hotel and marine, the predominant view is that medical should be within the marine department, with which it is more similarly aligned, given that its main responsibility is the well-being of the passengers and crew. To meet this responsibility, the health department performs a number of tasks: establishing outbreak prevention policies; administering preventive medicine to the crew through, for example, immunization clinics; conducting water tests in order to prevent devastating outbreaks, such as Legionnaire's disease (Jernigan et al., 1996) or E. coli poisoning; responding to common medical emergencies; and stabilizing patients in need of transfer to a nearby medical facility for specialized treatments or further care.

On smaller ships, the medical department is typically staffed with one doctor and two nurses, or two doctors and four nurses (Novaro et al., 2010), and sometimes medical secretaries on larger vessels. The medical professionals on cruise ships tend to wear one of two hats, depending on whether they are serving the passengers or the crew. Because of the urgent nature of the typical medical visit of a cruise ship passenger, it was found that the most useful background for medical personnel is a specialization in emergency medicine (Peake et al., 1999). However, for the crew members, the medical professionals are primary care providers, tracking crew health in the role of general practitioners. When consultations with specialists are required, appointments are arranged with shore facilities while the ship is in port. These facilities are often in a turnaround port or a large city with proper specialists available at a reasonable cost. For example, a ship on a run off the west coast of Mexico might use Puerto Vallarta as a specialist port as opposed to San Diego or Los Angeles, given the significant price differences.

Safety culture and structure

For all professional seafarers, safety at sea is paramount. Though they have chosen to dedicate their lives to a potentially dangerous career in seafaring, all want to retire healthy and with full mobility. It is no surprise, then, that on-board safety considerations, whether in the form of workplace

safety or fire prevention, are deeply entrenched in the marine department culture. For
a more detailed outline, see Neumann and
Ullrich (Chapter 18, this volume).

Ship safety

The bridge and the engine control room
monitor in real time a number of critical
systems designed to detect a possible safety
issue. Once detected, a problem is reported
to the ship's bridge, which serves as the
command and control centre to resolve any
situation properly.

In case of fire, a number of mobile fire
teams, composed of officers and seamen,
are pre-established, to be ready to respond
within minutes to a fire or other issue
requiring quickly mobilized manpower,
such as an oil spill or other environmentally hazardous situations.

For other issues, such as a man overboard, the bridge officers also coordinate
medical or security personnel. Each ship
establishes its specific emergency response
time and conducts drills several times per
month, in accordance with international
regulations and internal company policies.

Emergency plan

A key element of the coordination is the
emergency plan, which details everyone's
role in an emergency. The emergency plan
lists each crew member's emergency number and provides protocols to be followed in
case of a number of emergencies. Each ship
has its own customized plan with which
every crew member must become familiar
upon joining a vessel.

Workplace safety

On-board workplace safety is of paramount
importance. While safety is everybody's
business, as the popular slogan says, in reality on-board workplace safety is spear-
headed by the marine department, and
more specifically by the safety officer.
Monthly workplace safety meetings are
conducted by each supervisor on board,
and minutes are recorded. Any safety

concerns are passed upward, along with the
minutes, to the safety officer. Outside safety
meetings, any immediate workplace safety
concern can be brought to the attention of
the safety officer, whose job it is to address
the concern. Though the safety officer also
continually conducts rounds of the ship
with the help of other marine officers, usually bridge officers, everyday safety practice
is the responsibility of supervisors. They
are responsible for conducting training sessions on best practices, e.g. cutting meat,
washing windows, etc., and for monitoring.

Security

Security is of prime importance for cruise
ships (Roach, 2004). From the time of the
first incident of maritime terrorism on the
Achille Lauro (McCredie, 1986) to the recent
attack on the *Seabourn Spirit* off the coast of
Somalia (Warren, 2010), the security of
passengers has been a priority. Lately, the
on-board security of ships has come under
the harsh scrutiny of a number of organizations and book authors.

Every ship has a security officer and a
security team who reports to him, all under
the control of the staff captain. Bridge officers provide real-time information to the
security guards via handheld radios or the
internal wireless telephone system. Furthermore, as routine procedure, security
guards inform the watch officer of any
issues and seek from him authorization
when required. The watch officer is an official representative of the master; hence all
his orders are on behalf of the captain. If a
situation arises, the watchkeeping officer
awakens the captain, staff captain and security officer. A number of code words are
used rapidly to pass on emergency information to the guard and the crew over the PA
without alarming passengers.

Nowadays, there is very strict control
over everything taken on board the ship and
even landed ashore. Nothing gets on board
without being scanned through X-ray or
passed under the scrutiny of the canine
(K-9) detection team. All passenger luggage
is screened for security and for such things
as alcohol, drugs and weapons.

Conclusion

Marine department personnel work primarily 'backstage', outside the view of guests. Therefore, few people, even crew members, understand well what goes on in the 'other' department. Not only do the marine personnel have little interaction with guests, but many of the areas in which they work, such as the engine room, bridge and even mooring deck, are too sensitive and/or dangerous for non-marine personnel.

The disconnect between marine personnel and those 'onstage' can be exacerbated by the friction resulting from a marine department operational constriction that impacts hotel operations and, consequently, guest satisfaction. Therefore, many ships are renewing their efforts to establish a mutual understanding between marine and hotel operations, so that each side can better appreciate the other's challenges and both can appreciate their co-dependent roles. Crew activities hosted by one department but involving both, like waffle day (typically hosted by the marine department) and special themed activities (typically hosted by the hotel department), are encouraged to facilitate such a rapprochement of crew members.

The marine department plays an essential role in ensuring the operational consistency and longevity of high quality amenities and facilities on board. When a significant rapprochement exists between the hotel and marine personnel, benefits accrue to both sides of operations, benefits that translate into a positive ship rating. Synergy between the two departments is essential for any world-class operation; after all, without a marine department, a cruise ship would be a seaside hotel, and without a hotel department, it would be a ghost ship.

References

Boisson, P. (1994) Classification societies and safety at sea: Back to basics to prepare for the future. *Marine Policy* 18(5), 363–377.

Goulielmos, A.M. (1998) Flagging out and the need for a new Greek maritime policy. *Transport Policy* 5(2), 115–125.

IMO (1989) *Final Act of the Conference with Resolutions and the Protocol of 1988 Relating to the International Convention on Local Lines, 1966.* International Maritime Organization, London.

IMO (1996) *STCW 95: International Convention on Standards of Training, Certification, and Watchkeeping for Seafarers, 1978, as amended in 1995.* International Maritime Organization, London.

IMO (2002) *ISPS Code.* International Maritime Organization, London.

IMO (2005) *International Convention for the Safety of Life at Sea 2002.* International Maritime Organization, London.

Jernigan, D.B., Hofmann, J., Cetron, M.S., Genese, C.A., Nuorti, J.P., Fields, B.S., Benson, R.F., Carter, R.J., Edelstein, P.H., Guerrero, I.C., Paul, S.M., Lipman, H.B. and Breiman, R. (1996) Outbreak of Legionnaires' disease among cruise ship passengers exposed to a contaminated whirlpool spa. *The Lancet* 347(9000), 494–499.

Ketkar, K.W. (1995) Protection of marine resources: the US Oil Pollution Act of 1990 and the future of the maritime industry. *Marine Policy* 19(5), 391–400.

King, J. (2005) The security of merchant shipping. *Marine Policy* 29(3), 235–245.

McCarter, P. (1999) STCW '95: implementation issues: what is the pass mark? *Marine Policy* 23(1), 11–24.

McCredie, J.A. (1986) Contemporary uses of force against terrorism: The United States response to *Achille Lauro* – questions of jurisdiction and its exercise. *Georgia Journal of International and Comparative Law* 16, 435–467.

Novaro, G.M., Bush, H.S., Fromkin, K.R., Shen, M.Y., Helguera, M., Pinski, S.L. and Asher, C.R. (2010) Cardiovascular emergencies in cruise ship passengers. *The American Journal of Cardiology* 105(2), 153–157.

Peake, D.E., Gray, C.L., Ludwig, M.R. and Hill, C.D. (1999) Descriptive epidemiology of injury and illness among cruise ship passengers. *Annals of Emergency Medicine* 33(1), 67–72.

Roach, J.A. (2004) Initiatives to enhance maritime security at sea. *Marine Policy* 28(1), 41–66.

Thanopoulou, H.A. (1998) What price the flag? The terms of competitiveness in shipping. *Marine Policy* 22(4/5), 359–374.

US Customs and Border Protection (2010) The Passenger Vessel Services Act: An Informed Compliance Publication. Available at: www.cbp.gov/linkhandler/cgov/trade/legal/informed_compliance_pubs/pvsa_icp.ctt/pvsa_icp.pdf (accessed 15 June 2010).

Véronneau, S. and Cimon, Y. (2007) Maintaining robust decision capabilities: an integrative human-systems approach. *Decision Support Systems* 43(1), 127–140.

Warren, R. (2010) Piracy and shipowners' ethical dilemmas. *Society and Business Review* 6(1), 49–60.

Part VI

Cruise Futures

---

20 Cruise Sector Growth – Prospects, Challenges, Responsibilities

Alexis Papathanassis and Michael Vogel

The future influences the present just as much as the past.

> F. Nietzsche, 1844–1900
> (cited in Watson, 2008, p. 147).

Introduction

Contemplating and anticipating the future is not just good business practice, it is also endemic to human nature. Future scenarios probably reveal more about expectations, wishes and intentions than about the future itself. However, the degree to which those intentions are implemented inevitably influences the future. In this way, forecasts tend to have a self-fulfilling element in that they affect present, anticipation-related, actions.

Our intention in this final chapter is not to provide a mere forecast or scenario of cruise sector growth, but rather to add some transparency with regard to the main principles, drivers and experiences fuelling predictions of the future of cruising. In accordance with the educational character of this volume, we aim to equip our readers with sufficient background to enable them to critically evaluate the various forecasts and scenarios in industry reports and the trade press, and ultimately to empower them to construct their own.

To stimulate further thoughts and debates about the future of the cruise sector and its growth, our chapter closes with the formulation of five key cruise management challenges.

Exploring Cruise Sector Growth and its Forecasts

Indicators

Cruise sector growth is usually expressed in terms of passenger numbers per calendar year. This measure is misleading for at least two reasons. First, if the growth in passenger numbers is accompanied by a decline in the average length of cruises, the number of passenger cruise days may fall. Hence rising passenger numbers do not preclude a contraction of the cruise sector. Second, 'passenger numbers' are actually the numbers of cruises sold, ignoring the fact that a person may be a passenger on more than one cruise in the same year. In fact, 21% of the respondents of a recent survey, conducted by the Cruise Lines International Association (CLIA, 2008), stated that they had taken two or more cruises within the past 12 months. If this estimate is accurate, the number of cruise passengers might only amount to three-quarters of the number published.

Alternative measures of cruise sector growth include the rates of change in available cruise capacity (expressed in lower berths or passenger cruise days) and cruise ticket revenue. As long as occupancy rates remain close to 100%, capacity is proportional to the number of cruises sold. In times of overcapacity, however, capacity growth would become a dysfunctional indicator of cruise sector growth.

Ticket revenue growth, on the other hand, is a very useful indicator of cruise sector growth because it can be decomposed into three meaningful components. Let r denote cruise ticket revenue, c the number of cruises sold, l their average length in passenger cruise days and p the average price per passenger cruise day. Then revenue can be written as $r = c \cdot l \cdot p$. Total differentiation yields

$$\Delta r = \Delta c \cdot l \cdot p + c \cdot \Delta l \cdot p + c \cdot l \cdot \Delta p \quad (20.1)$$

where Δ represents a change in the respective variable. Dividing through by $r = c \cdot l \cdot p$ and simplifying the resulting expression leads to

$$\frac{\Delta r}{r} = \frac{\Delta c}{c} + \frac{\Delta l}{l} + \frac{\Delta p}{p}. \quad (20.2)$$

The term $\Delta r/r$ is the rate of change (or growth rate) of cruise ticket revenue. It is equal to the sum of the rates of change of the number of cruises sold ($\Delta c/c$), the average cruise length ($\Delta l/l$) and the average price per passenger cruise day ($\Delta p/p$). Note that the current practice is to take $\Delta c/c$ as the measure of cruise sector growth and to ignore $\Delta l/l$ and $\Delta p/p$. Since cruise prices have been falling in real terms by more than 2% every year over the past 10 years (see Vogel and Oschmann, Chapter 1, this volume), it is understandable that the cruise lines prefer less rather than more transparency in the figures they publish.

Patterns

The propagation of an ever-growing and all-promising cruise sector dominates the trade press and the media, rendering it a kind of 'business refuge' within the cutthroat competition and meagre profit margins characterizing mass tourism. As it seems, 'cruises are booming!' A simple look at Fig. 20.1 appears to confirm this point. However, when it comes to clarifying why it is growing and for how long, the discussion becomes more complicated and reserved. In Chapter 1, Vogel and Oschmann provide a more differentiated analysis of the cruise

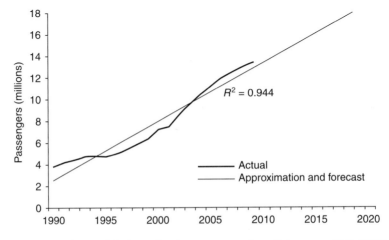

Fig. 20.1.   Linear extrapolation of CLIA members' passenger numbers. Data source: CLIA (2010).

sector's past and present growth, and of the demand enabling it. Yet how much can the past tell us about the future?

We begin our discussion with a simple statistical approach. By means of a linear extrapolation of the trend inherent in the CLIA data depicted in Fig. 20.1, we arrive at a forecast of 20 million passengers by 2022 and 30 million by 2041.

More statistically versed analysts would probably prefer to extrapolate an upward-curving quadratic trend (Fig. 20.2), since a parabola fits the data better than a straight line (R^2 is greater). In this case, the forecast would yield 20 million passengers by the year 2014 and 30 million passengers by 2022. For 2041, the statistically superior parabolic trend predicts 69 million passengers – 2.3 times the number forecasted by the linear trend!

The fundamental weakness of these two forecasts is their absurd assumption that the cruise sector will enjoy indefinite growth. Assumptions of this kind are usually the result of wishful thinking and greed, and they typically give rise to speculative bubbles. More realistically, the cruise sector will follow an S-shaped life cycle similar to the ones identified for tourist destinations (Butler, 1980, 2006) and segments (Zimmermann, 1997; see Fig. 20.3). Indeed, a cubic function fits the CLIA data

better than a linear or quadratic form. Still, forecasting the future of the cruise sector remains tricky. As Fig. 20.4 shows, the S-shaped trend reaches its maximum in 2017 and declines thereafter. The end is nigh – or not?

To be sure, CLIA does not represent the entire cruise industry. The time series could be extended to the 1960s. We might have analysed cruise data from North America (where the market shows tendencies of satiation) and from the 'rest of the world' (where vast untapped potential seems to exist) separately. And there are other mathematical forms that also produce S-shaped curves. Our point is that any forecast is sensitive to the underlying data and assumptions. At its most basic, forecasting 'takes historical fact and scientific knowledge ... to create images of what might happen in the future' (Cornish cited in Frechtling, 2002, p. 8). It is tempting to forecast by creating images of the future that are quantitatively different from the present but not qualitatively, because growth is easier to imagine than development. The result is that we simply project our experience of the as-is situation into the future. As Woody Allen puts it, 'I have seen the future, and it's very much like the present, only longer' (cited in Watson, 2008, p. 5).

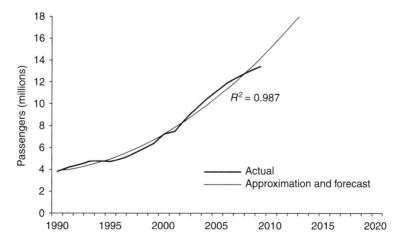

Fig. 20.2. Quadratic extrapolation of CLIA members' passenger numbers. Data source: CLIA (2010).

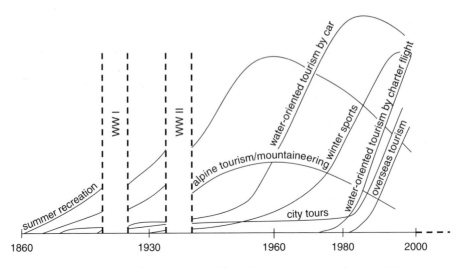

Fig. 20.3. European tourism products – a product life cycle approach. Source: based on Zimmermann (1997).

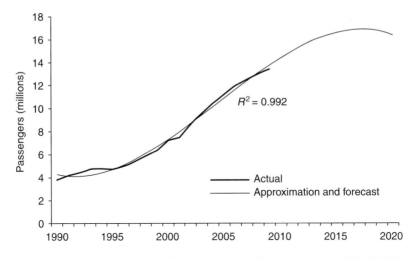

Fig. 20.4. Cubic extrapolation of CLIA members' passenger numbers. Data source: CLIA (2010).

Self-fulfilling prophecies

Forecasts are subject to uncertainty, always contain blind spots and, very importantly, affect decision makers, who in turn formulate policies that influence the future and therefore the accuracy of the forecast (Walonik, 1993). Nietzsche's quote at the outset of this chapter also emphasizes the expected influence of the future upon the present.

In the cruise sector, it is organizations with vested interests that conduct or commission the majority of market studies and forecasts. The cruise lines' lobbying organization CLIA, for instance, strives to keep travel agents and (potential) cruise line investors happy and secure their continued support for the cruise sector. Positive market outlooks can be of great help in this respect. The consulting firm GP Wild (2005,

2007), which generates much of its revenue from projects for the cruise sector, has an incentive to publish forecasts that are favourable to its clients. Banks that finance cruise ships are interested in making the cruise sector's prospects look particularly promising, to induce investors to build or buy more ships. And of course, each cruise sector analyst knows the forecasts of all the other analysts.

Not only does a brighter (projected) future of the cruise sector boost the business of CLIA, GP Wild, banks and other providers of services to the cruise sector today; the cruise sector itself also has a built-in amplifying feedback loop, which connects beliefs about the future with the present. A forecast of higher growth rates will induce cruise lines to expand their capacities faster, resulting in – yes – higher growth rates.

In our view, the cruise sector has benefitted from such self-fulfilling prophecies over the years. In Chapter 1 of this volume, Vogel and Oschmann argue that the demand for cruises is supply-led, that is, that product innovation and declining prices have fuelled demand. We believe that the supply side dominance in the cruise sector is partly the consequence of a long series of promising market potential analyses and roseate demand forecasts, triggering ambitious new-build programmes. The cruise lines then found ways of stimulating the necessary demand. High growth rates confirmed the accuracy of the earlier forecasts; high occupancy rates confirmed the existence of sufficient demand potential; and the cruise lines' profitability confirmed the viability of their business models. All three factors together led analysts to raise their expectations, to forecast more growth and thus, via the self-fulfilling prophecy mechanism, to cause their predictions to come true.

Forecasting methodology

In their analysis of forecasting methods applied in the cruise sector, Kollwitz and Papathanassis (2010) challenge the validity of certain assumptions and highlight methodological issues. Short-term forecasts for up to 5 years, for instance, are based on the assumption of market equilibrium, i.e. the price mechanism ensures that available capacity is fully utilized. The level of planned supply (new cruise ship capacity in the shipyards' order books) is interpreted as future demand. This approach delivers forecasts that are as accurate as trivial, since the cruise lines' revenue management departments make sure that full occupancy is maintained even if ticket prices have to be slashed (see Vogel, Chapter 10, this volume). To escape triviality, such forecasts would need to say something about the expected price level associated with market equilibrium.

Longer-term predictions tend to be made on the basis of statistical analyses of historical data, as exemplified by Figs 20.1, 20.2 and 20.4. Observed patterns are extrapolated into the future or transferred to other regions. An example of the latter is the argument that the European cruise market is following the North American market and reproducing its growth path with a couple of years' delay. The lower cruise market penetration rates in Europe serve as indicators of a large untapped potential. This need not be wrong, but the argument ignores important differences between North America and Europe with respect to the proximity of warm winter cruise destinations (winter cruises are more expensive for Europeans), to the households' budget per cruise day (Europeans have longer paid annual leaves and spread their holiday budgets over more days, resulting in lower budgets per cruise day), to cruise motives (casinos and shopping are less important for European cruisers) and to general leisure travel behaviour.

Relying on statistics whilst ignoring the fundamental questions leads to a dead end. In our view, fundamental questions are: What is the cruise demand potential under today's (economic, technological, competitive, product supply etc.) conditions? By how much and why is actual demand falling short of this potential? How and why will the demand potential change in the foreseeable future? What could cause actual cruise demand to fall short of this potential? And will this future be desirable for cruise companies and cruise passengers?

Boundary issues

In 2010, 1.2 million Germans went on an ocean cruise (DRV, 2011). A total of 0.5 million or 43% of them travelled with Aida Cruises, the German subsidiary of the Carnival Corporation. Originally, Aida's 'club ship' cruise concept was based on Germany's popular Robinson Club resorts. Over the years, the Aida concept has been developed further, but the cruise line still considers Robinson Club and similar land-based resorts as its competitors. This point is important because it challenges the relevance of the cruise sector's seemingly obvious boundaries.

The choice of boundaries implies discrimination between inside and outside. Inside is part of the relevant system and counts as pertinent in an analysis, whereas the outside is often simply subsumed under 'environment' and excluded from analysis. For example, when the cruise sector celebrates itself (e.g. 'The cruise industry is the most exciting growth category in the entire leisure market'; CLIA, 2010, p. 1), it does so largely at the expense of other tourism sectors which lose the demand that cruises gain. If boundaries were chosen to comprise the 'whole relevant system' (Churchman, 1970, p. B43) of tourism, it would become clear that overall, a zero-sum game does not give as much reason to celebrate. The choice of cruise sector boundaries is thus highly significant for the interpretation of market indicators and forecasts.

The example of Aida Cruises competing for new customers not only with other cruise lines, but also with land-based resorts, emphasizes the importance of 'pushing out' systemic boundaries of the cruise sector to overcome its self-referentiality. Cruises have become affordable alternatives to land-based package holidays. The cruise lines have tapped an enormous market potential, but now they play in a league where competi-

tion is price-dominated, cost pressures translate into standardization, and the scale of operations causes high management complexity. If the cruise lines compete for the same target customers and play the game by the same rules as the mass market tour operators and large hotel chains, how relevant is the cruise/non-cruise distinction? Why should the size of the market, the degree of market concentration, the intensity of competition etc. be determined separately for cruises and for other types of holidays if the customers regard them as increasingly close substitutes?

Traditional cruise sector boundaries cloud the fact that some cruise companies operate very distinct business models (see Gross and Lück, Chapter 5, this volume), which have little more in common with one another than a passenger ship. Do ships actually have to be a defining characteristic of the cruise sector, or is the association of cruises with ships a systemic boundary that should be overcome? In 1999, for instance, the German operator Hapag-Lloyd Cruises started offering so-called 'cruise flights' in a dedicated aircraft (HLKF, 2011). Even though the passengers spend the nights in different hotels, cruise flights retain several characteristic elements of cruises: a fixed multi-destination itinerary, 'shore' excursions, an elaborate service concept, the same 'vessel' and crew throughout the journey. Thus redefining cruise sector boundaries can open up new development horizons and reveal opportunities for growth.

Managing Cruise Sector Growth

So far, we have explored and critically discussed characteristics of cruise sector growth and its forecasts, almost as if this growth were something that just happens. This is, of course, not what the title of this volume, *The Business and Management of Ocean Cruises*, suggests, and we do not want to convey the impression that there is anything like a growth automatism.

However, the ways in which the cruise sector represents itself in its market studies, reports and forecasts strongly affects the ways in which cruise managers construct their mental models of the sector. Mental models are tacit and usually unexamined theories as to how the world works. They exist below the level of awareness and guide people in their decision making and actions. 'Why are mental models so powerful in affecting what we *do*? In part, because they affect what we *see*' (Senge, 1994, p. 175; original emphasis). We used the term self-referentiality earlier. The cruise sector is highly self-referential: it observes itself, interprets itself, learns from itself and celebrates itself. In this respect, it differs little from other sectors of the economy.

By pointing out some of the mechanisms at work in the cruise sector's self-construction – euphemistic performance indicators, growth myths, under-complex forecasting methods, power-induced feedback loops and reductionist systemic boundaries – we aimed to make present and future cruise managers more aware of the perceptive, cognitive and affective biases they are likely to develop over time, which will inescapably influence the priorities they set, the decisions they make and the actions they take.

The successful management of cruise sector growth will not only depend on managers' perceptions and mental models, but also on their approaches to handling specific key challenges facing the cruise sector. In the remainder of the chapter, we formulate five such challenges relating to different areas of cruise management, hoping to stimulate many critical and constructive debates.

Challenge 1: Developing cruise destinations sustainably

The growth of cruise capacity has not been matched universally by a similar growth in the carrying capacity of attractive cruise destinations. Unlike cruise ships, many kinds of attractions cannot be expanded or reproduced at will. Interesting historic sites and places of particular natural beauty, for example, are in fixed supply, and purpose-built

tourist attractions are imperfect substitutes. Moreover, attractions need to be accessible for cruise ship passengers. Cruise traffic concentrates in a few hot spots, which become literally overrun, whereas places without accessible attractions tend not to be included in cruise itineraries.

Overcrowded ports and attractions, infrastructure-challenged destinations, environmental degradation and antagonistic relationships between locals and visitors are clear indicators of an unsustainable development of cruising. It is unsustainable because this kind of cruise tourism gradually destroys the foundations of its own popularity: the passengers' cruise experience and satisfaction deteriorate, and for the local people the perceived costs of cruise tourism outweigh the perceived benefits (see Manning, Chapter 4, this volume).

This calls for a more intense cooperation between cruise operators, ports and destination management organizations, and for the consideration of stakeholder interests that extend beyond the purely economic. Destination carrying capacities need to be assessed and taken seriously, which may require the spatial and temporal dispersion of cruise tourism, the limitation or even the deliberate reduction of passenger numbers. This poses an enormous challenge, especially to the destination communities, which are typically less experienced, less organized and less decided than the cruise lines.

Challenge 2: Controlling scale effects

Cruise sector growth, especially in the volume segments, is associated with growing systemic tensions and contradictions. Cruises today cost less and offer more convenience, more on-board attractions, a wider choice of dining and entertainment options etc. than 10 or 20 years ago, yet many cruise passengers demand even more value for even less money. New cruise ships are equipped with better facilities and more advanced technology for reducing negative environmental impacts than older ships, yet, overall, the environmental problems related to cruising seem to be exacerbated rather than diminished. And despite very efficient processes for managing shore excursions and decades of experience with excursions in certain destinations, 'people pollution' is getting worse rather than better.

These examples demonstrate different scale effects. Economies of scale have permitted cruise lines to decrease prices. Occupancy risks associated with rapid capacity expansion put additional pressure on prices, and discounting has turned many cruise line customers into keen bargain hunters. This limits the cruise lines' ability and willingness to allocate sufficient resources to the mitigation of negative environmental impacts related to the growing scale of their operations. Scale may allow bringing down costs and reducing negative impacts per unit (passenger, berth, ship), but if scale increases at a higher rate than efficiency, the advances in technological and process efficiency get fully eaten up by increases in scale. As Daly and Farley (2011) point out, even an efficiently loaded ship will sink if it is overloaded.

From our perspective, growth of the cruise sector is desirable for the economic benefits it brings. However, the critical consequences of scale undermine the cruise sector's legitimacy. This poses a more profound and more general problem to cruise management than the challenge 1, because of the way the economic incentives are structured: the benefits of scale are privatized by the cruise lines, whereas the costs are socialized. The given incentive structures and competitive dynamics will not permit a solution to the problem of scale (and legitimacy) to come from within the cruise sector.

We therefore believe that it would be in the cruise sector's own best long-term interest if regulators such as the IMO put incentive mechanisms in place which align the cruise lines' profit maximizing behaviour with sustainability. The main challenge especially for senior cruise managers in this context will be to suppress their defensive reflexes, to remind themselves of their companies' corporate social responsibility, and

to participate in designing a framework that will help preserve the cruise sector's public acceptance and viability in the long run.

Challenge 3: Managing geographical shifts of demand

As Vogel and Oschmann (Chapter 1, this volume) show, today's most important market for cruises, North America, is growing more slowly than the European markets, not only in terms of growth rates, but even in absolute numbers of passengers. The British Passenger Shipping Association (PSA) state in their 2011 Cruise Review that 'there is now a genuine prospect of North America losing its position as the largest source market for the cruise sector' (PSA, 2011, p. 16). Moreover, from our point of view, it is only a matter of time before Asian markets become the third gravitational centre of the cruise sector.

This has far-reaching implications for the brand strategies, product development approaches and management structures of today's globally operating US cruise companies. Carnival Corporation already seems to have found a *modus operandi*, allowing it to serve heterogeneous local markets very effectively. Because of its significant external growth in the past (see Bjelicic, Chapter 2, this volume), Carnival has a diversified portfolio of ten cruise lines and brands, which are managed in a fairly decentralized manner.

> Our cruise brands appeal to the tastes and cultures of the vacationers in the countries in which they operate enabling us to achieve greater demand and market penetration. Our decentralized structure supports this foundation, operating as a collection of separately managed cruise brands. Management teams led by locally-based entrepreneurial executives are driven to grow and optimize their brands which fosters an ownership-oriented attitude that is rare in an organization our size.
>
> (Carnival, 2011, p. 2)

Cruise lines with global brands like Royal Caribbean International, Celebrity Cruises or

NCL, cannot easily replicate this management structure. Their need to serve several different markets with the same brands necessarily entails a higher degree of centralization, which is incompatible with local entrepreneurship. Global brands work best in the context of homogeneous local consumer preferences (Vogel, 2009b). If this is not the case – as in the cruise sector – a global brand strategy may still be justified if there is one dominant market (the US in the cruise sector) and a less significant periphery. However, with Europe outgrowing the North American market, and Asia likely to follow in a few years' time, this second condition may soon no longer be fulfilled either. The challenge will be to find brand-strategic and organizational answers to the geographical shifts of cruise demand over the next decades.

Challenge 4: Refining business models

The cruise sector is polarized. On the one hand, a handful of large corporations operate a large number of large vessels, sailing on mainstream routes and calling at mainstream destination ports. Their favourable cost structure (because of fleet size, ship size and standardization) and significant on-board business allow them to charge moderate ticket prices and thus to attract customer groups, which, in the past, would not have been able to afford a cruise. Production and consumption processes on 'supersized' ships have been found to correspond, in several respects, to Ritzer's (1993) McDonaldization thesis by being efficient, calculable, predictable, controlled and, despite their rationalization, susceptible to irrational consequences (Weaver, 2005).

For the cruise giants, we see the main management challenges in this context in counteracting the increasing commoditization of their products. Margins need to be protected through differentiation from competitors. In our earlier discussion of cruise sector boundaries we suggested that the relevant competitors may not all be cruise lines. If sustainable differentiation cannot be achieved, the cruise lines may have to capitalize more fully on their monopolistic

supplier position on board (Vogel, 2009a), which might not necessarily be welcomed by all passengers.

On the other hand, the cruise sector comprises many small and medium-sized cruise companies (SMCs), which offer niche products, serving special-interest customer groups, narrowly defined geographical markets, ultra luxury segments or combinations of these. Their small fleet and ship size is associated with high costs per unit of capacity, and spatial restrictions on board limit the possibilities to generate additional revenue. As a result, ticket prices tend to be high.

The main challenges for these SMCs, many of which are family-owned, will be to secure their financing and, not unrelated, to find suitable second-hand tonnage. Obtaining bank loans has become more difficult in recent years, since banks started reducing their risk exposure and requiring SMCs to have a larger equity base before lending to them. The 2008/09 financial crisis made the situation even more difficult. Financing is probably the most serious barrier to market entry and growth for SMCs today.

Because of their financial constraints, SMCs tend not to order new vessels but depend on second-hand tonnage. Since most cruise ships that have been built over the past two decades are too large for small niche players, there is now a shortage of smaller-scale tonnage, forcing SMCs to operate bigger vessels than they can fill with confidence, and to accept riskier financing arrangements with banks than they would otherwise.

Challenge 5: Enhancing professionalism

Learning by doing, supplemented by occasional training units, is still the dominant human resource development (HRD) strategy in the cruise lines' hotel departments. Most of today's hotel directors or general managers started their careers washing dishes in the galley before working their way up, which is why they tend to propagate this approach. Advantages of in-service, apprenticeship-type HRD are its low cost and its immediate practical relevance.

The downside of learning by doing, however, is that staff learn by copying existing practices rather than standard or even best practices, and by uncritically adopting their colleagues' and superiors' attitudes and habits in order to be accepted by them and to become part of the team.

If professionalism is defined as the 'ability to align personal and organizational conduct with ethical and professional standards that include a responsibility to the customer or guest and community, a service orientation, and a commitment to lifelong learning and improvement' (Sheldon *et al.*, 2011, p. 14; see also Haga, 1976), then professionalism can but need not result from learning by doing.

Given the cruise lines' high service quality ambitions, the complexity of hotel operations on large vessels and the very positive impact of competent leadership on staff motivation and working climate, we believe that enhancing professionalism through more systematic education and training would pay off in terms of greater customer and employee satisfaction, lower staff turnover rates and better solutions to operational problems. The particular managerial challenge here will be to overcome the inertia of an established and seemingly time-proven HRD and career model.

Final Word

The Preface of this volume starts with the remark that

> Cruise lines combine socio-economic, technological and environmental systems in unique ways to form their products.

Many managerial functions in the cruise sector deal with tensions, conflicts and uncertainties arising from the interaction of at least two of these systems.

The Business and Management of Ocean Cruises is about handling these tensions, conflicts and uncertainties professionally. However, it is no secret that the global cruise sector benefits substantially from legal, regulatory and taxation loopholes, from the authorities' inability to control cruise ships effectively in international waters, and from the economic dependency of many destinations on cruise tourism.

The increasing scale of the cruise sector means greater visibility, and greater visibility often entails more scrutiny, not only by the authorities, but also by non-governmental organizations and individual members of the public. With their critical books, authors like Chin (2008), Gaouette (2010) and Klein (2002, 2005, 2008) reach large audiences. Websites such as CruiseJunkie.com and cruise-critical user-generated contents on Facebook, Twitter, YouTube and other social networks enjoy high credibility in the public, making it increasingly difficult for the cruise sector to control cruise-related communication and to guarantee the public acceptance and legitimacy of some of the cruise lines' practices.

We welcome this development and wish to encourage our readers, and especially all present and future cruise managers, to commit themselves to the high standards of professionalism as defined earlier in this chapter. *The Business and Management of Ocean Cruises* is about big money, but it is also about big responsibility.

References

Butler, R.W. (1980) The concept of a tourism area cycle of evolution: implications for management resources. *The Canadian Geographer* 24(1), 5–16.

Butler, R.W. (2006) *The Tourism Area Life Cycle: Applications and Modifications*. Channelview Publications, Clevedon.

Carnival (2011) *Annual Report 2010*. Carnival Corporation & PLC, Miami, Florida.

Chin, C.B.N. (2008) *Cruising in the Global Economy: Profits, Pleasure and Work at Sea*. Ashgate, Aldershot.

Churchman, C.W. (1970) Operations research as a profession. *Management Science* 17(2), B37–B53.

CLIA (2008) *Cruise Market Profile Study*. Cruise Lines International Association, Fort Lauderdale, Florida.

CLIA (2010) Cruise Market Overview: Statistical Cruise Industry Data Through 2009. Available at: www.cruising.org/sites/default/files/misc/2010FINALOV.pdf (accessed 10 April 2011).

Daly, H.E. and Farley, J. (2011) *Ecological Economics: Principles and Applications*, 2nd edn. Island Press, Washington, DC.

DRV (2011) *Fakten und Zahlen zum deutschen Reisemarkt 2010*. Deutscher ReiseVerband, Berlin.

Frechtling, D.C. (2002) *Practical Tourism Demand Forecasting: Methods and Strategies*. Butterworth-Heinemann, Oxford.

Gaouette, M. (2010) *Cruising for Trouble: Cruise Ships as Soft Targets for Pirates, Terrorists, and Common Criminals*. Praeger, Santa Barbara, California.

Haga, W.J. (1976) Managerial professionalism and the use of organization resources. *American Journal of Economics and Sociology* 35, 337–347.

HLKF (2011) Kreuzflüge – die Welt exklusiv im Privatjet erleben. Available at: www.hl-kreuzfluege.de (accessed 12 April 2011).

Klein, R.A. (2002) *Cruise Ship Blues. The Underside of the Cruise Industry*. New Society Publishers, Gabriola Island, British Columbia.

Klein, R.A. (2005) *Cruise Ship Squeeze: The New Pirates of the Seven Seas*. New Society Publishers, Gabriola Island, British Columbia.

Klein, R.A. (2008) *Paradise Lost at Sea: Rethinking Cruise Vacations*. Fernwood Publishing, Halifax, Nova Scotia.

Kollwitz, H. and Papathanassis, A. (2010) Evaluating cruise demand forecasting practices: a Delphi approach. Paper presented at the 2nd International Cruise Conference, 18–20 February, University of Plymouth.

PSA (2011) *The Cruise Review*. Passenger Shipping Association, London. Available at: www.the-psa.co.uk/downloads/PSA_Cruise_Review_2011.pdf (accessed 27 April 2011).

Ritzer, G. (1993) *The McDonaldization of Society: an Investigation into the Changing Character of Contemporary Social Life*. Pine Forge Press, Newbury Park, California.

Senge, P. (1994) *The Fifth Discipline. The Art and Practice of the Learning Organization*. Currency Doubleday, New York.

Sheldon, P.J., Fesenmaier, D.R. and Tribe, J. (2011) The Tourism Education Futures Initiative (TEFI): activating change in tourism education. *Journal of Teaching in Travel & Tourism* 11, 2–23.

Vogel, M. (2009a) Onboard Revenue: The secret of the cruise industry's success? In: Papathanassis, A. (ed.) *Cruise Sector Growth: Managing Emerging Markets, Human Resources, Processes and Systems*. Gabler, Wiesbaden, pp. 3–15.

Vogel, M. (2009b) The economics of US cruise companies' European brand strategies. *Tourism Economics* 15(4), 735–751.

Walonik, D. (1993) An overview of forecasting methodology. Available at: www.statpac.com/research-papers/forecasting.htm (accessed 27 April 2011).

Watson, R. (2008) *Future Files: 5 Trends that will Shape the Next 50 years*. Nicholas Brealy Publishing, London.

Weaver, A. (2005) The McDonaldization thesis and cruise tourism. *Annals of Tourism Research* 32(2), 346–366.

Wild, G.P. (2005) *Cruise Industry Statistical Review*. G.P. Wild (International) Ltd., Haywards Heath.

Wild, G.P. (2007) Contribution of Cruise Tourism to the Economies of Europe. Available at: www.cruise-norway.no/viewfile.aspx?id=2213 (accessed 27 April 2011).

Zimmermann, F. (1997) Future perspectives of tourism: traditional versus new destinations. In: Oppermann, M. (ed.) *Pacific Rim Tourism*. CABI, Wallingford, pp. 231–239.

Index